Rogov's Guide to Israeli Wines
2007

Daniel Rogov

ROGOV'S GUIDE TO ISRAELI WINES

2007

The Toby Press

First Edition 2006
The Toby Press LLC

POB 8531, New Milford, CT 06776-8531, USA
& POB 2455, London W1A 5WY, England

www.tobypress.com

© Daniel Rogov 2006

The right of Daniel Rogov to be identified as the author
of this work has been asserted by him in accordance
with the Copyright, Designs & Patents Act 1988

All rights reserved. No part of this publication may be reproduced,
stored in a retrieval system, or transmitted in any form or by
any means, electronic, mechanical, photocopying or otherwise,
without the prior permission of the publisher, except in the case
of brief quotations embodied in critical articles or reviews.

ISBN 1 159264 171 7, *hardcover*

A CIP catalogue record for this title is
available from the British Library

Typeset in Chaparral by Jerusalem Typesetting

Printed in Israel

TABLE OF CONTENTS

FOREWORD VII

HOW TO USE THE GUIDE viii
   Key to Symbols and Scores viii

INTRODUCTION 1

The History of Wine in Israel 1
   Ancient Times 1
   Modern Times 4
   The Israeli Wine Revolution 6

The Current and Future State of Wine Production in Israel 7

The Phenomenon of the Boutique Wineries 8

Grape Growing Regions 9

Grape Varieties in Israel 11
   White Wine Grapes 12
   Red Wine Grapes 13

Vintage Reports: 1976–2005 16
   The Last Five Years 17
   Somewhat Older Vintages 18

Questions of Kashrut 19
   Some Israeli Wines are Kosher, Others are Not 19
   What Makes an Israeli Wine Kosher? 20
   The Question of Wines that are Mevushal 21

A Few Lists 22
   The Ten Best Wine Producers 22
   Ten New or Up-and-Coming Producers 23
   The Ten Fastest Improving Producers 23
   The 10 Best Value Producers 23

ROGOV'S GUIDE TO ISRAELI WINES

    The Ten Best Wines Released in the Last Twelve Months 24

Drinking Habits 24
    Within Israel 24
    Sacramental versus "Wine Culture" 25
    Within the "Jewish World" 25
    Israel as a Potential Supplier of "Niche Wines" 26

THE WINERIES AND THEIR WINES 27

AFTERWORD 343

Dessert Wines 343

A Guide to Tasting Wines 345
    Basic Rules for tasting wines 345
    Wine Appreciation 347

Several Words about Scores 350

GLOSSARY OF WINE TERMINOLOGY 353

CONTACTING THE WINERIES 361

INDEX 377

ABOUT THE AUTHOR 379

FOREWORD

Israeli wines from the 2004 and 2005 vintages are now making their way to market, and following the pattern of recent years, many of those wines are proving to be of enviably high quality. In 2006, Israeli wineries made unprecedented debuts and received glowing reviews in venues as diverse in character as Bordeaux, London, Moscow, New York, Toronto and London.

The days when Israel was producing primarily sweet red wines for sacramental purposes are long gone, and today Israel is acknowledged as a serious wine producer. Wines are being made from highly prized grape varieties at more than one hundred and fifty wineries scattered all over the country, from the Upper Galilee and the Golan Heights to the Judean Hills and the Negev Desert. The construction of state-of-the-art wineries, the ongoing import and cultivation of good vine stock from California and France, experimentation with new wine varieties and blends, and the enthusiasm and knowledge of young, well-trained winemakers has yielded an abundance of quality wines that can compete comfortably with the finest wines of the New World.

The purpose of this book is to provide readers with extensive knowledge about the wineries and wines of Israel, and to serve as a convenient guide for selecting and storing local wines. The introduction supplies the reader with the necessary historical and geographical background, while the major part of the guide is devoted to the wines, offering tasting notes and scores for wines that are now on the shelves or scheduled to appear within the next six to nine months, as well as wines that are still stored in the cellars of wine lovers.

How to Use the Guide

Wineries are arranged in the book by alphabetical order and in the few cases where wineries may be known by more than one name, especially outside of Israel, readers will find the alternative names listed in the index. Following a brief description of the location, history and production of each winery are the reviews, from the top-level series to the lower. Each series is arrayed from red wines to whites, and then sparkling and dessert wines. These are further divided into grape varieties such as Cabernet Sauvignon, Merlot, etc. Each variety is arranged according to vintage years, from the most current release to the most mature available, and each review concludes with a score and a suggested drinking window.

Key to Symbols and Scores

THE WINERIES

*****	A WORLD-CLASS WINERY, REGULARLY PRODUCING EXCELLENT WINES
****	CONSISTENTLY PRODUCING HIGH-QUALITY WINES
***	SOLID AND RELIABLE PRODUCER WITH AT LEAST SOME GOOD WINES
**	ADEQUATE
*	HARD TO RECOMMEND

SCORES FOR INDIVIDUAL WINES

96–100	Truly great wines
90–95	Exceptional in every way
85–89	Very good to excellent and highly recommended
80–84	Recommended but without enthusiasm
70–79	Average but at least somewhat faulted
Under 70	Not recommended

Special Note about Tentative Scores:
The scores of wines tasted only from the barrel, that is to say,

well before release and sometimes even before final blends have been made, are scored within a range and noted as *tentative*. Wines attaining such scores will be re-tasted and updated in future editions.

DRINKING WINDOWS
A drinking window is the suggested period during which the wine is at its very best. The notation "best 2008–2012" indicates that the wine needs further cellaring before it comes to its peak and will then cellar comfortably through 2012. "Drink now–2012" indicates that although the wine is drinking well now it will continue to cellar nicely until 2012. "Drink now" indicates that the wine is drinking well now but can be held for a year or so, and "drink up" suggests that the wine is at or past its peak and should not be cellared any longer. "Drink from release" refers to wines that are not yet on the market but will appear within the coming nine months.

KOSHER WINES
That there is no contradiction between making fine wine and the kosher laws is made apparent in the introduction to this guide. Within the guide, the reviews of all wines that have received a kashrut certificate from a recognized rabbinic authority are followed by the symbol K.

Introduction

The History of Wine in Israel

Ancient Times

The history of wine in the land of Israel is as old as the history of the people who have inhabited that land over the centuries. As early as five thousand years ago people cultivated vines and made, stored and shipped wines. The first mention of wine in the Bible is in a reference to Noah, who is said to have planted the first vineyard and to have become intoxicated when he drank the wine (Genesis 9:20–21). Another well known reference concerns the spies sent out by Moses to explore the land of Canaan. They returned after their mission with a cluster of grapes said to have been so large and heavy that it had to be borne on a carrying frame (Numbers 13:23). The vine is also mentioned as one of the blessings of the good land promised to the children of Israel (Deuteronomy 8:8).

The Bible lists the necessary steps to care for a vineyard:

> My beloved had a vineyard in a very fruitful hill;
> And he dug it; and cleared it of stones,
> And planted it with the choicest vine,
> And built a tower in the midst of it,
> And also hewed out a vat therein;
> And he looked that it should bring forth grapes.
> He broke the ground, cleared it of stone and
>   planted it with choice vines.
> He built a watchtower inside it,
> He even hewed a wine press inside it.
>
> *(Isaiah 5: 1–2)*

Vintners in ancient times knew as we do today that

locating vineyards at higher altitudes and thus in areas with greater temperature changes between night and day would cause the fruit to ripen more slowly, adding to the sweetness of the fruit and its ability to produce fine wines. Two ways of growing vines were known then; in one the vines being allowed to grow along the ground, and in the other being trained upward on trellises (Ezekiel 17:6–8). It was widely accepted then as today that vines cultivated by the second method almost always produce superior grapes.

Remains of ancient wine presses may be found today in all parts of the Land of Israel, from the Galilee to Jerusalem and the Negev Desert. In nearly every part of Israel, archeologists have discovered hundreds of jars for storing and transporting wine. Many of these amphorae indicate in detail where and by whom the wine was made, as well as the year of the vintage, this showing that even in antiquity the source of the grapes and the quality of the harvest were considered important.

It is known today that even during the Bronze Age, Egyptian Pharaohs enjoyed wines that were shipped from Canaan. The growing of grapes and the production of wine was a major agricultural endeavor during the period of the First and Second Temples, and the kings of Judah and Israel were said to have owned large vineyards as well as vast stores of wine. The vineyards and stores of King David in particular were so numerous that he is said to have appointed two officials, one to be in charge of the vineyards, and the other to be charge of storage.

In biblical times the harvest was a celebratory period as well as a period of courtship. The treading of the grapes was done most often on a *gat* or an *arevah*, the *gat* being a small, generally square pressing floor that had been cut into bedrock, and the *arevah* a smaller treading surface that could be moved from vineyard to vineyard. From either of these the must (that is to say, the fresh and as yet unfermented grape juice) ran into a *yekev*, which was a vat for collecting the must as it flowed from the treading floor through a hole carved in the stone. When natural bedrock was unavailable, an earthen treading surface lined with mosaics was used. In several areas, caves or large cisterns carved from natural bedrock have been found, which would have served two purposes—first for storing the grapes until they were pressed and then, because they were cool and dark, for storing the wine while it fermented and then aged in clay jugs.

Once fermentation had been completed, the wines were stored in pottery vessels which were sealed with wood, stone or clay stoppers. For purposes of shipping, the stoppers were wrapped in cloth and coated with clay. Since new clay vessels tend to absorb as much as 20 percent of the wines stored in them, it became common practice to store better wines in older jars. A major development, during the third century BCE was the discovery that stoppers made from cork were an effective way to seal amphorae.

As much as these wines were prized, it must be understood that they were very different from wines as we know them today. They were often so intense and coarse that they needed a fair amount of "adjustment" before they were considered drinkable. To improve the bouquet, the Romans were known to add spices and scents to their wines. To make the wine sweeter, they added a syrup made by heating grape juice in lead containers for a long period over a low flame, and to improve flavors and hide faults it was customary to add honey, pepper, chalk, gypsum, lime, resin, herbs and even sea water.

In the time of the First and Second Temples, wine was widely consumed by the local populace, but the very best wines were set aside for libations in the Temple. The Bible specifies the different types of offerings—a quarter of a *hin* (one *hin* was the equivalent of about 5.7 liters or 1.5 gallons) of wine when offering a sheep; a third of a *hin* for a ram; and half a *hin* for an animal from the herd such as a cow (Numbers 15:5). In addition, people were required to give tithes of new wine to the Temple (Deuteronomy 12:17). Wines were so central to the culture during the days of the first and second Temples that those who planted vineyards were exempt from military service, and illustrations of grapes, grape leaves, amphorae and drinking vessels were often used as symbols on seals and coins as well as for decorations on the friezes of buildings.

After the destruction of the second Temple, wine was integrated into all religious ceremonies including *brit milah* (circumcision), weddings, the Sabbath and high holidays, and is especially central in the Passover *seder* where it is customary to drink four glasses of wine.

Through the fourth to six centuries, during the late Roman and Byzantine periods, the wine industry shifted from Judea to the southern part of the land, where the port towns Ashkelon and Gaza became centers of wine trading. Those wines were so coveted by the Romans that they shipped them to their legions throughout the Mediterranean and North Africa, and Christian pilgrims brought them back to Europe.

The Moslem conquest of the Holy Land in the seventh century put an end to this prosperous industry. The Moslem rulers banned the drinking of alcohol and as a result the flourishing local wine industry almost ceased to exist. The only wines allowed were the small amounts that Christians and Jews required for sacramental use. Attempts were made by the Crusaders in the twelfth and thirteenth centuries to revive the wine industry in the Holy Land but these were short-lived, since they realized it would be easier to ship wines from Europe. It was only with the renewal of Jewish settlement in the nineteenth century that the local winemaking industry was reestablished.

Modern Times

The Jewish philanthropist Sir Moses Montefiore, who visited the Holy Land in the nineteenth century, encouraged the Jews living there to work the land and replant vines. One person who listened to his call was Rabbi Itzhak Schorr, who founded a new winery in Jerusalem in 1848. Rabbi Abraham Teperberg founded the Efrat winery in 1870 in the old city of Jerusalem, as well as an agricultural school in Mikveh

Israel, not far from Jaffa. This school was financed and run by *Alliance Israelite Universelle*, a Jewish organization based in France that aimed at training Jewish settlers in agricultural work. The school was the first to plant European grape varieties, and had a winery as well as large wine cellars. Many of its graduates became vine growers.

An important boost to the local industry came about when Baron Edmond de Rothschild, the owner of the famed Chateau Lafite in Bordeaux, agreed to come to the help of the Jewish colonies, and financed the planting of the first vineyards near Rishon Letzion in the coastal plain. Rothschild hoped that the Holy Land would serve as the source of kosher wines for Jews the world over, and that the wine industry would provide a solid economic basis for the new Jewish communities. He brought in experts from Europe and imported grape varieties from the south of France including Alicante Bouchet, Clairette, Carignan, Grenache, Muscat and Semillon. Rothschild funded the first wineries of the Jewish settlements—in 1882 the Rishon Letzion Winery, and in 1890 the Zichron Ya'akov winery in the Mount Carmel area, thus marking the beginning of the modern wine industry in the Land of Israel. Unfortunately, not all ran smoothly. The first harvests were lost to heat and in 1890–91 the land was overrun by phylloxera, a plague of aphid-like insects that destroyed all of the vines. The vineyards were dug up, and replanted with vines grafted onto phylloxera-resistant root stocks.

In 1906 Rothschild helped to set up a cooperative of grape growers that managed the two wineries, and in 1957 his heirs sold their share to the cooperative. It took the name Carmel Mizrachi, and continued to be the dominant factor in the local wine industry until the early 1980s. Rothschild's dream that viticulture would provide a major source of income for the region had been shattered with the advent of three major events—the Russian revolution, the enactment of Prohibition in the United States, and the banning of imported wines to Egypt, those virtually eliminating the fledgling industry's three largest potential markets and causing many vineyards to be uprooted. Still, in the following decades several new wineries opened, including Segal, Eliaz and Stock, but for the most part they and Carmel continued to produce wines largely destined for sacramental purposes. The 1948 records testifying to the annual consumption of a mere 3.9 liters of wine per person showed that wine had not yet become part of the culture of life in Israel.

The Israeli Wine Revolution

In 1972, Professor Cornelius Ough of the Department of Viticulture and Oenology at the University of California at Davis visited Israel and suggested that the soil and climate of the Golan Heights would prove ideal for the raising of grapes. In 1976 the first vines were planted in the Golan, and in 1983 the then newly established Golan Heights Winery released its first wines. Almost overnight it became apparent that Israel was capable of producing wines of world-class quality. During the early 1980s the Israeli wine industry endured an economic crisis, but the revolution had begun and there was no turning back.

Unfettered by outdated winemaking traditions or by a large stagnant corporate structure, the young winery imported excellent vine stock from California, built a state-of-the-art winery, and added to this the enthusiasm and expertise of young American winemakers who had been trained at the University of California at Davis. Equally important, the Golan winery began to encourage vineyard owners to improve the quality of their grapes and, in the American tradition, paid bonuses for grapes with high sugar and acid content, while rejecting substandard grapes. The winery was also the first to realize that wines made from Grenache, Semillon, Petite Sirah and Carignan grapes would not put them on the world wine map, and focused on planting and making wines from Cabernet Sauvignon, Merlot, Sauvignon Blanc, Chardonnay, white Riesling, Gewurztraminer and other noble grape varieties.

The Golan wines were a success from the beginning not only within Israel but abroad. This success had a great impact on other Israeli wineries, which have made major steps in improving the quality of their wines. There are now five major wineries, twelve medium-sized wineries and a host of small wineries in the country, many of which are producing wines that are of high quality, and several producing wines good enough to interest connoisseurs all over the world.

The Current and Future State of Wine Production in Israel

Accurate data about the local wine industry is difficult to come by due to lack of coordination between the Israeli Wine Institute, the Ministry of Agriculture, the Export Institute and the Grape Grower's Association. When wineries submit their production and export figures, for example, they make no distinction between exports of table wines, sacramental wines, grape juice and even brandy and liqueurs. It is estimated that today Israel produces about thirty-six million bottles of table wine a year, that amount representing continued growth over the last five years of five to ten percent annually. Approximately forty thousand dunams (twenty thousand acres) of land are currently under grape cultivation, an increase of fifty percent in cultivated land area since 1995. Approximately sixty percent of the table wines produced today are dry reds, while as recently as 1995 production was seventy percent whites and only thirty percent reds.

Following an extended period in which the imagination of the wine-drinking public within Israel was captured by boutique wineries and garagistes, the years 2003–2006 might be regarded as the years of the larger wineries. In 2003, the Golan Heights Winery released the country's first varietal wines made from Sangiovese, Pinot Noir and Gamay grapes, as well as the country's first single-vineyard organically grown Chardonnay. Under its Yarden label, the winery also produced the country's first Semillon-botrytis wine. During that same year, Carmel released the first wines from its new boutique winery Yatir, and has continued to give us exciting single-vineyard Cabernet Sauvignon, Syrah and Chardonnay wines. Barkan introduced the country's first Pinotage wine. During 2005, Recanati released the country's first wine made from Barbera grapes and several of the medium-sized wineries gave us the country's first Zinfandel wines.

Although the Golan Heights Winery, with its Katzrin, Yarden, Gamla and Golan series, remains the obvious quality leader among the large wineries in the country, a great deal of excitement continues to be generated by Carmel and several other wineries, large and small. Two other large wineries, Binyamina and Efrat, have now joined the ranks of those wineries on the way up. Both of these wineries, now with well-trained winemakers aboard, are in the process of modernizing their equipment, gaining better control over their vineyards and producing several series of wines that are successfully capturing the attention of sophisticated wine drinkers.

Despite these positive signs, at least some of the larger wineries continue to face potential problems, some structural and economic and others relating to a grape glut resulting from several years of overplanting (from 1998–2002) that included grapes that held no hope for producing fine wines.

The Phenomenon of the Boutique Wineries

In recent years, the country has seen a dramatic growth in boutique wineries, garagistes, micro-wineries and artisanal producers, each striving to produce world-class wines. Such wineries, producing anywhere from under five hundred to one hundred thousand bottles annually, can remain highly personalized affairs, the winemakers having full control over their vineyards, knowing precisely what wine is in what barrel at any given moment and what style they want their wines to reflect. The label of a boutique winery does not, however, guarantee quality. At the top end of the range, a handful of small wineries founded by competent, well-trained professionals are producing some of the very best wines in the country. At the bottom end are numerous wineries founded by hobbyists who produce wines that are barely acceptable.

Many local boutique wineries, continuing to grow but

feeling they may have peaked in their local sales, are now seeking to export their wines. To date, however, the various consortiums that have been formed to promote such foreign sales have not shown exciting results.

Grape Growing Regions

The ideal areas for the cultivation of wine grapes lie in the two strips between 30–50 degrees north and south of the equator. Israel, which is located on the southern side of that strip in the Northern Hemisphere, is thus ideally situated. Considering Israel's specific climate, it is important to note that the vine can thrive in many different types of soil, and can thrive in regions that receive little rainfall.

Although the land area of Israel is a mere 7,992 square miles (which is five percent of the land area of California), like many wine-growing nations or regions that have a long north-south axis (Italy, Chile or California, for example), the country has a large variety of microclimates. In the north, snow falls in winter and conditions are comparable to those of Bordeaux and the Northern Rhone Valley of France, yet within a few hours' drive one arrives at the Negev Desert, where the climate is similar to that of North Africa.

The country is divided into five vine-growing regions, the names of which are generally accepted by the European community and appear on all labels of varietal wines that are designated for sale both locally and abroad. Each region is divided into sub-regions, encompassing specific valleys, mountains or other locales. Although various governmental and quasi-governmental agencies are considering implementing a more stringent *appellation controlee* system, the major regions today remain as follows:

GALILEE: Located in the northern part of the country, this area extends to the Lebanese border and incorporates the Golan Heights. It is the region most suited for viticulture in Israel. The high altitude, cool breezes, marked day and night temperature changes and rich, well-drained soils make the area ideal for the cultivation of a large variety of grapes.

The area is divided into four sub-regions: the Upper Galilee, the Lower Galilee, Tabor and the Golan Heights. Some of the wineries located here are the Golan Heights Winery, Galil Mountain, Chateau Golan, Dalton, Saslove and Tabor. Development of new vineyards continues apace in the area, many of these owned by wineries located in other parts of the country.

SHOMRON (SAMARIA): Located near the Mediterranean coast south of Haifa, and including the Carmel Mountain Range and surrounding the towns of Zichron Ya'akov and Binyamina, this region remains the largest grape growing area in the country. The area has medium-heavy soils and a Mediterranean climate, with warm summers and humid winters. Wineries in the area include Margalit, Tishbi, Binyamina, and the Zichron Ya'akov branch of Carmel, all relying at least in part for their better wines on grapes grown in other areas.

SHIMSHON (SAMSON): Located between the foothills of the Jerusalem Mountains and the Mediterranean coast, this region encompasses the central plains including the area around Rishon Letzion and Rehovot. Although the area boasts many vineyards, the limestone, clay and loamy soils and the coastal Mediterranean climate of warm, humid summers and mild winters do not offer ideal conditions for the cultivation of fine varieties, and many of the wineries in the area rely on grapes from other parts of the country. Among the wineries located here are Carmel, Barkan, Karmei Yosef, and Soreq.

JERUSALEM MOUNTAINS: Sometimes referred to as the Judean Hills, this region surrounding the city of Jerusalem offers a variety of soil conditions and a cool Mediterranean climate due to its relatively high altitude. For many years the region served as home primarily to wineries that specialized in sweet sacramental wines, but about a decade ago it became clear that this area could prove excellent for raising noble varieties. The area underwent strenuous revitalization with the major planting of sophisticated vineyards and the opening of several medium-sized and an increasing number of small wineries. More than twenty-five wineries are found in the area, including Castel, Clos de Gat, Sea Horse, Flam, Ella Valley Vineyards, Mony, Tzora and Efrat. It is clear that a true *route de vins* is developing in this region

NEGEV: Ten years ago, few would have thought this semi-arid desert region appropriate for growing grapes, but now, sophisticated computerized drip-irrigation systems have made it possible to grow high quality grapes here, including among others Merlot, Cabernet Sauvignon and Chardonnay. The region is divided into two sub-areas: Ramat Arad, which is situated 600–700 meters above sea level and has impressive night-day temperature changes, and where results with noble varieties has been excellent; and the Southern Negev, a lower, more arid area where sandy to loamy soils and very hot and dry summers offer a special challenge to grape growers. Carmel was the first to plant extensive vineyards at Ramat Arad. More recently, Barkan has begun extensive development of vineyards at Mitzpe Ramon in the heart of the Negev. Among the wineries found here, some rely entirely on desert-raised grapes. Others that draw as well on grapes from other areas are Yatir and Sde Boker.

Grape Varieties in Israel

The last two decades have seen a major upheaval in the vineyards of Israel. Prior to 1985 the grapes planted were largely Carignan, Petite Sirah and Grenache for red and rosé wines, and Semillon, Emerald Riesling, and Colombard for whites. The wineries focused on light, white and often sweet wines, and only a handful of noble varieties were to be found in the country. The scene shifted dramatically with the development of vineyards planted with noble varieties, first on the Golan Heights, then in the Upper Galilee. Today, from the Negev Desert to the northernmost parts of the country, the focus is on many of those varieties that have proven themselves throughout the world.

Unlike many of the wine-growing regions, especially in

Wine Regions
Vineyard Areas

Galilee
 Upper Galilee
 Lower Galilee
 Golan Heights

Shomron
 Mt. Carmel
 Sharon

Samson
 Dan
 Adulam
 Latrun

Jerusalem Mountains
 Beit-El
 Jerusalem
 Southern Jerusalem Mountains

Negev
 Northern Negev Hills
 Central Negev

Europe, Israel does not have any indigenous grapes that might be considered appropriate for making wine. The closest the country came to having its own grape was the introduction of the Argaman grape, a cross between Souzao and Carignan grapes. Widely planted in the early 1980s, that experiment proved a fiasco; although the grape yielded wines deep in color, they lacked flavor, depth or body. In the list that follows, those grapes capable of producing quality wines in Israel are noted with an asterisk (*).

White Wine Grapes

CHARDONNAY: The grape that produces the great dry white wines of Burgundy and is indispensable to the production of Champagne. The most popular white wine grape in the world today, producing wines that can be oaked or un-oaked, and range in flavors from flinty-minerals to citrus, pineapple, tropical fruits and grapefruit, and in texture from minerally-crisp to creamy. (*)

CHENIN BLANC: Originating in France's central Loire Valley, this thin-skinned and acidic grape has a high sugar content that can give aromas and flavors of honey and damp straw. Within Israel the grape has largely produced wines best categorized as ordinary, and often semi-dry.

COLOMBARD: Known in Israel as French Colombard and producing mostly thin and acidic wines.

EMERALD RIESLING: A cross between the Muscadelle and Riesling grapes developed in California primarily for growth in warm climates, the grape produces mostly semi-dry wines of little interest.

GEWURZTRAMINER: This grape originated in Germany, came to its glory in Alsace and has now been transplanted to many parts of the world. Capable of producing aromatic dry and sweet wines that are often typified by their softness and spiciness, as well as distinctive aromas and flavors of litchis and rose petals. (*)

MUSCAT: There are many varieties of Muscat, the two most often found in Israel being the Muscat of Alexandria and Muscat Canelli, both of which are capable of producing wines that range from the dry to the sweet and are almost always typified by their perfumed aromas.

RIESLING: Sometimes known in Israel as Johannisberg Riesling, sometimes as White Riesling and sometimes simply at Riesling, this noble German variety has the potential to produce wines that although light in body and low in alcohol are highly flavored and capable of long aging. Typified by aromas and flavors of flowers, minerals, lime, and when aged, sometimes taking on a tempting petrol-like aroma. (*)

SAUVIGNON BLANC: At its best in the Loire Valley and Bordeaux for producing dry white wines, this successful transplant to Israel is capable of producing refreshing, sophisticated and distinctively aromatic and grassy wines, often best consumed in their youth. (*)

SEMILLON: Although this native French grape was used for many years in Israel to produce largely uninteresting semi-dry white wines, its susceptibility to noble rot is now being taken advantage of to produce sweet dessert wines with the distinctive bouquet and flavors of melon, fig and citrus. (*)

TRAMINETTE: A not overly exciting hybrid, a derivative of the Gewurztraminer grape, developed primarily for use in cold weather New York State and Canadian climates.

VIOGNIER: The most recent white wine transplant to Israel, this grape produces the fascinating Condrieu wines of France's Rhone Valley. Capable of producing aromatic but crisply dry whites and full-bodied whites, some of which have long aging potential. (*)

Red Wine Grapes

ARGAMAN: An Israeli-inspired cross between Souzao and Carignan grapes. Possibly best categorized as the great local wine failure, producing wines of no interest. Many of the vineyards that were planted with Argaman continue to be uprooted to make room for more serious varieties.

BARBERA: From Italy's Piedmont region, this grape has the potential for producing wines that although light and fruity are capable of great charm. (*)

CABERNET SAUVIGNON: The most noble variety of Bordeaux, capable of producing superb wines, often blended with smaller amounts of Merlot and Cabernet Franc. The best wines from this grape are rich in color and tannins, and have complex aromas and depth of flavors, those often typified by blackcurrants, spices and cedar wood. At their best, intriguing and complex wines that profit from cellaring. (*)

CABERNET FRANC: Less intense and softer than Cabernet Sauvignon, most often destined to be blended with Merlot and Cabernet Sauvignon, but even on its own capable of producing dramatically good, leafy, fruity and aromatic reds. (*)

CARIGNAN: An old-timer on the Israeli scene, this originally Spanish grape produces largely dull and charmless wines. Still commonly planted within Israel but increasingly destined for distillation in the making of brandy and liqueurs. Several smaller wineries are, however, demonstrating that old-vine Carignan grapes, especially those in fields that have been unwatered for many years, can produce interesting and high quality wines.

GAMAY: The well-known grape of France's Beaujolais region, this fairly recent introduction to Israel is capable of producing light to medium-bodied wines of fragrance and charm, intended primarily for drinking in their youth. (*)

GRENACHE: Although this grape has done well in France's Rhone Valley and Spain, it has not yielded sophisticated wines in Israel, most being somewhat pale, overripe and sweet in nature. Probably at its best for blending.

MALBEC: Well known in France's Bordeaux, the Loire and Cahors, this grape is capable of producing dense, rich, tannic and spicy wines that are remarkably dark in color. (*)

MERLOT: Softer, more supple and often less tannic than Cabernet Sauvignon, with which it is often blended, but capable of producing voluptuous, opulent, plummy wines of great interest. A grape that has proven popular on its own as it produces wines that are easier to drink and are approachable earlier than wines made from Cabernet Sauvignon. (*)

NEBBIOLO: The grape from which the Barolo and Barbaresco wines of Italy's Piedmont region are made. Still experimental in Israel but with the potential for producing perfumed, fruity and intense wines that are full-bodied, high in tannins, acidity and color, and have the potential for long-term cellaring. (*)

PETIT VERDOT: Planted only in small quantities and used in Israel as it is in Bordeaux, primarily for blending with other noble varieties to add acidity and balance. Capable on its own of producing a long-lived and tannic wine when ripe. (*)

PETITE SIRAH: Related only peripherally to the great Syrah grape, this grape at its best is capable of producing dark, tannic and well-balanced wines of great appeal and sophistication, but that potential has been obtained only once or twice in Israel, the grape being used too often to produce mass-market wines that tend to be hot, tannic and without charm. A few small wineries manage to obtain excellent wines from this variety.

PINOT NOIR: A relatively recent transplant to Israel, this grape, which is responsible for the great reds of Burgundy, is making a very good initial showing. At its best the grape is capable of producing smooth, rich and intricate wines of exquisite qualities, with flavors of cherries, wild berries and violets and, as they age, take on aromas and flavors of chocolate and game meat. Also used in Israel, as in the Champagne region of France, to blend with Chardonnay to make sparkling wines. (*)

PINOTAGE: A South African cross between Pinot Noir and Cinsault, capable of being flavorful and powerful, yet soft and full, with a pleasing sweet finish and a lightly spicy overlay. (*)

SANGIOVESE: Italy's most frequently planted variety, found in the simplest Chianti and most complex Brunello di Montalcino wines, this is another grape recently introduced to Israel, showing fine early results with wines that are lively, fruity and full of charm. (*)

SYRAH: Some believe that this grape originated in ancient Persia and was brought to France by the Romans, while others speculate that it is indigenous to France. Syrah found its first glory in France's northern Rhone Valley, and then in Australia (where it is known as Shiraz). Capable of producing deep royal purple tannic wines that are full-bodied enough to be thought of as dense and powerful, but with excellent balance and complex aromas and flavors of plums, berries, currants, black pepper and chocolate. First results from this grape have been exciting and plantings are increasing dramatically. (*)

TEMPRANILLO: The staple grape of Spain's Rioja area, with recent plantings in Israel, this is a grape with the potential for producing long-lived complex and sophisticated wines typified by aromas and flavors of black fruits, leather, tobacco and spices. (*)

ZINFANDEL: Zinfandel is not exactly new in Israel, but until recently the vines that had been planted were capable of producing only mediocre semi-dry blush wines. What is new are recently planted high-quality vines from California that offer the potential for producing full-bodied to massive wines, moderately to highly alcoholic, with generous tannins and the kind of warm berry flavors that typify these wines at their best. (*)

Vintage Reports: 1976–2005

The first formal vintage tables appeared in the 1820s and since then wine lovers have relied on them to help make their buying and drinking decisions. As popular as they are, however, it is important to remember that because all vintage tables involve generalizations, there are no firm facts to be found in them. In a sense, these charts are meant to give an overall picture and perhaps to supply clues about which wines to consider buying or drinking. In making one's decisions it is wise to remember that the quality of wines of any vintage year and in any region can vary enormously between wineries. Also worth keeping in mind is that vintage reports and tables such as those that follow are based on what most people consider "quality wines" and not those made for everyday drinking and thus not intended for aging. More than this, estimates of drinkability are based on wines that have been shipped and stored under ideal conditions.

Following are short reports on the last five vintage years, these followed by a listing of the years of interest going back to 1976. Vintage years are rated on a scale of 20–100, and these numerical values can be interpreted as follows:

100	=	Extraordinary
90	=	Exceptional
80	=	Excellentw
70	=	Very Good
60	=	Good But Not Exciting
50	=	Average But With Many Faulted Wines
40	=	Mediocre/Not Recommended
30	=	Poor/Not Recommended
20	=	Truly Bad/Not Recommended

The following symbols are used to indicate drinking windows (Predictions of drinking windows are based on ideal storage since the wine was released.):

C	=	Worthy of Cellaring
D/C	=	Drink or Cellar
D	=	Drink Now or in the Next Year or So
D–	=	Past Its Prime but Probably Still Drinkable
SA	=	Well Beyond Its Prime and Probably

Undrinkable

The Last Five Years

2005 VINTAGE RATING 89
One of the most promising years in the last decade, with a prolonged harvest of overall high quality, exceptionally good in many parts of the country for reds and whites alike.

Barrel tastings reveal wines of excellent balance, structure and aging potential. C

2004 VINTAGE RATING 88
Colder than average temperatures and heavy rainfall during the winter months followed by an unusually warm and dry period during March and April caused early budbreak in warmer vineyards. Relatively cool temperatures returned in May leading to a relatively short and hectic harvest but with an overall excellent crop. A very promising year. C

2003 VINTAGE RATING 90
A cold and wet winter with precipitation about one third higher than normal was followed by unusually warm weather in May, leading to strong and rapid shoot growth and a hectic month of shoot positioning. Due to moderate and stable summer temperatures, harvest was stretched out to 17 weeks, concluding on November 18th. Overall, an excellent vintage year for both reds and whites. C

2002 VINTAGE RATING 82
In the north of the country the warm weather in February and March followed by a particularly cold spell in April and May stretched out the ripening season and resulted in an extended 15-week harvest. May rains during blooming caused a 15% reduction to yields. In the rest of the country several prolonged hot spells caused some vineyards to lose as much as 80% of their crop. Overall, only few acceptable wines and fewer appropriate for long-term cellaring. D/C

2001 VINTAGE RATING 85
This was one of the earliest harvest years in recent history. Not an exciting year, but overall, a better year for reds than whites. D

Somewhat Older Vintages

2000	89	D/C
1999	86	D/C
1998	85	D/C
1997	90	D/C

1996	82	D-
1995	90	D-
1994	84	SA
1993	92	D/C
1992	85	SA
1991	82	SA
1990	91	D
1989	90	SA
1988	85	SA
1987	78	SA
1986	76	SA
1985	90	SA
1984	86	SA
1983	55	SA
1982	55	SA
1979	92	SA
1976	92	SA

Questions of Kashrut

For many years, wines that were kosher had a justifiably bad name, those in the United States being made largely from Concord grapes, which are far from capable of making fine wine, and many of those from Israel following the perceived need for kosher wines to be red, sweet, coarse and without any sign of sophistication. The truth is that those wines were not so much consumed by knowledgeable wine lovers as they were used for sacramental purposes. Such wines are still made but are today perceived largely as oddities, and with kosher wines now being made from the most noble grape varieties in state-of-the-art wineries by talented winemakers, there need be no contradiction whatsoever between the kosher laws and the production of fine wine.

Some Israeli Wines are Kosher, Others are Not

A look at the current Israeli wine scene indicates that the wines of every large winery and the majority of medium-sized wineries in Israel are kosher, but those of the smaller wineries are often not.

For many years, with the exception of those wines made in Christian monasteries, all of the wines produced in Israel were kosher. The reasons for this were and still are twofold. The first reason relates to the fact that a large proportion of the Israeli population, even among the non-observant, consume only foods and beverages that are kosher. The second, also with a clear economic basis, is that only kosher products can enter the large supermarket chains in the country. Because the majority of wines produced in the country continued to be purchased in supermarkets, no large winery can give up that large sales potential. Moreover, kashrut is maintained because many of the wineries continue to target their export sales largely toward Jewish consumers worldwide.

The wines of several medium-sized producers and many of the boutique wineries have a somewhat different goal in mind—that of producing upper-end wines that are targeted toward higher-end and not necessarily kashrut-observant wine consumers both in Israel and abroad. Especially for small wineries, the production of kosher wines, which more than anything adds the need for additional staff (for example, rabbinical supervisors), as well as fees to the rabbinical authorities, can add prohibitively to their costs and to the eventual retail price of their wines.

What Makes an Israeli Wine Kosher?

In order for an Israeli wine to be certified as kosher, several requirements must be met. As can easily be seen, none of these requirements has a negative impact on the quality of the wine being produced and several are widely acknowledged to be sound agricultural practices even by producers of non-kosher wines.

1. According to the practice known as *orla*, the grapes of new vines cannot be used for winemaking until the fourth year after planting.
2. No other fruits or vegetables may be grown in between the rows of vines (*kalai hakerem*).
3. After the first harvest, the fields must lie fallow every

seventh year. Each of these sabbatical years is known as *shnat shmita*.

4. From the onset of the harvest only kosher tools and storage facilities may be used in the winemaking process, and all of the winemaking equipment must be cleaned to be certain that no foreign objects remain in the equipment or vats.
5. From the moment the grapes reach the winery, only Sabbath observant Jews are allowed to come in contact with the wine. Because many of the winemakers in the country are not Sabbath observant, that means that they cannot personally handle the equipment or the wine as it is being made and are assisted in several of their more technical tasks by Orthodox assistants and kashrut supervisors (*mashgichim*).
6. All of the materials (e.g. yeasts) used in the production and clarification of the wines must be certified as kosher.
7. A symbolic amount of wine, representing the tithe (*truma vema'aser*) once paid to the Temple in Jerusalem must be poured away from the tanks or barrels in which the wine is being made.

The Question of Wines that are Mevushal

Some observant Jews demand that their wines be pasteurized (*mevushal*), especially in restaurants and at catered events, where there is the possibility that a non-Jew may handle the wine. This tradition dates to ancient times, when wine was used by pagans for idolatrous worship: the Israelites used to boil their wines, thus changing the chemical composition of the wine so that it was considered unfit for pagan worship. Wines that are *mevushal* have the advantage that they can be opened and poured by non-Jews or Jews who are not Sabbath observant.

Today, *mevushal* wines are no longer boiled. After the grapes are crushed, the common practice is to rapidly raise the temperature of the liquids to 176–194 degrees Fahrenheit

(80–90 Celsius) in special flash pasteurizing units, hold it there for under a minute and then return the temperature, equally rapidly, to 60 degrees Fahrenheit (15 Celsius).

There is no question but that modern technology has reduced the impact of these processes on the quality of the wine, but most winemakers and consumers remain in agreement that, with very few exceptions, wines that have been pasteurized lose many of their essential essences, often being incapable of developing in the bottle and quite often imparting a "cooked" sensation to the nose and palate.

Some wines are produced in both regular and *mevushal* versions, the *mevushal* editions destined for the export market or for the highly observant within Israel. Because it is almost impossible for anyone outside of the wineries to keep track of and taste all of those wines, no attempt is made within this book to report on such "double bottlings."

Simply stated, a wine that is *mevushal* is no more or less kosher than a wine that is not, and none of the better wines of Israel today fall into this category. Those who are concerned with such issues will find the information they require on either the front or rear labels of wines produced in the country.

A Few Lists

The Ten Best Wine Producers

1. Golan Heights Winery (Katzrin, Yarden, Gamla, Golan)
2. Castel
3. Flam
4. Margalit
5. Yatir
6. Galil Mountain
7. Saslove
8. Amphorae
9. Recanati
10. Carmel (Single Vineyard, Regional)

Ten New or Up-and-Coming Producers

1. Clos de Gat
2. Chateau Golan
3. Ella Valley
4. Sea Horse
5. Carmei Yosef
6. Alexander
7. Gustavo & Jo
8. Bazelet ha Golan
9. Orna Chillag
10. La Terra Promessa

The Ten Fastest Improving Producers

1. Carmel
2. Barkan (including Segal)
3. Tabor
4. Dalton
5. Zauberman
6. Vitkin
7. Gush Etzion
8. La Terra Promessa
9. Binyamina
10. Efrat

The 10 Best Value Producers

1. Galil Mountain
2. Golan Heights Winery
3. Dalton
4. Flam
5. Tabor
6. Amphorae
7. Recanati
8. Orna Chillag
9. Saslove
10. Tishbi

The Ten Best Wines Released in the Last Twelve Months

Margalit, Cabernet Sauvignon, Special Reserve, 2003
Flam, Cabernet Sauvignon Reserve, 2003
Carmel, Cabernet Sauvignon, Kayoumi, 2003
Golan Heights Winery, Cabernet Sauvignon, Yarden, 2002
Yatir, Yatir Forest, 2003
Sea Horse, Elul, 2003
Recanati, Special Reserve, 2003
Carmel, Merlot, Har Bracha, 2002
Dalton, Cabernet Sauvignon, Meron Vineyard, 2004
Ella Valley Vineyards, Cabernet Sauvignon, Vineyards Choice, 2003

Drinking Habits

Within Israel

Since the founding of the state in 1948 and until 1997, annual Israeli wine consumption held steady at about 3.9 liters per capita. Recent years have seen a major increase, and consumption now stands at close to 8 liters annually. This figure puts Israelis far behind the French and Italians, who consume 56 and 49 liters respectively, or even the Australians who consume 20 liters per year.

The increase in local consumption reflects of course the increasing quality of local wines, but at the same time it also reflects the fact that more and more Israelis are traveling abroad and dining in fine restaurants where wine is an integral part of the meal. Today many Israelis are touring the fine wineries of Bordeaux, Tuscany and the Napa Valley, and even though such wine appreciation is still limited to the upwardly mobile segment of the population, more and more people will now order wine to accompany their meal in a fine restaurant.

In addition to showing a growing appreciation of wine in general, Israelis are moving in several directions that can be seen in many other countries as well. Consumption is shifting from semi-dry to dry wines, from whites to reds, from light to heavier wines and most important, there is a movement toward buying higher quality wines. Twenty-five years ago, more than eighty percent of the wines produced in the country were sweet. Today, nearly eighty percent of the wines produced are dry.

Israelis have also dramatically increased their consumption of imported wines, and the better wine shops of the country stock wines from every region of France, Italy, Australia, New Zealand, California, Washington State, Spain, Portugal, Germany, Austria, Chile and Argentina. Some members of the local wine industry perceive this phenomenon as having a negative impact on the local industry. Others, perhaps with a greater sense of foresight, realize that imported wines pose a challenge to the local wine industry to continue to improve the quality of its products.

Sacramental versus "Wine Culture"

Within Israel, as in nearly every country with a Jewish population, some continue to drink wine entirely for sacramental purposes—for the *kiddush* blessing that begins the two main meals of the Sabbath and holidays. An increasing number have realized that any kosher wine is appropriate for such purposes, but others hold to the perceived tradition that such wines should be red, thick and sweet. Although those wines hold no interest for sophisticated wine drinkers, several of the large wineries continue to produce *kiddush* wines and there are wineries that focus entirely on these consumers.

Within the "Jewish World"

Nearly all of the better wine stores of the major cities of North America, the United Kingdom and France have at least a small section devoted to kosher wines, and in recent years the wines of Israel have taken a more prominent space on those shelves alongside kosher wines from California, France, Spain, Australia, Chile and Argentina. Israeli wines, both kosher and non-kosher, are receiving a warmer reception, now being reviewed more regularly in magazines devoted to wine as well as in the weekly wine columns of many critics, and also appearing on the menus of many prestigious restaurants.

Israel as a Potential Supplier of "Niche Wines"

Wine lovers enjoy few things more than hunting for previously unknown or little-known wines. So it has been in recent years, for example, with the wines of Sicily, and the Penedes region of Spain: when those wines first arrived on the shelves of wine stores in New York, London and Toronto, they filled an empty "niche." The first wines sold out quickly, those that proved to be of high quality were reordered, and those that came to be accepted as truly excellent moved out of the niche category and onto the regular shelves.

Many, including this critic, feel that Israeli wines are on the verge of being accepted, especially in North America and the United Kingdom, as niche wines. As that happens, the wines will move off those shelves limited only to kosher holdings and begin to appear in a special Israeli section. Their appeal to the broader population will come from their unique qualities, reflecting their Mediterranean and specifically Israeli character.

The Wineries and their Wines

For many years it was possible to group Israeli wine producers into one of two broad categories—large and small wineries. The last four years have seen dramatic changes, for during that time five new medium-sized producers have appeared on the local scene, several of the wineries that could be categorized as boutiques have expanded their production, and a host of small wineries continue to open. Within each category there are wineries that produce excellent and often exciting wines.

The wines reviewed in this guide include only those I have tasted—wines already on the market, wines due to be released within the next several months, or those still in the cellars or homes of wine lovers. Also listed are barrel tastings, some being those of wines scheduled to be released only in another 2–3 years. Not included in the guide are wineries that produce wines primarily for sacramental purposes, as those wines hold no interest for wine consumers at large. Nor, with only a few exceptions, does the guide rate the wines of those wineries producing under 1,500 bottles annually. Ratings for wineries (1–5 stars) are based on current status. For those wineries that have released only one or two vintages, the ratings should be considered as tentative, since they might move up or down in the next edition of this guide.

Agur ★★★

Set on Moshav Agur in the Judean plains, this small winery, owned by winemaker Shuki Yashuv, has grown from releasing 1,800 bottles in the 2000 vintage to about 7,000 from 2005. The winery has its own vineyards on the *moshav* and also draws on grapes from the Ella Valley, those including Cabernet Sauvignon and Merlot, with Cabernet Franc and Petit Verdot coming on line with the 2005 harvest. Grapes from each vineyard are fermented separately, some in stainless steel vats, others in new and used *barriques*.

Special Reserve

SPECIAL RESERVE, CABERNET SAUVIGNON, 2004: Full-bodied, with generous spicy oak and vanilla backed up by still firm tannins that yield nicely to show generous currant, blackberry and licorice aromas and flavors. Drink from release–2008. Tentative Score 86–88.

SPECIAL RESERVE, CABERNET SAUVIGNON, 2003: With 20 months in oak, this dark ruby, medium to full-bodied red shows still firm tannins that need time to integrate and reveal the generous aromas and flavors including cassis, blackberries and spices that are waiting to unfold. Drink now–2008. Score 86.

SPECIAL RESERVE, CABERNET SAUVIGNON, 2001: Deep garnet in color, this medium to full-bodied, firmly tannic and generously oaky wine offers up currant and berry fruits on a background of spices and Mediterranean herbs. Drink now. Score 86.

Agur

AGUR, CABERNET SAUVIGNON, 2004: Dark ruby towards garnet, medium-to full-bodied, with chunky country-style tannins and appealing blackberry, currant and spicy aromas and flavors. Drink now–2008. Score 86.

AGUR, CABERNET SAUVIGNON, 2003: Medium to full-bodied, deep garnet in color, with near-sweet tannins, gentle wood and appealing currant, berry and herbal aromas and flavors. Drink now–2008. Score 86.

AGUR, CABERNET SAUVIGNON, 2002: An oak-aged country-style blend of 85% Cabernet Sauvignon and 15% Merlot. Medium-bodied, with chunky tannins and appealing black fruit and herbal aromas and flavors. Not complex but pleasant. Drink up. Score 85.

AGUR, CABERNET SAUVIGNON, 2001: Deep ruby toward garnet in color, this medium-bodied blend of 95% Cabernet Sauvignon and 5% Merlot spent one year in new and older wood barrels. With somewhat chunky tannins, this country-style wine has a sweet herbal aroma along with currant and plum flavors. Drink up. Score 85.

AGUR, CABERNET SAUVIGNON-MERLOT, KESEM, 2004: Garnet red, medium-bodied, with soft tannins balanced by a gentle wood influence and forward berry, black cherry and cassis fruits. Drink now. Score 86.

AGUR, CABERNET SAUVIGNON-MERLOT, KESEM, 2003: Medium-bodied, with good balance between country-style tannins, spicy wood and berry, black cherry and currant fruits. Drink now. Score 85.

AGUR, CABERNET SAUVIGNON-MERLOT, 2002: Deep ruby red, this light to medium-bodied blend of 60% Cabernet and 40% Merlot has youthful plum, berry, mineral and smoky oak aromas and flavors. Perhaps best when served lightly chilled. Drink up. Score 85.

AGUR, CABERNET-MERLOT, 2001: A perhaps too powerful toasty oak flavor imparts a chewy texture, but given a chance to open in the glass the wine yields appealing currant and berry fruits. Past its peak. Drink up. Score 85.

Alexander ✦✦✦✦

Founded in 1996 by Yoram Shalom and located on Moshav Beit Yitzhak in the Sharon region, the winery receives grapes largely from contract vineyards at Kerem Ben Zimra in the Upper Galilee, and has full control over those vineyards. Primary output to date has been of Cabernet Sauvignon, Merlot, Chardonnay and Sauvignon Blanc and now coming on line are Syrah and Grenache.

Growth has been steady, increasing from about 12,000 bottles in 2002 to 45,000 in 2005. With the 2006 vintage the winery will switch over to kosher production and planned output for that harvest is 60,000–70,000 bottles. In addition to producing two top-of-the-line series, Alexander the Great and The Wine of Alexander, the winery also releases a second wine, Sandro, a Port-style wine, and private label wines for several restaurants.

Alexander the Great

ALEXANDER THE GREAT, CABERNET SAUVIGNON, 2005: Made from grapes from 26 year old vines, this medium to full-bodied dark garnet red wine shows soft tannins, spicy wood and a tempting array of mineral, black fruit, herbal and chocolate aromas. On the long finish, cloves and a hint of iodine. Best 2009–2013. Tentative Score 91–93.

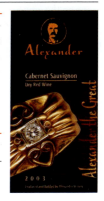

ALEXANDER THE GREAT, CABERNET SAUVIGNON, 2004: Full bodied and reflecting the oak in which it developed with firm, near-sweet tannins and hints of smoke. Generous and long with a complex array of currant, herbal and mineral aromas and flavors. Best 2008–2011. Tentative Score 88–90.

ALEXANDER THE GREAT, CABERNET SAUVIGNON, 2003: Generous wood and tannins in fine balance with currant, plum and herbal aromas and flavors, those complemented on the long finish by mocha and sweet cedar. Drink from release–2011. Tentative Score 89–91.

ALEXANDER THE GREAT, CABERNET SAUVIGNON, 2002: Full-bodied, with firm tannins and generous smoky oak, those coming together nicely with blackcurrant, blackberry and light hints of herbs and espresso. Generous and mouthfilling but with a hint of not entirely wanted bitterness that comes in on the finish. Drink now–2010. Score 89.

ALEXANDER THE GREAT, CABERNET SAUVIGNON, 2001: Almost massive in structure and body, the wine shows generous tannins nicely balanced by spicy wood, black fruits, herbs and a hint of eucalyptus. Drink now. Score 91.

ALEXANDER THE GREAT, CABERNET SAUVIGNON, 2000: This firm and concentrated blend of 95% Cabernet Sauvignon and 5% Merlot boasts a dark ruby toward garnet color and a rich, almost luxurious texture, along with layers of currants, wild berries, black cherries and plums. Good toasty oak flavors and a long opulent finish. Drink now. Score 91.

ALEXANDER THE GREAT, CABERNET SAUVIGNON, 1999: Deep purple, this medium to full-bodied blend of 95% Cabernet Sauvignon and 5% Merlot spent 24 months in American and French oak barrels. Rich and concentrated aromas and flavors of currants, plums and orange peel along with chocolate, vanilla, light spicy overlays and a distinct hint of mint on the long finish. A bit past its peak. Drink up. Score 89.

The Wine of Alexander

ALEXANDER, CABERNET SAUVIGNON, 2005: Medium to full-bodied, dark ruby in color, with generous soft tannins and showing vanilla and spices from the casks in which it is aging. On the nose and palate, rich blackcurrant and blackberry fruits along with hints of earthiness. Generous and long. Drink from release–2010. Tentative Score 88–90.

ALEXANDER, CABERNET SAUVIGNON, 2004: Medium to full-bodied, with gripping tannins and wood nicely balanced by generous black fruits, the wine promises to be elegant. Drink from release–2009. Tentative Score 87–89.

ALEXANDER, CABERNET SAUVIGNON, 2003: Not as aromatic as earlier vintages but opening to an array of flavors including black fruits, Mediterranean herbs and licorice. Medium to full-bodied, with soft tannins and a moderately long vanilla and mint finish. Drink now–2008. Score 89.

ALEXANDER, CABERNET SAUVIGNON, 2002: Deep royal purple in color, this young wine with still closing tannins shows good blackcurrant, berry and earthy-herbal aromas and flavors, but lacks somewhat in depth and length. Drink now. Score 86.

ALEXANDER, CABERNET SAUVIGNON, 2001: Spicy, earthy overlays complement rich plum and berry flavors and just a hint of vanilla. Soft tannins integrating well in this full-bodied wine. Drink now. Score 90.

ALEXANDER, CABERNET SAUVIGNON, 2000: Medium to full-bodied with well-integrated tannins, the wine shows warm blackcurrant, berry, toasty oak and vanilla flavors, all on a delicate spicy background. Mouth-filling and with a moderately long finish. Drink now. Score 89.

ALEXANDER, CABERNET SAUVIGNON, 1999: Full-bodied, with generous and well-integrated tannins, the wine offers aromas and flavors of currants, berries, herbs and a light earthiness. A bit past its peak but still elegant and complex. Drink up. Score 90.

ALEXANDER, CABERNET SAUVIGNON, 1998: This round Cabernet still shows freshness and good fruits but is now taking on overtones and a finish of bitter herbs. Past its peak. Drink up. Score 86.

ALEXANDER, MERLOT, 2005: Deep royal purple, with firm but nicely integrating tannins and hints of spicy wood and tobacco balanced nicely by a generous array of black plum, raspberry, cassis and chocolate aromas and flavors. Best from 2008. Tentative Score 89–91.

ALEXANDER, MERLOT, 2004: Dark cherry towards garnet, medium-bodied, with soft tannins integrating nicely. Round and generous, with cassis, blackberry and black cherry fruits accompanied by hints of pepper and nutmeg. Drink from release–2008. Tentative Score 86–88.

ALEXANDER, MERLOT, 2003: Well-balanced with ripe plum, black cherry, currant, sweet cedar and hazelnut aromas and flavors. Smooth and supple, with soft tannins and a hint of mocha on the finish. Drink now–2008. Score 88.

ALEXANDER, MERLOT, 2002: Medium to full-bodied, with anise and menthol aromas and flavors backing up cherry, plum and currant fruits, with hints of green olives, herbs and tobacco. Elegant and supple but not meant for long-term cellaring. Drink now. Score 89.

ALEXANDER, MERLOT, 2001: Intense, deep and elegant, with a solid core of cherry, currant and light oak, this now fully mature medium to full-bodied wine continues to show depth and complexity. Drink up. Score 90.

ALEXANDER, MERLOT, 2000: Medium to full-bodied, fully mature, with its tannins well integrated, this ripe cherry, berry and currant flavored wine continues to show good balance between oak, fruits and tannins. Look for a very appealing herbal finish. Drink now. Score 89.

ALEXANDER, MERLOT, 1999: Medium to full-bodied, with abundant soft tannins and berry, cherry and toasty oak aromas and flavors, those with appealing spicy notes leading to a moderately long finish. Drink up. Score 88.

ALEXANDER, SYRAH, 2005: Dark royal purple in color, full bodied, with deep but remarkably soft tannins. Hints of smoky wood, freshly turned earth, and spices, those on a background of black fruits, and on the finish, light smoked meat. Best from 2008. Tentative Score 89–91.

ALEXANDER, SHIRAZ, 2002: Dark garnet red, this medium to full-bodied wine was aged in French oak *barriques* for 15 months. Ripe berry-cherry fruits with soft tannins, spicy oak and a hint of vanilla. Drink up. Score 87.

ALEXANDER, ROSÉ, 2005: Made entirely from Grenache grapes, this deep pink towards ruby wine shows light to medium body, crisp acidity and an array of tutti-frutti aromas and flavors, those including bananas, raspberries, strawberries and chopped citrus peel. Drink up. Score 87.

ALEXANDER, CHARDONNAY, LIZA, 2005: Medium-bodied, showing an appealing oak influence. A lively wine, with citrus, melon, and apple aromas and flavors, those lingering on a long finish which shows hints of figs and pie crust. Drink now. Score 88.

ALEXANDER, CHARDONNAY, LIZA, 2004: Light golden straw in color and medium-bodied, with tantalizing hints of cream and yeast. Opens with a distinct pineapple hint but that turns in the glass to fig, pear and apples, all with a spicy and pleasingly light bitter overtone. Drink up. Score 87.

ALEXANDER, SAUVIGNON BLANC, 2005: Unoaked, straw colored and concentrated, with generous lime, citrus peel, green apple and grapefruit aromas and flavors matched by hints of herbs, honeysuckle and sweet peas on a tart and lively finish that lingers nicely. Drink now. Score 88.

Sandro

SANDRO, 2003: Medium-bodied, dark garnet in color, with soft tannins and reflecting a gentle hand with the wood, this blend of Cabernet Sauvignon and Merlot offers up currant, cranberry and red plum fruits. Soft and round. Drink up. Score 87.

SANDRO, 2002: A medium-bodied Cabernet-Merlot blend with soft tannins, generous black fruits and appealing vanilla and smoky oak overlays. Drink up. Score 85.

SANDRO, 2001: This medium-bodied oak-aged blend of 70% Cabernet Sauvignon and 30% Merlot, now fully mature, shows well integrated soft tannins, sweet wood and vanilla, and currant, black cherry and berry fruits. Drink up. Score 87.

Aligote ✲✲

Established by Tsvika Fante and located on Moshav Gan Yoshiya on the central Coastal Plain, the first wines released by this winery were 800 bottles from the 2002 harvest. Production in 2003 was 2,500 bottles and in 2004 and 2005 grew to 3,000 bottles.

ALIGOTE, CABERNET SAUVIGNON, 2004: A blend of 92.5% Cabernet Sauvignon and 7.5% Shiraz. Medium- to full-bodied, with generous soft tannins balanced nicely by toasty oak and appealing aromas and flavors of currants, wild berries and tobacco. Drink now–2008. Score 85.

ALIGOTE, CABERNET SAUVIGNON, 2003: Dark garnet, this full-bodied red shows good balance between soft tannins and sweet vanilla from the American oak in which it was aged. Round and mouth-filling, with blackcurrant, plum and orange peel aromas and flavors. Long and comfortable on the palate. Drink now. Score 86.

ALIGOTE, CABERNET SAUVIGNON, 2002: Deep ruby red, medium to full-bodied, with chunky tannins and pronounced acidity on berry, cherry and cassis fruits. Lacking balance. Drink up. Score 83.

ALIGOTE, MERLOT 2004: Garnet towards purple, this medium-bodied blend of 90% Merlot with 5% each of Cabernet Sauvignon and Shiraz shows chunky country-style tannins balanced nicely by spicy wood and appealing blackberry and black cherry aromas and flavors. Drink now. Score 85.

ALIGOTE, MERLOT, 2003: This deep garnet, medium-bodied softly tannic wine shows appealing berry, black cherry and orange peel aromas and flavors as well as light overlays of bittersweet chocolate and freshly picked tarragon on the long finish. Drink now. Score 85.

ALIGOTE, MERLOT, 2002: Medium-bodied, with generous, well-integrating tannins, this oak-aged blend of 93% Merlot and 7% Shiraz offers ample plum, berry and currant aromas and flavors, those backed up by spices and vanilla as well as a rather marked oaky note. Drink up. Score 84.

ALIGOTE, SANGIOVESE, 2003: Deep purple in color, medium-bodied, with soft tannins and raspberry and black cherry fruits, the wine is now falling apart and past its peak. Drink up. Score 79.

ALIGOTE, CABERNET SAUVIGNON-MERLOT, 2002: Medium-bodied, with chunky tannins and somewhat stingy black fruits. Lacking balance or length. Drink up. Score 82.

Alon *

Located on Moshav Alonei Aba, north of Haifa, this small winery recently changed hands. Under former owner Gal Segev the winery produced 3,000 bottles from the 2003 vintage. No wines have been released from the 2004 vintage but new owner-winemaker Chaim Cachala will release about 4,000 bottles from the 2005 vintage. To date the winery has released two varietal wines, Cabernet Sauvignon and Merlot. Drawing largely on grapes from the Galilee and the Jezreel Valley, the winery is currently experimenting with other varieties, those including Petit Verdot, Cabernet Franc, Shiraz, Sangiovese and Nebbiolo.

ALON, CABERNET SAUVIGNON, 2003: Dark ruby, medium-bodied, with a somewhat woody influence but also showing attractive cassis and berry fruits along with hints of vanilla. Firmly tannic on the finish. Drink now. Score 83.

ALON, CABERNET SAUVIGNON, 2002: Garnet toward purple, medium-bodied, with appealing currant and berry fruits, this is a simple country-style wine. Drink up. Score 80.

ALON, CABERNET SAUVIGNON, 2001: Medium-bodied, with fruits hidden under coarse tannins and the too-strong influence of wood. Drink up. Score 75.

ALON, CABERNET SAUVIGNON, 2000: Dark royal purple and medium-bodied, faulted, with aromas and flavors that are too reminiscent of concentrated fruit juice. Drink up. Drink up. Score 74.

ALON, CABERNET SAUVIGNON, 1999: Medium-bodied, with perhaps overly sweet plum and cherry flavors, this rather coarse country-style wine is showing age. Drink up. Score 72.

ALON, MERLOT, 2003: Dark ruby in color, a somewhat oaky and tannic country-style wine with a few black fruits and a hint of spiciness. Drink now. Score 83.

ALON, MERLOT, 2002: Ruby toward garnet in color, this simple medium-bodied, oak-aged wine has well integrated soft tannins and pleasant currant and berry fruits. Drink up. Score 82.

ALON, MERLOT, 2001: Deep ruby toward purple in color, medium-bodied, with chunky tannins and berry-black cherry fruits, the wine is well past its peak and no longer scoreable.

ALON, MERLOT 2000: Aged in oak for one year, this dark purple, medium-bodied wine offers up unusually tough tannins for a Merlot, and subdued aromas and flavors of stewed black fruits that fail to linger. Drink up. Score 76.

Amphorae *****

Set in a green and luxuriant mouth of a long dormant volcano on the Makura Ranch, on the western slopes of Mount Carmel, and using grapes from some of the best vineyards of the Golan Heights and the Upper Galilee, the winery is headed by winemaker Gil Shatzberg, one of the winemakers at the cutting edge of today's Israeli wine scene.

Production from the 2000 vintage was 23,000 bottles, from the 2003 vintage about 55,000 and in 2004 and 2005, 70,000 bottles. In 2005 the winery moved into a new, beautiful, state-of-the-art winery and target production is 80,000–100,000 bottles annually.

The winery's top-of-the-line series is Amphorae, and their second wines are under the Rhyton label. Both of these series are age-worthy, while wines in the Med.Red series are meant for relatively early drinking.

Amphorae is the Greek term for tall, double handled jugs with narrow necks and bases, often made of clay, that were used by the Greeks and later by the Romans for storing and shipping wine, and the original rhyton was an ancient Greek cup, most often shaped like a drinking horn.

Amphorae

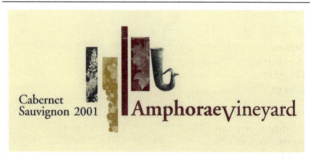

AMPHORAE, CABERNET SAUVIGNON, RESERVE, 2005: Still in embryonic form but already showing firm but comfortably yielding tannins and, on the nose and palate, generous black fruits. With the potential for true elegance. Best from 2009. Tentative Score 92–94.

AMPHORAE, CABERNET SAUVIGNON, 2005: In its formative stages, but already showing fine balance between wood, sweet tannins and earthy, lightly spicy plum and currant fruits. Best 2008–2011. Tentative Score 90–92.

AMPHORAE, CABERNET SAUVIGNON, 2004: Full-bodied and solid but soft enough to be thought of as caressing, with generous blackberry, plum, cherry, mineral and cocoa notes set off by vanilla and creamy oak. Forward but not vulgar and with structure and balance that bode well for its future. Drink from release–2011. Tentative Score 91–93.

AMPHORAE, CABERNET SAUVIGNON, 2003: Blended with a small percentage of Petite Sirah, this full-bodied, harmonious wine shows excellent balance between still firm tannins, wood, and juicy currant and cherry fruits and spices. With intriguing raspberry, chocolate and mocha flavors on the finish, this is a complex and delicious wine. Drink now–2011. Score 91.

AMPHORAE, CABERNET SAUVIGNON, 2002: A good effort from the spotty 2002 vintage year. An appealing medium to full-bodied wine with generous fruits well balanced by oak and moderate tannins but without the concentration or structure for long-term cellaring. Drink now. Score 88.

AMPHORAE, CABERNET SAUVIGNON, 2001: Delicious, traditional Cabernet with a small amount of Syrah blended in. This full-bodied, deep garnet toward royal purple wine shows a tempting array of blackcurrant and plum fruits, those backed up nicely by generous hints of spices and mocha, wood and fruits, and a long and luxurious finish. Drink now–2009. Score 91.

AMPHORAE, CABERNET SAUVIGNON, SPECIAL RESERVE, 2000: Deep red, remarkably rich, complex and aromatic. With excellent balance, tiers of currant, plum, Mediterranean herbs and sweet oak, and a long finish, this is a wine well worthy of cellaring. Drink now–2014. Score 93.

AMPHORAE, CABERNET SAUVIGNON, 2000: A full-bodied Cabernet so intense and powerful that you might be tempted to think of it as potent. With its firm tannins integrating nicely, this dark and deep wine is now showing currant, blackberry and plum aromas and flavors, all with generous overlays of pepper and chocolate. Drink now–2008. Score 93.

AMPHORAE, MERLOT, ORGANIC, 2005: From the organic vineyard at Makura Ranch and made entirely according to organic principles, this medium to full-bodied wine reflects its volcanic *terroir* with gentle layers of earth and ash serving as a comfortable background for purple plum and cassis aromas and flavors. Rich, elegant and long. Drink from release–2009. Tentative Score 90–92.

AMPHORAE, MERLOT, 2004: Dark royal purple in color, dense, with firm and chewy tannins and generous wood well balanced by ripe black cherry, plum, raspberry and briar flavors, all lingering nicely on the palate. Best 2008–2012. Tentative Score 91–93.

AMPHORAE, MERLOT, 2003: Blended with 10% of Cabernet, this outstanding Merlot offers cherry, currant, anise and cedar aromas and flavors, those coming together nicely with firm tannins and the judicious use of oak. Concentrated, elegant, graceful and long, the wine is now coming beautifully into its own. Drink now–2010. Score 91.

AMPHORAE, MERLOT, 2002: Supple and fruity, with soft tannins well balanced by gentle oak and appealing berry, cassis and plum fruits. Not complex and not for long-term cellaring but a good match to food. Drink now. Score 87.

AMPHORAE, MERLOT, 2001: Medium to full-bodied, with firm tannins integrating nicely, and with tempting berries, plums, herbs and light spices. Aromatic, rich and with a long ripe finish, the wine clearly reflects its Mediterranean *terroir*. Drink now–2008. Score 90.

AMPHORAE, MERLOT, 2000: Deep royal purple in color, this blend of 95% Merlot, 2% Cabernet Sauvignon and 3% Petite Sirah is well knit but not tight, firm but not muscular, and very well balanced, with dark fruits well set off by light and appealing herbal and vanilla aromas and flavors. Drink now. Score 91.

AMPHORAE, CABERNET SAUVIGNON-MERLOT, 2002: Tight, ripe and complex, with layers of black cherry, plum, berry and spices, and with hints of herbs and black olives that come in near the finish, this medium to full-bodied wine offers well-integrated tannins, a smooth texture and a moderately long fruity finish. Drink now. Score 90.

AMPHORAE, CABERNET FRANC, 2004: Deep garnet, with bright raspberry and plum flavors, this dark, rich and plush wine shows thick, earthy tannins and gamy currant and cedar wood aromas and flavors. Perhaps not elegant but certainly powerful and complex. Drink now–2012. Score 90.

AMPHORAE, SYRAH, 2005: Still in embryonic form but showing the kind of balance and structure that may make this Israel's longest lived Syrah to date. Round, ripe and generous, with an almost tangy balance between plum, blackberry, black cherry and exotic spices, those backed up by generous soft tannins. On the long finish touches of black pepper and citrus peel. Best 2008–2015. Tentative Score 92–94.

AMPHORAE, SYRAH, 2004: Firm and well structured tannins now integrating and showing a core of leather, spicy wood and earthiness that highlight rich currant, wild berry, anise and lightly beefy flavors. On the long finish generous hints of espresso coffee, violets and toffee. Destined for elegance. Drink now–2012. Tentative Score 90–92.

AMPHORAE, SHIRAZ, 2003: Medium to full-bodied, a deep almost inky purple in color, with tempting plums and violets from the first sip, those yielding to smoke, chocolate and earthy-herbal aromas and flavors. Long and intriguing. Drink now–2009. Score 91.

AMPHORAE, CHARDONNAY, 2005: Golden straw in color, with harmony and elegance instead of power, this gently oaked white shows good acidity and a gentle minerality together with aromas and flavors of pear, apple and kiwi fruits, all leading to a long, fresh finish. Drink now–2008. Score 90.

AMPHORAE, CHARDONNAY, 2003: Deep gold in color with orange reflections, this medium to full-bodied white reflects its 12 months in *barriques* with complex, rich and concentrated aromas and flavors of figs, mandarin oranges, nectarines and spicy nuts. Light buttery-oak shadings on the finish add understated elegance. Drink now–2008. Score 91.

AMPHORAE, CHARDONNAY, 2002: Ripe and subtle, with pear, pineapple, butterscotch and vanilla aromas and flavors matched by spices, creamy oak and a long mineral-rich finish. Still delicious but now taking on a deeper, almost bronze color and not for further cellaring. Drink up. Score 88.

AMPHORAE, VIOGNIER, 2005: Unoaked and with no malolactic fermentation, this medium-bodied, lively wine offers crisp tropical fruits, peaches, melon and a floral accent. Lightly spicy, aromatic, generous and delicious. Drink now. Tentative Score 89.

AMPHORAE, ROSÉ DE MERLOT, 2005: Light to medium bodied, with the color of the first reddish-orange blush that a ripe peach attains, this rosé shows as dry, crisp and fresh as one could want. Pleasant and understated, with hints of black cherries, licorice and spices. Hardly a typical rosé. Drink now–2008. Score 88.

Rhyton

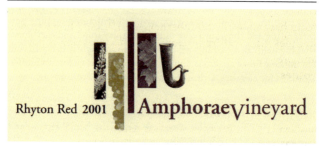

RHYTON, 2003: A blend of 82% Cabernet Sauvignon, 10% Petite Sirah and 4% each Shiraz and Merlot, this wine reflects its nearly 24 months in used oak *barriques* with gentle oak, well integrating tannins and medium-body. On the nose and palate are black fruits, white chocolate and a welcome hint of spiciness. Drink now–2008. Score 89.

RHYTON, 2002: Developed in *barriques* for 18 months, this well-balanced, round and generous blend of Cabernet Sauvignon, Merlot and Petit Sirah shows soft tannins, gentle wood and near-sweet currant and berry aromas and flavors, those with an appealing hint of spiciness. Drink now. Score 88.

RHYTON, 2001: This medium-bodied blend of Cabernet Sauvignon, Merlot and Petite Sirah from 25–30-year-old vines has soft, well-integrated tannins and abundant currant and berry aromas and flavors, all leading to an almost sweet fruity finish. Drink now. Score 89.

Med.Red

MED.RED, 2004: Dark garnet towards royal purple and medium-bodied, with soft, well integrating tannins and fine balance between those, gentle spicy wood and black fruits. Soft, round and delicious. Drink now–2008. Score 88.

MED.RED, 2003: Deep garnet red, medium-bodied, with spicy oak and soft tannins backed up nicely by blackcurrant and black cherry fruits. An oak aged blend of 97% Cabernet Sauvignon and 3% Shiraz. Drink now. Score 88.

Amram's *

Founded in 2001 on Moshav Ramot Naftali in the Upper Galilee by grape grower Amram Azulai and his son Ehud, the team has vineyards of Cabernet, Merlot and Shiraz grapes in Emek Kadesh. Production from 2004 was 2,800 bottles and projected release from the 2005 vintage is about 6,000 bottles.

AMRAM'S, CABERNET SAUVIGNON, 2004: Ruby towards garnet, medium-bodied, with near-sweet tannins and hints of wood (the wine was aged in stainless steel with exposure to oak chips). Soft and round, with straightforward berry, cherry and currant fruits. Drink now. Score 83.

AMRAM'S, CABERNET SAUVIGNON, 2003: Dark garnet red, medium-bodied, with soft tannins and spicy cedar hints showing appealing currant and wild berry aromas. Drink now. Score 84.

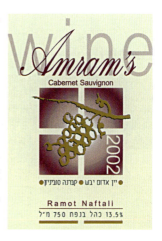

AMRAM'S, MERLOT, 2004: Light to medium-bodied, with soft, almost unfelt tannins and basic berry, cherry aromas and flavors. Drink up. Score 80.

AMRAM'S, CABERNET SAUVIGNON-MERLOT, 2003: Ruby towards garnet red, with chunky, country-style tannins and a spicy oak influence. Flavors of blackberries, plums and black cherries. Straightforward and without complexities. Drink up. Score 76.

AMRAM'S, CABERNET SAUVIGNON-SHIRAZ, 2004: Dark and somewhat cloudy garnet towards brick red, medium-bodied, with chunky tannins A country-style wine with basic black fruits. Drink up Score 78.

AMRAM'S CABERNET SAUVIGNON-SHIRAZ, 2003: Dark garnet towards brick-red in color, medium-bodied, with more of an herbal, vegetable character than a fruity one. Drink up. Score 70.

Anatot *

Founded in 1998 by Aharon Helfgot and Arnon Erez, the winery, which is located in Anatot, a community north of Jerusalem, is currently producing 17,500 oak-aged bottles annually from Cabernet Sauvignon and Merlot grapes. Wines are produced in two series, Anatot and Notera, and grapes come primarily from vineyards in the Lachish and Shiloh regions.

Anatot

ANATOT, CABERNET SAUVIGNON, 2003: Dark garnet, with chunky, country-style tannins and generous smoky oak yielding in the glass to reveal appealing currant and plum fruits. Drink now–2008. Score 84

ANATOT, CABERNET SAUVIGNON, 2002: This pleasant deep ruby toward garnet medium-bodied red shows moderate tannins, a hint of spicy oak, and appealing plum, black cherry and currant fruits. Drink up. Score 81.

ANATOT, CABERNET SAUVIGNON, 2001: Dark ruby toward purple in color and medium-bodied, the wine has subdued tannins and oak and dull aromas and flavors of black fruits. It is stingy on the palate and already showing age. Score 76.

ANATOT, MERLOT, 2003: Dark royal purple in color, with firm tannins and an underlying earthiness but with appealing black fruits. Meant for early drinking. Drink now. Score 76.

ANATOT, MERLOT, 2002: Dark garnet in color, medium-bodied, with chunky tannins and some berry, black cherry and currant fruits.

One dimensional and finishing with exaggerated earthiness. Drink up. Score 72.

ANATOT, MERLOT, 2001: This somewhat cloudy deep ruby wine seems muddy on the palate with its muted fruits, far too much earthiness and a barnyard aroma that creeps in over time. Score 68.

Notera

ANATOT, NOTERA, 2003: A medium to full-bodied blend of 60% Merlot and 40% Cabernet Sauvignon. Reflects its 24 months in oak with very generous smoky wood and coarse tannins that tend to hide the berry-cherry fruits. Drink now. Score 80.

ANATOT, NOTERA, 2002: Medium-bodied, with far too generous oak, coarse almost burning tannins and skimpy berry and black cherry fruits. Drink up. Score 76.

NOTERA, 2001: A medium-bodied oak-aged blend of 60% Merlot and 40% Cabernet Sauvignon. Appealing in its youth with soft tannins, and black fruits but now showing age. Drink up. Score 78.

Assaf ★★★

Founded in 2004 by Assaf Kedem (formerly a partner in the Bazelet Hagolan Winery) and located in the village of Kidmat Tzvi on the Golan Heights, the winery has its own vineyards containing Cabernet Sauvignon, Cabernet Franc, Pinotage and Sauvignon Blanc grapes. Production from the 2004 vintage was 11,000 bottles.

ASSAF, CABERNET SAUVIGNON, RESERVE, 2004: Garnet towards deep purple, medium to full-bodied, this blend of 85% Cabernet Sauvignon and 15% Cabernet Franc was aged in partly French, partly American *barriques* for 12 months. Good balance between mouth-coating tannins, spicy and vanilla tinged oak, and acidity. On the palate wild berries, red currants and a light but appealing mineral hint, all lingering nicely. Drink now–2009. Score 90.

ASSAF, CABERNET FRANC, ROSÉ, 2004: Made entirely from Cabernet Franc grapes allowed only minimal skin contact, this medium-bodied, rose-petal pink wine shows appealing berry, cassis and mineral aromas and flavors, as well as a tempting light bitter-almond finish. Drink now. Score 88.

ASSAF, SAUVIGNON BLANC, 2005: Light golden straw in color and medium-bodied, the wine lacks acidity and shows too stingy fruits and a somewhat heavy earthy overlay. Drink up. Score 84.

Avidan ✯✯✯

Located on Kibbutz Eyal in the Sharon region, this boutique winery relies on Chardonnay, Shiraz, Cabernet Sauvignon, Petite Sirah and Merlot grapes selected from various vineyards in the Upper Galilee. The winery produced 2,500 bottles in 2003 and is currently producing about 10,000 bottles annually.

AVIDAN, CABERNET SAUVIGNON, 2005: Still in embryonic form but already showing firm tannins well balanced by spicy wood, herbaceousness and currant and plum fruits. Firm but near-elegant. Drink from release–2009. Tentative Score 87–89.

AVIDAN, CABERNET SAUVIGNON, RESERVE, 2004: Dark garnet in color, medium to full-bodied, with soft tannins, this blend of 85% Cabernet Sauvignon and 15% Merlot spent 16 months in oak. Wild berry and blackcurrant fruits on the nose and palate, with a hint of spiciness on a moderately long finish. Drink now–2008. Score 89.

AVIDAN, CABERNET SAUVIGNON, 2004: Aged in oak for 10 months, this medium-bodied, softly tannic, dark garnet blend of 85% Cabernet Sauvignon, 10% Merlot and 5% Shiraz offers up jammy plum and red and black berry flavors and aromas. Drink now. Score 85.

AVIDAN, CABERNET SAUVIGNON, 2003: Dark ruby towards garnet in color, this medium-bodied blend of Cabernet Sauvignon and Merlot shows generous oak and firm tannins, those matched nicely by currant, berry and black cherry fruits. Drink now. Score 86.

AVIDAN, CABERNET SAUVIGNON, 2002: Deep garnet in color, this blend of 85% Cabernet Sauvignon and 15% Merlot spent 18 months in oak. Ripe and plummy, with fleshy tannins and medium body, backed up by supple cherry, berry and spice notes and a nice fruity finish. Drink up. Score 86.

AVIDAN, MERLOT, 2005: Soft and round, with silky tannins that allow berry, black cherry and currant notes to make themselves felt on a background of spicy cedar. Drink now–2008. Score 86.

AVIDAN, SHIRAZ, 2005: Full-bodied but not dense, a rich, polished and thoroughly modern style, with generous plum and blackberry fruits backed up nicely by dark chocolate, pepper and hints of licorice. Drink from release–2008. Tentative Score 89–91.

AVIDAN, SHIRAZ, LIMITED EDITION, 2004: Dark garnet in color, medium-bodied, this oaked, unfiltered wine shows good balance between soft tannins, spicy oak and berry, currant and cassis aromas and flavors. Moderately long. Drink now. Score 86.

AVIDAN, SHIRAZ, 2003: Medium-dark ruby, medium to full-bodied, with good balance between soft tannins, wood and plum, cherry and earthy aromas and flavors. On the moderately-long finish look for a hint of leather. Drink now. Score 86.

AVIDAN, PETITE SIRAH, 2005: Blended with a small amount of Shiraz and showing deep garnet in color, with full body and firm tannins, those in fine balance with spicy wood and plum, currant and berry fruits. Drink from release–2008. Tentative Score 87–89.

AVIDAN, BLEND DE NOIRS, 2004: Dark cherry red, this medium-bodied blend of 70% Shiraz and 30% Merlot spent ten months in oak. Fresh, fruity and aromatic, with plum and spicy wood aromas and flavors. Drink now. Score 85.

AVIDAN, CHARDONNAY, PETIT SOLEIL, 2004: Deep gold in color, reflecting six months in Burgundy style oak barrels. With gentle smoky wood and spices, those overlaying tropical fruits, citrus peel and a light herbal essence. Full-bodied, with a near crème-fraiche finish. Drink now. Score 88.

Bar ✶✶

Established in 2002 by Ilan Bar in the town of Binyamina in the Sharon area, and drawing largely on grapes from the surrounding vineyards, this family-owned winery produces Cabernet Sauvignon, Merlot, Carignan, Sauvignon Blanc and Chardonnay wines as well as Jonathan Red, a blend of Merlot and Cabernet. The winery is currently producing about 4,500 bottles annually.

BAR, CABERNET SAUVIGNON, 2004: Dark ruby in color, medium-bodied, with too generous smoky wood and firm tannins hiding the black fruits that struggle to make themselves felt. Drink now–2008. Score 83.

BAR, CABERNET SAUVIGNON, 2003: Medium-bodied, dark garnet in color, with soft tannins integrating nicely with aromas and flavors of spicy wood, blackcurrant, plum and oriental spices. Drink now. Score 85.

BAR, CABERNET SAUVIGNON, 2002: Soft and round, medium-bodied and with soft, well-integrated tannins, the wine offers appealing currant and berry flavors. Drink now. Score 85.

BAR, JONATHAN RED, 2004: A country-style, medium-bodied blend of Merlot and Cabernet Sauvignon with chunky tannins and spicy cedar. Aromas and flavors of wild berries, cassis liqueur and herbaceousness. Drink now. Score 83.

BAR, JONATHAN RED, 2002: Aged in used oak barrels for 9 months, this blend of 70% Merlot and 30% Cabernet Sauvignon shows good balance between blackberries, earthiness and spices. Medium-bodied, with chunky tannins, a pleasing country-style wine. Drink up. Score 85.

BAR, MERLOT, 2002: Soft and round with forward black cherry, raspberry and herbal aromas and flavors. Soft tannins and an earthy-tobacco and smoky wood finish to add charm. Drink now. Score 86.

BAR, CARIGNAN, 2002: Medium-bodied, well-balanced with smooth, almost sweet tannins and black cherry and herbal aromas and flavors. Soft and lively. Drink up. Score 85.

BAR, SAUVIGNON BLANC, 2003: Bright and lively, with citrus, earthy and grassy overtones. Not complex but a well made and enjoyable wine. Drink up. Score 85.

Baram ✷✷

Located on Kibbutz Baram in the Upper Galilee, this small winery released its first wines from the 2004 vintage. Winery owned vineyards contain Cabernet Sauvignon and Merlot grapes. First releases were of 1,800 bottles and 2,500 bottles will be released from the 2005 vintage.

BARAM, CABERNET SAUVIGNON, 2004: Dark ruby towards garnet, medium-bodied, with generous tannins integrating nicely with appealing spicy wood and black fruits. Score 85.

BARAM, MERLOT, 2004: Medium-bodied, with soft tannins and smoky oak influences. Showing simple but appealing berry, red plum and spices on the nose and palate. Drink now. Score 84.

Barkai **

Located on Moshav Roglit in the Ella Valley at the foothills of the Jerusalem Mountains, and headed by winemaker Itai Barkai, the winery relies on Cabernet Sauvignon, Merlot and Shiraz grapes from its own vineyards. Production for 2002 and 2003 was under 1,000 bottles annually and 2004 production was 2,400 bottles. A new winery is currently being constructed with a capacity for 10,000 bottles annually.

BARKAI, CABERNET SAUVIGNON-MERLOT, 2004: Deep ruby towards garnet, medium-bodied with generous near-sweet tannins and flavors and aromas of sur-ripe berries, cherries, and cassis. Drink now. Score 84.

BARKAI, CABERNET SAUVIGNON-MERLOT, 2003: Medium-bodied, with soft, near-sweet tannins and hyper-ripe, almost jammy berry and plum aromas and flavors. Drink now. Score 83.

BARKAI, CABERNET SAUVIGNON-MERLOT, 2002: Dark garnet red in color, medium-bodied, with chunky, country-style tannins and appealing blackberry and cassis fruits. A bit earthy and alcoholic and starting to show age. Drink up. Score 83.

BARKAI, CABERNET SAUVIGNON-MERLOT, 2001: A simple but pleasant country-style wine, with generous berry and black cherry fruits backed up by earthiness and hints of Mediterranean herbs. Showing age. Drink up. Score 82.

Barkan ★★★

Founded in 1990 by Shmuel Boxer and Yair Lerner with the buyout of the former wine and liqueur producer, Stock, the winery was first located in the industrial area of Barkan, not far from Kfar Saba on the Trans-Samaria Highway. In 1999 Barkan started to plant vineyards in Kibbutz Hulda, on the central plain near the town of Rehovot, where it now has a state-of-the-art winery. Under the supervision of winemakers Ed Salzberg, Yotam Sharon and Itay Lahat, the first of whom studied in California, the second in France, and the third in Australia, this is now the second largest winery in Israel, with current production of 7.5–9 million bottles annually and projected growth to ten million by 2010.

With an investment exceeding $20 million in the winery and adjoining vineyards (1500 dunams owned jointly by the winery and the *kibbutz*, making this the largest single vineyard in the country), and ongoing construction of a visitors' center and underground barrel room, Barkan is also now the parent company of Segal Wines. The winery releases varietal wines in five series: Superieur, Millennium, Reserve, Classic, and Domaine, the last an upgrade on what was formerly the Lachish series. The winery is currently developing a vineyard of 150 dunams (75 acres) in Mitzpe Ramon in the Negev Desert, and starting to release wines from there under the label Negev Project.

Superieur

SUPERIEUR, CABERNET SAUVIGNON, 2002: Full-bodied, with generous spicy oak and lively acidity. Features a core of ripe blueberry, cassis and blackcurrant fruits, those matched nicely by overlays of spices and cocoa and, on the long finish, appealing hints of minerals and licorice. Drink now–2008. Score 89. **K**

SUPERIEUR, CABERNET SAUVIGNON, 2000: Made from grapes harvested on the Golan and in the Upper Galilee. Aged first in new oak and transferred later to used oak, this full-bodied and concentrated, deep royal toward purple wine offers up generous blackcurrant, blackberry and chocolate aromas, all with an appealing overlay of Mediterranean herbaceousness. Drink now. Score 89. K

SUPERIEUR, CABERNET SAUVIGNON, 1999: Medium to full-bodied, round and well balanced, with soft, well-integrated tannins and aromas and flavors of currants, berries and white chocolate. Drink up. Score 88. K

SUPERIEUR, CABERNET SAUVIGNON, 1996: Aged in new oak casks for 18 months, this medium-bodied, moderately tannic wine is a bit too simple and earthy, and from its youth has shown slightly sour flavors that tend to hide the cherry, berry and plum fruits which never fully succeeded in bursting forth. Now well past its peak and no longer scoreable. K

SUPERIEUR, CABERNET SAUVIGNON, 1995: Even after having spent 18 months in oak casks, this wine showed only modest cedar, spice and berry flavors. Lacking in balance and too tight and austere, this medium-bodied wine has rather flat tannins and a notable lack of ripe fruit flavors. Now past its peak and no longer scoreable. K

SUPERIEUR, PINOTAGE, 2002: Full-bodied, with sur-ripe blackberry, black cherry and currant fruits, those backed up nicely by moderately-firm tannins and generous spicy, meaty and herbal aromas and flavors. Deep, round and long. Drink now–2008. Score 90. K

SUPERIEUR, CHARDONNAY, 2002: Complex and full-bodied, with juicy pear, spice, vanilla, hazelnut and honeyed aromas and flavors that reveal hints of earth and mineral on the long finish. Drink up. Score 88. K

Reserve

RESERVE, CABERNET SAUVIGNON, 2004: Dark royal purple in color, dense and intense, with layers of blackcurrants, plums, raspberries and spices, those in fine tune with firm tannins. Best 2008–2011. Tentative Score 89–91. **K**

RESERVE, CABERNET SAUVIGNON, ALTITUDE +412, 2003: Made from 85% of grapes harvested at the Avnei Eitan vineyards on the Southern Golan Heights and 15% from Kerem Dishon in the Upper Galilee, this deep garnet, full-bodied wine was aged in primarily French *barriques* for 14 months. Near-sweet tannins and a gentle influence of the wood reveal generous cassis, blackberry and raspberry fruits, those backed up by spices and a light mineral overlay. Drink now–2011. Score 89. **K**

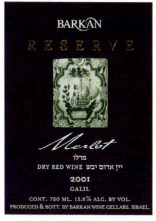

RESERVE, CABERNET SAUVIGNON, ALTITUDE +720, 2003: Made from grapes from the Har Godrim vineyard near the Lebanese border and aged for 12 months in primarily French oak casks. Full-bodied, concentrated, and deep royal-purple in color, with firm tannins that are integrating nicely, Showing red currants and purple plums on a tantalizing earthy-herbal background. Best 2008–2012. Score 90. **K**

RESERVE, CABERNET SAUVIGNON, ALTITUDE +624, 2003: Deep garnet towards royal purple in color, made from grapes from the vineyards at Moshav Alma in the Upper Galilee, and oak-aged for 15 months. On first attack firm, drying tannins but those receding to add a near-sweetness to the black fruits, oriental spices and hints of white truffles and green olives. Long and generous. Best 2008–2012. Score 91. **K**

RESERVE, CABERNET SAUVIGNON, 2002: Dark garnet to royal purple, medium to full-bodied, with good balance between wood, tannins and blackcurrant and blackberry fruits. Look as well for light hints of spices, vanilla and earthiness, those lingering nicely. Drink now–2008. Score 88. **K**

RESERVE, CABERNET SAUVIGNON, 2001: Dark garnet in color, medium to full-bodied, with generous but not exaggerated toasty oak and acidity, soft tannins and an appealing array of cassis, black cherry and plum fruits. Drink now–2008. Score 90. **K**

RESERVE, CABERNET SAUVIGNON, 2000: Maturing nicely, the once almost searing tannins now soft and integrating nicely and the perhaps too generous wood receding. On the nose and palate near-elegant currant, black cherry and light peppery smoky overlays. Drink now. Score 87. K

RESERVE, CABERNET SAUVIGNON, 1999: Showing better now and clearly at its peak. Medium to full-bodied, with firm tannins receding in the glass to show spicy blackcurrant and plum fruits as well as hints of smoky wood that play nicely on the palate and hints of vanilla on the finish. Drink up. Score 89. K

RESERVE, CABERNET SAUVIGNON, 1998: Medium to full-bodied, now mature, with its tannins well integrated and the once spicy oak receding into the background. Still showing good balance and structure, with aromas and flavors of blackcurrants and purple plums, those followed by hints of vanilla and licorice. Past its peak. Drink up. Score 85. K

RESERVE, CABERNET SAUVIGNON, 1997: Rich, generous and with abundant and mouth-filling blackcurrant, black cherry and spice overtones that linger nicely on the palate, the wine continues to show style, grace and a long finish, but is now past its peak. Drink up. Score 86. K

RESERVE, CABERNET SAUVIGNON, 1996: Dark garnet, showing signs of browning, and with somewhat chunky tannins that have never quite integrated and still work hard to hide berry, currant and plum fruits. Past its peak. Drink up. Score 84. K

RESERVE, MERLOT, 2004: Medium-dark ruby towards garnet, full-bodied, with youthfully firm tannins. On the nose and palate, ripe, near-sweet berries, chocolate and eucalyptus coming nicely to the surface of what has the potential to be an elegant wine. Drink now–2009. Score 88. K

RESERVE, MERLOT, 2003: Medium-dark garnet in color, full bodied, with soft tannins and spicy oak integrating well with aromas and flavors of blackberries, currants, plums and appealing hints of mint and minerals all of which linger nicely. Drink now–2009. Score 89. K

RESERVE, MERLOT, 2002: Dark garnet in color, with soft, well-integrated tannins and overall good balance, the once powerful and dominating oak now receding to let the plum and berry fruits make themselves felt. Drink up. Score 85. K

RESERVE, MERLOT, 2001: Medium to full-bodied and medium dark garnet in color, this wine is still showing plenty of tannins and oak, but given time to open in the glass reveals an appealing core of currant, black cherry, and herbs. Fully mature. Drink up. Score 86. K

RESERVE, MERLOT, 2000: Showing better now than at earlier tastings. Medium-bodied, with soft tannins and a generous core of currant, black cherry and plums, and appealing overlays of spicy oak and tea. Somewhat past its peak. Drink up. Score 86. K

RESERVE, MERLOT, 1999: Deep royal purple with clearing at the rim, this medium-bodied wine offers up soft tannins, light wood and a few currant and berry fruits. One dimensional, lacking length and now well past its peak. Drink up. Score 80. K

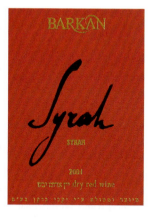

RESERVE, PINOT NOIR, NEGEV PROJECT, 2003: Subdued ruby in color, medium-bodied, with soft, well-integrated tannins and appealing berry and black cherry fruits backed up by light herbal and earthy sensations. Drink now. Score 88. K

RESERVE, PINOT NOIR, 2002: This medium-bodied red spent 10 months in small oak barrels and reflects dusty plum and berry fruits together with an appealing earthy finish. Look as well for a pleasing lightly bitter herbal sensation on the finish. Drink now. Score 88. K

RESERVE, PINOTAGE, 2003: Dark and deep, full-bodied, with fine balance between generous tannins, not-exaggerated wood, and tempting plum, black cherry, blueberry and chocolate aromas and flavors all lingering nicely. Drink now–2008. Score 89. K

RESERVE, PINOTAGE, 2002: Garnet to royal purple in color, this medium to full-bodied red is packed with lush raspberry, blackberry, black cherry and currant fruits, those matched nicely by sweet spices and dark chocolate. A tantalizing hint of smoked bacon on the moderately long finish. Drink now. Score 90. K

RESERVE, PINOTAGE, JUDEA, 2001: Medium to full-bodied, with generous but soft and well-integrated tannins, the wine shows a bare hint of sweetness overlaying its blackcurrant and black cherry fruits, with dashes of smoked meat and herbs. Soft, round and appealing. Drink up. Score 88. K

RESERVE, TEMPRANILLO, 2005: Still in its infancy but already showing deep color, a near-muscular structure and mouth-coating tannins. A generous array of ripe plum, red cherry, licorice, tobacco and prune aromas and flavors, all ending with a hint of sweet cedar wood. Best from 2008. Tentative Score 90–92. K

RESERVE, CHARDONNAY, 2003: Golden straw in color, medium to full-bodied and satisfyingly mouth-filling, with citrus, apple and melon fruits that blend nicely with toasty oak and vanilla. Look for a hint of cinnamon on the moderately-long finish. Drink now. Score 88. K

RESERVE, CHARDONNAY, NEGEV PROJECT, 2003: Medium-bodied, this unoaked white shows a stony dryness together with white peaches, green apples and citrus fruits on an herbaceous background. Unusual and delicious. Drink now. Score 89. K

RESERVE, CHARDONNAY, 2002: Light gold in color, medium-bodied and fully mature, but still showing good balance between fruits, wood and acidity. Citrus, melon and pear aromas and flavors along with spices lead to a mouthfilling finish. Drink up. Score 87. K

RESERVE, SAUVIGNON BLANC, 2005: Light-straw colored, light to medium-bodied, with crisp clean aromas and flavors of citrus and tropical fruits, all of which linger nicely on the palate. Drink now. Score 86. K

RESERVE, SAUVIGNON BLANC, 2004: Bright and lively, golden-straw in color, medium-bodied, with ample acidity and tempting melon and apple fruits. Generous grassy-mineral hints throughout. Drink now. Score 86. K

RESERVE, SAUVIGNON BLANC, 2003: Medium to full-bodied, light golden straw in color with green reflections and melon, gooseberry and apple fruits on a mineral-rich background. Appealing spiciness and lively acidity carry through to a moderately long finish. Drink up. Score 87. K

RESERVE, SAUVIGNON BLANC, 2002: Bright light straw in color, fruity, with grassy and mineral notes and flinty dryness, this aromatic wine was wisely left in oak for only two months before bottling. Fragrant and refreshing, it shows tropical fruit, citrus and fig aromas and flavors, as well as a long finish. Past its peak. Drink up. Score 85. K

RESERVE, EMERALD RIESLING, 2005: Light to medium-bodied, with mild sweetness set off by balancing acidity and fresh aromas and flavors of pineapple, citrus fruits and dried apricots. Drink up. Score 84. K

RESERVE, EMERALD RIESLING, 2004: Medium-bodied, with a light, not-offensive level of sweetness and good balancing acidity. Appealing citrus and summer fruits. Drink up. Score 84. K

RESERVE, EMERALD RIESLING, 2003: Medium-bodied, with a fruity nose and lacking the often cloying floral aromas of Emerald Riesling, the wine shows only a light hint of sweetness, as well as tempting citrus and peach aromas and flavors. Overall good balance although lacking a bit in liveliness. Past its peak. Drink up. Score 82. K

Classic

CLASSIC, CABERNET SAUVIGNON, 2004: Medium-bodied, with once firm tannins now integrating nicely and showing simple but appealing traditional Cabernet aromas and flavors of peppery currant and black cherry fruits. Drink now. Score 85. K

CLASSIC, CABERNET SAUVIGNON, 2003: Deep ruby red, medium-bodied, with chunky tannins and appealing berry, cherry and currant fruits. Not complex but appealing. Drink now. Score 84. K

CLASSIC, CABERNET SAUVIGNON, 2002: Medium-bodied, with plum and berry aromas and flavors, hints of spices and a bit of chocolate that comes in near the end. A simple but pleasant enough little wine. Drink up. Score 84. K

CLASSIC, CABERNET SAUVIGNON, 2001: This medium-bodied deep purple wine offers up plum, currant and black cherry aromas and flavors, but is low in tannins and lacking in depth and breadth. Past its peak. Drink up. Score 81. K

CLASSIC, MERLOT, 2004: Medium-bodied, with soft, well integrated tannins. Lightly oak aged, showing just hints of smoky wood and vanilla, and on the nose and palate appealing blackberry, plum and berry fruits and a pleasant hint of herbaceousness. Drink now. Score 85. K

CLASSIC, MERLOT, 2003: Medium-bodied, dark ruby in color, with dark plum fruits and soft, just gripping-enough tannins to add backbone and a hint of bitter herbs on the finish. Drink up. Score 84. K

CLASSIC, MERLOT, 2002: Light to medium-bodied, international in style with berry, plum and spice aromas and flavors. Past its peak. Drink up. Score 80. K

CLASSIC, MERLOT, 2001: Firm and tight, this compact Merlot has warm currant, herb and earthy notes and a short, tannic finish. Look for nice peppery notes as the wine sits on the palate. Somewhat past its peak. Drink up. Score 82. K

CLASSIC, PINOT NOIR, 2004: After 10 months in oak this medium-dark garnet, medium-bodied, and softly tannic wine shows clean and fresh, but is somewhat skimpy on its fruits and has an unwelcome bitter-herb finish. Drink now. Score 83. K

CLASSIC, PINOT NOIR, 2000: Made entirely from Pinot Noir grapes grown in the vineyards of Mitzpeh Ramon in the Negev Desert and aged in oak casks for 11 months, this medium-bodied red is now showing signs of browning and even though it maintains its black cherry and berry fruits as well as hints of spices and licorice, it is now past its peak. Drink up. Score 83. K

CLASSIC, SYRAH, 2004: Light garnet red in color, light to medium-bodied, with soft tannins and some appealing plum and berry aromas and flavors backed up by a hint of spiciness. Drink now. Score 84. K

CLASSIC, SYRAH, 2003: Medium-bodied, with appealing black fruits and spices, a not-at-all complex but simple and appealing little wine. Drink now. Score 84. K

CLASSIC, SYRAH, 2002: Not much bouquet in this medium-bodied wine, but good plum and currant fruits and hints of mint and juniper berry. Drink up. Score 83. K

CLASSIC, PINOTAGE, 2004: Dark ruby, medium-bodied, with soft tannins, gentle hints of spicy wood and cherry and wild berry fruits. Nothing complex here and precious little to remind us of Pinotage but an easy to drink wine. Drink now. Score 84. K

CLASSIC, PETITE SIRAH, 2004: Dark in color, with brooding tannins and somewhat skimpy black fruits. Somewhat flat and one dimensional. Drink up. Score 82. K

CLASSIC, PETITE SIRAH, 2003: Deep ruby in color, with chunky, country-style tannins and a few cherry-berry fruits. Drink up. Score 83. K

CLASSIC, PETITE SIRAH, 2002: Lightly earthy, firm and tight, this medium-bodied and tannic wine shows good cherry-berry fruits, and earthy-cedar notes. Not long or overly complex but a good Israeli Petite Sirah. Somewhat past its peak. Drink up. Score 83. **K**

CLASSIC, ROSÉ, 2005: A blend of 85% Shiraz and 15 % Tempranillo. Medium-bodied, dry and refreshing, with cherry, peach pit and mineral aromas and flavors. Drink up. Score 85. **K**

CLASSIC, CHARDONNAY, 2003: With its golden color and forward pear, apple and summer fruit aromas and flavors, this appealing medium-bodied wine shows good balance but lacks depth. Drink up. Score 85. **K**

CLASSIC, SAUVIGNON BLANC, 2005: Bright and lively, this unoaked white shows lime, grapefruit and passion fruits, those opening on the finish to reveal hints of herbs and pears. Drink now. Score 85. **K**

CLASSIC, SAUVIGNON BLANC, 2004: Light to medium-bodied, with low acidity and a hint of sweetness but clean and appealing as a summertime quaffer. Drink up. Score 84. **K**

CLASSIC, SAUVIGNON BLANC, 2003: Light to medium-bodied, somewhat flat on the nose, the wine had appealing citrus and summer fruits and good balancing acidity but now is past its peak. Drink up. Score 84. **K**

CLASSIC, EMERALD RIESLING, 2005: Semi-dry, with not quite enough acidity to add liveliness. Floral and with tropical and citrus fruits. Drink up. Score 82. **K**

CLASSIC, EMERALD RIESLING, 2004: Semi-dry, with simple but pleasant tropical fruit and flowery aromas and flavors. Serve well chilled. Drink up. Score 84. **K**

CLASSIC, EMERALD RIESLING, 2003: Off dry, with its light sweetness nicely balanced by acidity and with appealing tropical and citrus fruit flavors and aromas. Past its peak. Drink up. Score 78. **K**

Domaine

DOMAINE, CABERNET SAUVIGNON, 2005: Light and acidic and showing none of the true Cabernet Sauvignon traits, this light to medium-bodied wine has scarcely any tannins. Score 79. **K**

DOMAINE, MERLOT, 2005: Medium-bodied, soft and round, without complexity or depth but with appealing spicy berry and black cherry fruits. For those just switching from semi-dry whites to reds. Drink now. Score 82. **K**

DOMAINE, SHIRAZ, 2005: Medium-dark royal-purple in color, medium-bodied and with soft tannins. Plum, cassis and berry flavors on a soft and round background make this an easy-to-drink entry level wine. Drink now. Score 84. **K**

DOMAINE, PETITE SIRAH, 2005: Dark garnet towards royal purple, unoaked, showing good balance between soft tannins and generous berry and black cherry fruits. Not complex but a pleasant entry level quaffer. Drink now. Score 85. **K**

DOMAINE, EMERALD RIESLING, 2005: To put it politely, a "restrained" wine, not showing much on the nose or palate but at least avoiding the sin of being too flowery and too sweet. Drink up. Score 78. **K**

Millennium

MILLENNIUM, CABERNET SAUVIGNON, 2004: Medium-bodied, with soft, almost unfelt tannins and simple but pleasant berry and cherry fruits. A pleasant quaffer. Drink now. Score 85.

MILLENNIUM, CABERNET SAUVIGNON, 1999: Bright garnet red in color, medium-bodied, with soft tannins and generous currant and berry fruits. Somewhat past its peak. Drink up. Score 85. **K**

MILLENNIUM, CABERNET SAUVIGNON, 1996: Dark cherry red toward garnet, medium to full-bodied, with somewhat coarse tannins and stingy berry and plum fruits. Well past its peak and no longer scoreable. **K**

Bashan ✶✶

Founded by Uri Rapp and Emmanuel Dasa and located on the southern Golan Heights, with their first releases from the 2004 vintage, the winery produces kosher wines that are fully organic and to date is based entirely on Cabernet Sauvignon grapes raised in its own vineyards. Current releases are about 6,000 bottles annually, and tentative plans are to grow to production of 25,000 bottles.

BASHAN, CABERNET SAUVIGNON, 2005: Medium to full-bodied, this organic wine shows good balance between sweet oak, generous yeasts and on the nose and palate appealing ripe and spicy black fruits. Best from 2008. Tentative Score 86–88. **K**

BASHAN, CABERNET SAUVIGNON, 2004: Oak-aged for 18 months with spicy and vanilla laded smoky wood backed up by soft, nicely integrating tannins and forward currant and blackberry fruits. A moderately-long finish with hints of chocolate and Mediterranean herbs. Drink now–2008. Score 86. **K**

Bazelet Hagolan ✶✶✶✶

Founded in 1998 by Yo'av Levy on Moshav Kidmat Tsvi in the Golan Heights, the first facility of this winery was located in a cow shed and initial production from that vintage year was 1,800 bottles. Today, working with Australian trained winemaker Tal Pelter, the winery produces 25,000 bottles annually, all from Cabernet Sauvignon grapes grown in their own vineyards on the Golan Heights, and target production is 50,000. The wines are in two series: Reserve and Bazelet Hagolan, the first aged in oak for about 20 months, the second for 8–10 months. The winery released its first Chardonnay wine in 2005, and since the 2004 vintage all the production is kosher.

Reserve

RESERVE, CABERNET SAUVIGNON, 2005: Rich, ripe, smooth, generous and well-balanced with currant, berry and plum flavors coming together with near-sweet tannins and tempting smoky oak. Best 2008–2012. Tentative Score 89–91. **K**

RESERVE, CABERNET SAUVIGNON, 2004: This dark garnet, medium to full-bodied oak-aged red shows excellent balance between acidity, firm tannins, wood and fruits. On the nose and palate ripe blackcurrants, wild berries and cassis matched by hints of herbs and licorice. Long and generous. Drink from release–2011. Tentative Score 89–91 **K**

RESERVE, CABERNET SAUVIGNON, 2003: Full-bodied, with soft tannins well balanced by spicy oak and a rich array of aromas and flavors, those including currants, berries, black cherries, orange peel, star anise and white pepper. Round and generous, with a long, near-sweet finish. Drink now–2008. Score 89.

RESERVE, CABERNET SAUVIGNON, 2002: Inky dark purple, with firm tannins and generous wood, those integrating nicely to reveal complex aromas and flavors of blackcurrant and black cherry fruits and Mediterranean herbs. Drink now. Score 87.

MILLENNIUM RESERVE, CABERNET SAUVIGNON, 2000: Medium to full-bodied, this dark garnet wine shows good balance between firm tannins, oak and fruits, those including concentrated layers of currants and berries. Look for mint, minerals and earthy flavors on the long finish. Drink up. Score 89.

Bazelet Hagolan

BAZELET HAGOLAN, CABERNET SAUVIGNON, 2005: Soft, round and delicious even at this embryonic stage, showing a solid core of currants, wild berries, toasty oak, vanilla and minerals. Fleshy and long. Drink from release–2010. Tentative Score 88–90. **K**

BAZELET HAGOLAN, CABERNET SAUVIGNON, 2004: Dark ruby towards garnet, medium-bodied and reflecting its 10 months in French and American *barriques* with smoky oak and soft tannins. Good balance and an appealing array of cherry, raspberry and currant fruits, those with a light spicy overlay that lingers nicely. Drink now–2008. Score 88. **K**

BAZELET HAGOLAN, CABERNET SAUVIGNON, 2003: Deep garnet in color, medium to full-bodied with aromas and flavors of spicy cherries, currants, Mediterranean herbs and chocolate leading to a medium-long lightly spicy finish. Mouthfilling and generous. Drink now–2010. Score 89.

BAZELET HAGOLAN, CABERNET SAUVIGNON, 2002: Deep cherry-red towards garnet in color, medium to full-bodied, with concentrated currant, blackberry, spice and peppery notes. Good balance between wood and soft tannins and a moderately long finish. Drink now. Score 87.

BAZELET HAGOLAN, CABERNET SAUVIGNON, 2001: Dark garnet toward inky black in color, this full-bodied, firmly tannic wine shows rich aromas and flavors of blackcurrants and blackberries, generous spiciness and nice earthy-olive hints, as well as a long finish. Drink now. Score 90.

BAZELET HAGOLAN, CABERNET SAUVIGNON, 2000: Medium-bodied and with moderate levels of smooth tannins, the wine's dark purple color is starting to brown, but it maintains its tempting currant, plum, mint and earthy aromas and flavors. Somewhat past its peak, so drink up. Score 88.

BAZELET HAGOLAN, CABERNET SAUVIGNON, 1999: Full-bodied, with its once firm tannins now well integrated and with light overlays of spices and smoke from the oak in which it aged, the wine shows still youthful currant and plum fruits. Long and mouth-filling but now well past its peak. Drink up. Score 86.

Beit-El *

Established by California trained winemaker Hillel Manne in 2001 and located in the settlement of Beit-El, north of Jerusalem, this small winery has been producing Cabernet Sauvignon and Merlot wines from their own vineyards. The winery is currently producing about 3,000 bottles annually, nearly all of those destined for export to the United States.

BEIT-EL, CABERNET SAUVIGNON, 2005: Medium-bodied, with chunky country-style tannins and aromas and flavors of cooked fruits on a sweet, alcoholic and coarse background. Score 65. K

BEIT-EL, CABERNET SAUVIGNON, 2004: Medium to full-bodied, with coarse tannins that seem not to want to integrate and, despite being categorized as dry, an unwanted touch of sweetness. Aromas and flavors of stewed plums, a foxy sensation on the palate and an alcoholic finish. Drink up. Score 72. K

BEIT-EL, MERLOT, 2005: Medium-bodied, showing signs of oxidation despite its youth, and with stewed, sweet fruits on the palate. Score 70. K

BEIT-EL, MERLOT, 2004: Medium-bodied, with chunky tannins, too generous wood influence and forward aromas and flavors of ripe black fruits. Drink up. Score 77. K

Benhaim ✦✦

Founded in 1997 by the Benhaim family on Moshav Kfar Azar in the Sharon region, the winery is currently producing about 40,000 bottles annually from Cabernet Sauvignon, Merlot, Petite Sirah, Chardonnay, Muscat Canelli, Muscat of Alexandria, and Traminette grapes as well as a Port-style wine. With their own vineyards now planted on the eastern slopes of Mount Meron in the Upper Galilee, the winery is planning to expand its production to 50,000–60,000 bottles. Wines are released in three series—Grande Reserve, Reserve and Benhaim and have been kosher since the 2001 vintage.

Grande Reserve

GRANDE RESERVE, CABERNET SAUVIGNON, 2003: With more than two years in new oak this full-bodied and firmly tannic wine may still be in its infancy but the oak seems to be rising, the tannins becoming more biting and the fruits receding. Some plum, currant and chocolate flavors but those nearly buried under the onslaught of the wood. Drink now. Score 84. **K**

GRANDE RESERVE, CABERNET SAUVIGNON, 2001: Deep royal purple in color and reflecting its 26 months in oak casks with very generous vanilla-flavored wood and with rather coarse tannins that seem not to want to integrate. Stingy on its currant and black fruits and somewhat short. Drink up. Score 83. **K**

GRANDE RESERVE, CABERNET SAUVIGNON, 2000: Although showing considerably better than at earlier tastings, the wine still has firm tannins and solid and almost chunky wood after having spent 26 months in oak, which makes it more of an herbal-earthy-mineral wine than a fruity one, Drink up. Score 86.

GRANDE RESERVE, CABERNET SAUVIGNON, 1999: Dark ruby in color, light to medium-bodied, with firm tannins and a too-generous hand with the oak that throw the wine out of balance and allow it to show only overripe plum flavors and aromas. Past its peak. Drink up. Score 78.

Reserve

RESERVE, CABERNET SAUVIGNON, 2003: Medium to full-bodied, this blend of 88% Cabernet Sauvignon, 7% Merlot and 5% Petite Sirah reflects 20 months in new oak with generous smoky and spicy wood influences. Still firm tannins but those and the wood opening in the glass to reveal ripe currants and berries and moderate length. Drink now. Score 88. **K**

Benhaim

BENHAIM, CABERNET SAUVIGNON, 2003: A blend of 88% Cabernet Sauvignon, 7% Merlot and 5% Petite Sirah, this dark garnet, medium to full-bodied wine reflects its 14 months in *barrique*s with generous spicy oak and tannins that are still firm but now integrating nicely. An appealing array of blackcurrant, wild berry, coffee and dark chocolate notes, those leading to a long finish. Drink now. Score 89. **K**

BENHAIM, CABERNET SAUVIGNON, 2002: A blend of 85% Cabernet Sauvignon rounded out by the addition of Merlot and Petite Sirah. Medium to full-bodied, with soft tannins and generous spicy oak matched by wild berry, cassis and on the moderate finish a hint of minty-chocolate. Drink now. Score 85. **K**

BENHAIM, CABERNET SAUVIGNON, 2001: After 18 months in oak this medium-bodied wine has smooth tannins and appealing currant, berry and cassis flavors and an almost sweet finish. Drink up. Score 84. **K**

BENHAIM, MERLOT, 2003: Medium-dark garnet in color, medium-bodied, with generous soft tannins and wood, those in good balance with fruits and acidity. On first attack, plums and spices,

those opening to reveal black cherries and cassis fruits together with hints of smoke, all leading to a pleasing hint of bitterness on the finish. Drink now. Score 87. **K**

BENHAIM, MERLOT, 2002: Dark royal purple in color, medium-bodied, with soft tannins integrating nicely, this blend of 85% Merlot and 15%

Cabernet Sauvignon and Petite Sirah that was oak-aged for 14 months is soft and round, with aromas and flavors of currants, purple plums and wild berries. Somewhat one-dimensional. Drink up. Score 85. K

BENHAIM, MERLOT, 2001: This medium-bodied, not overly complex red shows moderate, well-integrated tannins along with generous plum and cassis fruits. Drink up. Score 85. K

BENHAIM, PINOT NOIR, 2003: Cherry red towards light garnet, medium-bodied, with soft tannins, bended with 15% of Merlot and oak-aged for 14 months. On the nose and palate berry, cherry and plum fruits. Lacking complexity. Drink now. Score 84. K

BENHAIM, LA PETITE SIRA, 2003: Not a mis-spelling of Petite Sirah but a play on words, *sira*, meaning boat in Hebrew and the winery owners being fans of yachting. Oak-aged for 12 months, this garnet-red blend of 60% Petite Sirah and 40% Merlot offers up soft tannins that allow the currant and black cherry fruits to make themselves nicely felt. A good quaffer. Drink now. Score 85. K

BENHAIM, LA PETITE SIRA DE BENHAIM, 2002: This unusual and not successful blend of Petite Sirah and Merlot is somewhat musky and too earthy on the nose and palate, and has only stingy black fruits. Drink up. Score 76. K

BENHAIM, ROSÉ DE CABERNET, 2003: This rosé, made entirely from Cabernet Sauvignon grapes kept on the skins for only a short time and then allowed to develop in 500 liter barrels for 2 months, shows refreshing aromas and flavors of strawberries and raspberries. Drink up. Score 84. K

BENHAIM, CHARDONNAY, 2004: Medium-bodied, light golden in color, reflecting 12 months in oak with just enough spicy wood to set off aromas and flavors of green apples and pears. Crisp and generous. Drink now. Score 87. K

BENHAIM, CHARDONNAY, SINGLE VINEYARD, HAR MERON, 2003: Light golden in color, medium-bodied and with moderate wood-influence, this lightly buttery white shows melon, pineapple and summer fruits. Drink up. Score 84. K

BENHAIM, CHARDONNAY, 2003: Light to medium bodied, with refreshing acidity and pineapple, melon fruits. Somewhat past its peak. Drink up. Score 82. K

BENHAIM, CHARDONNAY, 2002: Medium-bodied, without much depth and somewhat on the tart side, with green apple and citrus aromas and flavors, and just a hint of minerals. Well past its peak. Drink up. Score 75. K

BENHAIM, MUSCAT ALEXANDRONI, 2004: After 12 months in oak this wine was reinforced to bring it to 15.4% alcohol. Generous sweetness here but that well balanced by acidity and showing appealing summer and tropical fruits. An appealing dessert wine. Drink now–2008. Score 87. K

BENHAIM, MUSCAT CANELLI, DESSERT, 2003: This golden colored medium-bodied dessert wine offers up plenty of sweetness and fruity-floral aromas and flavors, those matched nicely by acidity. Drink up. Score 81. K

BENHAIM, MUSCAT, 2002: Unabashedly sweet, this light, golden medium-bodied wine has aromas and flavors of ripe white peaches and spring flowers but lacks the balancing acidity that might have kept it lively. Drink up. Score 80. K

Ben-Hanna ✯✯✯

Located in Moshav Kfar Ruth in the central plains near the city of Modi'in, and receiving Cabernet Sauvignon, Merlot, Grenache, Petit Verdot and Cabernet Franc grapes from the Judean Mountains, this winery is the venture of Shlomi Zadok, who is also the winemaker at Nachshon Winery. The winery's first release was of 2,500 bottles. Releases from the 2005 harvest will be about 3,000 bottles and plans are to grow to 20,000–30,000 bottles annually. The winery is currently relocating to new facilities on Moshav Gefen.

BEN-HANNA, CABERNET SAUVIGNON, 2005: Deep purple in color, with firm tannins starting to integrate and good balance between wood and fruits. On the nose and palate spicy blackcurrants, blackberries and light herbal leading to a long and mouthfilling finish. Best from 2008. Tentative Score 88–90.

BEN-HANNA, CABERNET SAUVIGNON, 2003: Aged in barrels originally used for Chardonnay, this dark cherry red, medium to full-bodied and still firmly tannic wine shows currant, blueberry and mineral aromas and flavors all well balanced by lightly spicy oak. Drink now. Score 85.

BEN-HANNA, CABERNET SAUVIGNON, ORCA SELECTION, 2003: Aged in *barriques* for 24 months, with firm tannins and generous wood. Opening in the glass to reveal fine balance and ripe blueberry, plum and currant fruits, all lingering nicely on the palate. Drink now–2008. Score 91.

BEN-HANNA, CABERNET SAUVIGNON, BREISHEET, 2002: After eight months in oak, this medium-bodied light adobe brick red wine shows light tannins and a bare hint of wood along with currant and black cherry fruits and a light touch of Mediterranean herbs. Drink now. Score 84

BEN-HANNA, MERLOT, 2004: Deep garnet in color, light to medium-bodied, this straightforward but pleasant little wine has focused cherry, vanilla and toasty oak notes. Drink now–2008. Score 86.

BEN-HANNA, SINGLE-HUMPED MERLOT, 2004: The name of this wine makes sense when you see the picture of a camel on the label. Based largely on grapes from the Negev, this is a soft, round and generous wine showing blueberry, blackberry and currant notes along with hints of mint and sweet herbs, all coming together harmoniously. Drink now–2009. Score 91.

BEN-HANNA, MERLOT, BAMIDBAR, SDE BOKER, 2003: Made from grapes from both the Negev and the Jerusalem Hills and aged in oak for 14 months, an appealing medium-bodied red, with soft tannins and aromas of plums and currants on a mineral-rich background. Drink now. Score 87.

BEN-HANNA, CABERNET FRANC, 2005: Medium garnet towards purple in color, with soft, near-sweet tannins. Rich in black fruits and hints of citrus peel and mint, the wine promises to be deep and long. Drink from release–2009. Tentative Score 88–90.

BEN-HANNA, PETIT VERDOT, 2005: Bright garnet red in color, with silky tannins, medium-body and generous black fruits, this wine promises to be round, generous and elegant. Drink from release–2009. Tentative Score 87–89.

BEN-HANNA, MEDITERRANEAN BLEND, 2005: Deep royal purple in color, with soft tannins, spicy wood and appealing blackberry, currant and cassis aromas and flavors. An oak aged blend of 50% Grenache, 12% Syrah, 33% Petit Verdot and 5% Cabernet Franc, this soft and elegant wine will drink nicely from release–2010. Tentative Score 88–90

BEN-HANNA, CABERNET SAUVIGNON-MERLOT, SHALEM, 2003: Dark ruby towards royal purple, medium to full-bodied, with still firm tannins nicely balanced by spicy wood and tempting berry, currant and black cherry fruits, those showing light hints of earthiness and herbaceousness. Drink now–2008. Score 87.

Binyamina ✯✯✯

First established in 1952 as Eliaz Wineries, the winery is located in the town of Binyamina at the foothills of the Carmel Mountains. In 1994 a group of investors bought out the outdated winery, replaced the existing management, and is still gradually introducing modern technology and equipment. Quality has been improving year by year thanks to increasing quality control in the vineyards and the recently remodeled *chais* (barrel room), one of the most attractive in the country.

Under the supervision of winemaker Sasson Ben-Aharon, the winery is now the fourth largest in the country and produces nearly 2.8 million bottles annually from a large variety of grapes, those from vineyards in nearly every part of the country. To the winery's credit, they were the first in the country to introduce Viognier and Tempranillo varietals. Wines of interest are produced in the Special Reserve, Hachoshen, Yogev and regular Binyamina series as well as in the recently released non-vintage wines in the upswing Tiltan series. The winery also has a boutique arm, The Cave, which has a separate entry.

Special Reserve

SPECIAL RESERVE, CABERNET SAUVIGNON, 2005: Medium to full-bodied, with firm but yielding tannins and generous red berry and cassis fruits, those on a background of oriental spice and light herbaceousness. Drink from release–2009. Tentative Score 86–88. K

SPECIAL RESERVE, CABERNET SAUVIGNON, 2004: Dark garnet in color with orange reflections, made from grapes harvested on the Golan Heights. Full-bodied, with generous spicy oak and blackcurrant and blackberry fruits backed up nicely by hints of tobacco and earthiness. Drink from release–2010. Tentative Score 87–89. K

SPECIAL RESERVE, CABERNET SAUVIGNON, 2003: Medium to full-bodied, dark garnet in color, with firm tannins and showing ripe plum, blackberry and cherry fruits, a gentle overlay of spicy oak and an appealing herbal overtone on the finish. Drink now. Score 87. K

SPECIAL RESERVE, CABERNET SAUVIGNON, 2002: This medium to full-bodied wine continues to show firm tannins that seem not to want to integrate and a hint of sweetness that runs through. There are some dark, minty fruits here but those are a bit stingy. Drink now. Score 85. K.

SPECIAL RESERVE, CABERNET SAUVIGNON, 2001: Reflecting its 18 months in new and old *barriques*, this deep royal purple wine shows good balance between fruits, tannins and wood. Generous but well-integrated tannins, a modicum of spicy oak and good currant and berry fruits as well as a warm herbal overlay that lingers nicely. Drink up. Score 85. K

SPECIAL RESERVE, CABERNET SAUVIGNON, 2000: Dark cherry-red toward purple, this medium to full-bodied wine spent 18 months in French oak *barriques*. Currant and black berry fruits dominate on the first sip, but let the wine open and it reveals an appealing herbal-earthy background and a moderately long finish. Starting to show age but still good balance between fruits, wood, acidity and tannins. Drink up. Score 88. K

SPECIAL RESERVE, MERLOT, 2005: Still in embryonic form but already showing medium to full-body and firm tannins, those opening to reveal a good array of ripe and spicy plum, cassis and berry fruits. Drink from release. Tentative Score 86–88. K

SPECIAL RESERVE, MERLOT, 2004: Medium to full-bodied, with moderately firm, near-sweet tannins well balanced by currant, wild berry and cherry fruits. Now a bit acidic on the palate. Drink now. Score 88. K

SPECIAL RESERVE, MERLOT, 2003: This dark cherry red medium-bodied wine is not overly complex but has soft tannins and good balance between those, wood and fruits. Look for hints of licorice and chocolate on the berry-cherry fruits. Drink now. Score 87. K

SPECIAL RESERVE, MERLOT, 2002: The heavy wood once felt here has now settled down nicely and the wine shows good balance between lightly smoky oak, soft tannins and fruits. Look for black plums, black cherries and berries, all with a light spicy overlay. Not complex but appealing. Drink now. Score 85. K

SPECIAL RESERVE, SHIRAZ, 2005: Deep garnet in color, with still firm near-sweet tannins and generous spicy wood, those showing balance and harmony and revealing generous plum, wild berry and currant fruits. On the background, hints of leather and chocolate. Drink from release. Tentative Score 87–89. K

SPECIAL RESERVE, SHIRAZ, 2004: Dark garnet towards royal purple, reflecting its 14 months in oak with firm tannins and generous smoky wood and vanilla. Blended with 2% of Viognier grapes, medium to full-bodied and showing clean blueberry, blackberry and plum fruits along with hints of spices, smoked meat and earthiness. Drink now–2008. Score 89. K

SPECIAL RESERVE, SHIRAZ, 2003: Royal purple in color, medium to full-bodied, with soft tannins, sweet cedar wood, black cherries, plums and a lightly earthy background. Well balanced, long and generous. Drink now. Score 87. K

SPECIAL RESERVE, CABERNET SAUVIGNON-MERLOT-SHIRAZ, 2003: Dark garnet red, full-bodied and deeply tannic at this stage but showing good balance between tannins, wood and fruits, already opening to show currant, berry and plum fruits, those intertwining nicely with hints of tobacco and chocolate. Drink now. Score 88. K.

SPECIAL RESERVE, CHARDONNAY, 2005: Medium to full-bodied, with generous but not overdone acidity and appealing pineapple, peach and tropical fruit aromas and flavors, and a tempting hint of cream on the finish. Drink from release–2008. Tentative Score 87–89. K

SPECIAL RESERVE, CHARDONNAY, 2004: Aged *sur lie* in French *barriques*, with a lively golden color and crisply refreshing spicy pear and apple fruits, this medium to full-bodied white shows appealing nectarine and vanilla flavors on the moderately long finish. Drink now. Score 87. K

SPECIAL RESERVE, CHARDONNAY, 2003: Bright shining gold in color, with orange and green reflections, this oak-aged medium-bodied white offers up melon, peach and apple fruits and reflects its aging *sur lie* with hints of toasted white bread and spicy oak. Drink now. Score 87. K

SPECIAL RESERVE, SAUVIGNON BLANC, 2005: Medium-bodied and light golden straw in color, this crisp and lively unoaked white shows appealing apple and pineapple aromas and flavors. Not complex but very pleasant. Drink now. Score 87. **K**

SPECIAL RESERVE, SAUVIGNON BLANC, 2004: Unoaked, medium-bodied, with grassy, herbaceous and citrus flavors, this clean, crisp and refreshing wine opens nicely on the palate. Drink up. Score 85. **K**

SPECIAL RESERVE, SAUVIGNON BLANC, 2003: Light straw colored, medium-bodied and with crisp acidity, this unoaked white offers up generous pineapple, citrus and grassy flavors along with a light and appealing asphalt overlay. Drink up. Score 85. **K**

SPECIAL RESERVE, VIOGNIER, 2005: Medium-bodied, light golden in color, with appealing aromas and flavors of citrus and apricot as well as hints of cinnamon and minerals, all with good balancing acidity and a warm earthy finish. Drink now–2008. Score 86. **K**

SPECIAL RESERVE, VIOGNIER, 2004: Aged *sur lie*, with gentle acidity that yields to buttery-mineral nuances and with lemon and apple aromas and flavors as well as a lightly earthy note on the finish. Drink now. Score 86. **K**

SPECIAL RESERVE, VIOGNIER, 2003: This unoaked light to medium-bodied wine shows light golden color and lively aromas of grapefruit, apricot and mint, as well as good balancing acid and a green apple note. Drink up. Score 86. **K**

SPECIAL RESERVE, GEWURZTRAMINER, 2004: Golden straw in color, medium-bodied, barely off-dry and with good balancing acidity to keep it lively. Appealing spicy aromas and flavors of citrus, litchis and summer fruits. Drink now. Score 86. **K**

SPECIAL RESERVE, GEWURZTRAMINER, 2003: A pleasant half-dry white, with fresh citrus and tropical fruits, and good balancing acidity to set off the sweetness. Drink up. Score 83. **K**

SPECIAL RESERVE, GEWURZTRAMINER, DESSERT WINE, 2003: Medium-bodied, with tropical fruits, citrus peel and floral aromas. Lacking the spiciness that should typify the variety and the acidity that might have made the wine more lively. Drink now. Score 83. **K**

Avnei Hachoshen

HACHOSHEN, CABERNET SAUVIGNON, 2004: Full-bodied, with spicy, vanilla-rich wood and near-sweet tannins in good balance with blackcurrant, wild berries and minerals, all leading to a long and appealing spicy finish. Drink now–2008. Score 88. **K**

HACHOSHEN, CABERNET SAUVIGNON, TARSHISH, 2003: Deep garnet towards purple, full-bodied, with mouthcoating tannins that are opening to show harmony, and in addition to traditional blackcurrants, sweet berries and spices, generous mineral, toasty and vanilla notes. Best 2008–2011. Score 91. K

HACHOSHEN, SYRAH, 2004: With 14 months in oak, showing medium to full-bodied, with soft, well integrated tannins and light herbal-earthy aromas and flavors complemented nicely by plum, berry and cassis fruits. Hints of tobacco and chocolate on the finish. Drink now–2008. Score 87. K

HACHOSHEN, SYRAH, ODEM, 2003: Blended with 2% of Viognier, full-bodied, firm and concentrated, dark garnet in color, with firm and mouthcoating tannins opening in the glass to reveal near-sweet berry, plum, meaty and earthy aromas and flavors, all leading to a long finish. Drink now–2012. Score 91. K

HACHOSHEN, CABERNET SAUVIGNON-SHIRAZ-MERLOT, SAPIR, 2003: A full-bodied, firmly tannic blend of 40% each of Cabernet and Shiraz and 20% Merlot. Oak aged for 15 months, showing good balance between wood, tannins and a tempting array of aromas and flavors, those including chocolate, tobacco, dusty-oak and minerals, all on a warm background of blackcurrants, blackberries and spices. Drink now–2009. Score 90. K

HACHOSHEN, CHARDONNAY, SHOHAM, 2004: Developed for 16 months in oak. Deep golden straw in color, with smoky oak on the ascendant but with appealing citrus, tropical and melon fruits. Drink now. Score 87. K

HACHOSHEN, SAUVIGNON BLANC FUMÉ, LESHEM, 2004: Light golden in color, medium-bodied, lively, vibrant and focused, reflecting 6 months in oak with hints of spices and vanilla along with aromas and flavors of pears, melon, honeysuckle and fresh cut hay. Drink now. Score 88. K

HACHOSHEN, CHARDONNAY-VIOGNIER-SAUVIGNON BLANC, YASHFEH, 2004: Medium-bodied and crisply dry but losing its flush of youth, its golden color now a bit darker but no less fruity (look for pears, apples and citrus) but the once appealing hint of licorice now taking on an earthy-herbal nature. Drink up. Score 86. K

Yogev

YOGEV, CABERNET SAUVIGNON, 2005: Medium to full-bodied, with soft tannins and sur-ripe plum and berry fruits and generous alcohol that gives the wine a near-sweet finish. Drink now. Score 85. K

YOGEV, CABERNET SAUVIGNON-MERLOT, 2004: Medium-bodied, with soft, almost unfelt tannins, this lightly oaked blend of 50% each of Cabernet Sauvignon and Merlot shows straightforward berry, cassis and plum fruits. A good quaffer. Drink now. Score 85. K

YOGEV, CABERNET SAUVIGNON-SHIRAZ, 2004: A blend of 50% each of Cabernet Sauvignon and Shiraz, oak-aged for 8 months. Medium-bodied, with soft tannins and tempting hints of vanilla and smoky oak and appealing spicy currant, berries, and light earthiness. Drink now–2008. Score 88. K

YOGEV, ROSÉ, 2005: A blend of 50% each Cabernet Sauvignon and Zinfandel, this light to medium-bodied peach colored towards pale pink rose shows clean and refreshing berry, cherry and strawberry aromas and flavors. Simple but pleasant. Drink now. Score 85. K

YOGEV, CABERNET-SAUVIGNON-ZINFANDEL, ROSÉ, 2004: With a deep red berry color, this light to medium-bodied rosé shows tempting red berry, strawberry and spicy aromas and flavors. Charming. Drink now. Score 87. K

YOGEV, SAUVIGNON BLANC-CHARDONNAY, 2005: Light golden straw colored, this aromatic, medium-bodied, unoaked blend of 70% Sauvignon Blanc and 30% Chardonnay shows appealing pineapple, peach and apple aromas and flavors. A well-done quaffer. Drink now. Score 86. K

YOGEV, SAUVIGNON BLANC-CHARDONNAY, 2004: Light straw colored with green tinges, this light to medium bodied unoaked blend offers up aromas and flavors of pineapple, citrus and mango, those on an appealing lightly herbal background. Just the barest hint of sweetness here but that with good balancing acidity. Drink now. Score 87. K

Tiltan

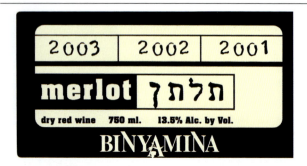

TILTAN, N.V.: The third release in this series and the best to date. Made from Cabernet Sauvignon grapes from the 2002, 2003 and 2004 vintages, this medium to full-bodied blend shows generous wood and tannins, those in good balance with spicy and lightly earthy black fruits. On the finish, nice hints of herbs and vanilla. Drink now–2008. Score 88. K

TILTAN, CABERNET SAUVIGNON, N.V.: Made from grapes harvested in 2001, 2002 and 2003 and then blended after oak-aging, this medium-bodied red shows softening but still-chunky tannins and moderate wood influence, balanced nicely by plum, blackcurrant and earthy aromas and flavors. Drink up. Score 85. K

TILTAN, MERLOT, N.V.: A blend of Merlot grapes from the Upper Galilee that were harvested in 2001, 2002 and 2003, the first batch aged in oak for fourteen months, the second for ten months and the third for three months. Soft tannins but somewhat heavily oaked and with only moderate aromas and flavors of currants, berries. Drink up. Score 85. K

Binyamina

BINYAMINA, CABERNET SAUVIGNON, 2005: Medium-bodied, with gentle smoky and spicy influences from the wood and with soft, nicely integrating tannins. Not complex but with appealing currant, black cherry and berry fruits backed up nicely by a hint of spiciness. Drink now. Score 85. **K**

BINYAMINA, CABERNET SAUVIGNON, 2004: Light wood influences and chunky tannins give this medium-bodied wine a distinctly rustic touch. Simple berry, cherry and cassis aromas and flavors. Drink up. Score 83. **K**

BINYAMINA, CABERNET SAUVIGNON, 2003: Aged partly in American and partly in French oak, this medium to full-bodied-wine shows dusty tannins that promise to integrate well, along with currant, berry and light earthy notes. Look for a hint of cinnamon on the moderately long finish. Drink up. Score 86. **K**

BINYAMINA, MERLOT, 2005: Soft and round, medium-bodied, with silky tannins integrated nicely with gently spicy oak and berry-cherry aromas and flavors. Not complex but a good quaffer. Drink now. Score 84. **K**

BINYAMINA, MERLOT, 2004: Lightly oaked, blended with a small amount of Cabernet Sauvignon, this medium-bodied wine shows near-sweet tannins and a few black fruits on the nose and palate. A bit musky on the nose. Drink up. Score 80. **K**

BINYAMINA, MERLOT, 2003: Dark royal purple in color, this lightly oaked, medium-bodied wine shows generous but yielding tannins well balanced by wood and fruits. Good currant, raspberry and plum aromas and flavors along with a hint of cocoa on the finish. Drink up. Score 86. K

BINYAMINA, SHIRAZ, 2003: Blended with 2% of Viognier, this medium-bodied, deep garnet wine reflects its twelve months in oak with soft tannins and a light vanilla overlay with spicy plums on a light herbal-earthy background. Drink now. Score 85. K

BINYAMINA, TEMPRANILLO, 2005: Medium-bodied and supple, with soft tannins and a hint of spice from the oak, along with black cherry, mineral and light earthy flavors and a hint of rhubarb on the finish. Drink now. Score 85. K

BINYAMINA, TEMPRANILLO, 2004: Ruby towards garnet in color, medium-bodied, with firm tannins and black cherry, grape, mineral and earthy aromas and flavors. A simple quaffer. Drink up. Score 84. K

BINYAMINA, CHARDONNAY, 2005: Not complex, but fresh, fruity and appealing, with green apple, citrus and peach fruits set off nicely by good balancing acidity. Drink now. Score 85. K

BINYAMINA, CHARDONNAY 2004: Unoaked, youthful, fruity, fresh and friendly, not particularly strong on the nose but with tempting flavors of peaches and nectarines. Drink up. Score 85. K

BINYAMINA, CHARDONNAY, 2003: Light gold in color, this simple but pleasant white reflects its short time in oak with a spicy overlay on appealing citrus and green apple fruits. Drink up. Score 85. K

BINYAMINA, SAUVIGNON BLANC, 2005: Clean and crisp, light-straw colored, with tropical fruits, citrus and spring flowers on the nose and palate. Simple but appealing. Drink now. Score 84. K

BINYAMINA, SAUVIGNON BLANC, 2004: Fresh and well balanced, unoaked and with generous acidity to keep it lively and backing up tropical fruit, green apple and light floral aromas and flavors. An unoaked good quaffing wine. Drink now. Score 84. K

BINYAMINA, GEWURZTRAMINER, DESSERT, 2004: Dark straw towards honeyed golden in color, with generous sweetness set off nicely by floral aromas and flavors of litchi and tropical fruits. Drink now. Score 84. K

BINYAMINA, MUSCAT, 2005: Floral, with hints of peppermint backing up its lemon and grapefruit personality. Moderately sweet but lacking the acidity that would have made it more lively. Drink now. Score 82. K

BINYAMINA, MUSCAT, 2004: Semi-dry, not so much floral as it is herbal, with hints of mint on the citrus and summer fruits. Not overly sweet and perhaps best as an aperitif. Drink up. Score 83. K

BINYAMINA, MUSCAT, 2003: Light and bright in color, this medium-bodied white shows flavors of dried summer fruits and light pepper, its moderate sweetness offset nicely by natural acidity. Drink up. Score 83. K

BINYAMINA, EMERALD RIESLING, 2005: Aromatic and floral, with flavors of citrus and summer fruits. Moderately but not offensively sweet. Drink up. Score 83. K

BINYAMINA, EMERALD RIESLING, 2004: Semi-dry, with floral aromas and flavors of nectarines and citrus, but a bit on the sweet side without enough balancing acidity. Drink up. Score 82. K.

Birya **

Founded by Moshe Porat in the community of Birya near the town of Safed in the Galilee and drawing on grapes from Ramot Naftali in the Upper Galilee, the winery released its first wines from the 2003 vintage. Current production is about 4,500 bottles, two-thirds of which were released in April 2004 and the remainder given additional time in barrels.

BIRYA, CABERNET SAUVIGNON, 2004: Deep garnet towards royal-purple in color, medium to full-bodied, with soft tannins integrating nicely with wood and fruits. Aromas and flavors of blackcurrants and berries on a light herbal background. Drink now. Score 84. **K**

BIRYA, CABERNET SAUVIGNON, PORAT WINE, 2003: Medium to full-bodied with firm but well integrating tannins and traditional Cabernet fruits of blackcurrants and berries and hints of herbs and spices on the finish. Drink now. Score 85. **K**

BIRYA, MERLOT, 2004: Medium-bodied, soft and round, with forward berry, black cherry and currant fruits. Drink now. Score 85. **K**

BIRYA, MERLOT, PORAT WINE, 2003: Dark cherry-red toward garnet, this medium-bodied red offers up soft tannins and a berry-cherry-currant personality. Drink now. Score 84. **K**

Bnai Baruch ✶

Founded in 2002 by Emmanuel Goldstein and the members of the Bnai Baruch Yeshiva, a school devoted to study of the Talmud and Kabbalah, grapes are received and undergo initial fermentation at the Nachshon winery before being transferred to the yeshiva for further development. The winery is currently producing about 3,000 bottles of Cabernet Sauvignon, Merlot and Chardonnay annually.

Special Edition/Reserve

SPECIAL EDITION, CABERNET SAUVIGNON, 2003: Oak aged for one year, this medium-bodied, 100% Cabernet Sauvignon shows chunky tannins, high acidity and some hyper-ripe berry-cherry aromas and flavors. Drink now. Score 80. **K**

Bnai Baruch

BNAI BARUCH, CABERNET SAUVIGNON, 2003: Developed with oak chips, this medium-bodied dark garnet and somewhat coarsely tannic wine offers up a few currant and plum flavors. One dimensional and short. Drink up. Score 78. **K**

BNAI BARUCH, MERLOT, 2003: With dusty oak from the oak chips, a somewhat coarse and simple wine with a few black fruits. Drink up. Score 76. **K**

BNAI BARUCH, CHARDONNAY, 2004: Dark golden, going to bronze, with a hint of unwanted sweetness running through and with a few citrus and pineapple fruits. Drink up. Score 72. **K**

Bustan ★★★★

Founded in 1994 by Ya'akov Fogler, this small winery situated on Moshav Sharai Tikva near Tel Aviv draws Cabernet Sauvignon and Merlot grapes from the Jerusalem and Judean Mountains, and produces about 2,000 bottles annually. The winery has earned a good name for its distinctly French-style wines, which have had a formal kashrut certificate since 1999.

BUSTAN, CABERNET SAUVIGNON, 2003: Dark ruby to garnet, medium-bodied, with soft tannins integrating well and with generous but not overwhelming spicy oak. Spicy currant and berry fruits along with chocolate and tobacco on the finish. Drink now–2011. Score 90. K

BUSTAN, CABERNET SAUVIGNON, 2002: Medium to full-bodied, deep garnet towards royal purple, with firm tannins now integrating nicely to reveal sweet cedar wood, currants, wild berries and hints of chocolate, espresso and anise. Drink now–2008. Score 89. K

BUSTAN, CABERNET SAUVIGNON, 2000: Medium-bodied, lacking balance between too soft tannins, heavy acidity and black fruits that seem too sweet on the palate, this is the first disappointing wine from an otherwise excellent winery. Drink now. Score 84. K

BUSTAN, CABERNET SAUVIGNON, 1999: An intense wine with rich and vibrant currant, black cherry and mocha aromas and flavors, these unfolding on the palate to reveal complexity and depth. After losing the rough edges of youth, the wine is now long and elegant and is starting to reveal delicious chocolate, tobacco and anise notes. Drink now. Score 90. K

BUSTAN, CABERNET SAUVIGNON, 1998: Full-bodied and rich, the wine shows aromas and flavors of black cherries, currants and oak as well as spicy overtones, all sitting comfortably on the palate. Deep, long and complex, the wine opens in the glass to reveal its elegance. Drink now. Score 91.

BUSTAN, CABERNET SAUVIGNON, 1997: With 21 months in small oak casks, this ripe and generous wine has distinctive mouth-filling aromas and flavors of blackcurrants and black cherries as well as minty and spicy overtones that linger on and on. Well structured, stylish and graceful, and with soft, now well-integrated tannins. Drink now. Score 90.

BUSTAN, CABERNET SAUVIGNON, 1996: During its youth this wine was searingly tannic but even then showed balance that boded well for its future. Now full-bodied and deep, with the tannins having taken on a softer, sweeter nature and with aromas of black and red currants, wild berries, tobacco, coffee and oak, the wine is drinking beautifully. Drink up. Score 92.

BUSTAN, CABERNET SAUVIGNON, 1995: Oak-aged for 20 months, now fully mature and showing tempting blackcurrant, plum and berry fruits, those matched nicely by aromas and flavors of toasty oak, espresso coffee and black olives on the finish. Drink up. Score 92.

BUSTAN, CABERNET SAUVIGNON, 1994: Oak-aged for 19 months, with its tannins and wood now fully integrated, this well balanced wine from a problematic vintage still shows complex aromas and flavors of currants, berries and black cherries, those matched nicely by minerals, while the finish yields spices and a hint of mint. Drink up. Score 89.

BUSTAN, MERLOT, 2002: Aged in oak for 22 months, this dark garnet, full-bodied, firmly tannic and concentrated wine shows generous black fruits, spices and sweet cedar, all coming to a long licorice and chocolate finish. Best 2008–2011. Score 92. **K**

BUSTAN, MERLOT, 2000: Dark royal purple in color, this medium to full-bodied red shows good balance between soft tannins, sweet cedar, plum and blackberry aromas and flavors. Softening nicely on the palate, this is a round and flavorful wine. Drink now. Score 89. **K**

BUSTAN, MERLOT, 1999: Deep, dark, rich and full-bodied, with spicy currant, mocha, nut, herbal and coffee aromas and flavors, this well-balanced wine has firm but well-integrated tannins and a long complex finish. The best Merlot from Bustan to date. Drink now. Score 93. **K**

BUSTAN, MERLOT, 1998: Round and soft, and with deep layers of wild berries, black cherries, mint and spices that open nicely in the glass, the wine has generous but well-integrated tannins, a good hand with the oak and a long, mouth-filling finish. Drink now. Score 91.

BUSTAN, MERLOT, 1997: Bold, ripe and delicious, with layers of rich plums, currants and black cherries along with a bare herbal accent.

The wine has deep flavors that linger comfortably on the palate, good balance between fruits, acids and tannins, and a long finish. Drink up. Score 90.

BUSTAN, MERLOT, 1996: When first released, the wine was so dense and tannic that one might easily have taken it for a Rhone Syrah. The wine still shows firm tannins but those are now well integrated with smoky-spicy oak, natural acidity and appealing black cherry and wild berry fruits, all coming together in a long finish. Drink up. Score 91.

BUSTAN, MERLOT, 1995: Medium-bodied, with silky tannins and holding nicely to the caressing texture of its youth, the wine yields stewed black fruits, tobacco and chocolate, those matched well by light herbal overtones. Past its peak. Drink up. Score 88.

BUSTAN, SYRAH, 2003: Aromatic enough to be thought of as perfumed, this full-bodied, chewy and richly tannic wine offers up flavors of blackberries, currants, and boysenberry jam, those with tempting overlays of pepper, wet earth, and just a hint of grilled meat. Deep and intense, with a long, complex finish. Best 2008–2012. Score 92. **K**

Bustan Hameshusheem *

Located on Moshav Had Ness on the Golan Heights, winemaker-owner Benny Josef released his first wines to the market from the 2001 vintage. Production of 8,000 bottles annually is primarily of Cabernet Sauvignon, Merlot, Barbera and Sangiovese, and the grapes are drawn from the upper Galilee and nearby vineyards.

BUSTAN HAMESHUSHEEM, CABERNET SAUVIGNON, 2004: Dark in color, with generous firm tannins, those balanced nicely by spicy oak, currant and wild berry aromas and flavors. Drink now. Score 84.

BUSTAN HAMESHUSHEEM, CABERNET SAUVIGNON, 2003: Deep royal purple in color, medium-bodied, with country-style chunky tannins matched nicely by smoky oak, plum and blackberry aromas and flavors. Drink now. Score 84.

BUSTAN HAMESHUSHEEM, CABERNET SAUVIGNON, 2002: Medium to full-bodied, with somewhat coarse tannins that mark it as country-style, and with ripe plum and berry fruits. Simple but pleasant. Drink up. Score 82.

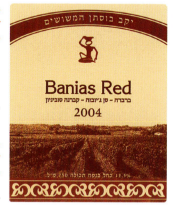

BUSTAN HAMESHUSHEEM, BARBERA, SANGIOVESE-CABERNET SAUVIGNON, BANIAS, 2004: As light in color as in body, reflecting its 8 months in oak with only the barest hint of spiciness and stingy and overripe black fruits. Drink up. Score 75.

BUSTAN HAMESHUSHEEM, BARBERA-SANGIOVESE-CABERNET SAUVIGNON, BANIAS, 2003: Not fully clear garnet in color, medium-bodied, with unyielding tannins. On the nose and palate red fruits that are sweet, coarse and foxy. Score 62.

BUSTAN HAMESHUSHEEM, SANGIOVESE-CABERNET SAUVIGNON-MERLOT, 2002: Medium-bodied, dark cherry red in color, and with soft tannins but somewhat diffuse aromas and flavors, the wine is quite acidic and doesn't reflect the nature of any of the varieties in the blend. Drink up. Score 78.

Carmel ✦✦✦✦

Carmel was founded as a cooperative of vintners in 1882 with funding provided by the Baron Edmond de Rothschild. Its first winery was constructed that same year in Rishon Letzion, in the central coastal region of the country, followed in 1890 by a winery in Zichron Ya'akov, in the Mount Carmel area. Carmel receives grapes from about 300 vineyards throughout the country, some owned by the winery, others by individual vintners and by *kibbutzim* and *moshavim*. Even though their share of the local wine market has dropped from over ninety percent in the early 1980s to somewhat under fifty percent today, Carmel remains the largest wine producer in the country, currently producing over 13 million bottles annually.

For many years, Carmel was in a moribund state, producing wines that while acceptable, rarely attained excellence and failed to capture the attention of more sophisticated consumers. In the last four years, Carmel took dramatic steps to improve the level of their wines. Senior winemaker Lior Laxer is now overseeing a staff of five talented winemakers, most of whom have trained and worked outside of Israel; the winery is developing new vineyards in choice areas of the country and gaining fuller control over contract vineyards; and a new state-of-the-art winery has been partly completed at Ramat Dalton in the Upper Galilee. In the 1990s Carmel was the first winery to plant major vineyards in the Negev Desert, has more recently established an in-house boutique arm in Zichron Ya'akov, and is also a partner in the new Yatir winery. Despite all of this, it is no secret that Carmel is undergoing serious economic difficulties and, with nearly all new faces at the helm of the company, many are now waiting to see precisely what the future holds in store.

Current releases include the top-of-the-line varietal Single Vineyard series, the wines in the Regional series (sometimes referred to as the Appelation Series) and the Private Collection series. Other wines are in the Zichron Ya'akov series, the Selected series (sometimes known as Vineyards or Vineyards Selected Series outside of Israel) and the Hiluleem series.

Limited Edition

LIMITED EDITION, 2003: A blend of 50% Cabernet Sauvignon, about 24% each of Merlot and Petit Verdot and 2% of Cabernet Franc. Generous but not overpowering wood, well balanced by soft tannins and well-tuned acidity. On the nose and palate blackcurrants, gooseberries, spices and sweet cedar wood all coming together in a long, intense and elegant finish. Best 2008–2012. Score 92. K

LIMITED EDITION, 2002: Deep royal-purple in color, with orange reflections, a Bordeaux blend of 60% Cabernet Sauvignon, 30% Merlot and 10% Cabernet Franc, each variety vinified separately and developed for fourteen months in French oak. Medium to full-bodied, with soft tannins and good balance between sweet and smoky wood, aromas and flavors of blackcurrants, berries and dark chocolate all leading to a long finish. Drink now–2012. Score 92. K

Single Vineyard

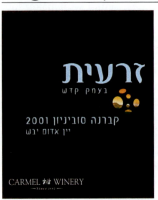

SINGLE VINEYARD, CABERNET SAUVIGNON, KEREM ZARIT, 2004: Full-bodied, with solid tannins and with fine balance between those, spicy wood and fruits. On the nose and palate ripe cassis, blackcurrant and blackberry notes, with vanilla, mineral, eucalyptus and tobacco, all coming together in a complex, well-focused and long finish. Drink from release–2012. Tentative Score 91–93. K

SINGLE VINEYARD, CABERNET SAUVIGNON, KEREM ZARIT, 2003: Dark garnet, with firm, near sweet tannins that yield nicely in the glass to reveal an appealing touch of rustic earthiness that adds dimension to rich, ripe black fruits. Complex, concentrated and elegant. Drink now–2011. Score 90. K

SINGLE VINEYARD, CABERNET SAUVIGNON, KEREM ZARIT, 2002: Dark cherry-red, this medium to full-bodied wine shows soft tannins and generous vanilla and smoky overtones. First impressions are of berries and eucalyptus, those yielding to currants, vanilla, black tea, green peppers and a light spiciness that lingers nicely on the moderately long finish. Warm, round and well balanced. Drink now–2009. Score 90. **K**

SINGLE VINEYARD, CABERNET SAUVIGNON, KEREM ZARIT, 2001: Made entirely from Cabernet Sauvignon grapes and aged in French oak *barriques* for 12 months, the wine has a lively cherry-ruby color. The opening impression on the nose is of eucalyptus and black fruits, and on the palate, of sweet berries. Medium-bodied and with soft tannins, the wine opens nicely in the glass and has a medium-long finish. Drink now–2009. Score 87. **K**

SINGLE VINEYARD, CABERNET SAUVIGNON, KAYOUMI, 2004: Full-bodied, with firm tannins integrating nicely to reveal a rich array of cassis, blackberry, purple plum, sage and mineral aromas and flavors, those coming together in a long, somewhat tannic but elegant finish. Drink from release–2012. Tentative Score 90–92. **K**

SINGLE VINEYARD, CABERNET SAUVIGNON, KAYOUMI, 2003: Luscious and elegant, deep garnet, full-bodied and softly tannic, the nose and palate still showing the blackcurrant, berry and spicy wood that was here but now also showing smoked bacon together with oriental spices and tobacco. Drink now–2014. Score 92. **K**

SINGLE VINEYARD, CABERNET SAUVIGNON, KEREM BEN ZIMRA, 2002: Deep garnet-purple towards black, full-bodied, reflecting its fourteen months in new and used French oak with generous tannins and spicy oak, well balanced by berry, plum and currant fruits set off nicely by hints of vanilla and eucalyptus. On the long finish of this round and complex wine look for yields of tobacco and green olives. Drink now–2009. Score 91. **K**

SINGLE VINEYARD, CABERNET SAUVIGNON, RAMAT ARAD, 2002: Dark garnet red, full-bodied, with abundant but soft, near-sweet and well integrating tannins. Opens with black fruits and sweet cedar wood, those yielding to currants, berries and vanilla and finally to a tempting herbal-earthy sensation. Long and complex. Drink now–2009. Score 92. **K**

SINGLE VINEYARD, CABERNET SAUVIGNON, RAMAT ARAD, 2000: Aged in French *barriques* for 14 months, deep red toward garnet in color, this full-bodied red boasts excellent balance between abundant but soft and well-integrated tannins, just the right hints of vanilla and smoke from the wood, and tempting aromas and flavors that start off with stewed black fruits and then lead to a long earthy-spicy finish. Drink now–2008. Score 92. K

SINGLE VINEYARD, CABERNET SAUVIGNON, SCHECH, 2004: From a not yet well known vineyard on the Golan Heights, this red lives up nicely to the stereotypes of what makes a wine "feminine." Soft, round and caressing, elegant without being intense, full-bodied without being concentrated and with tempting aromas and flavors of black cherries, currants and anise. Drink from release–2012. Tentative Score 88–90. K

SINGLE VINEYARD, MERLOT, HAR BRACHA (IN THE USA, KEREM SHOMRON), 2002: Full-bodied and complex, this dark purple towards black wine shows still rather firm tannins but has balance and structure that bode well for the future. In time look for black cherry, currant and plum fruits, those on a spicy cedar-wood background. Drink now–2009. Score 92. K

SINGLE VINEYARD, SHIRAZ, KAYOUMI, 2004: Intense and concentrated, dense and fragrant, with silky-smooth ripe tannins. On the nose and palate raspberries, black cherries, black pepper, licorice as well as generous but well balanced doses of spicy oak and earthiness. Needs time to show its supple and stylish elegance. Best 2008–2015. Tentative Score 91–93. K

SINGLE VINEYARD, SHIRAZ, KAYOUMI, 2003: Firm and well-structured, a soft, caressing and elegant wine. Generous soft tannins highlight a tempting array of currant, plum, blackberry and anise flavors and aromas, all of which culminate in a long, mouthfilling finish. Best 2008–2012. Score 91. K

SINGLE VINEYARD, SYRAH, RAMAT ARAD, 2003: Oak aged for about nine months, this dark cherry red towards purple, medium to full-bodied wine shows excellent balance between soft tannins, smoke, spices, and aromas and flavors of currants, plums and chocolate. Long, smooth and generous. Drink now–2008. Score 90. K

SINGLE VINEYARD, SYRAH, RAMAT ARAD, 2002: Made from the grapes of young vines, this fresh and lively medium-bodied wine was wisely placed in oak for only 4 months and now shows soft tannins, generous plum, currant and berry fruits as well as a nice layer of spiciness, and just the barest hint of freshly turned earth. Drink now. Score 89. K

SINGLE VINEYARD, CHARDONNAY, KAYOUMI, UPPER GALILEE, 2005: Gentle pressing and cold fermentation, aged partly in new and partly one-year-old 300 liter French barrels. Showing elegance and focus. Crisp and fresh, and on the nose and palate rich apple, pear, fig and light toasty notes coming together very nicely indeed. Drink from release–2008. Tentative Score 89–91. **K**

SINGLE VINEYARD, CHARDONNAY, KAYOUMI, 2004: Bright and lively and with enough complexity to catch your attention. Developed in 300 liter barrels, this medium-bodied white shows aromas and flavors of citrus peel, vanilla pastry cream and brioche, all lingering nicely. Drink now. Score 88. **K**

SINGLE VINEYARD, CHARDONNAY, MERON, 2003: After fermenting in stainless steel, the wine was transferred to new oak casks to develop *sur lie*. Medium to full-bodied, showing appealing buttery and vanilla flavors on a background of pears, spices and citrus, all with just the right level of smoky, toasty oak. Rich, mouth-filling and long. Drink now. Score 90. **K**

SINGLE VINEYARD, CHARDONNAY, HAR TAVOR, 2002: Medium-bodied, smooth and supple, the wine offers up ripe pear, pineapple and grapefruit fruits backed up nicely by hints of oak, spices, and a wisp of honey that comes in on the finish. Look as well for light hints of vanilla and nutmeg. Drink up. Score 88. **K**

SINGLE VINEYARD, SAUVIGNON BLANC, RAMAT ARAD, 2005: Lightly oak-aged, medium-bodied, lively and with grapefruit and passion fruits backed up by grassy and floral input that makes the wine harmonious and tempting. Drink now–2008. Score 88. **K**

SINGLE VINEYARD, SAUVIGNON BLANC, RAMAT ARAD, 2004: Light golden-straw in color with a surprising tinge of pink, medium-bodied, unoaked and remarkably light on the palate. Bright, clean and crisp, with fresh citrus, tropical fruits and appealing herbal overtones leading to a moderately-long finish. Drink now. Score 88. **K**

SINGLE VINEYARD, SAUVIGNON BLANC, RAMAT ARAD, 2003: Bright golden straw in color, medium-bodied and with fresh nectarine, citrus and floral aromas and flavors on a mineral-rich background. Rich, clean and refreshing. Drink up. Score 89. **K**

SINGLE VINEYARD, JOHANNISBERG RIESLING, KAYOUMI, UPPER GALILEE, 2005: Off-dry but bright and lively, with fine focus and balancing acidity. Unoaked, with tempting peach and apple flavors set off nicely by floral and mineral edges. Elegant and satisfying. Drink now–2008. Score 90. **K**

SINGLE VINEYARD, GEWURZTRAMINER, LATE HARVEST, KEREM SHUAL, 2004: Made from grapes harvested in the upper Golan Heights, some affected by botrytis. Medium-bodied, with generous sweetness set off by good balancing acidity, and on the nose and palate apricot, cinnamon, rose petal and honeyed flavors. Rich, spicy and elegant, with a long silky finish. Drink now–2009. Score 92. **K**

Regional (Appelation)

REGIONAL, CABERNET SAUVIGNON, UPPER GALILEE, 2003: Dark ruby towards royal purple in color, medium to full-bodied, with firm tannins integrating nicely, and appealing blackberry and currant fruits matched well by hints of minerals and mint. Moderately long. Drink now–2008. Score 88. **K**

REGIONAL, CABERNET SAUVIGNON, UPPER GALILEE AND RAMAT ARAD, 2002: Deep garnet towards purple, medium to full-bodied and reflecting generous but well integrated tannins after aging in new French oak for fourteen months. Compact and well focused, showing aromas and flavors of cedary oak, red currants, violets and dark chocolate. On the medium-long finish look for appealing hints of spices and tobacco. Drink now. Score 87. **K**

REGIONAL, CABERNET SAUVIGNON, UPPER GALILEE AND RAMAT ARAD, 2001: Aged for 14 months in small oak barrels, this deep purple, medium to full-bodied red shows good balance between wood, soft tannins and fruits. On the nose and palate red and black berries, purple plums and a hint of eucalyptus on the medium-long finish. Drink now. Score 88. **K**

REGIONAL, MERLOT, UPPER-GALILEE, 2004: Deep garnet in color, medium to full-bodied, with tannins integrating nicely. Opens slowly but when it does, offers up appealing black currant and blueberry fruits, those with a light overlay of oak and appealing green pepper and eucalyptus aromas and flavors. Fresh, generous and elegant. Drink from release–2010. Tentative Score 90–92. **K**

REGIONAL, MERLOT, UPPER GALILEE, 2003: Garnet towards brick red in color, with somewhat chunky tannins and a bit skimpy with its berry, cherry and cassis aromas and flavors. Lacking complexity but pleasant. Drink now. Score 87. **K**

REGIONAL, MERLOT, UPPER GALILEE AND RAMAT ARAD, 2001: Deep garnet towards purple in color, medium to full-bodied, with well integrated tannins after aging in new French oak for 14 months. Compact and well focused, showing aromas and flavors of cedary oak, red currants, violets and dark chocolate. On the medium-long finish appealing hints of spices and tobacco. Drink up. Score 87. **K**

REGIONAL, CABERNET FRANC, JERUSALEM MOUNTAINS, 2002: Made entirely from Cabernet Franc grapes, this deep ruby towards garnet wine shows good balance between medium to full-body, generous soft tannins and currant and berry fruits together with the lead-pencil sensation one often finds in the wines of Bordeaux. Drink now. Score 88. **K**

REGIONAL, CARIGNAN, ZICHRON YA'AKOV, 2004: Made from low yield, 30 year old vines, this full-bodied, firmly tannic wine shows ripe cherry, berry, peppery and spicy aromas and flavors, those on a light earthy and smoky background Drink now–2009. Score 88. **K**

REGIONAL, PETITE SIRAH, JUDEAN HILLS, 2004: Deep ruby towards garnet, this is an intense and vibrant wine, full-bodied, still rough around the edges but worth watching as it should open to reveal ample tannins well balanced by wood, and flavors and aromas of black cherries, currant and mocha. Drink now–2009. Score 87. **K**

REGIONAL, CABERNET SAUVIGNON-SHIRAZ, UPPER GALILEE, 2004: Full-bodied, with soft tannins and spicy wood coming together nicely with wild berry, black cherry and plum fruits on a licorice and vanilla rich background. Drink now–2008. Score 87. **K**

REGIONAL, REHES RED, ZICHRON, 2005: A distinct step-down in the Regional series, this blend of Merlot, Carignan and Petite Sirah (75%, 16% and 9% respectively) shows some black and red fruits but is a far too simple and acidic wine. Drink up. Score 80. **K**

REGIONAL, CHARDONNAY, HAR TAVOR, 2004: Medium-bodied, buttery, and with appealing aromas and flavors of bitter oranges and tropical fruits. Good balance between acidity, wood and fruits. Drink up. Score 86. **K**

REGIONAL, CHARDONNAY, UPPER GALILEE, 2004: Simple and austere, medium-bodied, with earthy and woody flavors that dominate the pear and melon fruit flavors. Could use more fruit and more acidity to make it livelier. Drink up. Score 84. **K**

REGIONAL, CHARDONNAY, GALILEE, 2003: Oak fermented and then developed *sur lie* for nine months, this light gold, medium-bodied white offers up a generous mouthful of summer and tropical fruits, those matched nicely by crisp minerals and just the right feel of oak. Drink up. Score 88. K

REGIONAL, SAUVIGNON BLANC-CHARDONNAY, UPPER GALILEE AND RAMAT ARAD, 2003: A blend of 80% Sauvignon Blanc from Ramat Arad and 20% Chardonnay from the Upper Galilee, fermented in stainless steel and then transferred to new French oak *barriques* to develop *sur lie* for six months. Clean, light to medium-bodied, with generous acidity and appealing grapefruit and melon flavors. Drink up. Score 85. K

REGIONAL, JOHANNISBERG RIESLING, 2005: Generously aromatic, with peach, apple and floral aromas and flavors. Good acidity to keep it lively and interesting. Drink now. Score 86. K

REGIONAL, REHES WHITE, UPPER GALILEE, 2005: An odd blend of Chardonnay, Sauvignon Blanc and Gewurztraminer (50%, 40% and 10% respectively). Unoaked, with aromas simultaneously flowery and grassy along with muted citrus, kiwi and earthy flavors. On the finish, a too pronounced hint of sweetness. Drink now. Score 78. K

Private Collection

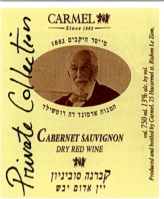

PRIVATE COLLECTION, CABERNET SAUVIGNON, 2004: Aged partly in French and American oak, partly in stainless steel, this dark garnet, medium-bodied red shows near-sweet tannins and generous currant and blueberry aromas and flavors. Not complex but lithe and easy to drink. Drink now–2008. Score 86. K

PRIVATE COLLECTION, CABERNET SAUVIGNON, 2003: Dark royal-purple in color, medium to full-bodied, with tannins integrating nicely and appealing aromas and flavors of currants, wild berries, spicy oak. Drink now. Score 85. K

PRIVATE COLLECTION, CABERNET SAUVIGNON, 2002: Dark royal purple, this medium to full-bodied oak-aged red shows appealing aromas and flavors of currants, black cherries and spices. Good balance between moderate tannins, acidity and wood. Drink now. Score 87. **K**

PRIVATE COLLECTION, CABERNET SAUVIGNON, 2001: Medium to full-bodied, this dark cherry red toward garnet wine shows firm tannins and a rather generous hand with the oak beyond. Given time to open in the glass the wine shows wild berry, currant and lightly spicy aromas and flavors. Drink up. Score 85. **K**

PRIVATE COLLECTION, MERLOT, 2004: Deep garnet towards royal purple in color and medium-bodied, with soft tannins and appealing ripe cherry-berry flavors as well as a hint of root beer. Drink now. Score 86. **K**

PRIVATE COLLECTION, MERLOT, 2003: Deep garnet in color, medium-bodied, reflecting its ten months in oak with hints of vanilla and spices along with firm tannins that may yield in time but now hold back the plum and berry fruits. Drink now. Score 85. **K**

PRIVATE COLLECTION, MERLOT, 2002: This medium-bodied soft and round wine has stingy aromas but offers up generous and appealing flavors of black cherries and plums. Drink up. Score 85. **K**

PRIVATE COLLECTION, MERLOT, 2001: Medium-bodied, soft and round, with generous berry, cherry and currant fruits along with light hints of oak and fresh herbs. Not overly complex but pleasant. Past its peak. Drink up. Score 83. **K**

PRIVATE COLLECTION, MERLOT, 2000: Not a classic Merlot but a solid and well made wine that boasts plenty of currant, wild berry, black cherry and spicy flavors as well as good balance and abundant firm tannins. Past its peak. Drink up. Score 82. **K**

PRIVATE COLLECTION, CABERNET SAUVIGNON-MERLOT, 2004: Dark garnet red, medium-bodied, with chunky, country-style tannins but those opening to reveal moderate levels of black cherry, tar and spicy notes. Drink up. Score 85. **K**

PRIVATE COLLECTION, CABERNET SAUVIGNON-MERLOT, 2003: Medium to full-bodied, with soft tannins and appealing currant and plum fruits backed up by hints of spices and sweet herbs. Drink now. Score 85. **K**

PRIVATE COLLECTION, CABERNET SAUVIGNON-MERLOT, 2002: This medium-bodied red shows just enough cherry, plum and spicy notes on a smooth, moderately tannic background. Drink now. Score 86. **K**

PRIVATE COLLECTION, CABERNET SAUVIGNON-MERLOT, 2000: Medium-bodied, with an attractive ruby-garnet color, this lightly herbal wine shows a modest range of plum, cherry, earth and anise aromas and flavors as well as a cedary, moderately tannic finish. Drink up. Score 85. K

PRIVATE COLLECTION, CABERNET SAUVIGNON-SHIRAZ, 2003: Dark garnet in color, medium-bodied, with wood, soft tannins and acidity in fine balance with appealing berry, black cherry and cassis fruits. Drink up. Score 84. K

PRIVATE COLLECTION, CABERNET SAUVIGNON-SHIRAZ, 2002: The abundant wood and tannins are backed up by enough berry, black cherry and earthy-herbal aromas and flavors to pull the wine together. Needs time to open in the glass. Drink up. Score 83. K

PRIVATE COLLECTION, GIVAT ZAMARIN, RED, 2004: An unoaked blend of Cabernet Sauvignon, Merlot, Carignan and Petite Sirah. Medium-bodied, with soft tannins and some blackberry, currant and spicy aromas and flavors. Lacking complexity but an acceptable quaffer. Drink now. Score 84. K

PRIVATE COLLECTION, CHARDONNAY, 2004: Light-golden straw in color, medium-bodied with a core of green apple and pineapple flavors. Crisp and clean with some appealing mineral overtones. Drink up. Score 84. K

PRIVATE COLLECTION, CHARDONNAY, 2002: Fermented in the barrels and allowed to develop *sur lie* for eight months, the wine has attractive aromas and flavors of citrus fruits and peel, a hint of pineapple, and a light underlying spiciness. Somewhat past its peak. Drink up. Score 84. K

PRIVATE COLLECTION, SAUVIGNON BLANC, 2005: Light-straw colored, medium-bodied, fresh and fruity with appealing green apple, peach and light grassy aromas and flavors. Drink up. Score 85. K

PRIVATE COLLECTION, SAUVIGNON BLANC, 2003: After undergoing long, low temperature fermentation to keep its fresh fruity character, this crisply refreshing unoaked white shows a core of nectarine, citrus, floral and light grassy aromas and flavors. Drink up. Score 86. K

PRIVATE COLLECTION, CHARDONNAY-SAUVIGNON BLANC, 2005: Light-straw in color, light to medium-bodied, with sweet apple and spicy spring flower aromas. Not complex but an acceptable quaffer. Drink now. Score 84. K

PRIVATE COLLECTION, CHARDONNAY-SAUVIGNON BLANC, 2003: Medium-bodied, clean and crisp, the wine shows summer fruit, pineapple and citrus aromas and flavors. Drink up. Score 84. K

PRIVATE COLLECTION, EMERALD RIESLING, 2005: Clear light straw in color, light in body, with sweetness that lacks acidity to keep it lively. Floral and pineapple aromas and flavors. Drink up. Score 79. K

PRIVATE COLLECTION, EMERALD RIESLING, 2004: Light golden straw in color, light to medium-bodied, floral on the nose, with thankfully restrained sweetness, good liveliness and flavors citrus and tropical fruits. Drink up. Score 80. K

PRIVATE COLLECTION, WHITE, GIVAT ZAMARIN, 2004: Pale golden straw with green tints, this flowery but dry blend of Sauvignon Blanc, French Colombard, Chardonnay and Emerald Riesling shows appealing aromas and flavors of citrus and summer fruits. Not complex but a good quaffer. Drink up. Score 85. K

Selected (Vineyard)

SELECTED, CABERNET SAUVIGNON, 2005: Garnet red in color, medium-bodied, with soft tannins and simple but appealing black fruits. Drink now. Score 82. K

SELECTED, CABERNET SAUVIGNON, 2004: Dark garnet, medium-bodied, with somewhat coarse tannins and rather stingy currant and plum notes. Drink up. Score 82. K

SELECTED, CABERNET SAUVIGNON, 2003: Dark in color, medium-bodied and with soft tannins and appealing plum, currant and black cherry fruits, those with appealing hints of spices and Mediterranean herbs. Drink up. Score 83. K

SELECTED, MERLOT, 2005: Medium-bodied, soft, round and with generous black plum and cherry fruits. Nothing complex but a good entry-level wine. Drink now. Score 82. K

SELECTED, MERLOT, 2004: Medium-bodied, with soft tannins and forward black fruits. A simple entry-level wine. Drink now. Score 82. K

SELECTED, MERLOT, 2003: Medium-bodied, with silky tannins and generous black fruits and a hint of spiciness. Somewhat one dimensional but good with food. Drink up. Score 83. K

SELECTED, PETITE SIRAH, 2005: Soft and round, with forward blackberry, cassis and earthy aromas and flavors. Drink now. Score 80. K

SELECTED, PETITE SIRAH, 2004: Medium-bodied, with country-style tannins and a hint of overall coarseness but generous berry and earthy aromas and flavors. Drink now. Score 83. K

SELECTED, PETITE SIRAH, 2003: Dark cherry red in color, this medium-bodied wine offers up chunky tannins and appealing plum and berry flavors. Drink now. Score 84. K

SELECTED, ZINFANDEL, 2004: As always a semi-dry blush or "white" Zin. Light to medium-bodied, with more of a resemblance to cherry-berry juice than to wine. Drink up. Score 74. K

SELECTED, ZINFANDEL, 2003: A semi-dry blush Zinfandel of medium body with some appealing fresh berry-cherry aromas and flavors but with sweetness that is not matched by acidity or depth. Drink up. Score 78. K

SELECTED, CHARDONNAY, 2005: Nothing complex here but a pleasant little white with pineapple and citrus fruits. An entry-level quaffer. Drink up. Score 82. K

SELECTED, CHARDONNAY, 2004: A simple little wine, light in color, with citrus and pineapple flavors. Drink now. Score 82. K

SELECTED, SAUVIGNON BLANC, 2005: Light, simple, fresh and fruity with green apple, pineapple and peach fruits on a lightly floral background. Drink now. Score 84. K

SELECTED, EMERALD RIESLING, 2005: As light in color as in body and a bit too sweet, with floral and citrus aromas dominating. Drink up. Score 78. **K**

SELECTED, EMERALD RIESLING, 2004: Light straw in color, light to medium-bodied, with its sweetness not fully balanced by acidity and only skimpy citrus and pineapple aromas and flavors. Drink up. Score 79. **K**

SELECTED, MOSCATO, 2005: Half-sweet, light, with primarily citrus and pineapple aromas and flavors and not quite lively enough to make it truly *frizzante*. Drink up. Score 78. **K**

SELECTED, MOSCATO, 2004: In the style of Moscato d'Asti but so fizzy that it calls to mind soda more than *frizzante* wine. Too sweet, lacking balancing acidity and with too forward pineapple aromas and flavors. Drink up. Score 74. **K**

SELECTED, WHITE ZINFANDEL, 2005: Beyond the appealing pink color, far too sweet without balancing acidity and not much in the way of fruits or anything else to add charm. Drink up. Score 74. **K**

Zichron Ya'akov

ZICHRON YA'AKOV, MERLOT, 2003: Dark garnet in color, medium-bodied, with soft, well-integrated tannins and appealing black cherry and currant fruits. Not complex but a good quaffer. Drink now. Score 84. **K**

ZICHRON YA'AKOV, MERLOT, 2002: Bright purple toward garnet in color, the wine has up-front plum, black cherry and light spicy aromas and flavors, but lacks a balance between those fruits, tannins and wood. Drink up. Score 79. **K**

ZICHRON YA'AKOV, RED, 2004: An unoaked blend of Merlot, Carignan, Cabernet Sauvignon and Petit Sirah. Garnet to purple in color, medium-bodied with soft tannins and berry-cherry fruits. An appealing quaffer. Drink up. Score 85. K

ZICHRON YA'AKOV, SAUVIGNON BLANC, 2004: Light straw towards gold in color, medium-bodied, this unoaked blend of 87% Sauvignon Blanc and 13% Chardonnay proves acidic but refreshing, with crisp, clean citrus, pear and pineapple aromas and flavors matched by an appealing hint of bitterness. Drink now. Score 86. K

ZICHRON YA'AKOV, WHITE, 2004: A somewhat disconnected potpourri of Sauvignon Blanc, French Colombard, Chardonnay, Emerald Riesling and Semillon. Very fruity and flowery, with tropical fruits, citrus and a hint of sweetness. Drink up. Score 80. K

Not Part of a Specific Series

CARMEL, HILULEEM RED, 2005: As light in body as it is in tannins, this super-young blend of Merlot, Carignan and Petite Sirah shows pleasant cherry, berry and violet flavors, all on a slightly tart edge. Drink up. Score 83. K

CARMEL, HILULEEM WHITE, 2005: A blend of Sauvignon Blanc, Semillon and Chardonnay, so light and acidic that you might even think you were drinking a glass of lightly alcoholic orange and grapefruit juice. Drink up. Score 81. K

CARMEL, MUSCAT DESSERT WINE, 2002: Made from late harvested Muscat of Alexandria grapes that were fermented slowly and then reinforced with alcohol to stop the fermentation, this sweet, fruity and fresh wine offers up ripe pear, litchi and honeyed aromas and flavors. Balanced, elegant and a good match to fruit based desserts. Drink now. Score 88. K

CARMEL, THE PRESIDENT'S WINE, N.V.: Carmel's attempt at producing a sparkling wine has far too much acidity, its flavors and aromas are too similar to a nectar made from tropical fruits, lemon and grapefruit, and its bubbles are far too "fat" and not long-lasting enough. Score 75. K

Castel ★★★★★

Starting as a micro-winery, the Domaine du Castel grew gradually and now produces approximately 100,000 bottles annually. That change in output, however, has not affected the quality of the wines, and since releasing a mere 600 bottles of his first wine in 1992, owner-winemaker Eli Ben Zaken, now working with his son Ariel, has consistently made some of the best wines in the country. The physically beautiful winery, with an exquisite cellar holding more than 500 *barriques*, is located on Moshav Ramat Raziel in the Jerusalem Mountains. The winery relies entirely on grapes grown in the area of the winery, mostly in their own vineyards, others in vineyards under their full supervision. Grape varieties include Cabernet Sauvignon, Merlot, Petit Verdot, Cabernet Franc, Malbec and Chardonnay.

The winery produces wines in three series—the first label, Grand Vin Castel, is an often exquisite Bordeaux-style blend with distinct Italian overtones; the fine second label, Petit Castel, is meant for earlier drinking; and then there is "C", which is consistently one of the most exciting Chardonnay wines produced in the region. The winery produced a first kosher version of its Grand Vin in 2002 and from the 2003 vintage all of Castel's wines have been kosher.

Grand Vin Castel

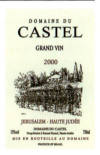

GRAND VIN CASTEL, 2005: Full-bodied, tannic enough to be thought of as muscular but with structure and balance that promise concentration and elegance. On the nose and palate blackcurrants, red plums and blackberries, those matched nicely by spicy wood and hints of Mediterranean herbs. Best 2009–2013. Tentative Score 92–94. **K**

GRAND VIN CASTEL, 2004: Deep garnet towards black in color and full-bodied, with firm tannins integrating nicely with smoky wood. On the nose and palate, raspberries, blackcurrants, vanilla, and chocolate, those yielding on a long finish to hints of licorice, tobacco and chocolate. Generous and elegant. Best 2008–2012. Tentative Score 93–95. **K**

GRAND VIN CASTEL, 2003: Dark garnet towards royal purple in color and full-bodied, with firm tannins integrating nicely. Multilayered, on first attack revealing blackcurrants, blackberries and spices, those yielding to purple plums and near-sweet cigar tobacco and on the long finish hints of mint and a tantalizing earthy-herbal overtone. Approachable now but best from 2008–2012. Score 94. **K**

GRAND VIN CASTEL, 2002 (KOSHER EDITION): Full-bodied, bold, concentrated, and with layer after layer of aromas and flavors that linger on. Look for currants, cherries, plums and spices on first attack, those yielding nicely to cedar, minerals and tobacco leaf. Drink now–2009. Score 91. **K**

GRAND VIN CASTEL, 2002: Rich and round, with ripe currant, black cherry and anise, with still firm tannins on a green olive, cedar and mineral background. Full-bodied, intense and long. Drink now–2008 Score 91.

GRAND VIN CASTEL, 2001: Developing beautifully, this still young wine is now showing earthy currant, black cherry, sage and cedar wood aromas and flavors. Full-bodied and concentrated, the wine possesses great elegance and features long lingering flavors rich in hints of coffee and chocolate. Drink now. Score 91.

GRAND VIN CASTEL, 2000: With once firm tannins now well-integrated, this medium to full-bodied wine is showing excellent balance between spicy blackcurrant, plum and blackberry fruits, those matched nicely by hints of Mediterranean herbs and clean earthy aromas and flavors. Muscular, with firm tannins with as well as a long, spicy finish. Drink now. Score 92.

GRAND VIN CASTEL, 1999: This full-bodied, deep ruby toward dark purple wine reveals good balance between generous, well-integrated tannins and elegant black fruits including currants, plums and blackberries. Look also for aromas and flavors of mint and red licorice, all coming together in a just spicy enough finish with tobacco aromas and flavors. Drink now. Score 90.

GRAND VIN CASTEL, 1998: A near-elegant wine, slow to open during its youth and now aging somewhat more quickly than anticipated. With now softened tannins, some spicy-smoky wood and plum and currant fruits, all leading to a moderately-long vanilla flavored finish. Drink up. Score 90.

GRAND VIN CASTEL, 1997: Perhaps Castel's most luxurious wine in its youth, with remarkably intense blackcurrant and black cherry fruits, Mediterranean herbs, an abundant but very well balanced oak and a long finish with pepper and anise. Supple and harmonious but now starting to fade. Drink up. Score 89.

GRAND VIN CASTEL, 1996: Fully mature now, this complex full-bodied wine shows excellent balance between wood, ample tannins, and an array of aromas and flavors of currants, herbs, tobacco and hints of mint and sweet cedar that unfold nicely on the palate. Past its peak so drink up. Score 89.

GRAND VIN CASTEL, 1995: Concentrated, intense and elegant, this medium to full-bodied wine shows deep currant, purple plum and black cherry fruits on a background of chocolate, and what has developed into earthy, tobacco and cedar wood flavors. Still harmonious but now somewhat past its peak and not meant for further cellaring. Drink up. Score 88.

GRAND VIN CASTEL, 1993: Now taking on a deep adobe brick red color, this still rich and round wine with ample blackcurrants, a light bitter nuttiness and deeper herbaceousness than it had earlier is clearly past its peak and not meant for further cellaring. Drink up. Score 90.

Petit Castel

PETIT CASTEL, 2004: Medium to full-bodied and with soft tannins, this caressing red opens with a chocolate and berry-rich nose, joined by cassis, black cherries, dark plums and black pepper, all lingering on a long, polished and round finish. Elegant and supple. Drink now–2010. Score 92. **K**

PETIT CASTEL, 2003: Softer, smoother and more approachable than the Grand Vin of this vintage. Medium to full-bodied, with forward black fruits, soft tannins already integrating nicely and a pleasing array of currant, wild berry and earthy-herbaceous aromas and flavors. Mouthfilling and moderately long. Drink now–2008. Score 90. **K**

PETIT CASTEL, 2002: Dark ruby toward garnet in color, this medium-bodied red shows soft, well-integrated tannins and generous currant and wild berry fruits together with generous touches of sweet cedar, spices and herbs on the moderately long finish. Drink now–2008. Score 89.

PETIT CASTEL, 2001: Medium to full-bodied, with soft and well-integrated tannins and excellent balance between wood and fruit, this wine is living up to its earlier promise. Blackcurrant and blackberry fruits come together very nicely with lightly smoky cedar and an appealing underlying hint of earthiness. Drink now–2008. Score 91.

PETIT CASTEL, 2000: Medium to full-bodied, this deep garnet toward royal purple wine reveals smooth, well-integrated tannins and an attractive array of fruits including currants, black cherries and plum to which generous hints of oak and a dash of spiciness add charm. Drink now. Score 89.

PETIT CASTEL, 1999: Medium to full-bodied, this appealing wine offers currant and cherry-berry notes integrated well with lightly smoky-toasty and spicy aromas and flavors. With moderate levels of smooth tannins, tantalizing bittersweet and herbal notes that emerge at the finish, and just the right touch of oak. Drink up. Score 89.

PETIT CASTEL, 1998: Well balanced and with a spicy finish, this wine is living up to its full potential. Ripe, rich and harmonious, the wine shows fine balance between smooth tannins, smoky wood and blackcurrant-black cherry fruits. Drink up. Score 90.

"C" Chardonnay

"C", CHARDONNAY, 2005: Rich, complex and opulent, with layer after layer of citrus, fig, pear, apricot, spices and smoky, toasty oak, this is a wine that opens beautifully on the palate, offering up forward flavors and aromas while maintaining its sense of finesse and elegance. Drink from release–2010. Tentative Score 92–94. K

"C", CHARDONNAY, 2004: Light gold in color, medium to full-bodied, with generous but intentionally subdued influences of wood. Deeply aromatic, with tempting citrus, melon, pear and tropical fruit aromas and flavors, those coming to a creamy and long finish. Drink now–2010. Score 92. K

"C", CHARDONNAY, 2003: A Burgundy style Chardonnay, full-bodied, showing complex ripe pear, green apple and hazelnut aromas and flavors on a lightly smoky background. Drink now–2008. Score 91. K

"C", CHARDONNAY, 2002: A full-bodied, elegant Burgundy style white, showing citrus, pineapple, green apple, toasted bread and fig aromas and flavors along with a comfortably nutty finish. Drink now–2008. Score 91.

"C", CHARDONNAY, 2001: Not showing as rich now as it did during its youth, this medium to full-bodied mouth-filling wine has depth, length and elegance, with tempting white peach, nectarine, pineapple and citrus aromas and flavors, all on a just firm enough toasty oak background and with an appealing nut and vanilla flavored long finish. Drink up. Score 90.

"C", CHARDONNAY, 2000: Medium to full-bodied, now taking on a somewhat darker golden straw color, the wine boasts generous pear, fig and citrus aromas and flavors, all on a background that at one moment feels like butterscotch and at another like toasty bread. An elegant wine but now somewhat past its peak. Drink up. Score 91.

"C", CHARDONNAY, 1999: This complex, elegant and full-bodied white calls to mind the Burgundy whites of Montrachet and Meursault with its nutty, mineral and summer fruit aromas and flavors, all unfolding beautifully on the palate. Drink up. Score 94.

"C", CHARDONNAY, 1998: Deep golden in color, this full-bodied, velvety and lush wine continues to show rich summer fruit and pear along tempting spicy oak flavors. Long on the palate, with a hint of bitter almonds creeping in. Drink up. Score 93.

The Cave ✯✯✯

Founded in 1997 as a daughter company of Binyamina Wineries, this small winery has its barrel storage facilities in a cave at the foothills of Mount Carmel, not far from the town of Zichron Ya'akov. The artificial cave, which was built in the sixteenth century, is nine meters high and maintains a constant natural temperature and humidity. The winery is releasing 6,000 bottles annually of a Cabernet Sauvignon-Merlot blend, the grapes coming from a single vineyard in Kerem Ben Zimra in the Upper Galilee, the wines being made by the winemaker of Binyamina.

THE CAVE, CABERNET SAUVIGNON-MERLOT, 2003: Full-bodied, firmly tannic, with generous spicy oak integrating nicely and showing elegant blackcurrant, plum and blackberry aromas and flavors. Drink now–2009. Score 89. K

THE CAVE, CABERNET SAUVIGNON-MERLOT, 2002: This blend of 65% Cabernet Sauvignon and 35% Merlot was oak-aged for 20 months. Medium to full-bodied, with solid tannins that yield in the glass to reveal a generously fruity and elegant wine. On the nose and palate blackcurrants, blackberries and vanilla matched nicely by hints of Mediterranean herbs. Drink now–2008. Score 89. K

THE CAVE, CABERNET SAUVIGNON-MERLOT, 2001: This moderately-deep garnet, well balanced, medium to full-bodied red was oak-aged for 18 months. Continuing to show tempting aromas and flavors of currants, plums and berries, those with overlays of coffee, Mediterranean herbs and spicy oak. Drink now. Score 88. K

THE CAVE, CABERNET SAUVIGNON-MERLOT, 2000: This blend of 60% Cabernet Sauvignon and 40% Merlot was aged in small oak barrels for 24 months. The barnyard-aromas and somewhat firm tannins felt when the wine is first poured will yield to ripe plum and blackberry aromas and flavors. Full-bodied and sturdy, the wine offers generous oak and a perhaps overly herbal finish. Drink up. Score 85. K

Chateau Golan ★★★★★

A fully modern winery located on Moshav Eliad on the Golan Heights, Chateau Golan released their first wines from the 2000 vintage under the hand of Oregon and California trained winemaker Uri Hetz. Vineyards owned by the winery currently yield Cabernet Sauvignon, Merlot, Cabernet Franc, Petite Sirah, Petit Verdot, Grenache, Sauvignon Blanc, Mouvredre and Viognier grapes. Other grapes being planted include Rousanne and Grenache Blanc. Production is currently between 70,000–75,000 bottles and future production is estimated at somewhat over 100,000 bottles annually. To date the winery has released wines in one series, Royal Reserve, that including the proprietary blend known as Eliad.

Royal Reserve

ROYAL RESERVE, CABERNET SAUVIGNON, 2005: Showing a firm, full-bodied but vibrant style, with spicy, mocha-tinged blackcurrant, blackberry and herbal aromas and flavors, all finishing with hints of leather. Best 2008–2011. Tentative Score 89–91.

ROYAL RESERVE, CABERNET SAUVIGNON, 2004: Blended with 15% of Cabernet Franc, dark garnet towards royal purple in color, medium to full-bodied, with layers of blackcurrants and plums matched nicely by minerals, toasty oak and hints of spices. On the long finish generous hints of cocoa and nutmeg. Best 2008–2012. Score 91.

ROYAL RESERVE, CABERNET SAUVIGNON, 2003: Deep, young and tight, but showing excellent focus and concentration. Full-bodied and packed with nicely integrating tannins, the wine shows aromas and flavors of currants, black cherries and anise, along with attractive earthy-herbal overtones and hints of green olives. Drink now–2012. Score 90.

ROYAL RESERVE, CABERNET SAUVIGNON, 2002: Medium to full-bodied, well-balanced, concentrated and long, this blend of Cabernet Sauvignon with 9% Cabernet Franc offers an appealing array of ripe cherry, currant, red plum, jammy strawberry and spicy flavors overlaid by light toasty oak, and a near-sweet finish with a hint of tobacco. Drink now–2008. Score 89.

ROYAL RESERVE, CABERNET SAUVIGNON, 2001: Oak-aged for ten months, this deep garnet toward purple, medium-bodied wine shows smooth tannins, just the right hints of earth and spices and appealing blackberry and blackcurrant fruits leading to a clean and medium-long finish. Drink now. Score 88.

ROYAL RESERVE, CABERNET SAUVIGNON, 2000: Intense and deep with cherry, currant and mocha aromas and flavors, and with good balance between tannins and fruits, this medium to full-bodied 100% Cabernet fills the mouth nicely and with near-elegance. Drink now. Score 88.

ROYAL RESERVE, CABERNET SAUVIGNON, 1999: Medium to full-bodied, with an appealing royal purple color, this Cabernet Sauvignon was blended with 4% Merlot to give it some softness. Reflecting ten months in new French oak barrels, the wine is rich and well balanced, with smooth tannins and with currant, mineral, pepper and smoky oak aromas and flavors. Drink now. Score 89.

ROYAL RESERVE, MERLOT, 2005: A modern wine with soft tannins, forward fruits and generous wood. Plush and delicious, packed with fruits, Mediterranean herbs, mocha and vanilla, those coming together nicely and opening on the long, gently spicy finish to show hints of currants and blueberries. Drink from release–2010. Tentative Score 89–91.

ROYAL RESERVE, MERLOT, 2004: Blended with 5% Cabernet Franc and 6% Syrah. Complex, concentrated and elegant, showing a rich array of currant, blackberry and wild berry fruits, those supported by hints of earthy minerals, sage and anise. Well focused, generous and long. Best 2008–2012. Score 91.

ROYAL RESERVE, MERLOT, 2003: Aged in oak for 12 months, this deep garnet towards royal purple, medium to full-bodied blend of Merlot, Syrah and Cabernet Sauvignon (86%, 13% and 1% respectively) shows fine balance between generous tannins, spicy wood and currants, berry fruits and herbaceousness. On the long finish hints of licorice and green olives. Concentrated and well focused. Drink now–2010. Score 90.

ROYAL RESERVE, MERLOT, 2002: This deep royal-purple oak-aged blend of 85% Merlot and 15% Cabernet Sauvignon shows firm, well-integrated tannins and appealing currant, wild berry and plum aromas and flavors, together with gentle overlays of spicy chocolate and vanilla. Drink now. Score 88.

ROYAL RESERVE, MERLOT, 2001: Medium to full-bodied, this elegant and intense Merlot, blended with 15% of Cabernet Sauvignon, was aged in French oak casks for one year. Dark in color, the wine has deep, still firm tannins, well balanced by raspberry, plum and currant fruits, those on a complex background of dark chocolate and vanilla, and a long, sweet finish. Drink now–2008. Score 91.

ROYAL RESERVE, MERLOT, 2000: Remarkably similar in style to the Merlot-based wines of Bordeaux, this medium to full-bodied, ripe and juicy oak-aged blend of 89% Merlot and 11% Cabernet Sauvignon has plenty of ripe cherry and currant fruits along overlays of vanilla, green olives and toasted oak. Drink up. Score 88.

ROYAL RESERVE, SYRAH, 2005: Bold, dark-hued and rich, thick and plush on first attack, opening to reveal a tempting array of spicy blackberry, boysenberry, pomegranate and citrus peel aromas and flavors, those with light green and meaty notes as the wine lingers comfortably on the palate. Drink from release–2012. Tentative Score 90–92.

ROYAL RESERVE, SYRAH, 2004: On first attack, dense and muscular, but opening nicely in the glass. Ripe, with firm tannins in fine balance with acidity, wood and minerals. On the nose and palate blackberries, red currants, licorice, Oriental spices and mineral aromas and flavors that go on to a long and supple finish. Drink now–2009. Score 90.

ROYAL RESERVE, SYRAH, 2003: Blended with 15% of Grenache this is a classic and elegant Syrah with distinct Mediterranean overtones. Assertive and complex, this spicy, gamy wine offers up appealing smoke and black pepper along with deep raspberry and floral aromas and flavors. Drink now–2009. Score 90.

ROYAL RESERVE, SYRAH, 2002: Big, rich, dense and tannic, and already showing roundness and richness, this wine is a deep garnet to purple color and has generous plum, herbal and earthy aromas and flavors. Somewhat astringent in its youth but integrating very nicely now. Drink now–2008. Score 90.

ROYAL RESERVE, SYRAH, 2001: Dark royal purple in color, this medium to full-bodied blend of 85% Syrah and 15% Cabernet has inherent good balance and structure. Still young but already showing soft tannins and tempting plum and berry fruits with generous hints of earthiness and herbaceousness. In time it will show olive and mushroom aromas as well. Drink now–2008. Score 91.

ROYAL RESERVE, SYRAH, CUVEE NATUREL, 2001: Intense, tannic and concentrated, medium to full-bodied. Deep purple in color, reflecting its 14 months in French oak with spices and a generous dash of vanilla, those complemented nicely by jammy black fruits. Drink now. Score 90.

ROYAL RESERVE, GRENACHE, 2005: Ripe, rich and with generous oak-accented blackberry, black cherry, spicy and black pepper flavors. True to its variety, with an attractive hint of greenness. Drink from release–2010. Tentative Score 89–91.

ROYAL RESERVE, GRENACHE-SYRAH, 2004: A blend of 39% Grenache and 61% Syrah, still waiting for a proprietary name. Deep purple in color, with gripping tannins well balanced by spicy wood, chocolate and an array of black cherry, plum, tar, and spice aromas and flavors, all lingering nicely on the finish. Drink now–2009. Score 89.

ROYAL RESERVE, GRENACHE, 2003: Loyal to its varietal traits, an attractive pale ruby wine, medium-bodied, with soft tannins and tempting blackberry, black cherry and red currant fruits as well as spicy oak. Drink now–2009. Score 89.

ROYAL RESERVE, CABERNET FRANC, 2005: Subtle and seductive, with generous tannins integrating nicely. On the nose and palate fresh currant, dark berry and black cherry fruits matched nicely by bell peppers, cigar box and lead pencil notes. Promising length, depth and elegance. Best 2008–2011. Tentative Score 90–92.

ROYAL RESERVE, CABERNET FRANC, LIMITED EDITION, 2003: Full-bodied, earthy and aromatic with an appealing array of currant, plum and wild berry fruits, those backed up nicely by vanilla and spices from the oak as well as an appealing hint of earthiness on the moderately long finish. Rich and concentrated. Drink now–2010. Score 90. **K**

ROYAL RESERVE, MERLOT-CABERNET, 2000: Dark purple toward black in color, this medium to full-bodied blend of 65% Cabernet and 35% Merlot was aged in French and American oak barrels for 12 months. Well balanced and with tempting black cherry, currant, plum and hazelnut aromas and flavors, this smooth wine has just a hint of coffee on the finish. Drink up. Score 89.

ROYAL RESERVE, ROSÉ, 2005: As it was last year, made entirely from Cabernet Franc grapes. With the color of peaches in their first bloom, medium-bodied and far more complex than one usually anticipates in a rosé. On the nose and palate peaches, strawberries, rosewater and wild berries. Crisply dry but with an irresistible near-honeyed finish. Drink now. Score 88.

ROYAL RESERVE, CABERNET FRANC, ROSÉ, 2004: Somewhere in color between bright cherry red and that of red rose petals and far deeper than a standard rosé, this medium-bodied, soft and round rosé shows appealing aromas and flavors of raspberries, cassis and cranberries, turning almost sweet on the surprisingly long finish. Drink up. Score 87.

ROYAL RESERVE, SAUVIGNON BLANC, 2005: Developed partly in oak and partly in stainless steel, this is a medium-bodied wine, delightfully aromatic, with a tempting array of spices and a peppery character, showing pear, apple, melon and mineral flavors that linger very nicely. Impeccably balanced and long. Drink now–2008. Score 90.

ROYAL RESERVE, SAUVIGNON BLANC, 2004: Light golden straw in color, with aromas and flavors of summer fruits, pears and citrus, those on an appealing grassy-spicy background. Drink up. Score 88.

ROYAL RESERVE, SAUVIGNON BLANC, 2003: Made entirely from Sauvignon Blanc grapes from the northern Golan, fermented in stainless steel and then partly oak aged, a multi-layered wine, showing at first citrus and pineapple, those yielding nicely to pear, floral and herbal aromas and flavors. Generous alcohol (14%) but that balanced by natural acidity. Long, mouthfilling and elegant. Drink now. Score 91.

ROYAL RESERVE, SAUVIGNON BLANC, 2002: Fermented partly in stainless steel vats and partly in oak and then allowed to rest *sur lie* for six months, this medium-bodied, deep golden straw white offers up aromas and flavors of melons and pears on the first attack, those then yielding to tropical fruits, all with generous herbal-tobacco overlays. Crisp, long and elegant. Drink up. Score 89.

Eliad

ELIAD, 2005: Showing deeper, more earthy and with more of a generous hint of tobacco than in earlier releases. With rich currant and plum aromas and flavors set off nicely by smoky wood and fine-grained tannins, those in fine balance and blossoming on a long finish to reveal red cherries and a hint of licorice. Best 2008–2012. Tentative Score 90–92.

ELIAD, 2004: A blend this year of Cabernet Sauvignon, Merlot, Cabernet Franc and Petit Verdot (70%, 21%, 3% and 6% respectively), this may be the most intense wine released to date by the winery. Dark garnet in color, ripe and complex, showing deep plum, berry, floral, coffee and earthy aromas and flavors all coming together beautifully in a long and graceful finish. Best 2008–2012. Score 92.

ELIAD, 2003: Oak aged, this deep garnet blend of 66% Cabernet Sauvignon, 20% Merlot and 14% Cabernet Franc is already showing rich, intense and complex. Concentrated plum, berry, currant and spicy oak aromas and flavors matched nicely by spices and a hint of tobacco. Best 2008–2012. Score 92.

ELIAD, 2002: Still young and tight, this blend of 91% Cabernet Sauvignon and 9% Merlot has crisp tannins and generous currant, black cherry and cedar as well as leathery-earthy aromas and flavors, with a long finish in which the tannins and wood meld beautifully. Drink now–2009. Score 90.

ELIAD, 2001: A blend of Cabernet Sauvignon, Merlot and Syrah (85%, 10% and 5% respectively), each aged separately, some in French and some in American oak. This dark, almost inky royal purple medium-bodied wine shows soft tannins that are nicely balanced by jammy plum and blackberry fruits, and appealing layers of chocolate and smoky-toasty aromas and flavors. Drink now. Score 90.

Chillag ★★★★

After studying oenology in Piacenza, Italy, and working at the Antinori wineries in Tuscany, Orna Chillag released her first wines in Israel in 1998. Now located in a new facility in the industrial area of the town of Yahud, on the central plain, the winery relies on Merlot and Cabernet Sauvignon grapes from the Upper Galilee and recently planted its own Syrah, Petit Verdot and Petit Sirah. Production has grown from 4,000 bottles in 2002 to 12,000 each in 2003 and 2004 and 15,000 in 2005. Plans are to grow to 20,000 bottles annually.

In addition to regular releases in two series, Primo Riserva and Giovani, Chillag also produces a line of kosher wines under the label Orna at the Carmel winery in Rishon Letzion. Made from grapes grown in the Zar'it vineyards in the Upper Galilee, 15,000 bottles of Chillag's kosher Cabernet Sauvignon were released for sale in the United States from the 2003 and 2004 vintages.

Primo Riserva

PRIMO RISERVA, CABERNET SAUVIGNON, 2005: Delicious. Full-bodied, deeply tannic and even now with generous but judicious wood in fine balance with tempting blackberry, red currant and oriental spices, all leading to a rich, long and blueberry-laden finish. Best 2008–2012. Tentative Score 89–91

PRIMO RISERVA, CABERNET SAUVIGNON, 2004: Deep garnet towards purple in color, with firm tannins well balanced with smoky wood and fruits. Rich blackberry,

cherry and licorice flavors with overlays of spicy oak and licorice. Long and elegant. Best 2008–2012. Tentative Score 90–92.

PRIMO RISERVA, CABERNET SAUVIGNON, 2003: Aged in French oak for 18 months, with a small amount of Merlot added, this full-bodied red shows appealing aromas and flavors of blackcurrant and ripe berry fruits, those matched nicely by spicy oak and, on the long finish, a hint of freshly turned earth. Drink now–2009. Score 90.

PRIMO RISERVA, CABERNET SAUVIGNON, CASTELLANA, 2002: Dark royal purple in color, this full-bodied wine was made by blending 70% Cabernet Sauvignon and 30% Merlot together in the same oak barrels. Aromas and flavors of spicy currants, anise and cedary oak come together in a complex, mouth-filling, supple wine. Drink now. Score 89.

PRIMO RISERVA, CABERNET SAUVIGNON, 2001: Full-bodied, with real weight and grip and with plenty of tannins, this concentrated blend of 90% Cabernet Sauvignon and 10% Merlot shows a deep purple color. Now opening to reveal fine balance between tannins, wood and fruit, yielding currants, plums and blackberries with meaty and toasty accents. Drink now–2008. Score 89.

PRIMO RISERVA, MERLOT, 2004: Impressive aromas and flavors of blackcurrants, minerals and toasty oak, with somewhat firm tannins that seem not to want to integrate and a somewhat medicinal aroma that lingers. Drink now. Score 86.

PRIMO RISERVA, MERLOT, 2002: Medium to full-bodied, with velvety tannins, this elegant and harmonious red shows tempting fresh blackcurrant, berry and plum flavors, those with hints of cedary, spicy notes. Look for a long, vanilla and berry rich aftertaste. Drink now. Score 90.

Giovane

GIOVANE, CABERNET SAUVIGNON, 2005: Relying on Montalcino yeasts to give the wine a distinct Italian flair, this deep, dark and round wine already shows soft tannins and temptingly forward fruits, those including cherries, wild berries and cassis all on a warmly spicy background. Drink from release–2009. Tentative Score 88–90.

GIOVANE, CABERNET SAUVIGNON, 2004: Deep garnet towards royal-purple, medium-bodied, with firm but well integrating tannins and tempting black fruits, spices and a long lightly herbal finish. Generous and elegant. Drink now–2009. Score 89.

GIOVANE, MERLOT, 2005: As deep in its rich garnet-red color as it is in tannins and reflecting the oak casks in which it is developing with a gentle hand, this medium to full-bodied wine shows berry, black cherry and cassis fruits, those matched with gentle hints of bitter herbs and, on the long finish, a hint of peppermint. Drink from release–2009. Tentative Score 88–90.

GIOVANE, MERLOT, 2004: Dark royal purple in color, full-bodied and with firm but caressing near-sweet tannins opening to reveal lush blackberry, currant, plum, vanilla and mocha aromas and flavors, those leading to a fruit-loaded long herbal finish. Soft, round, and long. Drink now–2008. Score 89.

GIOVANE, MERLOT, 2003: Dark royal purple with orange and violet reflections, needing some time for the still firm tannins to integrate but already showing an elegant array of currants, cherries and spices along with a gentle modicum of oak. On the finish, hints of coffee and herbs. Drink now–2009. Score 90.

Orna

CHILLAG, CABERNET SAUVIGNON, ORNA, 2004: Dark royal purple in color, full-bodied, with near-sweet tannins integrating nicely. Look for aromas and flavors of blackcurrants, plums and berries, those with a nice spicy overlay. Drink now–2008. Score 88. **K**

CHILLAG, CABERNET SAUVIGNON, ORNA, 2003: Aged in French oak for 14 months, this ripe and chewy wine shows soft tannins and plum and blackcurrant fruits. Drink now. Score 89. **K**

Clos de Gat ★★★★★

Located on Kibbutz Har'el in the Jerusalem Mountains, this joint project of the *kibbutz* and Australian-trained winemaker Eyal Rotem, released its first wines from the 2001 vintage. The name, "Clos de Gat" is a play on words—the French *clos* is an enclosed vineyard surrounded by stone walls or wind-breaks, while the Hebrew *gat* is an antique wine press. With the exception of the Chardonnay grapes in the 2002 wine, all the grapes have come from the winery's own vineyards, which now include Cabernet, Merlot, Petit Verdot, Syrah and most recently the winery's own Chardonnay. Production in 2002 was 22,000 bottles, in 2004 approximately 60,000 bottles and in 2005, due to reduced yields, about 45,000 bottles. The winery has two series, the top label, Clos de Gat and the second label, Har'el, and, starting with the 2003 vintage, all the wines have been made with wild-yeasts.

Clos de Gat

CLOS DE GAT, 2004: A blend containing 65% Cabernet Sauvignon flushed out with Petit Verdot and Merlot. Medium to full bodied, with soft tannins that promise to integrate nicely, temptingly spicy oak and on the nose and palate, blackcurrants, plums, oriental spices and light hints of freshly turned earth and licorice. Best from 2008. Tentative Score 91–93.

CLOS DE GAT, 2003: Full-bodied, with firm tannins integrating nicely, this oak-aged blend of Cabernet Sauvignon, Merlot and Petit Verdot (66%, 30% and 4% respectively) reveals generous blackcurrant, black cherry and berry fruits on a spicy and vanilla tinted background. Good balance and with structure that bodes well for an elegant future. Drink now–2012. Score 92.

CLOS DE GAT, 2002: Full-bodied, with generous but soft tannins, this dark red towards black in color, medium to full-bodied blend of 70% Cabernet Sauvignon and 30% Merlot reflects its 18 months in oak with spicy but not exaggerated wood. On the nose and palate ripe currants and plums matched nicely by hints of coffee, sweet-cedar, vanilla and Mediterranean herbs. Drink now–2009. Score 90.

CLOS DE GAT, 2001: A deep ruby-garnet full-bodied unfiltered blend of 70% Cabernet Sauvignon and 30% Merlot, with generous soft tannins that integrate beautifully, this is a wine that can honestly be said to reflect its *terroir*. Overlaying traditional Cabernet blackcurrants are generous hints of green olives, basil, tarragon and other Mediterranean herbs. The wine shows good balance and structure, with chocolate and leather coming in on the long finish. Drink now–2009. Score 90.

CLOS DE GAT, CHARDONNAY, 2004: Oak-aged for 12 months, full-bodied, ripe, floral and creamy but with pleasing acidity and spiciness, this intense and opulent wine shows appealing layers of pear, green apple and figs, all with a hint of ginger that tantalizes. Long and generous. Drink now–2008. Score 92.

CLOS DE GAT, CHARDONNAY, 2003: Delicious medium to full-bodied Chardonnay with ripe pineapple, citrus, apple and spicy notes. Enough mineral crispness here to make one think of fine Chablis, with a good touch of toasty oak but with balancing acidity that carries the wine very well indeed. Drink now–2009. Score 91.

CLOS DE GAT, CHARDONNAY, 2002: Full-bodied with ripe pear and pineapple aromas and flavors on the first attack, these yielding beautifully to citrus flowers, apple, and ripe apricots, all on a spicy background. Fermented and aged *sur lie* in French oak barrels, the wine has very good balance between lively acidity, intentionally underplayed oak and minerals, and a creamy, mouth-filling sensation. Drink now. Score 91.

CLOS DE GAT, ROSÉ, 2005: This medium-bodied, barely-sweet deep pink blend of one-third Syrah and two-thirds Cabernet Sauvignon offers up blackcurrant and blackberry fruits, those with light earthy and spicy hints and far more complexity than one usually expects in a rosé. Drink now. Score 89.

Har'el

HAR'EL, CABERNET SAUVIGNON, 2004: Blended with small amounts of Merlot and Petit Verdot, aged in oak for about 12 months, and showing good balance between near-sweet soft tannins, spicy wood and fruits. Look for black cherries and plums, those yielding to currants and hints of chocolate and tobacco. Drink now–2012. Score 89.

HAR'EL, CABERNET SAUVIGNON, 2003: Medium to full-bodied, an oak-aged blend of 93% Cabernet Sauvignon, 4% Merlot and 3% Petit Verdot, with soft tannins that highlight generous raspberry, ripe cherry and blackcurrant fruits, those matched nicely by moderate oak and a hint of anise. Drink now–2008. Score 90.

HAR'EL, MERLOT, 2004: Deep and dark, with near-sweet oak-accented tannins and generous currant, plum and berry aromas and flavors, those coming to a well-focused, lightly smoky and mouthfilling finish. Drink now–2010. Score 90.

HAR'EL, MERLOT, 2003: A dense, muscular wine that needs time to settle down but promising to be deep, dark and absolutely beautiful. Complex oak-accented blackberry, currant and black cherry aromas and flavors on a background of chewy tannins, sweet cedar, and hints of pepper and vanilla, all of which linger beautifully. Best 2008–2012. Score 92.

HAR'EL, SYRAH, 2004: Dark garnet red in color, this medium to full-bodied blend of 85% Syrah and 15% Cabernet Sauvignon shows soft, well integrating tannins and tempting black plum and cassis aromas and flavors set off nicely by hints of spices and fresh herbs. Long and elegant. Drink now–2009. Score 90.

HAR'EL, SYRAH, 2003: Deep ruby colored, this blend of 85% Syrah and 15% Cabernet Sauvignon shows generous peppery overtones. Medium to full-bodied, with firm but nicely integrating tannins and complex plum, red berry and earthy aromas and flavors, all with a hint of leather on the finish. Drink now–2009. Score 91.

Dalton ★★★★

Founded by Mat Haruni in 1993, this fully modern winery located in the industrial park of Dalton in the Upper Galilee has vineyards in Kerem Ben Zimra and several high altitude sites along the Lebanese border. Australian and Californian trained winemaker Na'ama Mualem is currently producing wines in three series, Reserve, Dalton and Canaan, the first of age-worthy varietal wines, the second, of similar varieties, is intended for earlier drinking, and the third, a popularly priced series. Grapes include Cabernet Sauvignon, Merlot, Shiraz, Barbera, Zinfandel, Chardonnay and Sauvignon Blanc. First production was 50,000 bottles, current production is about 800,000 and the target for 2007 is one million bottles. Dalton has earned an especially good name for quality wines providing excellent value for money.

Single Vineyard

SINGLE VINEYARD, CABERNET SAUVIGNON, MERON, 2004: Perhaps the best wine to date from Dalton. Deep youthful cherry towards garnet, medium to full-bodied, this well balanced wine was aged in French oak for eight months and then  bottled without filtration. Generous soft tannins and ample wood, those already integrating nicely to reveal a very appealing array of red currant, raspberry and citrus peel on a peppery, lightly herbal, minty background. Round, long and mouthfilling. Drink now–2010. Score 92. **K**

Reserve

RESERVE, CABERNET SAUVIGNON, 2005: In its infancy and tasted from components but already showing medium to full-body, firm tannins and hints of spicy-smoky wood, those balanced nicely by currant, plum and berry fruits. Best from 2008. Tentative Score 88–90. K

RESERVE, CABERNET SAUVIGNON, 2004: Medium to full-bodied, with soft tannins and a layer of spicy-toasty wood, coming together in fine balance to reveal aromas and flavors of blackberries, currants and spices and, on the long finish, an appealing hint of mint. Drink from release–2009. Tentative Score 88–90. K

RESERVE, CABERNET SAUVIGNON, 2003: Darker garnet than in its youth, medium to full-bodied, still firmly tannic and with generous oak well balanced by fruits and natural acidity. On the nose and palate blackcurrant, black cherry and herbal-spicy aromas and flavors. Drink now–2009. Score 89. K

RESERVE, CABERNET SAUVIGNON, 2002: As during its youth, medium-bodied, ripe and harmonious. Now showing sweet cedar and herbaceousness that open to reveal currant, ripe plum and black cherry fruits. Drink now–2008. Score 87. K

RESERVE, CABERNET SAUVIGNON, 2001: Medium-bodied, with barely any tannins and marked too strongly by the oak in which it aged, the black fruits here fail to make themselves felt adequately. Drink up. Score 84. K

RESERVE, CABERNET SAUVIGNON, 1999: After two years in oak, this deep royal purple, medium to full-bodied wine opens in the glass to reveal aromas and flavors of ripe wild berry, black cherry and currant fruits along with generous hints of mint and vanilla. Mature now but still well focused and concentrated. Drink now. Score 89. K

RESERVE, CABERNET SAUVIGNON, 1998: This medium to full-bodied wine opens nicely in the glass to reveal ripe black cherry, currant, vanilla and light spicy overtones. Well focused and with smooth tannins and good balance. Drink up. Score 86. K

RESERVE, CABERNET SAUVIGNON, 1997: Aged for over 12 months partly in American and partly in French oak barrels, this well-made medium to full-bodied wine has plenty of plum, currant and cherry flavors, along with vanilla and oak notes and just the right hint of herbs and spices that linger on the palate. Past its peak. Drink up. Score 86. K

RESERVE, MERLOT, 2004: Destined to spend about 14 months in oak, showing appealing spicy and vanilla notes and moderately firm tannins, those balanced well with fruits and natural acidity. On the nose and palate plum, blueberry and herbal aromas and flavors and, on the long finish, hints of cigar tobacco. Drink now–2009. Score 88. K

RESERVE, MERLOT, 2003: Aged in oak for 14 months, dark garnet in color, with currant, plum, cherry and herbal aromas and flavors all with a light overlay of vanilla. Showing complexity and finesse. Drink now. Score 89. K

RESERVE, MERLOT, 2002: Smooth and elegant, with a core of ripe plum and black cherry fruits, those on a background of toasty oak, spices and very appealing hints of sage and tea. As the wine continues to develop, look for a leathery note on the long finish. Drink now. Score 89. K

RESERVE, MERLOT, 2001: Not fully living up to its earlier promise, the toasty oak seems to overshadow the plum, berry and currant fruits and a rather strong white chocolate overlay now hiding the anise and cedar wood that were once there. Drink up. Score 85. K

RESERVE, MERLOT, 2000: Intense and lively, with generous plum, wild berry and light hints of oak and vanilla, this rich and complex wine borders comfortably on elegance. The wine aged in small oak casks for a year and has a nice lingering finish. Drink up. Score 90. K

RESERVE, SHIRAZ, 2003: Medium to full-bodied and solidly tannic, reflecting its 10 months in new American oak with generous hints of smoke and vanilla, those on tempting black fruits, mint and earthiness. Needs time to open and show its elegance. Drink now–2009. Score 89. K

RESERVE, CHARDONNAY, 2005: Barrel fermented, developed on its lees, showing generous oak at this stage but that in fine balance with fruit and acidity. Medium to full-bodied, with ripe summer and tropical fruits. Drink now–2008. Score 88. K

RESERVE, CHARDONNAY, 2003: After 8 months *sur lie* in new French oak *barriques*, this medium-bodied white shows appealing earthy, buttery and vanilla aromas backed up nicely by flavors of melons and pears.

Drink now. Score 88. ĸReserve, Chardonnay, 2002: Deep, complex and harmonious, this tempting wine shows ripe, rich pear, spice, apple and hazelnut aromas and flavors, with an elegant finish yielding notes of figs, butterscotch and spices. Drink up. Score 88. ĸ

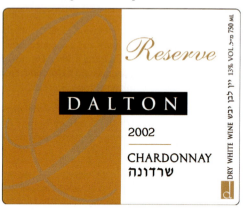

RESERVE, CHARDONNAY, 2001: Fully mature but still lively and elegant, showing an abundance of citrus, ripe pear, melon and spicy flavors. Light toasty oak and hints of minerals add charm to the long finish. Drink up. Score 87. ĸ

RESERVE, SAUVIGNON BLANC, 2005: Medium-bodied, unoaked, and with aromas and flavors of grapefruit peel, green apples and hints of grassiness, coming together in a vigorous, fresh and lively but just complex enough wine. Drink now. Score 89. ĸ

RESERVE, SAUVIGNON BLANC, 2004: Unoaked, fresh, crisp and aromatic, with light herbal hints. On first sip dominated by grapefruit flavors but those yielding to aromas and flavors of apples, melons, spices and minerals. Drink now. Score 87. ĸ

RESERVE, SAUVIGNON BLANC, 2003: The color of golden straw, with appealing tropical fruits, citrus and melon flavors, those on a lightly floral-herbaceous background; a very nice wine indeed. Drink up. Score 86. ĸ

RESERVE, SAUVIGNON BLANC, 2002: Light gold in color, this unoaked white has hints of tropical fruits and a low-keyed grassiness felt on the long finish. Past its peak. Drink up. Score 85. ĸ

RESERVE, SAUVIGNON BLANC, 2001: One of the best Sauvignon Blanc varietals made in Israel. Pale gold in color, this unoaked white is smooth and elegant, with fresh herbal aromas and flavors overlaying citrus and peach notes. Look for light hints of grass as the wine lingers on the palate. Somewhat past its peak. Drink up. Score 91. K

Dalton

DALTON, CABERNET SAUVIGNON, 2004: Dark garnet, medium-bodied, with moderately firm tannins, spicy oak and appealing currant and plum fruits. Not complex but pleasant. Drink now. Score 85. K

DALTON, CABERNET SAUVIGNON, 2003: Medium-bodied, with soft, well-integrated tannins and a solid core of currant, wild berry and minty flavors. An appealing wine. Drink now. Score 87. K

DALTON, CABERNET SAUVIGNON, SAFSUFA, 2003: A *mevushal* wine targeted entirely towards the observant Jewish population outside of Israel. Medium-bodied, with somewhat coarse tannins and with ripe, almost cooked berry and plum flavors, those with a hint of unwanted bitterness. Drink up. Score 79. K

DALTON, CABERNET SAUVIGNON, 2002: Well focused and with good balance between moderate tannins and plum, cherry and currant flavors, this appealing wine has a medium-long finish with hints of mocha and cedar wood. Drink now. Score 87. K

DALTON, CABERNET SAUVIGNON, 2001: Medium-bodied and with smooth tannins, this deep ruby toward garnet red offers good currant and plum fruits. Drink up. Score 86. K

DALTON, CABERNET SAUVIGNON, 2000: Young, fresh and supple, this medium-bodied, not overly complex white shows well-focused earthy, currant, black cherry and cedar flavors. Drink up. Score 85. K

DALTON, MERLOT, 2004: Medium-bodied, with soft tannins and a hint of toasty oak that highlights black cherry, raspberry and plum fruits. Lingers nicely with toasty and floral notes. Drink now. Score 87. K

DALTON, MERLOT, 2003: Moderate levels of complexity, soft tannins, medium-body and a band of berry and black cherry fruits and a tempting hint of spices. Good backbone here. Drink now. Score 87. K

DALTON, MERLOT, 2002: Distinctly New World in style, this medium to full-bodied fruit-driven wine shows generous plum, currant and blackberry flavors on a firm tannic background. A nice hint of bitterness on the finish. Drink up. Score 88. K

DALTON, MERLOT, 2001: Showing soft tannins, hints of sage and tea and a medium-long finish, the wine needs time to open in the glass to reveal its currant and berry flavors. Somewhat past its peak. Drink up. Score 85. K

DALTON, MERLOT, 2000: Aged in French oak barrels for 14 months and blended with 5% Cabernet Sauvignon, this tempting medium-bodied wine offers smooth tannins and generous aromas and flavors of wild berries and plums with appealing toasty, vanilla overtones. Somewhat past its peak. Drink up. Score 87. K

DALTON, SHIRAZ, 2003: Deep, almost impenetrable purple in color, medium to full-bodied, with generous but yielding tannins, this lightly oak-aged wine shows a generous array of earthiness, tobacco and milk chocolate on a background of wild berries and plums. Drink now. Score 88. K

DALTON, SHIRAZ, SAFSUFA, 2003: Medium to full-bodied, with firm tannins integrating nicely and with generous smoky oak, those well balanced with plum, blackberry, mint and earthy aromas and flavors leading to a long vanilla and currant finish. *Mevushal* and made only for export. Drink now–2008. Score 88. K

DALTON, BARBERA, 2004: A very nice first Barbera release. Developed in oak casks for 9 months, dark cherry red in color, medium-bodied, soft and round, with good balancing acidity and tempting aromas and flavors of ripe berries, cherries and minerals, ending on a lightly spicy finish. Drink now. Score 87. K

DALTON, CHARDONNAY, 2005: As always, unoaked, medium-bodied and lovely, with crisp dryness highlighting citrus, apple and tropical fruits. Drink now. Score 86. K

DALTON, CHARDONNAY, 2004: Unoaked, medium-bodied, with tempting tropical fruits, citrus and minerals, a crisply dry, lightly floral and delicious wine meant for early consumption. Drink up. Score 86. K

DALTON, SAUVIGNON BLANC FUMÉ, 2004: Light-straw colored, medium-bodied, with hints of toasted white bread from having spent about 3 months in oak. Appealing aromas and flavors of grapefruit, melon and tropical fruits. Lively and refreshing. Drink now. Score 86. K

DALTON, SAUVIGNON BLANC FUMÉ, 2003: Light in color but packed with fresh tropical fruit and citrus flavors, those with a lightly smoky overlay and hints of roasted nuts. Meant for youthful drinking. Drink up. Score 86. K

DALTON, SAUVIGNON BLANC FUMÉ, 2002: Toasty-smoky aromas and flavors along with appealing peach and apricot fruits on a clean, just lively enough background. Somewhat past its peak. Drink up. Score 84. K

DALTON, ROSÉ, 2005: Semi-dry, light to medium-bodied, with skimpy berry and strawberry aromas and flavors. A bit flat on the palate. Drink up. Score 83. K

DALTON, MOSCATO, 2005: Light in body, *frizzante*, with ripe nectarine and apricot fruits, this soft and generously sweet but lively wine hints of litchis and pears. Light and fun. Drink now. Score 85. K

Canaan

CANAAN, RED, 2005: Medium-bodied, softly tannic, developed in stainless steel with the addition of oak chips that add a hint of spicy wood matched nicely by black cherry and cassis fruits. Not complex but fresh and generous. Drink now. Score 86. K

CANAAN, RED, 2004: A not complex but pleasant little blend of Cabernet Sauvignon and Merlot. Soft, round and with appealing black fruits. Drink up. Score 85. K

CANAAN, RED, 2003: A basic Cabernet-Merlot blend, light to medium-bodied, with soft tannins and generous fruits. Somewhat past its peak. Drink up. Score 85. K

CANAAN, SAUVIGNON BLANC-CHARDONNAY-WHITE RIESLING, 2002: Light straw in color, this semi-dry, light to medium-bodied white offers simple and low-level citrus, pineapple and apple aromas and flavors. Drink up. Score 83. K

CANAAN, SAUVIGNON BLANC-CHARDONNAY-WHITE RIESLING, 2001: Light and refreshing, with clean aromas and flavors of citrus, pears, green apples and an appealing hint of spiciness on the finish. Past its peak. Drink up. Score 82. K

CANAAN, WHITE, 2004: Pale straw in color, light to medium-bodied, with citrus and melon fruits on a lightly spicy background. Drink now. Score 84. K

Dico's *

Founded by David Ben-Arieh in 2001 on Moshav Ginaton on the central plains, this winery relies on Cabernet Sauvignon grapes from Kerem Ben Zimra and Merlot from the Gedera area. Current production is about 2,500 bottles annually.

DICO'S, CABERNET-MERLOT, 2004: Dark but not clear garnet in color, with firm tannins and overly generous spicy wood that hides the berry, cherry and currant flavors that fail to make themselves adequately felt. Drink up. Score 78.

DICO'S, CABERNET-MERLOT, 2003: A country-style wine, deep cherry red towards purple, medium-bodied, with chunky tannins, smoky wood and aromas and flavors of ripe berries and plums. Drink up. Score 79.

DICO'S, CABERNET-MERLOT, 2002: A medium-bodied blend of 85% Cabernet Sauvignon and 15% Merlot, this soft, simple, country-style wine has a ripe black cherry flavor, somewhat coarse tannins and a vague hint of sweet cedar wood. Drink up. Score 78.

DICO'S, CABERNET-MERLOT, 2001: Medium-bodied, with a modest array of cedar and cherry flavors that fade on the too-short finish. Drink up. Score 79.

Efrat ✶✶✶

Founded in 1870 by the Teperberg family in the Jewish quarter of the old city of Jerusalem, and then relocating outside of the walls, the winery moved in 1964 to Motza, on the outskirts of the city. For many years the winery produced primarily sacramental wines for the ultra-Orthodox community, but in the 1990s they also started producing table wines. More recently, under the supervision of California-trained winemaker Shiki Rauchberger, the winery has been trying to appeal to a more sophisticated audience and with the recent release of their Teperberg Reserve series may be succeeding.

The winery currently releases wines in several series—Teperberg Reserve, Teperberg Selection, Terra, Israeli, and Collage. Annual production is currently about 3.7 million bottles and grapes are drawn from the Judean Mountains, the Central Plain and other regions, including several new and well tended vineyards. Construction of a new modern winery to replace the largely outmoded existing facilities is now underway, and anticipated production within five years is scheduled to attain 7,000,000 bottles. With the exception of the wines in the Teperberg series, all of the wines are *mevushal*.

Teperberg Reserve

TEPERBERG RESERVE, CABERNET SAUVIGNON, 2005: Dark ruby in color, with generous tannins balanced by smoky oak and forward fruits. Medium to full-bodied, with aromas and flavors of spicy cherry, plum and mocha, all lingering nicely. Best 2008–2010. Tentative Score 88–90. **K**

TEPERBERG RESERVE, CABERNET SAUVIGNON, 2004: Dark royal purple, full-bodied, with soft tannins set off by sweet cedar, black currants, red berries, sage and espresso coffee aromas and flavors. On the finish, hints of lead-pencil and asphalt, all coming together in burly but subtle ways. Drink from release–2009. Tentative Score 87–89. **K**

TEPERBERG RESERVE, CABERNET SAUVIGNON, 2003: Dark garnet in color, with its once firm tannins now integrating nicely to show tempting berry, black cherry and currant fruits, those matched by hints of spices, leather and earthiness and, on the generous finish, an appealing overlay of chocolate. Drink now–2009. Score 88. **K**

TEPERBERG RESERVE, CABERNET SAUVIGNON, 2002: Now showing dark garnet in color, full-bodied, with soft, well-integrated tannins and appealing aromas and flavors of currants, black cherries and plums. Well balanced and long. Drink now. Score 87. **K**

TEPERBERG RESERVE, MERLOT, 2005: Dark garnet towards purple in color, medium-bodied, with soft tannins, rich earthiness and red fruits on the nose, those opening to show generous tangy blackcurrants, minerals and cocoa powder, all lingering nicely. Drink from release–2008. Tentative Score 87–89. **K**

TEPERBERG RESERVE, MERLOT, 2004: Medium-dark ruby, medium-bodied, with soft, near-sweet tannins and appealing blackcurrant, cassis and purple plums complemented nicely by hints of chocolate and Mediterranean herbs. Drink from relese-2008. Tentative Score 87–89. **K**

TEPERBERG RESERVE, CHARDONNAY, 2005: Bright, light and fragrant, with grapefruit, mango, litchi and pear aromas and flavors, those reflecting *sur lie* development with nice hints of cedar and musky spices. Drink now–2008. Score 87. **K**

TEPERBERG RESERVE, CHARDONNAY, 2004: Fermented and developed *sur lie* for 6 months in new French oak *barriques*, this deep golden, medium-bodied wine shows an appealing array of citrus, peach and pear fruits. Drink now. Score 87. **K**

TEPERBERG RESERVE, CHARDONNAY, 2003: Fermented and developed *sur lie* in French oak *barriques* for six months, this medium to full-bodied white shows appealing citrus, pear and melon fruits, those on a round and creamy background. Fully mature. Drink up. Score 87. K

TEPERBERG RESERVE, CHENIN BLANC, 2005: Golden straw in color, with a deep herbal, earthy and citrus peel nose opening to reveal a light to medium-bodied lively white with generous orange marmalade, nectarine and cardamom flavors. Drink now. Score 88. K

TEPERBERG RESERVE, CHENIN BLANC, 2004: A bit of bottle stink when first opened but that blows off nicely. Golden straw in color, medium-bodied, reflecting oak treatment with a light creamy overlay on aromas and flavors of peaches, pears, melons and spring flowers, those complemented by a hint of citrus peel on the finish. Drink now. Score 87. K

TEPERBERG RESERVE, CHENIN BLANC, 2003: Golden-straw colored, medium to full-bodied, with good balance between tropical fruits and citrus, crisp acidity and light creamy and nutty overtones from the oak in which the wine was aged. Drink up. Score 87. K

Teperberg Selection

TEPERBERG SELECTION, MERITAGE, 2005: A medium to full-bodied lightly oaked blend of 70% Cabernet Sauvignon, 25% Merlot and 5% Cabernet Franc. Chunky tannins tend to hold back cedar, tobacco, currant and sage aromas and flavors. Perhaps better with time. Drink now–2010. Score 86. K

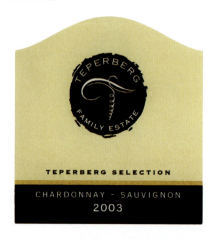

TEPERBERG SELECTION, MERITAGE, 2004: Lightly oaked, this dark garnet medium to full-bodied blend of Cabernet Sauvignon, Merlot and Cabernet Franc offers up spicy oak and blackcurrant, blackberry and orange-peel notes. Round and generous. Drink now–2008. Score 87. **K**

TEPERBERG SELECTION, MERITAGE, 2003: A full-bodied, softly-tannic Bordeaux blend of 50% Cabernet Sauvignon, 40% Merlot and 10% Cabernet Franc. Deep ruby towards garnet in color, with spicy oak and appealing plum, currant and berry fruits. Round and well-balanced. Drink now. Score 87. **K**

TEPERBERG SELECTION, MERITAGE, 2002: Deeply tannic, acidic and wood-laded on opening, but given time in the glass the wine opens to show appealing blackberries, plums and fresh forest floor aromas and flavors. Drink up. Score 85. **K**

Terra

TERRA, CABERNET SAUVIGNON, 2004: Medium-bodied, with moderate wood influences, this soft, round and generous wine shows plum, red currant and spices on the nose and palate as well as a touch of herbaceousness on the finish. Drink now. Score 86. **K**

TERRA, CABERNET SAUVIGNON-MERLOT, 2005: Dark cherry towards garnet red in color, with soft tannins, just the barest hint of wood, and appealing plum, currant and blueberry aromas and flavors. Not complex but easy to drink. Drink now. Score 85. **K**

TERRA, CHARDONNAY, 2005: Developed *sur lie* in French barrels for three months, this light-straw colored, medium-bodied and lively white shows straightforward but appealing aromas and flavors of citrus and summer fruits. Drink now. Score 85. **K**

Collage

COLLAGE, DRY RED, 2005: A blend of 50% Cabernet Sauvignon and 25% each of Shiraz and Petite Sirah. Dark ruby in color, medium-

bodied, with soft almost unfelt tannins, and simple but clean aromas and flavors of black fruits. An acceptable entry-level wine. Drink now. Score 83. K

COLLAGE, CABERNET SAUVIGNON-PETITE SIRAH, 2005: Light and lively, ruby towards garnet in color, earthy on first attack but this followed by a lightly spicy berry, black cherry personality. Drink now. Score 83. K

COLLAGE, CHARDONNAY-SEMILLON, 2005: Clean and freshly acidic, with pineapple, tropical and floral aromas and flavors. An entry-level white. Drink now. Score 83. K

Israeli Series

ISRAELI, CABERNET SAUVIGNON, 2005: Medium-bodied, with soft tannins and a light hint of spicy wood. Look for aromas and flavors of blueberry, cherries and sweet red peppers. Lacking complexity but easy to drink. Drink now. Score 84. K

ISRAELI, CABERNET SAUVIGNON, 2004: Dark royal purple in color, medium-bodied, with soft tannins and berries and black cherry fruits. Drink up. Score 85. K

ISRAELI, MERLOT, 2005: Medium-bodied, with gentle tannins and showing forward plum, raisin and toasty aromas and flavors. An internationalized but pleasant enough little red. Drink now. Score 83. K

ISRAELI, MERLOT, 2004: Dark cherry red, medium-bodied with dusty tannins, perhaps too generous acidity and hints of spices. A bit skimpy on its currant and berry fruits. Drink up. Score 83. K

ISRAELI, SHIRAZ, 2005: Soft and round, light and lively, with raspberry, plum and dusty spicy aromas and flavors that linger nicely. Drink now. Score 85. K

ISRAELI, SHIRAZ, 2004: Bright garnet in color, medium-bodied, with country-style chunky tannins but those opening nicely in the glass to reveal pleasant enough plum and wild berry fruits. Drink now. Score 84. K

ISRAELI, CABERNET SAUVIGNON-MERLOT, 2004: Fresh and lively, with soft tannins and an appealing berry-cherry personality. Hints of spices and Mediterranean herbs add complexity. Drink up. Score 85. K

ISRAELI, ZINFANDEL, BLUSH, 2004: Light, fresh and fruity, off-dry and packed with berry, cherry and strawberry flavors. A pleasant picnic wine. Drink up. Score 83. K

ISRAELI, CHARDONNAY, 2005: Light gold in color, medium-bodied, with tangy citrus, apple and pear fruits and light toasty oak and buttery notes on the finish. Drink now. Score 86. K

ISRAELI, CHARDONNAY, 2004: Light-golden straw in color, medium-bodied, with appealing citrus and tropical fruits backed up nicely by good natural acidity and hints of spiciness. Drink up. Score 85. K

ISRAELI, EMERALD RIESLING, 2005: Half-dry, light to medium-bodied, very floral, a fruit-cocktail set of flavors and with marked but not overpowering sweetness. Drink up. Score 79. K

Ella Valley ★★★★

Located on Kibbutz Netiv Halamed Hey in the Jerusalem Mountains, the winery has vineyards that might well serve as a model of efficiency and beauty anywhere in the world. Cultivation started in 1997 in the Ella and Adulam Valleys in the Judean Hills, and now includes Cabernet Sauvignon, Cabernet Franc, Merlot, Shiraz, Pinot Noir, Petite Sirah, Chardonnay, Sauvignon Blanc, Semillon and Muscat grapes. Under the supervision of French-trained winemaker Doron Rav Hon, the winery released its first wines, 90,000 bottles, from the 2002 harvest, and current production is about 200,000 bottles annually. Projected production for 2010 is 300,000 bottles. At this stage wines are being released in three series: Vineyard's Choice, Ella Valley Vineyards and Ever Red.

Vineyard's Choice

VINEYARD'S CHOICE, CABERNET SAUVIGNON, 2005: Full-bodied, moderately firm tannins and fine balance. On first attack near-sweet berries and spices, those opening to reveal lush currant and blackberry aromas and flavors. Best 2008–2013. Tentative Score 90–92. K

VINEYARD'S CHOICE, CABERNET SAUVIGNON, 2003: Aged in oak for 17 months, blended with 3% of Cabernet Franc, a deep and brooding wine. Deep royal purple in color, full-bodied, with ripe, rich fruits showing harmony and finesse. Layers of currants, juicy cherries and tempting oak shadings. Drink now–2011. Score 91. K

VINEYARD'S CHOICE, MERLOT, 2005: Deep, dark and with blockbuster tannins but those promising to soften with time to show the wine's complexity and balance. A tempting array of black cherry, blackberry and currant flavors all coming together in a long finish. Best 2008–2012. Tentative Score 91–93. **K**

VINEYARD'S CHOICE, MERLOT, 2004: Dark, deep and firmly tannic but with balance that bodes well for the future. Reflecting 16 months in oak with spicy and sweet-cedar notes, those opening to reveal raspberry, currant, chocolate and herbal notes that linger on a long finish. Best 2008–2012. Score 91. **K**

VINEYARD'S CHOICE, MERLOT, 2003: Full-bodied and firmly structured, with dark black cherry, berry, anise and spice flavors that stand up nicely to the tannins and moderate oak influences. Needs time but promises to soften and develop beautifully. Best 2008–2010. Score 90. **K**

VINEYARD'S CHOICE, MERLOT, 2002: Full-bodied, with deep but yielding tannins and a complex array of plum, currant and berry fruits, together with rewarding black olive and earthy overlays. Excellent balance between oak, tannins and fruits. Drink now–2008. Score 92. **K**

VINEYARD'S CHOICE, MERLOT-CABERNET SAUVIGNON, 2004: A blend of 60% Merlot and 40% Cabernet Sauvignon, oak-aged for 16 months. Showing generous oak, firm but well integrating tannins, plums and black cherries on a spicy and harmonious background and with hints of vanilla that rise on the moderately-long finish. Drink now–2009. Score 88. **K**

Ella Valley Vineyards

ELLA VALLEY VINEYARDS, CABERNET SAUVIGNON, 2005: Still in embryonic form but already showing a ripe and polished potential with rich raspberry, blackberry and blackcurrant fruits backed up nicely by cocoa and toasty oak. Generous and long. Drink from release–2011. Tentative Score 89–91. **K**

ELLA VALLEY VINEYARDS, CABERNET SAUVIGNON, 2004: Full-bodied, ripe and complex, with ripe cherry, currant and plum aromas and flavors, those with a dash of anise and oak. Developing nicely, with supple tannins and overall excellent balance. Drink now–2010. Score 90. **K**

ELLA VALLEY VINEYARDS, CABERNET SAUVIGNON, 2003: Firm and tight, big and somewhat rustic, with notes of minerals and sweet cedar on a background of chewy tannins. Concentrated and now softening to reveal its rich plum and currant fruits. Drink now–2008. Score 89. **K**

ELLA VALLEY VINEYARDS, CABERNET SAUVIGNON, 2002: Dark garnet toward purple in color, this medium to full-bodied wine shows rich, ripe currant, plum, cherry, anise and mint aromas and flavors. Generous and long, but with a light bitterness that runs through to the finish. Drink now. Score 88. K

ELLA VALLEY VINEYARDS, MERLOT, 2005: Dark and brooding, with still muscular tannins needing time to integrate, this dense wine offers up generous currant and black cherry aromas and flavors. Best from 2008–2012. Tentative Score 90–92. K

ELLA VALLEY VINEYARDS, MERLOT, 2004: A Merlot firm enough in tannins that it needed 5% of Cabernet Sauvignon to soften it somewhat. Supple and with good balance spicy wood and fruit, a full-bodied red showing black cherry, currant and cedary oak. Best 2008–2011. Score 90. K

ELLA VALLEY VINEYARDS, MERLOT, 2003: Medium to full-bodied, deep garnet in color, with tannins now integrating nicely. Supple and elegant, with plum, blackberry, currant and berry fruits going to hints of cedar and spices on the long finish. Drink now–2009. Score 90. K

ELLA VALLEY VINEYARDS, MERLOT, 2002: Dark garnet towards royal purple in color, full-bodied and with firm tannins but those well in balance with wood and fruits. Rich, ripe and harmonious, with plum, cherry and blueberry fruits on a spicy finish that hints of freshly roasted coffee. Drink now–2008. Score 91. K

ELLA VALLEY VINEYARDS, PINOT NOIR, 2005: The first varietal Pinot Noir to be released by the winery. With soft tannins and just the right hint of toasty oak, showing generous cherry, raspberry and blueberry fruits, those overlaid with hints of currants and sweet spices, all leading to a long and elegant finish. Drink from release–2010. Tentative Score 90–92. K

ELLA VALLEY VINEYARDS, CABERNET FRANC, 2005: Made from 100% Cabernet Franc grapes, with generous wood and tannins needing time to integrate. A seductive wine with a generous nearly sur-ripe black cherry, peppery and herbal nature supporting mocha and vanilla on a harmonious finish. Best 2008–2011. Tentative Score 89–91. K

ELLA VALLEY VINEYARDS, CABERNET FRANC, 2004: Medium to full-bodied with austere tannins but already showing finesse. Sharply focused cherry, currant and wild berry flavors open slowly on the palate along with a generous but well-tempered dose of smoky oak. Drink now–2009. Score 89. K

ELLA VALLEY VINEYARDS, CABERNET FRANC, 2003: Blended with 15% of Cabernet Sauvignon, this almost impenetrably dark garnet, oak-aged full-bodied red shows firm tannins and generous wood influence, those balanced nicely by a generous array of black fruits, coffee, vanilla and tobacco, all leading to a long leathery finish. Drink now–2008. Score 91. K

ELLA VALLEY VINEYARDS, SHIRAZ, 2004: Full-bodied, dark, rich and complex with an array of spicy, smoky and meaty plum, berry, currant and anise notes set off nicely by near sweet tannins. Well-balanced and flavorful. Drink from release–2008. Tentative Score 88–90. K

ELLA VALLEY VINEYARDS, CABERNET SAUVIGNON-SYRAH, 2004: A full-bodied, firmly tannic blend of 70% Cabernet Sauvignon and 30% Syrah. Meaty hints from the Syrah, and black cherry and currants from the Cabernet, all with overlays of cedar wood and Mediterranean herbs. Drink now–2009. Score 88. K

ELLA VALLEY VINEYARDS, CHARDONNAY, 2005: Medium to full-bodied and aromatic, opening with green apples and figs, those yielding to lush pears and summer fruits. Focused with a long mineral and toasted white bread finish. Drink now–2008. Score 89. K

ELLA VALLEY VINEYARDS, CHARDONNAY, 2004: Deeply aromatic, reflecting ten months in oak with hints of smoke and spices. Soft and round, with generous pear, melon, citrus and mineral aromas and flavors that develop a near creamy note on the finish. Complex and long. Drink now–2008. Score 90. K

ELLA VALLEY VINEYARDS, CHARDONNAY, 2003: Ripe and complex, with spicy pear, apple and hazelnut notes. Reflecting its 10 months *sur lie*, this deep golden wine fills the palate with complex and long lingering flavors and just the right hints of toasted white bread and yeast. A good dose of oak here but that well integrated. Drink now–2008. Score 91. K

ELLA VALLEY VINEYARDS, SAUVIGNON BLANC, 2005: Aromatic, with gentle hints of spicy wood and steely minerals underlying generous grapefruit, guava and nectarine aromas and flavors, those lingering nicely to a long, lively and lightly grassy finish. Drink now–2008. Score 90. K

ELLA VALLEY VINEYARDS, SAUVIGNON BLANC, 2004: Smooth, rich and buttery, with a light grassiness matched by good spices and layers of pear, honey and minerals. A very appealing hint of light bitterness comes in on the long finish. Drink now–2008. Score 91. K

ELLA VALLEY VINEYARDS, MUSCAT DESSERT, 2003: Medium-bodied, unabashedly sweet but with fine balance between sugar, acidity and alcohol. On the nose and palate aromas and flavors of honeyed summer fruits, stewed pears, sesame seeds and spring flowers. Generous, mouthfilling and long. Drink now–2009. Score 90. K

ELLA VALLEY VINEYARDS, MUSCAT OF ALEXANDRIA, DESSERT WINE, 2002: Medium-bodied, with honeyed sweetness set off nicely by lively acidity, the wine offers generous and ripe apricot, peach and dried apple fruits matched nicely by spices and floral aromas and flavors. Equally good as an aperitif. Drink up. Score 89. K

Ever Red

ELLA VALLEY VINEYARDS, EVER RED, 2004: A medium-bodied blend of Cabernet Sauvignon, Merlot and Petite Sirah (60%, 33% and 7% respectively), with gentle tannins and an appealing array of plum and currant fruits, all with just a hint of spiciness that lingers nicely. Drink now. Score 88. K

ELLA VALLEY VINEYARDS, EVER RED, 2003: Deep purple in color, medium-bodied, this blend of Cabernet Sauvignon and Merlot opens in the glass to reveal gentle wood, soft tannins and appealing currant and wild berry fruits, and chocolate. A lightly spicy finish. Drink now. Score 87. K

ELLA VALLEY VINEYARDS, EVER RED, 2002: A medium to full-bodied oak-aged blend of 80% Cabernet Sauvignon and 20% Merlot, this supple and harmonious wine has an attractive core of plum, berry and cherry fruits. Finishes with a nice touch of spices, mild tannins and toasty oak. Drink up. Score 87. K

Essence ✯✯

Located in the community of Ma'aleh Tsvi'a in the Western Galilee, the winery was founded by Yaniv Kimchi, Eitan Rosenberg and Itzhak Avramov, and released its first wines in 2001. Grapes, including Cabernet Sauvignon, are raised in the winery's organic vineyards at the foothills of Mount Kamon, and the wines are made in accordance with international organic standards. The winery's output was 3,000 bottles in 2001 and about 5,000 annually since.

ESSENCE, CABERNET SAUVIGNON, 2004: Garnet red in color, medium-bodied, with firm tannins integrating nicely. On the nose and palate berry and currant fruits with hints of toasted oak. Drink now. Score 85.

ESSENCE, CABERNET SAUVIGNON, 2003: Deep ruby towards garnet, medium-bodied, with chunky tannins, spicy cedar wood and aromas and flavors primarily of ripe berries. Pleasant but somewhat one dimensional. Drink now. Score 84.

ESSENCE, MERLOT, 2003: Cloudy purple in color, with chunky tannins that seem not to want to integrate and stingy black fruits dominated by an overly alcoholic finish. Drink up. Score 79.

ESSENCE, MERLOT, 2002: Dark garnet toward purple in color, this medium-bodied wine has firm tannins that fail to integrate along with some appealing black fruit aromas and flavors and a hint of smoky oak. Somewhat past its peak. Drink up. Score 82.

ESSENCE, ELECTRIUM, 2003: Medium-bodied, with generous oak, this blend of Cabernet Sauvignon and Merlot shows soft but chunky country-style tannins and appealing blackberry and cassis aromas and flavors. Drink now. Score 84.

ESSENCE, ELECTRUM, 2002: This medium-bodied oak-aged blend of Cabernet Sauvignon and Merlot offers up soft tannins and generous blackcurrant and plum flavors. Drink now. Score 84.

Flam *****

Located in a sparkling new state-of-the-art facility not far from the town of Beit Shemesh at the foothills of the Jerusalem Mountains, the Flam winery has produced consistently excellent and exciting wines since its first releases from the 1998 vintage. Established by brothers Golan and Gilad Flam, Golan being the winemaker, after having trained and worked in Australia and Tuscany, and Gilad in charge of the business aspects. The winery is currently producing age-worthy varietal Cabernet Sauvignon and Merlot wines in their Reserve series, and also has a second wine, Classico, a blend of Cabernet Sauvignon and Merlot that is meant for relatively early drinking. Production from the 1998 vintage was less than 1,000 bottles, 25,000 bottles were released in 2002, 45,000 in 2003 and 55,000 in 2004 and 2005. Grapes come primarily from the vineyards in the Judean Mountains and the Galilee over which the winery has full control. Production potential at the new winery is for 90,000 bottles annually.

Reserve

RESERVE, CABERNET SAUVIGNON, 2005: Full-bodied, with chewy tannins balanced nicely by generous wood and already showing blackcurrant, mint and chocolate. On the long, elegant finish, hints of eucalyptus and Mediterranean herbs. Drink from release–2012. Tentative Score 91–93.

RESERVE, CABERNET SAUVIGNON, 2004: Deep garnet towards black in color, full-bodied, with still firm tannins but even now giving hints of the toasty and smoky plum, blackcurrant and lead-pencil aromas and flavors that will make this a long, elegant and generous wine. Best 2008–2012. Tentative Score 91–93.

RESERVE, CABERNET SAUVIGNON, 2003: This full-bodied, dark garnet towards deep purple wine was oak-aged for about 14 months. Generous blackcurrant and cherry fruits come together elegantly with mineral, herbal and light earthy aromas and flavors, all with a hint of smoky-toasty oak. Super-smooth tannins and a long finish. Drink now–2012. Score 92.

RESERVE, CABERNET SAUVIGNON, 2002: Made from Cabernet Sauvignon grapes from the upper Galilee and blended with a small amount of Merlot from Karmei Yosef, this elegant deep garnet towards black wine shows good integration between wood, soft tannins, sweet cedar and generous currant and ripe red fruits. Drink now–2010. Score 92.

RESERVE, CABERNET SAUVIGNON, 2001: Deep royal purple toward garnet, with deep extraction but still showing a remarkable softness, this full-bodied, distinctly Mediterranean red has excellent balance between wood, tannins and fruit. Traditional Cabernet blackcurrants are well set off by black cherries, spices and hints of black olives and leather. Drink now–2009. Score 94.

RESERVE, CABERNET SAUVIGNON, 2000: Well focused, this deep purple, medium to full-bodied blend of 90% Cabernet Sauvignon and 10% Merlot spent 15 months in oak casks. A wine so deep you feel you can get lost in it, with flavors and aromas of red currants, ripe red fruit and delicious spices. Drink now–2008. Score 94.

RESERVE, CABERNET SAUVIGNON, 1999: This deep and profound oak-aged blend of 85% Cabernet Sauvignon and 15% Merlot has intense berry, mint and cassis aromas and flavors, along with ample hints of spicy oak. Perhaps a bit past its peak but still elegant and refined, with silky tannins and a succulent finish. Drink up. Score 94.

RESERVE, CABERNET SAUVIGNON, 1998: Aged in new oak casks for 14 months, this delicious blend of 85% Cabernet Sauvignon and 15% Merlot is as assertive, rich and lush today as it was during its youth. Spicy and peppery tones overlay deep aromas and flavors of currants, black cherries and plums, along with floral accents and a clean, long finish. Drink now. Score 90.

RESERVE, MERLOT, 2005: Deep garnet in color, medium-bodied, with soft tannins integrating nicely with wood and generous black fruits. Long and elegant. Drink from release–2010. Tentative Score 91–93.

RESERVE, MERLOT, 2004: Medium to full-bodied, with silky smooth, near-sweet tannins, and with overlays of dusty cedar wood and spices highlighting currant and blackberry fruits. On the long finish, generous spices and a hint of white chocolate. Drink from release–2010. Tentative Score 90–92.

RESERVE, MERLOT, 2003: Dark, deep and intense, with soft, almost sweet tannins and layer after layer of berry, black cherry, anise and spice aromas and flavors that linger nicely on the palate. The once marked wood influence is now receding and the wine is showing soft and long. Drink now–2012. Score 92.

RESERVE, MERLOT, 2002: Deep royal purple and full-bodied, this dark, rich and luxurious wine has an array of flavors that open in the glass to reveal spicy currants, wild berries, mocha and herbs Once firm tannins now integrated nicely and showing a careful hand with smoky oak. On the long finish, anise and light tar overtones. Drink now–2010. Score 91.

RESERVE, MERLOT, 2001: Subdued and elegant, this full-bodied wine shows smooth, well-integrated tannins together with delicious plum, black cherry and light olive fruits, all coming together with smoky oak. An appealing, almost sweet herbal finish adds to the charm of the wine. Drink now–2008. Score 92.

RESERVE, MERLOT, 2000: Made entirely from Merlot grapes and aged for 15 months in small oak casks, the wine shows deep and concentrated black fruits overlaid with generous mocha, chocolate and vanilla aromas and flavors, as well as a pleasing sensation of herbaceousness that comes in on the long finish. With smooth tannins and excellent balance, a mouth-filling, ripe and elegant wine. Drink now. Score 91.

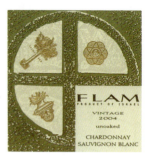

RESERVE, MERLOT, 1999: This medium to full-bodied wine has silky tannins and remarkably harmonious aromas and flavors of cassis, violets, berries and toasty oak. Rich, with flavors that linger on and on, Merlot lovers will find this wine irresistible. Fully mature. Drink now. Score 91.

RESERVE, SYRAH, 2005: Dark garnet in color, with hints of dusty wood on first attack, those yielding to appealing plum, wild berry and mint. Full-bodied and chewy but soft and elegant. Drink from release–2010. Tentative Score 90–92.

RESERVE, SYRAH, 2004: Youthful royal purple, aged in French and American *barriques*, this aromatic, medium to full-bodied wine shows firm but yielding tannins, gentle wood and a tempting array of berry and plum fruits, those backed up by hints of oriental spices, chocolate and light earthiness. Drink from release–2010. Tentative Score 90–92.

RESERVE, SYRAH, 2003: Aged in oak for about 10 months, this deep purple wine shows tempting earthy, mineral aromas and flavors, those backed up nicely by berries, currants and spices. Drink now–2009. Score 91.

RESERVE, CHARDONNAY-SAUVIGNON BLANC, 2005: Lively and refreshing but with generous complexity. Unoaked, with crisp clean aromas and flavors of melon, citrus, peaches and a tantalizing hint of wild flowers on the long finish. Drink now–2008. Score 90.

RESERVE, CHARDONNAY-SAUVIGNON BLANC, 2004: Unoaked and retaining the fresh and unalloyed aromatic flavors of both varieties (70% Chardonnay, 30% Sauvignon Blanc), this crisply dry, medium-bodied wine shows delicious citrus, pear and summer fruit aromas and flavors, those with tempting overlays of melon, herbs and flowers. Harmonious and expressive. Drink now. Score 90.

Superiore

SUPERIORE, 2004: A blend of 80% Syrah and 20% Cabernet Sauvignon showing toasty oak, smoke and soft tannins, those matched nicely by spicy plum and cassis fruits. Look for a round and elegant finish. Best 2008–2012. Score 90.

SUPERIORE, 2003: A blend of 77% Syrah and 23% Cabernet Sauvignon, each fermented separately in French oak before blending. Medium to full-bodied, with soft tannins and a generous earthy-herbal Syrah background coming together nicely with plum, tobacco and blackberry fruits. Round, long, and elegant. Calls to mind a Rhone Cornas. Drink now–2009. Score 90.

Classico

CLASSICO, 2005: Gently oaked, this blend of Cabernet Sauvignon and Merlot shows a dark ruby towards garnet color, near-sweet tannins and appealing blackberry and currant fruits. Soft and round. Drink now–2008. Score 89.

CLASSICO, 2004: As always, a blend of 50% each of Cabernet Sauvignon and Merlot, developed in oak for 6 months. A bit of bottle stink immediately on opening fades quickly to reveal tempting aromas of tobacco and dark chocolate matched nicely by flavors of blackberries and currants. Round and mouthfilling. Drink now. Score 90.

CLASSICO, 2003: A medium-bodied blend of equal parts of Cabernet Sauvignon and Merlot, with soft already well integrated tannins, a well balanced dose of wood and aromatic red berries and currants all coming together nicely with light smoky vanilla and a hint of spices. Drink now. Score 90.

CLASSICO, 2002: This medium to full-bodied Cabernet Sauvignon-Merlot blend shows plenty of smooth tannins, just the right influence of the wood to pass on generous smoky and vanilla flavors, and fruits that include red currants and wild berries along with a nice hint of herbaceousness. Drink up. Score 90.

CLASSICO, 2001: This medium-bodied Cabernet Sauvignon-Merlot blend spent 7 months in small oak casks and shows generous smooth tannins and tempting flavors of currants, plums, wild berries and spices. Look as well for a tempting hint of leather that is creeping in. A well-balanced and seductive wine, now fully mature. Drink up. Score 91.

CLASSICO, 2000: Surprisingly full-bodied and tannic but simultaneously smooth, elegant and well balanced, this blend of Cabernet and Merlot has vanilla, berry and coffee aromas and flavors, and a long delicious finish. Somewhat beyond its peak so drink up. Score 90.

CLASSICO, 1999: A blend of 50% each of Cabernet Sauvignon and Merlot that was aged for 6 months in new French oak barrels, this medium to full-bodied wine is remarkably smooth for its age, well balanced and packed with ripe black cherry, currant and berry flavors that linger nicely on the palate. Past its peak. Drink up. Score 88.

Galai ✶✶

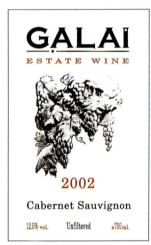

Sigalit and Asaf Galai established this small winery at Moshav Nir Akiva in the northern part of the Negev Desert in 2002. The winery has vineyards containing Cabernet Sauvignon and Merlot as well as experimental sections of Cabernet Franc, Shiraz and Zinfandel. In 2004 and 2005 production was 7,500 bottles.

GALAI, CABERNET SAUVIGNON, 2004: Dark ruby towards royal purple, medium to full-bodied, with chunky country-style tannins. Appealing currant, plum and smoky oak flavors but somewhat one-dimensional. Drink now. Score 85.

GALAI, CABERNET SAUVIGNON, 2003: Deep garnet in color, with firm tannins integrating nicely, this soft and round medium-bodied wine is a blend of Cabernet Sauvignon, Merlot and Cabernet Franc (85%, 11% and 4% respectively). Well balanced, with appealing black fruits and a moderately long finish. Drink now. Score 86.

GALAI, CABERNET SAUVIGNON, 2002: Medium-bodied, with the once firm tannins now nicely integrated. Supple and fruity, with just enough plum and cherry flavors to hold your interest. Drink up. Score 84.

GALAI, MERLOT, 2004: Medium to full-bodied, with firm tannins integrating nicely and an appealing array of berry, cherry and plum, those matched nicely by hints of spices and smoke. A bit of bitterness creeps in on the finish. Not meant for cellaring. Drink now. Score 84.

GALAI, MERLOT, 2003: Dark ruby towards garnet, this medium-bodied wine blended with 15% Cabernet Sauvignon spent 13 months in oak. There are some nice berry and cherry flavors here but with flabby tannins and high acidity the wine fails to come together. Drink now. Score 83.

GALAI, MERLOT, 2002: Medium-bodied, with soft almost unfelt tannins. Berry-cherry flavors and a hint of spices but short and one-dimensional. Drink up. Score 79.

GALAI, CABERNET SAUVIGNON-SHIRAZ, 2003: Aged for 20 months in oak, this medium to full-bodied blend of 67% Cabernet Sauvignon and 33% Shiraz offers appealing currant, plum and earthy-mineral aromas and flavors, all leading to a moderately long finish. Drink now. Score 85.

GALAI, CABERNET SAUVIGNON-SHIRAZ, 2002: Deep cherry-red in color, medium to full-bodied, with soft tannins, a hint of smoky oak, and generous plum and berry fruits. Drink now. Score 83.

GALAI, BACCHUS, 2003: Light to medium-bodied, this blend of 60% Cabernet Sauvignon and 40% Merlot has light tannins and somewhat diluted flavors and aromas of berries and black cherries. Short and one-dimensional. Drink up. Score 83.

Galil Mountain ★★★★

With its physically beautiful state-of-the-art winery located on Kibbutz Yiron in the Upper Galilee, this joint venture between the Golan Heights Winery and the *kibbutz* has vineyards located in some of the best wine-growing areas of the Upper Galilee, including Yiron, Meron, Misgav Am, Yiftach and Malkiya. Talented Micha Vaadia recently took over as the winemaker and continues to produce distinctly *terroir*-based wines in two series. The first label, Yiron, is a blend of Cabernet Sauvignon and Merlot, and the second, the Galil Mountain series, contains varietal releases of Cabernet Sauvignon, Merlot, Pinot Noir, Syrah, Sangiovese, Chardonnay and Sauvignon Blanc. Production from the 2000 vintage was about 300,000 bottles. Since then the winery has grown to an output of 650,000–700,000 bottles annually and expects to meet its target production of 1–1.2 million bottles annually by 2010.

Yiron

YIRON, 2003: A blend of 60% Cabernet Sauvignon, 35% Merlot and 5% Syrah. Young and vibrant but already showing complexity, depth and elegance. Dark royal purple in color, with firm but nicely integrating tannins, judicious wood and layers of spicy currant, anise, tar and

GALIL MOUNTAIN

cedary oak aromas and flavors blending nicely on the long finish. Drink now–2010. Score 92. K

YIRON, 2002: A medium to full-bodied oak-aged blend of 54% Cabernet Sauvignon and 46% Merlot. Deeply aromatic, dark purple toward black in color, with still muscular tannins integrating well, the wine shows abundant blackcurrant, plum, black cherry and berry fruits as well as sweet cedar wood. A generous and mouth-filling finish with an appealing light herbal-earthy overtone. Drink now–2009. Score 90. K

YIRON, 2001: Dark garnet, showing somewhat more full-bodied than in its youth, this blend of 78% Cabernet Sauvignon and 22% Merlot offers still generous tannins and oak but those now in fine tune with blackberry, currant and black cherry fruits. Also on the nose and palate gentle spiciness and now showing a hint of tobacco. Maturing beautifully and with elegance. Drink now–2008. Score 90. K

YIRON, 2000: Deep red toward purple, this medium to full-bodied blend of 60% Cabernet Sauvignon and 40% Merlot shows smooth, well-integrating tannins, and generous but not overpowering oak, reflecting 16 months in small oak barrels. Plum, cherry-berry and eucalyptus aromas and flavors are felt on the first attack, yielding to an appealing and gentle herbal-earthy overlay and a moderately long finish. Matured nicely. Drink up. Score 90. K

Galil Mountain

GALIL MOUNTAIN, CABERNET SAUVIGNON, 2005: Deep and dark, with full-body and generous near-sweet tannins highlighting ripe plum and berry fruits, spices and a tantalizing overlay of porcini mushrooms. Drink now–2008. 89. K

GALIL MOUNTAIN, CABERNET SAUVIGNON, 2004: Dark garnet red, with near-sweet tannins already integrating nicely, and traditional Cabernet currant, berry and light herbal aromas and flavors. Approaching elegance. Drink now–2008. Score 88. **K**

GALIL MOUNTAIN, CABERNET SAUVIGNON, 2003: Inky-black in color, full-bodied, with muscular tannins that have started to soften and with good balance and excellent structure. Tempting currant, cranberry and rhubarb aromas and flavors make this a long, round and quietly elegant wine. Drink now–2008. Score 89. **K**

GALIL MOUNTAIN, CABERNET SAUVIGNON, 2002: Medium to full-bodied, with generous well-integrated tannins, those well balanced by cassis and blackberry fruits. Drink up. Score 87. **K**

GALIL MOUNTAIN, CABERNET SAUVIGNON, 2001: Deep royal purple, medium-bodied and aromatic, this unoaked 100% Cabernet Sauvignon shows plenty of soft tannins as well as aromas and flavors of wild berries, black plums and herbs, along with a hint of cigar tobacco. Drink up. Score 87. **K**

GALIL MOUNTAIN, MERLOT, 2005: Deep, almost inky black garnet in color, full-bodied, with ripe berry, green pepper and light herbal aromas and flavors, those coming together in a deep and complex *terroir*-driven wine. Best from 2008. Score 89. **K**

GALIL MOUNTAIN, MERLOT, 2004: Dark ruby towards garnet in color, medium-bodied, with soft tannins, and with berry and plum fruits, all on a light peppery background. Round and smooth. Drink now–2009. Score 88. **K**

GALIL MOUNTAIN, MERLOT, 2003: Medium to full-bodied and rich in currant, berry and grapefruit peel aromas and flavors, smoky overlays and generous soft tannins, this unoaked wine promises to develop nicely. Drink now–2008. Score 88. **K**

GALIL MOUNTAIN, MERLOT, 2002: Deep, almost inky purple in color, medium to full-bodied, with generous aromas and flavors of herbs, berries and spring flowers on a softly tannic background and a medium-to-long, almost sweet finish highlighted by cedar and chocolate. Drink up. Score 86. **K**

GALIL MOUNTAIN, PINOT NOIR, 2005: Deep garnet, medium-bodied, with firm but nicely yielding tannins. Concentrated and with just enough muscle, with layers of wild berry, black cherry, currant, raspberry, violet and mineral notes. Best from 2008. Tentative Score 91–93. **K**

GALIL MOUNTAIN

GALIL MOUNTAIN, PINOT NOIR, 2004: Dark ruby towards garnet in color, with firm tannins well balanced with wood, the two needing time to come together with red berries and plums, black cherries, light herbal notes and, on the finish, fresh strawberries. Long and elegant. Drink now–2009. Score 90. **K**

GALIL MOUNTAIN, PINOT NOIR 2003: With six months in oak, this medium-bodied wine shows well-integrated soft tannins and appealing plum, cherry and wild berry fruits together with a bare meaty-herbal overtone. Drink now. Score 86. **K**

GALIL MOUNTAIN, PINOT NOIR, 2002: The darkest, most deeply extracted and most fruity of the Pinot Noir wines from Galil Mountain, with hints of cedar wood, soft and well-integrated tannins, and black cherry and oriental spices now showing nicely. Drink up. Score 86. **K**

GALIL MOUNTAIN, SYRAH, 2005: Depth, darkness and light earthy-mineral overtones in this remarkably full-bodied and still firmly tannic wine, but with enviable balance and structure. Showing a generous array of black fruits, oriental spices and black pepper. Best 2008–2011. Tentative Score 91–93. **K**

GALIL MOUNTAIN, SYRAH, 2004: Dark, full and bold, with layers of blackberry, blueberry, cocoa, mineral and chocolate complemented by hints of smoky oak. As this one develops look for hints of anise and licorice unfolding on the palate. Drink from release–2010. Tentative Score 89–91. **K**

GALIL MOUNTAIN, SYRAH, 2003: Made entirely from Syrah grapes from a low yield vineyard. Full bodied, tannic and concentrated, with generous but not overpowering oak all integrating nicely to show peppery black fruits, hints of grilled meat, and an appealing herbal-chocolate finish. Drink now–2009. Score 90. **K**

GALIL MOUNTAIN, SANGIOVESE, 2005: Dark, almost impenetrable garnet in color, rich, complex and with remarkable finesse for a pure

Sangiovese. On the nose and palate plum, cherry, blackberry, anise, currants and wild berries. Drink from release. Tentative Score 91–93. K

GALIL MOUNTAIN, SHIRAZ-CABERNET SAUVIGNON, 2005: Concentrated blackberry, blackcurrant and black cherry fruits weaving together beautifully with spicy, peppery notes. All of the potential for a complex, elegant and cellar-worthy wine. Best from 2008. Tentative Score 90–92. K

GALIL MOUNTAIN, SHIRAZ-CABERNET, 2003: Dark garnet, medium-bodied, with soft tannins and showing smooth and supple aromas and flavors of creamy currants, black cherries and coffee. Distinctly New World in style. Drink now. Score 87. K

GALIL MOUNTAIN, ROSÉ, 2005: A blend of 65% Sangiovese, 22% Cabernet Sauvignon and 13% Syrah. On the nose and palate, strawberries, wild berries, spices and a hint of mint that comes in on the finish. Medium-bodied and crisp with a 13.5% alcohol content. Perhaps the best rosé ever from Israel. Drink now. Score 90. K

GALIL MOUNTAIN, ROSÉ, 2004: A blend of Sangiovese, Cabernet Sauvignon and Syrah (92%, 5% and 3% respectively), this crisply dry light to medium-bodied rosé is refreshing and lively, with berries and light spices, while maintaining a surprising level of sophistication. Lightly *frizzante* when well chilled. Drink up. Score 86. K

GALIL MOUNTAIN, CHARDONNAY, 2005: Golden straw in color, with orange reflections, medium-bodied with fine balance and an appealing array of citrus, apple and melon aromas and flavors. Crisp and refreshing. Score 88. K

GALIL MOUNTAIN, CHARDONNAY, 2004: Bright golden straw in color, medium-bodied, with tempting aromas and flavors of loquats, tropical fruits and minerals. Good balance between light wood, crisp balancing acidity and mouthfilling fruits. Drink now. Score 88. K

GALIL MOUNTAIN, CHARDONNAY, 2003: The color of golden straw, with grapefruit, green apple and floral aromas and flavors and good balancing acidity to keep it lively, this is a refreshing wine, with appealing hints of vanilla and minerals. Give the wine ten minutes to open in the glass to show its best. Drink now. Score 86. K

GALIL MOUNTAIN, SAUVIGNON BLANC, 2005: Delicious! Medium-bodied, pale greenish yellow, with a generous citrus nose and on the palate, passion fruit, flinty minerals and the hint of an English rose garden after a summer shower. Crisp, lively and elegant. Drink now–2008. Score 91. K

GALIL MOUNTAIN

GALIL MOUNTAIN, SAUVIGNON BLANC 2004: Light straw in color, with orange and green reflections, this medium-bodied unoaked white shows fine balance between crisp acidity and fruits. On the nose and palate, peach and melon fruits and towards the finish a hint of grassiness Drink now. Score 89. **K**

Gat Shomron ✶

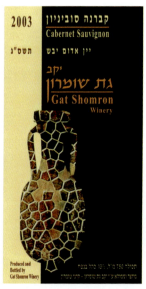

Founded by Avigdor Sharon and Limor Nachum on the settlement of Karnei Shomron, not far from Kfar Saba, in 2003, and releasing their first wines from that harvest in 2005, this small winery is currently producing about 2,000 bottles annually of oak-aged Cabernet Sauvignon, Merlot and Chardonnay.

GAT SHOMRON, CABERNET SAUVIGNON, 2004: Garnet red, with chunky tannins and a few currant, berry and plum fruits. Drink now. Score 80. **K**

GAT SHOMRON, CABERNET SAUVIGNON, 2003: Dark ruby towards garnet, with somewhat overgenerous tannins and oak, and ripe plum and berry fruits. Drink now. Score 82. **K**

GAT SHOMRON, MERLOT, 2004: A somewhat cloudy garnet red, with firm tannins and very generous oak hiding whatever black fruit flavors try to make themselves felt. Drink up. Score 79. **K**

GAT SHOMRON, MERLOT, 2003: Garnet red, medium-bodied, with chunky country-style tannins and generous oak set off nicely by aromas and flavors of plums, cassis and sweet herbs. Drink now. Score 84. **K**

GAT SHOMRON, CHARDONNAY, 2005: Golden-straw colored, with tart pineapple and citrus flavors. Floral with a hint of sweetness. Drink up. Score 78. **K**

GAT SHOMRON, CHARDONNAY, 2004: Medium-bodied, light golden in color, with aromas and flavors of pineapple, citrus and spring flowers. Somewhat alcoholic and coarse on the palate. Drink up. Score 82. **K**

Gesher Damia *

Founded in 1999 by Moshe Kaplan in the town of Pardes Hannah on the northern Coastal Plain, this small winery receives Cabernet Sauvignon, Merlot, Argaman, Petite Sirah, Gewurztraminer and Chardonnay grapes from Gush Etzion, the Jerusalem Hills and the center of the country. Production in 2002 was 4,000 bottles and the winery released 5,000 bottles in 2003 and 2004.

GESHER DAMIA, CABERNET SAUVIGNON, 2004: Dark ruby in color and medium-bodied, with chunky tannins, smoky oak and skimpy black fruits. Drink now. Score 79.

GESHER DAMIA, CABERNET SAUVIGNON, 2003: Deep ruby in color, medium-bodied, with gripping tannins and generous sweet and smoky oak and a few berry-cherry fruits. Drink up. Score 78.

GESHER DAMIA, CABERNET SAUVIGNON, 2002: This medium-bodied wine has firm tannins and abundant sweet cedar wood but lacks the fruits, depth or length to carry it. Drink up. Score 77.

GESHER DAMIA, CABERNET SAUVIGNON, 2001: Medium-bodied, with soft tannins and an appealing fruity character of currants and red plums, this country-style wine shows exaggerated wood that adds an unnecessary coarseness. Drink up. Score 84.

GESHER DAMIA, MERLOT, 2004: Medium-bodied, with soft, near-sweet tannins and blackberry, cherry and cassis fruits, those on a lightly spicy background. Drink now. Score 80.

GESHER DAMIA, MERLOT, 2002: Smooth and soft, this dark ruby toward garnet wine shows appealing currant, berry and cherry fruits but proves somewhat one-dimensional and short. Drink up. Score 78.

Ginaton ✯✯

Founded in 1999 by Doron Cohen and Benju Duke on Moshav Ginaton on the central plains not far from the city of Lod, and drawing Cabernet Sauvignon, Muscat and Chardonnay grapes from Karmei Yosef and Kerem Ben Zimra, the first commercial releases of the winery were 3,000 bottles from the 2000 vintage. Production from the 2005 vintage was about 5,500 bottles and the winery is holding temporarily at that number.

GINATON, CABERNET SAUVIGNON, NUMBERED SERIES, 2003: Reflecting 18 months in oak with generous spicy and smoky cedar and moderately-firm tannins. Medium to full-bodied, with some black fruits. Lacking complexity. Drink now. Score 84.

GINATON, CABERNET SAUVIGNON, KEREM BEN ZIMRA, 2003: Clear ruby towards purple, medium-bodied, with soft, almost unfelt tannins. Aromas and flavors of berries, cassis and black cherries on a lightly herbaceous background. Drink now. Score 84.

GINATON, CABERNET SAUVIGNON, KEREM BEN ZIMRA, 2002: Medium-bodied, with currant, berry and cherry fruits all on a lightly spicy background and with hints of Mediterranean herbs that come in on the finish. Drink now. Score 85.

GINATON, CABERNET SAUVIGNON, KEREM BEN ZIMRA, 2001: Medium-bodied, with berry, cherry and some currant fruits and a hint of toasty oak. Drink up. Score 83.

GINATON, CABERNET SAUVIGNON, KEREM YOSEF, 2001: Ripe plum and cherry flavors make this medium-bodied and moderately tannic wine just engaging enough to hold your interest. Drink now. Score 83.

GINATON, CABERNET SAUVIGNON, KEREM YOSEF, 2000: Medium-bodied, firm and with berry and chocolate notes but with too many earthy, cedary flavors. Somewhat past its peak. Drink up. Score 82.

GINATON, MERLOT, KEREM YOSEF, 2003: Medium-bodied, with soft, well integrating tannins and appealing aromas and flavors of blackberries and purple plums on a lightly spicy background. Drink up. Score 84.

GINATON, MERLOT, KEREM YOSEF, 2002: Medium-bodied, with good focus and nice wild berry and herbal flavors, but turning thin on the finish where it picks up a smoky, mineral accent. Drink up. Score 80.

GINATON, MERLOT, KEREM YOSEF, 2001: Medium-bodied with very soft tannins, with some ripe plum and cherry flavors, but turning simple on the finish. Drink up. Score 83.

GINATON, MERLOT, KEREM YOSEF, 2000: Not complex but with juicy ripe cherry and berry flavors and hints of cedar. Soft tannins make this an acceptable quaffer. Past its peak. Drink up. Score 82.

GINATON, SHIRAZ, 2003: Developed in oak for 18 months, medium to full-bodied, with firm tannins just starting to yield and revealing berry, black cherry and plum fruits on a lightly spicy and herbal background. Drink now. Score 84.

GINATON, CABERNET SAUVIGNON-MERLOT, 2003: Aged for 14 months in oak, a somewhat sharp and chunky country-style wine but showing appealing red berry and cassis aromas and flavors. Drink now. Score 84.

GINATON, CABERNET SAUVIGNON-SHIRAZ, 2003: Dark garnet, medium-bodied, with soft tannins and currant, plum and meaty-earthy aromas and flavors. Simple but appealing. Drink now. Score 84.

GINATON, CABERNET SAUVIGNON-MERLOT-PETITE SIRAH, 2003: Medium-dark garnet in color, with chunky tannins and a hint of country-style coarseness. A few wild berry, currant and leafy aromas and flavors. Drink up. Score 82.

Givon ✶

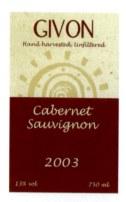

Established by Nir Ernesti and Shuki Segal in the village of Givon, north of Jerusalem in the Judean Mountains, and relying on Cabernet Sauvignon and Merlot grapes from nearby vineyards, this winery released its first wines from the 2002 vintage. Current production is about 4,000 bottles annually.

GIVON, CABERNET SAUVIGNON, 2004: Dark cherry red in color, medium-bodied, with soft tannins and appealing black cherry and plum fruits. Not typical for the variety but an acceptable quaffing wine. Drink now. Score 83.

GIVON, CABERNET SAUVIGNON, 2003: Medium-bodied, with soft tannins and simple but appealing flavors of berries and black cherries, but faulted somewhat by a too generous acidity. Drink up. Score 78.

GIVON, CABERNET SAUVIGNON, SOLO, 2003: Made entirely from Cabernet Sauvignon grapes, this medium-bodied, softly tannic red is somewhat one-dimensional but with appealing plum and berry fruits. Drink up. Score 84.

GIVON, MERLOT, 2004: Medium-bodied, low in tannins and on the simple side, with only skimpy berry and plum fruits. Score 80.

GIVON, MERLOT, 2003: This simple country-style wine, a blend of 90% Merlot and 10% Cabernet Sauvignon, has forward black fruits and medium-body but with its somewhat chunky tannins and rasping acidity it is not at all reminiscent of Merlot. Drink now. Score 78.

GIVON, NEBBIOLO, 2004: Dark cherry red, medium-bodied, with soft tannins and appealing raspberry and cherry fruits. A simple quaffer. Drink now. Score 82.

Golan Heights Winery *****

From the moment they released their first wines in 1984, there has been no doubt that the Golan Heights Winery was and is still today largely responsible for placing Israel on the world wine map. The winery, with its state-of-the-art facilities located in Katzrin on the Golan Heights, and fine vineyards on the Golan and in the Upper Galilee, is owned by eight of the *kibbutzim* and *moshavim* that supply them with grapes. Maintaining rigorous control over the vineyards and relying on a combination of New and Old World knowledge and technology, senior winemaker Victor Shoenfeld and his staff of winemakers, all of whom trained in California or France, produce wines that often attain excellence.

The winery has three regular series, Yarden, Gamla and Golan, the wines in the first two series often being age-worthy while those in the Golan series are meant for early drinking. There is also the top-of-the-line Katzrin series that includes a red Bordeaux-style blend that is released only in years considered exceptional and a Chardonnay that has been released annually since 1995.

The winery is currently producing more than six million bottles annually and of this production nearly thirty percent is destined for export. Among the regularly released varietal wines are Cabernet Sauvignon, Merlot, Pinot Noir, Gamay, Sangiovese, Sauvignon Blanc, Chardonnay, Johannisberg Riesling, Muscat Canelli and Gewurztraminer, and the winery is currently cultivating experimental plantings of Nebbiolo and Malbec. The winery also produces sparkling Blanc de Blanc and Brut, which are made in the traditional Champenoise method, Heightswine (a play on the words Ice Wine) and several dessert wines.

Katzrin

KATZRIN, 2003: A blend of Cabernet Sauvignon, Merlot and Cabernet Franc. Velvety and well-balanced to show off a rich core of blackcurrant, blueberry, peppery and herbal flavors, those with an overlay of soft tannins and gently smoky oak. Promising length, depth and elegance. Best from 2009. Tentative Score 92–94. **K**

KATZRIN, 2000: Elegant, ripe, bold and concentrated, with still tight tannins reflecting its youth but with the kind of balance and structure that bodes very well for the future, the wine shows currants, black cherries and purple plums along with spices and smoky wood. Drink now–2015. Score 92. **K**

KATZRIN, 1996: Vibrant and complex, with an array of aromas and flavors that include currants, cherries and plums overlaid by smoky oak, chocolate, spices and tobacco, this full-bodied, young tannic red is only now beginning now to reveal its charms. Excellent integration between fruit, tannins and oak indicates that the wine will continue to develop beautifully. Drink now–2015. Score 93. **K**

KATZRIN, 1993: Deep, broad, long and complex, this full-bodied Cabernet-Merlot blend continues to live up to its promise. Abundant tannins are well balanced by wood and fruits that include cassis, black cherries and orange peel, along with generous overlays of milk chocolate and toasty oak. Elegant and graceful, the wine is drinking nicely now and will cellar comfortably until 2012. Score 94. **K**

KATZRIN, 1990: A blend of 90% Cabernet Sauvignon and 10% Merlot, this deep, elegant full-bodied wine has a dark garnet color and excellent balance between fruits, wood, acidity and tannins. Look for a complex array of aromas and flavors, including blackcurrants, cherries, vanilla, cloves and chocolate. Lingering long on the palate, the wine is drinking beautifully now and should continue to cellar well until 2010. Score 95. **K**

KATZRIN, CHARDONNAY, 2003: Rich, ripe, concentrated and complex with generous layers of figs, tangerines, summer fruits and hazelnuts. Generous but not imposing oak on the finish makes it especially elegant as does a hint of butterscotch that comes in on the long finish. Drink now–2010. Score 92. **K**

KATZRIN, CHARDONNAY, 2002: Full-bodied, concentrated and complex, the wine was fermented in French oak *barriques* and then allowed to age *sur lie* for seven months. It shows layer after layer of fruits, those including orange, grapefruit, ripe pears and passion fruit, along with tiers of hazelnuts, minerals, vanilla and smoky, toasty oak. Rich, mouth-filling and long. Drink now–2009. Score 92. **K**

KATZRIN, CHARDONNAY, 2000: Aged for 10 months *sur lie*, this full-bodied, elegant and complex white still maintains a young and enthusiastic deep golden color and has layers of aromas and flavors that include poached pears, apples and passion fruit. Intense and concentrated, it shows tantalizing hints of spices, vanilla and oak, all culminating in a long finish. Drink now–2010. Score 92. **K**

KATZRIN, CHARDONNAY, 1999: Featuring complex pear, apple and buttery notes, but the spices now fading and the vanilla rising. Continuing to be stylish and appealing but not meant for much further cellaring. Drink up. Score 90. **K**

KATZRIN, CHARDONNAY, 1998: Generous, round and beautifully proportioned, this buttery, full-bodied wine has an abundance of spicy pear and apple flavors on a frame of rich oak, as well as hints of minerals and earthiness. Fully mature. Drink up. Score 91. **K**

KATZRIN, CHARDONNAY, 1997: This full-bodied deep golden wine was aged *sur lie* in new French barrels for nine months. Remarkably deep, concentrated and complex, it reveals an intense bouquet of cooked apples and pears, plenty of buttery overtones, and just the right amount of oak. Somewhat past its peak. Drink up. Score 88. **K**

Yarden

YARDEN, CABERNET SAUVIGNON, 2005: Showing excellent extraction and depth. Firmly tannic and with generous oak influences now but with the promise that those will integrate comfortably with black fruits, spices and earthy-minerality, perhaps with hints of chocolate and mocha. Look forward to a wine that will develop elegance as it ages. Best 2009–2014. Tentative Score 89–91. **K**

YARDEN, CABERNET SAUVIGNON, 2004: Excellent balance and structure. Generous tannins and spices and with those smoky oak, hints of asphalt and earthiness supporting an appealing array of blackcurrant, blackberry and purple plum aromas and flavors. Drink from release–2012. Tentative Score 90–92. **K**

YARDEN, CABERNET SAUVIGNON, 2003: Dark garnet red, showing an appealing balance between ripe soft tannins, spicy currant, anise and cedar wood aromas and flavors, all leading to a long and complex finish. Drink now–2012. Score 92. **K**

YARDEN, CABERNET SAUVIGNON, 2002: Dark garnet towards royal purple in color, full-bodied, with firm tannins and spicy oak yielding nicely to reveal flavors and aromas of red currants and berries on first attack, those giving way to layers of sweet cedar, vanilla, leather and, on the long finish, a hint of anise. Generous and elegant. Drink now–2012. Score 92. **K**

YARDEN, CABERNET SAUVIGNON, ELROM VINEYARD, 2001: Dark, almost impenetrable garnet-purple in color, full-bodied and with finely-tuned balance between generous well-integrated tannins and judicious oak, this exquisite wine shows complex tiers of aromas and flavors of red currants, berries, and spices on the first attack those later opening to include light earthy and herbal overlays. Plush and opulent, with a long, complex finish. Among the best ever made in Israel. Drink now–2013. Score 95. **K**

YARDEN, CABERNET SAUVIGNON, 2001: This delicious full-bodied red has good balance between wood, tannins and fruits. With plum, wild berry and currant fruits reflecting its 18 months in oak, with appealing overlays of vanilla, cedar and violets. Drink now–2010. Score 91. **K**

YARDEN, CABERNET SAUVIGNON, 2000: This full-bodied young red has firm tannins and abundant oak well balanced by currants, black cherries and what at one moment feels like plums, at another like black cherries, all matched nicely with vanilla and an appealing herbal overlay, and followed by a long finish. Drink now–2010. Score 92. **K**

YARDEN, CABERNET SAUVIGNON, 1999: With once firm tannins now softening and showing fine balance between wood and fruits, the wine is opening beautifully. Deep royal purple toward garnet in color with delicious aromas and flavors of black berries and cherries on a background of vanilla and sweet cedar wood as well as a hint of freshly roasted coffee on its long finish. Drink now–2009. Score 92. **K**

YARDEN, CABERNET SAUVIGNON, 1998: Full-bodied, deep in color and remarkably intense, with aromas and flavors of currant, plum, black cherry, vanilla and lightly toasted oak as well as excellent balance between fruits, wood and tannins. On the long finish mineral-earthy overtones and an appealing hint of anise. Maturing beautifully. Drink now–2008. Score 91. **K**

YARDEN, CABERNET SAUVIGNON, 1997: This traditional Yarden blend of 94% Cabernet Sauvignon, 5% Merlot and 1% Cabernet Franc is now fully mature but continues to show an overall firm structure and good balance between soft tannins, fruits, wood and acidity. Plenty of Cabernet currants along with blackberries and plums on the first attack, those yielding to gentle overlays of spices and Mediterranean herbs. Not for further cellaring. Drink up. Score 89. **K**

YARDEN, CABERNET SAUVIGNON, 1996: A blend of 98% Cabernet Sauvignon and 2% Cabernet Franc, this concentrated and intense medium to full-bodied wine with sweet tannins is now showing plum, currant and cherry fruits, those complemented nicely by vanilla and anise on the mid-palate, and appealing herbal sensations on the finish. Drink now. Score 91. **K**

YARDEN, CABERNET SAUVIGNON, 1995: The wine needs time to open in the glass but as it does it reveals luscious layers of aromas and flavors of blackcurrants, plums, tobacco and vanilla. Full-bodied, with concentrated but well-integrated tannins, and a hint of raspberries on the long finish. Drink now. Score 92. **K**

YARDEN, CABERNET SAUVIGNON, 1994: Because 1994 was not a great vintage year in Israel, this wine never attained the heights of the best wines of this series. Medium-bodied, it shows flavors of stewed prunes, black fruits and floral-earthy overtones. Fully mature. Drink up. Score 87. **K**

YARDEN, CABERNET SAUVIGNON, 1993: Royal purple in color, this full-bodied wine is concentrated, full-bodied and powerful, and in its maturity has now attained enviable levels of roundness, depth and complexity along with impeccable balance and an elegant bouquet. Silky tannins that give the wine just the right bite, flavors that unfold comfortably on the palate. Drink now. Score 94. K

YARDEN, CABERNET SAUVIGNON, 1992: Full-bodied, with fully integrated tannins and abundant black fruits, vanilla and appealing herbal, earthy, and tobacco overlays, this well balanced and generous wine shows a moderately long near-sweet finish. Past its peak. Drink up. Score 88. K

YARDEN, CABERNET SAUVIGNON, 1991: Deep purple in color and medium to full-bodied, the wine continues to reveal traditional Cabernet aromas and flavors of blackcurrants, cedar wood and black cherries along with herbal-mineral overtones on the finish. Past its peak. Drink up. Score 87. K

YARDEN, CABERNET SAUVIGNON, 1990: When young, this superb wine showed almost massive tannins and intensity but due to its excellent structure and good balance the wine has maintained its rich concentration along with its traditional blackcurrant, oak and vanilla aromas and flavors, those overlaid by aromatic cedar, leather and tobacco, and a remarkably long finish. Drink now. Score 92. K

YARDEN, CABERNET SAUVIGNON, 1989: Fully mature, delicious and elegant, the wine continues to show aromas and flavors that open seemingly without end on the palate. Look for blackberries, cherries, coffee, leather, toasted bread, smoky oak, vanilla and a hint of tobacco. Drink up. Score 92. K

YARDEN, CABERNET SAUVIGNON, 1988: Darkening and starting to brown at the rim, and with dark fruits, currants, vanilla and spices now clearly overlaid with aromas and flavors of damp earth, herbs and smoked meats, the wine continues to drink nicely even though it is somewhat past its peak. Drink up. Score 87. K

YARDEN, CABERNET SAUVIGNON, 1987: Never attaining excellence, the wine blossomed for a short while several years ago in what may have been its swan song. Still showing some currants and a few black fruits, the leather now has a rather sweaty aroma and the cinnamon and vanilla are becoming just a bit caramelized. Past its peak. Drink up. Score 85. K

YARDEN, CABERNET SAUVIGNON, 1986: Far lighter than most of the other Cabernet wines in this series, this wine has now passed whatever peak it may have attained and is now browning. Drink up. Score 84. K

YARDEN, CABERNET SAUVIGNON, 1985: Deep and warm, concentrated, heady and exotic, with spicy plums, blackcurrants and blackberries all overlaid with stewed fruits, chocolate and leather, along with flavors of coffee and chocolate that linger nicely, this is a wine that although fully mature and now clearly beyond its peak continues to belie its age. Drink up. Score 92. K

YARDEN, MERLOT, 2005: Still in embryonic form but showing the potential for a medium to full-bodied spicy red, with currant and plum aromas and flavors, and overlays of smoke and herbaceousness. Anticipate an elegant and long wine. Best 2008–2011. Tentative Score 89–91 K

YARDEN, MERLOT, 2004: Medium to full-bodied, with a generous array of currant, plum and berry fruits, those with overlays of minerals, bittersweet chocolate, cedar and soft but peppery tannins. Drink from release–2010. Tentative Score 88–90. K

YARDEN, MERLOT, 2003: This soft, smooth and polished wine shows tempting ripe cherry and currant fruits, those supported nicely by layers of Mediterranean herbs, vanilla and light hints of smoky oak. Complex, long and elegant. Drink now–2010. Score 90. K

YARDEN, MERLOT, 2002: Deep ruby towards garnet, medium to full-bodied, with soft, already well-integrating tannins and generously spicy oak. Shows tempting sweet black plum and wild berry fruits on an appealing herbal and chocolate background as well as black cherries and a hint of vanilla on the medium-long finish. Drink now–2008. Score 88. K

YARDEN, MERLOT, ORTAL VINEYARD, 2001: Loads of character in this rich, plush, full-bodied wine. On the first attack, a tempting array of currant, mocha, hazelnut and spices, those later joined by almost jammy plum and berry fruits. Reflecting its 14 months in new and used *barriques* with seamless tannins, generous but not at all overpowering oak and a long and complex milk chocolate and herbal finish. Drink now–2014. Score 94. K

YARDEN, MERLOT, 2001: Garnet toward royal purple in color, this medium to full-bodied wine has soft, integrated tannins and a tempting array of black fruits, vanilla and spices on the first attack, these yielding nicely to almost sweet cassis and light Mediterranean herbs on the finish. Drink now. Score 89. K

YARDEN, MERLOT, 2000: Somewhat less full-bodied than in its youth but still rich and tempting, generous in plum, berry and black cherry fruits as well as in overlays of chocolate and even a hint of citrus on its finish. Drink now. Score 89. K

YARDEN, MERLOT, 1999: Silky smooth tannins, and upfront fruit aromas and flavors of wild berries and currants, along with generous hints of vanilla and spices make this medium to full-bodied wine smooth and tempting. Drink up. Score 88. K

YARDEN, MERLOT, 1998: Ripe, complex, and simultaneously bold and elegant, the wine has tiers of rich plum, currant and blackberry aromas and flavors, overlaid by vanilla, chocolate and tobacco, together with smooth tannins and a deep long finish. Drink up. Score 92. K

YARDEN, MERLOT, 1997: Smooth, bright and striving for elegance, this blend of 85% Merlot and 15% Cabernet Sauvignon was aged for 14 months in oak. Full-bodied and with still chewy tannins, it offers tempting black cherry, raspberry, currant, floral and chocolate notes that open nicely on the palate. Drink up. Score 90. K

YARDEN, MERLOT, 1996: A blend of 85% Merlot, 14% Cabernet Sauvignon and 1% Cabernet Franc, this now fully mature wine continues to reflect rich prunes, berries and oriental spices in its aromas and flavors. With sweet tannins integrated nicely, the wine continues to drink well but is clearly beyond its peak. Drink up. Score 90. K

YARDEN, MERLOT, 1995: Now mature, the fully integrated tannins and oak make the wine round and comfortable on the palate. Still showing appealing wild berry, currant and spicy flavors and a moderately long finish. Clearly past its peak. Drink up. Score 87. K

YARDEN, MERLOT, 1994: From a mediocre vintage year, this is not the most exciting Merlot released by the winery. The wine is now showing age, its black fruits quite subdued and somewhat shadowed by what seems to be a light caramelization process. No longer scoreable. K

YARDEN, MERLOT, 1993: This well-balanced, well-structured wine is now showing a hint of browning and has hints of leather and coffee sneaking in at the end, but still maintains its ample plums and blackcurrants as well as a long, lightly herbal finish. Past its peak. Drink up. Score 87. K

YARDEN, MERLOT, 1992: Full-bodied and tannic in its youth, the wine has evolved beautifully from deep royal purple to an adobe brick red with a hint of browning at the rim. Still showing generous plum, vanilla, orange peel and spices, it now has hints of herbs and earthiness coming in. Past its peak. Drink up. Score 87. K

YARDEN, MERLOT, 1991: Leaving the grapes in the autumn sun for a prolonged time in order to attain a good level of ripeness contributed to the special success of this wine. Full-bodied and concentrated, with aromas and flavors of black cherries, currants, orange peel, chocolate and exotic spiciness, the wine is still drinking well but not meant for further cellaring. Drink up. Score 91. K

YARDEN, SYRAH, 2005: Medium to full-bodied, supple and generous with silky soft tannins, and plum, berry and rhubarb fruits on a rich mineral background. Drink from release. Tentative Score 89–91. K

YARDEN, SYRAH, 2004: A medium to full-bodied, firmly tannic wine with good balance, and aromas and flavors of blackberries, currants, anise and spicy oak. Drink from release. Tentative Score 88–90. K

YARDEN, SYRAH, 2003: Supple, with fresh and appealing sweet berry and vanilla flavors as well as peach pits, spring flowers and light earthiness. Look for a hint of tar on the moderately long finish. Drink now–2009. Score 90. K

YARDEN, SYRAH, 2002: Medium to full-bodied, concentrated and packed with tannins but those soft and already integrating nicely. Multiple layers of green berry, plums and hints of spices, chocolate and vanilla. Plenty of oak here but that will settle down in time and the wine will soften and show increased complexity with tobacco and floral overtones. Drink now–2010. Score 91. **K**

YARDEN, SYRAH, 2001: Medium to full-bodied, with its tannins integrating beautifully with spicy wood and vanilla, and continuing to show fine balance and structure. On the nose and palate an appealing array of black cherries, plums, licorice and hints of earthiness that come in on the generous finish. Drink now–2009. Score 90. **K**

YARDEN, SYRAH, 2000: Dark garnet towards royal-purple in color, this softly tannic, medium to full-bodied wine features aromas and flavors of red currants, plums and spices and, reflecting its 18 months in oak, shows tobacco, herbal and an appealing light meaty-earthy sensation. Long and mouth-filling. Drink now–2009. Score 91. **K**

YARDEN, PINOT NOIR, 2004: A tasty fruit-driven wine with complex flavors including toasted pine nuts, herbs, plums and black cherries. As this one develops look as well for anise and wild berry on a long mouth-filling finish. Drink from release–2012. Tentative Score 89–91. **K**

YARDEN, PINOT NOIR, 2003: Dark, almost impenetrably garnet red in color, with a generous hint of spicy oak complementing and not at all hiding aromas and flavors of plums, blackberry, and black cherry fruits, those matched nicely by a hint of violets that makes its way through the wine to its long, lightly earthy finish. Seamless and elegant. Drink now–2012. Score 92. **K**

YARDEN, PINOT NOIR, 2002: Medium to full-bodied, with soft, near-sweet tannins and fine balance between wood and fruit, and now coming into its own. On the nose and palate red berries, cherries, violets and cassis, those matched nicely by hints of espresso coffee and vanilla. With a long, lightly spicy and mouth-filling finish the wine is drinking beautifully now and will continue to cellar comfortably until 2009. Score 91. **K**

YARDEN, PINOT NOIR, 2001: Leaning from medium towards somewhat fuller-bodied, and with increased complexity showing now, this floral red shows well-integrating soft tannins and hints of sweet-and-smoky oak that highlight floral, spicy cherry, cassis and raspberry fruits. Look as well for lightly earthy and dark chocolate aromas. Drink now–2009. Score 90. **K**

GOLAN HEIGHTS WINERY

YARDEN, PINOT NOIR, 2000: Garnet towards royal purple in color, with tannins now almost fully integrated and with its once rich aromas and flavors now receding and showing only the skimpiest of black fruits and a light peppery overlay. Not living up to its earlier promise. Drink up. Score 87. **K**

YARDEN, PINOT NOIR, 1999: Medium-bodied, dark in color, now fully mature but still showing plum, black cherry and currant fruits. With mushroom and nutty flavors on the ascendant, still complex and rewarding but not for further cellaring. Drink up. Score 89. **K**

YARDEN, MOUNT HERMON RED, 2005: As nearly always, this dark cherry red, medium-bodied blend of Merlot, Cabernet Sauvignon and Cabernet Franc offers soft tannins that make the wine ready to drink in its youth. A few berry, currant and black cherry fruits here but those a bit too subdued. An entry-level wine. Drink up. Score 84. **K**

YARDEN, MOUNT HERMON RED, 2004: Cherry towards garnet red, medium-bodied with soft tannins, this blend of Merlot, Cabernet Sauvignon and Cabernet Franc shows appealing plum and berry fruits along on a light herbal background. Not complex but a good quaffer. Drink up. Score 85. **K**

YARDEN, CHARDONNAY, ODEM ORGANIC VINEYARD, 2005: Ripe and floral, with aromas and flavors of apricots, citrus and figs set off nicely by hints of ginger and pears that come in on the long and complex finish. Drink from 2008. Tentative Score 90–92. **K**

YARDEN, CHARDONNAY, ODEM ORGANIC VINEYARD, 2004: Rich and complex, full-bodied and creamy, with ripe apricot, citrus and pear fruits backed up nicely by an appealing spicy note. Drink now–2010. Score 92. **K**

YARDEN, CHARDONNAY, ODEM ORGANIC VINEYARD, 2003: Rich and elegant, with ripe pear, honeysuckle and melon flavors coming together beautifully with minerals, nutmeg and hazelnut hints on the long finish. Drink now–2009. Score 91. **K**

YARDEN, CHARDONNAY, ODEM ORGANIC VINEYARD, 2002: Maturing gracefully, showing deep golden straw in color. Ripe and complex flavors of pears, tropical fruits, hazelnuts and spices opening on the palate to reveal flinty and floral overtones along with generous but well-integrated oak and a long finish. Drink now–2008. Score 92. **K**

YARDEN, CHARDONNAY, 2003: Medium to full-bodied, fresh, vibrant and complex, with an array of pear, fig, citrus, honey and melon aromas and flavors coming together nicely with toasty oak and hints of spices. Drink now–2009. Score 90. **K**

YARDEN, CHARDONNAY, 2002: Light gold in color, this complex, medium to full-bodied oak-aged white offers up abundant pear, spice, hazelnut and citrus flavors, as well as hints of minerals, spicy oak and earth on the finish. Drink up. Score 90. **K**

YARDEN, CHARDONNAY, 2001: Medium to full-bodied, aged *sur lie* for seven months in partly new, partly old French *barriques*, this tempting light golden wine shows excellent balance between wood, natural acidity and fruits. Notable pear aromas and flavors yield comfortably to apples, lightly toasted bread and vanilla. Drink up. Score 89. **K**

YARDEN, CHARDONNAY, 2000: Smooth and rich, this medium to full-bodied white shows subtle pear, fig and citrus aromas and flavors along with the barest hints of butter and spices, and an appealing overlay of smoke imparted by the oak barrels in which it aged for seven months. Not for further cellaring. Drink up. Score 89. **K**

YARDEN, CHARDONNAY, 1999: Subtle and delicious, this deep golden colored wine has lovely spice and butterscotch aromas, all on a solid core of apple, quince and pear flavors. Well balanced and bordering on elegance. A bit past its peak. Drink up. Score 86. **K**

YARDEN, SAUVIGNON BLANC, 2005: Well-balanced and aromatic, with a personality bursting with spices, herbs and peppery wood, those matched nicely by pear, apple, melon and mineral aromas and flavors. Drink now. Score 89. **K**

YARDEN, SAUVIGNON BLANC, 2004: Light straw in color, medium-bodied, with straightforward aromas and flavors of lemon and lime and ripe peaches. Marred somewhat by unwanted hints of bitterness and earthiness that develop on the palate. Drink up. Score 85. **K**

YARDEN, SAUVIGNON BLANC, 2003: Not showing as well now as during earlier tastings. Straw-colored, medium-bodied, with muted tropical fruit aromas and flavors and what many will perceive as personality that is crisply dry but somewhat flat. Drink up. Score 85. **K**

YARDEN, VIOGNIER, 2005: Medium-bodied, ripe, lively and generous, combining spicy and floral notes nicely with nectarine, peach and kiwi fruits and with an intriguing hint of oak on the finish. Rich, concentrated and long. Drink from release–2008. Tentative Score 89–91. **K**

YARDEN, VIOGNIER, 2004: Round, ripe and lightly floral, aged partly in oak, with classic Viognier litchi, apricot and lime aromas and set off by hints of coconut, with a gentle spiciness. Harmonious, lively, long, and complex. Drink now. Score 91. K

YARDEN, VIOGNIER, 2003: The winery's first Viognier, released only in limited quantities. Fermented partly in new oak and partly in stainless steel, this medium-bodied rich and ripe wine shows spring flowers, vanilla, and orange blossoms on a background of pineapple, nectarine and apricots, all complemented by lively acidity. Drink up. Score 88. K

YARDEN, MOUNT HERMON WHITE, 2005: Medium-bodied, a simple entry-level dry wine with citrus and pineapple fruits. Drink now. Score 82. K

YARDEN, MOUNT HERMON WHITE, 2004: An unoaked blend of Chardonnay, Sauvignon Blanc and a small amount of Semillon that shows light spiciness and pleasant aromas and flavors of citrus and tropical fruits. An entry-level wine. Drink up. Score 83. K

YARDEN, JOHANNISBERG RIESLING, 2003: Medium-bodied, semi-dry, with a light golden-straw color and appealing summer fruits well balanced by good acidity. On the moderately-long finish look for green apples and a hint of spiciness. Drink up. Score 87. K

YARDEN, JOHANNISBERG RIESLING, 2002: Pale yellow toward gold in color, this medium-bodied semi-dry wine shows appealing aromas and flavors of peaches and apricots along with a long mineral laden finish. Plenty of natural acidity setting off the light sweetness makes it a good choice as an aperitif. Drink now. Score 89. K

YARDEN, JOHANNISBERG RIESLING, 2001: Even though this wine is categorized as semi-dry, it has just the barest hint of sweetness on the palate. Lively, well balanced and delicious, the wine has tempting aromas and flavors of peaches, apples and citrus. Drink up. Score 87. K

YARDEN, GEWURZTRAMINER, 2005: Silky and spicy on the palate, with grapefruit, summer fruits and spices. Medium-dry, with an appealing hint of rose petals on the finish. Drink now–2008. Score 86. K

YARDEN, GEWURZTRAMINER, 2004: Perhaps the most representative Gewurztraminer released by the winery, semi-dry but crisp, medium-bodied but mouthfilling, with traditional litchi and tropical fruits set off nicely by an appealing spiciness. Well balanced and generous. Drink now. Score 88. K

YARDEN, GEWURZTRAMINER, 2003: An appealing semi-dry, medium-bodied white with litchi, summer fruits and spices but lacking the acidity that might have made it more refreshing. Best as an aperitif. Drink now. Score 86. K

YARDEN, NOBLE SEMILLON, BOTRYTIS, 2004: Golden in color, with fine concentration and balance and developing deep honeyed botrytis-impacted spices and funkiness. On the nose and palate dried apricots, orange peel, toasty oak, and tropical fruits that come in towards the long caressing finish. Drink from release–2018. Score 92. K

YARDEN, NOBLE SEMILLON, BOTRYTIS, 2003: Deep and rich, with a concentrated personality of citrus peel, honeyed peaches, botrytis spice. Generously sweet, with fine balancing acidity and a long sweet and caressing finish on which tropical fruits and butterscotch arise. Drink now–2015. Score 91. K

YARDEN, NOBLE SEMILLON, BOTRYTIS, 2002: Golden towards subdued orange in color, medium to full-bodied and showing generous botrytis influence. Honeyed sweetness complemented nicely by aromas and flavors of orange peel and apricots. Soft, round and creamy on the palate, with good balancing acidity and hints of heather and white pepper on the moderately-long finish. Drink now–2015. Score 90. K

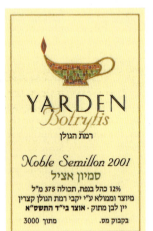

YARDEN, NOBLE SEMILLON, BOTRYTIS, 2001: This lively golden medium-bodied dessert white offers up unabashed honeyed sweetness along with aromas and flavors of orange marmalade, pineapple and ripe apricots that meld comfortably into a soft, almost creamy texture. Plenty of balancing natural acidity and a medium-long finish boasting hints of spring flowers and spices. Promises to darken and attain greater complexity and depth in the future. Drink now–2012. Score 90. K

YARDEN, HEIGHTSWINE, 2003: As always, a tantalizing dessert wine, light to medium-bodied with delicate honeyed apricot and peach aromas and flavors, good balancing acidity and an elegantly lingering finish. Drink now–2008. Score 90. K

YARDEN, HEIGHTSWINE, 2002: Light gold in color, medium-bodied, and with excellent balance. Plenty of natural acidity to back up the sweetness and keep it lively while allowing the peach, apricot, and quince fruits to make themselves nicely felt. Honeyed and floral, generous and round. Drink now–2008. Score 90. K

YARDEN, HEIGHTSWINE, 2001: Well balanced, generous and elegant, this honeyed dessert wine is made entirely from Gewurztraminer grapes treated to sub-freezing temperatures at the winery. It has a lively golden color and offers up a generous array of yellow peaches, apricots, melon, orange marmalade and quince, all on a floral and just spicy enough background. Drink now–2008. Score 91. K

YARDEN, HEIGHTSWINE, 2000: Well chilled, this delicious sweet wine reveals honeyed flavors of pears and quince. Let it warm in the glass and you will feel ripe apricots and white peaches. Let it linger on the palate and you will sense kiwi, pineapple and other tropical fruits. Made entirely from Gewurztraminer grapes, the wine is well balanced by plenty of natural acidity. Drink now. Score 92. K

YARDEN, HEIGHTSWINE, 1999: Unlike German or Canadian ice wines, in which grapes are allowed to freeze on the vine, the Gewurztraminer grapes used in this wine were frozen at the winery. The result is a sweet, almost thick mineral-rich dessert wine packed with aromas of peaches, apples, mangoes and pineapple that sit very comfortably on the palate. Drink now. Score 88. K

YARDEN, HEIGHTSWINE, 1998: Showing 40% sugar content to the pressed grape juice, this pleasingly sweet dessert wine offers up aromas and flavors of ripe peaches, apricots and tropical fruits. Drink up. Score 88. K

YARDEN, MUSCAT DESSERT WINE, 2003: Reinforced lightly with brandy, this floral wine shows tempting aromas and flavors of citrus and summer fruits. Good balance between generous sweetness, acidity and fruits. Drink now. Score 87. K

YARDEN, MUSCAT DESSERT WINE, 2002: Lightly reinforced with brandy, a floral wine, rich with citrus peel, pineapple and white peach aromas and flavors. Smooth and round, with generous sweetness and good balancing acidity to keep it fresh and lively. Drink now. Score 87. K

YARDEN, BLANC DE BLANCS, 1999: Made by the traditional *methode Champenoise*, just yeasty enough to enchant, with rich citrus, peach and tropical fruits along with a hint of mineral crispness. Sharp bubbles, a long mousse and a long and tempting near-creamy finish. Drink now–2009. Score 90. K

YARDEN, BLANC DE BLANCS, 1998: Ripe and vibrant with crisp apple and citrus aromas and flavors along with hints of vanilla, toasted white bread and nuts. The mousse is somewhat short but the bubbles are long-lasting and the lingering nutty-grapefruit finish lingers nicely. Drink now. Score 90. K

YARDEN, BLANC DE BLANCS, 1997: Made entirely from Chardonnay grapes in the traditional *Champenoise* method, this lovely and sophisticated sparkling wine has just the right hint of yeast on a background of delicious citrus, white peach, spring flowers and mint. Sharp, concentrated bubbles, a long lasting mousse and a lingering nutty finish. Drink now. Score 90. K

YARDEN, BLANC DE BLANCS, 1996: Made entirely from Chardonnay grapes, this medium-bodied sparkling wine is simultaneously rich and subdued. With concentrated long-lasting bubbles, a bouquet of dried and exotic fruits, spring flowers and the barest hints of coffee beans and herbs, this remains a refined, fresh and vibrant wine. Drink now. Score 91. K

YARDEN, BRUT, N.V.: Made in the traditional *Champenoise* method from a blend of Chardonnay and Pinot Noir grapes, this wine shows good balance, an abundance of citrus and white peach fruits, nutty flavors, just the right hints of yeast and sharp, long-lasting bubbles. Score 89. K

YARDEN, LATE HARVEST SAUVIGNON BLANC, 1988: Not many bottles are left, and not many of those are still drinking well, but a wine memorable for its past greatness. At its best the wine earned 94 points. K

Gamla

GAMLA, CABERNET SAUVIGNON, 2004: As in the past, a traditional Bordeaux blend, medium-bodied, with good balance between tannins, spicy oak and currant and berry fruits, those matched nicely by hints of spices on the moderately long finish. Drink now–2008. Score 87. K

GAMLA, CABERNET SAUVIGNON 2003: Always reliable, this oak aged medium to full-bodied blend of Cabernet Sauvignon, Cabernet Franc and one percent of Malbec shows good balance between tannins, wood and black fruits, all with hints of vanilla and an appealing spicy finish. Drink now. Score 87. K

GAMLA, CABERNET SAUVIGNON, 2002: The usual Bordeaux blend of Cabernet Sauvignon, Merlot and Cabernet Franc. Medium to full-bodied, a gentle touch of oak, soft tannins and with appealing blackcurrant, blackberry and vanilla aromas and flavors. Drink up. Score 87. K

GAMLA, CABERNET SAUVIGNON, 2001: This Bordeaux blend of Cabernet Sauvignon, Merlot and Cabernet Franc was oaked for about 12 months. Medium to full-bodied with soft tannins, generous currant and berry fruits and hints of spices and vanilla running throughout. On the moderately-long finish, light earthy overtones. Drink now. Score 87. K

GAMLA, CABERNET SAUVIGNON, 2000: A Bordeaux blend of 85% Cabernet Sauvignon, 11% Merlot and 4% Cabernet Franc, this medium to full-bodied red was aged for 12 months in oak and is now showing tempting currant, berries and black cherry fruits along with light vanilla and spicy overtones imparted by wood and a long, lightly spicy finish. Drink up. Score 87. K

GAMLA, CABERNET SAUVIGNON, 1999: A blend of 85% Cabernet Sauvignon, 12% Merlot and 3% Cabernet Franc, this deep red, medium to full-bodied wine spent one year in small oak barrels and is now showing appealing red fruit, currant and herbal notes, those overlaid by vanilla and white pepper. Drink up. Score 87. K

GAMLA, MERLOT, 2003: Deep garnet, medium to full-bodied, with still firm tannins but with balance and structure that bode well for the future. Generous berry, currant and plum fruits here, with overlays of sweet cedar, hints of milk chocolate and an appealing herbaceous overlay. Drink now–2009. Score 89. K

GAMLA, MERLOT, 2002: Dark ruby towards garnet, medium to full-bodied, with tannins well-balanced by spicy wood, black plum and wild berry fruits. Not overly complex. Drink up. Score 85. K

GAMLA, MERLOT, 2001: Elegant, well balanced and supple, this deep garnet medium-bodied wine offers up tempting berry and plum fruits, those complemented nicely by aromas and flavors of milk chocolate, vanilla and sweet cedar wood. Drink now. Score 89. K

GAMLA, MERLOT, 2000: Lean and with still-taut tannins, this deep royal purple toward garnet wine is more in the country-style than one usually anticipates from the Golan Heights Winery. Somewhat coarse and earthy, the wine shows plenty of plum and blackberries, and hints of orange peel and mint to carry it. Drink now. Score 87. K

GAMLA, MERLOT, 1999: This medium-bodied garnet to purple blend of 93% Merlot and 7% Cabernet Sauvignon was aged for 9 months in small oak barrels and shows plenty of black fruit and currants. Drink up. Score 86. K

GAMLA, PINOT NOIR, 2004: Cherry red, medium-bodied, lightly oaked with berry, black cherry and floral aromas. Soft, round tannins integrating nicely leading to a medium-long and generously fruity finish. Score 87. K

GAMLA, PINOT NOIR, 2003: Dark cherry red towards garnet, medium-bodied, reflecting its 7 months in oak with a hint of spicy wood. Well-balanced, smooth and ripe, with cherry, raspberry and cola aromas and flavors on a lightly spicy background. Long and rich, with soft, well-integrated tannins. Drink now. Score 88. K

GAMLA, PINOT NOIR, 2002: Light colored and medium-bodied, this smooth wine shows aromas and flavors of currants, berries and spring flowers as well as gentle overlays of oak and a hint of chocolate on the finish. Drink now. Score 86. K

GOLAN HEIGHTS WINERY

GAMLA, SANGIOVESE, 2005: Tempting aromas and flavors of sweet oak, berry and tea, those on a full-bodied and chewy background with a medium-long finish. Drink from release. Tentative Score 88–90. **K**

GAMLA, SANGIOVESE, 2004: Showing firm tannins, those integrating nicely, and appealing berry and black cherry fruits along with generous hints of licorice, chocolate and spicy oak. Drink now–2008. Score 87. **K**

GAMLA, SANGIOVESE, 2003: Dark garnet in color, medium-bodied, with soft tannins integrating nicely, and appealing spicy plum, berry and violet aromas and flavors. Soft, round, moderately long and although lacking great complexity, very appealing. Drink now–2008. Score 89. **K**

GAMLA, SANGIOVESE, 2002: Surprisingly concentrated considering the vintage. Dark, deep and rich with intense berry and black cherry fruits, smoky aromas and flavors. Medium to full-bodied with fine tannins and a long finish. Drink now. Score 88. **K**

GAMLA, SANGIOVESE, 2001: Dark garnet in color, with a hint of browning at the edges, but still showing nicely, the tannins well-integrated and offering ripe plum and currant fruits. Showing more distinct hints of tobacco and sweet oak and not meant for further cellaring. Drink up. Score 85. **K**

GAMLA, SANGIOVESE, 2000: A blend of 85% Sangiovese and 15% Cabernet Sauvignon, medium-bodied and oak-aged. Showing blackberries, chocolate and cinnamon along with distinctive and generous hints of black cherries and sage, smooth tannins, good overall balance, and a long finish highlighted by hints of mocha. Drink up. Score 88. **K**

GAMLA, CHARDONNAY, 2005: Tempting citrus, summer fruits and light spices on a crisp, mineral-rich background. Drink now. Score 87. **K**

GAMLA, CHARDONNAY, 2004: Light gold, medium-bodied, with generous summer fruit, citrus and citrus flower aromas and flavors, those on a lightly spicy background. Good balancing acidity to keep it lively. Drink now. Score 87. **K**

GAMLA, CHARDONNAY, 2003: Medium-bodied, with appealing citrus, summer fruit and mineral aromas and flavors. Drink now. Score 87. **K**

GAMLA, CHARDONNAY, 2002: Light golden straw in color, medium-bodied, with refreshing natural acidity and appealing peach, pineapple and tropical fruits. Not a complex wine but a very pleasing one. Drink up. Score 85. **K**

GAMLA, SAUVIGNON BLANC, 2005: Fresh and crisp, with minerals and a hint of citrus peel leading to rich melon, citrus and tropical fruit aromas and flavors. Drink now. Score 87. **K**

GAMLA, SAUVIGNON BLANC, 2004: Light straw in color, medium-bodied, with appealing pear, tropical fruit and melon flavors, those with a nice hint of spiciness and a light herbaceousness. Drink now. Score 87. **K**

GAMLA, SAUVIGNON BLANC, 2003: Light golden straw colored, medium-bodied, with generous aromas and flavors of tropical fruit, melon and a light overlay of grassiness. Good balancing acidity makes for a refreshing drink. Drink up. Score 86. **K**

GAMLA, WHITE RIESLING, 2004: Frankly sweet even though categorized as semi-dry, the wine has enough natural acidity to keep it lively and to highlight tempting citrus, pineapple and apricot flavors. Look for a hint of mint on the moderately-long finish. Drink now. Score 87. **K**

Golan

GOLAN, CABERNET SAUVIGNON, 2004: Dark ruby red, medium-bodied, with soft tannins and only the gentlest hint of wood. Fresh and fruity, with currant and berry fruits. Drink now. Score 85. **K**

GOLAN, CABERNET SAUVIGNON, 2003: Ruby red towards purple in color, medium-bodied, with bare hints of oak and soft, well-integrated tannins and appealing spicy cherry-berry aromas and flavors. A nice quaffer. Drink up. Score 86. **K**

GOLAN, CABERNET SAUVIGNON, 2002: Made entirely from Cabernet Sauvignon grapes and aged in American oak for six months, this medium-bodied red boasts soft tannins and tempting berry, currant and plum fruits, along with hints of spices and vanilla. Drink up. Score 87. **K**

GOLAN, MERLOT, 2004: The first Merlot release in the Golan series. Nothing overly complex here and not a wine meant for cellaring but pleasant, medium-bodied, with soft tannins and lively plum, currant and berry fruits, those on a lightly spicy background. Drink now. Score 85. K

GOLAN, GAMAY NOUVEAU, 2005: Made from Gamay Noir grapes, treated to carbonic maceration and bottled within weeks after completion of the harvest. Light in body, lively dark cherry towards purple in color, with scarce tannins and an abundance of wild berry, cherry, and even citrus peel and apple aromas and flavors. Drink up. Score 85. K

GOLAN, SION CREEK, RED, 2005: Light to medium-bodied, with almost unfelt tannins and fruity enough to make one think more of fruit-juice than of fine wine. Drink up Score 80. K

GOLAN, SION CREEK, RED, 2004: A simple entry-level wine, light to medium-bodied, with soft tannins, a floral aroma and a berry-cherry personality. Drink up. Score 80. K

GOLAN, CHARDONNAY, 2004: As always, a lively, clean and refreshing wine, medium-bodied with aromas of citrus, citrus peel and green apples. Drink now. Score 86. K

GOLAN, CHARDONNAY, 2003: Clean, crisp and refreshing, medium-bodied, with aromas and flavors of green apples, citrus and spring flowers. Drink up. Score 85. K

GOLAN, SION CREEK, WHITE, 2004: A light to medium-bodied potpourri of white grapes with citrus, pineapple aromas and flavors. Drink up. Score 80. K

GOLAN, SION CREEK, WHITE, 2003: A rather unlikely blend of Sauvignon Blanc, Gewurztraminer, Johannisberg Riesling and Muscat of Alexandria, this semi-dry white shows tropical fruits and pineapple aromas and flavors. Drink up. Score 79. K

GOLAN, MOSCATO, 2005: As it has been since 1999, light, fresh, lightly *frizzante*, generously sweet but with good balancing acidity and appealing pineapple, lemon and lime aromas and flavors. A simple but fun wine. Drink up. Score 86. K

GOLAN, MOSCATO, 2004: Fresh, lightly alcoholic, just barely *frizzante* in the style of Moscato d'Asti. Generously sweet but with good natural acidity to keep it lively and appealing, with pineapple, melon, and citrus flavors. Drink up. Score 87. K

GOLAN, EMERALD RIESLING, 2004: As to be anticipated with this grape, half-dry, floral and fruity. Drink up. Score 80. K

Greenberg ★★★

Located in the town of Herzliya Pituach, not far from Tel Aviv, this micro-winery owned by Motti Greenberg is now producing about 750 bottles annually. First wines were released from the 2003 vintage, using Cabernet Sauvignon, Merlot and Shiraz grapes from the Karmei Yosef vineyards at the foothills of the Jerusalem Mountains.

GREENBERG, CABERNET SAUVIGNON, 2004: Medium-bodied, with still firm tannins and generous smoky oak, those opening in the glass to reveal currant, black cherry and berry fruits on a light vanilla background. Drink now–2008. Score 87.

GREENBERG, CABERNET SAUVIGNON, 2003: Deep garnet toward purple, this medium to full-bodied red is a fine first effort, the wine showing generous but well integrating tannins, and blackcurrant and wild berry fruits with moderate overlays of spicy oak, vanilla and a light herbaceousness. Drink now. Score 86.

GREENBERG, MERLOT, 2004: Medium to full-bodied, with soft tannins integrating nicely and light spicy wood highlighting currant, berry and citrus peel aromas and flavors. Drink now–2008. Score 86.

GREENBERG, MERLOT, 2003: Medium-bodied, with soft, sweet tannins. Blackberry and cherry fruits are complemented nicely by spiciness and hints of vanilla and eucalyptus. Drink now. Score 87.

GREENBERG, SHIRAZ, 2004: Dark cloudy garnet red, this medium-bodied wine shows black fruits and light earthy aromas and flavors that linger nicely. Drink now. Score 86.

GREENBERG, SHIRAZ, 2003: This tempting medium-bodied wine shows floral and earthy aromas and flavors matched well by moderate tannins, wood and appealing black fruits. Mouthfilling and long. Drink now. Score 87.

GREENBERG, ANIN, 2004: A medium-bodied, dark garnet towards royal purple blend of 50% Merlot and 25% each of Shiraz and Cabernet Sauvignon. Soft, well-integrated tannins highlight forward berry, black cherry and cassis aromas, those with an appealing spicy hint on the finish. Drink now–2008. Score 87.

Gush Etzion ✯✯✯

Located at the Gush Etzion Junction near Jerusalem and owned largely by vintner Shraga Rozenberg and partly by the Tishbi family, the winery has its own vineyards in the Jerusalem Mountains, those with Cabernet Sauvignon, Merlot, Pinot Noir, Shiraz, Cabernet Franc and Petit Verdot as well as Chardonnay, Viognier and Johannisberg Riesling grapes. The winery released its first wines, 3,000 bottles, in 1998 and currently produces about 30,000 bottles annually. A new winery is now under construction with the potential for future production of up to 100,000 bottles.

GUSH ETZION, CABERNET SAUVIGNON, 2002: Deep royal purple in color, full-bodied, with generous soft tannins and spicy oak well balanced by ripe currants and cassis. Appealing overlays of chocolate and tobacco on the long finish. Drink now–2008. Score 88. K

GUSH ETZION, CABERNET SAUVIGNON, 2001: Dark, almost inky garnet toward royal purple, this full-bodied wine shows excellent balance between generous but soft tannins, just the right touch of smoky-spicy oak and elegant blackcurrant and wild berry fruits and spices along with Mediterranean herbs and green olives coming in toward the finish. Drink now–2008. Score 87. K

GUSH ETZION, CABERNET SAUVIGNON, 2000: Deep ruby medium to full-bodied wine with generous tannins and wood blending well with currant, plum and herbal aromas and flavors. Look for light hints of spices and smoky wood as well. Drink now. Score 86. K

GUSH ETZION, CABERNET SAUVIGNON, 1999: Aged in new oak barrels for 12 months, this medium-bodied, hearty, somewhat herbal and now fully mature wine yields appealing plum, black cherry and olive flavors, and has a lightly smoky character. Drink up. Score 86. K

GUSH ETZION, CABERNET SAUVIGNON-MERLOT, 2000: Medium to full-bodied, this country-style wine shows chunky tannins, plenty of wood, plum and black cherry fruits, all with hints of dill and other Mediterranean herbs. Drink now. Score 85. K

GUSH ETZION, CHARDONNAY 2005: Light-straw colored, this unoaked white shows tempting tropical and citrus fruits on a light mineral background. Fresh, crisp and refreshing. Drink now. Score 86. K

GUSH ETZION, CHARDONNAY, ORGANIC, 2003: Light golden straw in color, medium-bodied, with generous balancing acidity and apple and peach fruits. Lightly *frizzante* which may indicate that a second fermentation is taking place in the bottle and with a somewhat odd spearmint flavor. Drink up. Score 85. K

GUSH ETZION, CHARDONNAY, 2002: Golden colored, this ripe and full flavored wine shows a pleasant earthy accent to its pineapple, hazelnut and citrus aromas and flavors as well as a surprisingly long and complex finish. Past its peak. Drink up. Score 88. K

GUSH ETZION, CHARDONNAY, 2001: Clean, ripe and fruity, the wine has a solid core of pear, apple and melon flavors as well as hints of spices that linger nicely on the palate. Drink up. Score 87. K

GUSH ETZION, DESSERT WINE, 2000: This blend of organically raised Chardonnay and Sauvignon Blanc grapes spent 8 months in small oak barrels. Deep gold toward orange in color, this wine is markedly sweet and has plenty of natural acids. Drink up. Score 85. K

Gustavo & Jo ✶✶✶✶

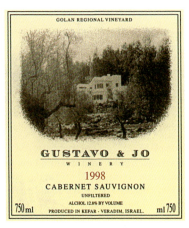

Located in the village of Kfar Vradim in the Western Galilee, and drawing on grapes from the Golan Heights and the Upper Galilee, this small winery was founded in 1995 by Gideon Boinjeau and produced only Cabernet Sauvignon wines until the release of a first white in 2005. Production of two series, Premium and Gustavo & Jo, averages 3,000 bottles annually, with a future target of 10,000 bottles. Starting with the 2006 vintage all the wines will be kosher.

Premium

PREMIUM, CABERNET SAUVIGNON, 2003: Dark garnet towards black in color and full-bodied, with firm tannins integrating nicely, those well balanced by spicy wood and blackcurrant, blackberry and cassis fruits all on a background of minty-chocolate. Long and complex. Best 2008–2012. Score 91.

PREMIUM, CABERNET SAUVIGNON, 2002: Deep garnet towards black in color and full-bodied, with still firm but well-integrating tannins. Excellent balance between wood, tannins and an appealing array of black and red fruits, those yielding to spices, chocolate and mint. Long and complex. Drink now–2012. Score 91

PREMIUM, CABERNET SAUVIGNON, 2001: Full-bodied, with once firm tannins now integrating nicely and continuing to show the fine balance and structure of its youth. On the nose and palate currant, black cherry and plum fruits, those backed up nicely by hints of Mediterranean herbs and a gentle overlay of mint. Drink now. Score 91.

PREMIUM, CABERNET SAUVIGNON, 2000: Full-bodied and with its once firm tannins now well integrated, the wine reveals a complex set of aromas and flavors that include currants, wild berries, leather and spices. Deep, rich, and bordering on elegance. Drink now. Score 90.

Gustavo & Jo

GUSTAVO & JO, CABERNET SAUVIGNON, 2004: Medium-dark garnet in color, with grapes primarily from the Upper Galilee, this spicy, generously oaked and tannic wine shows fine balance and structure and appealing black fruits. Hints of licorice and green olives come together nicely on a long and mouthfilling finish. Best 2008–2013. Tentative Score 89–91.

GUSTAVO & JO, CABERNET SAUVIGNON, 2003: Dark garnet towards black, full-bodied, with still firm tannins well balanced by spicy wood and blackcurrant, blackberry and cassis fruits all on a background of minty-chocolate. Long and complex. Drink from release–2010. Tentative Score 89–91.

GUSTAVO & JO, CABERNET SAUVIGNON, 2002: This deep inky purple full-bodied still young red has firm, somewhat tight tannins and a tempting array of currant and black cherry fruits, those coming together nicely with spicy oak, eucalyptus and generous hints of chocolate and tobacco on the long finish. Long, complex and mouth-filling. Drink now–2008. Score 89.

GUSTAVO & JO, CABERNET SAUVIGNON, 2001: Dark purple toward garnet, full-bodied, with distinct Cabernet aromas and flavors including blackcurrants, black cherries, and a generous hint of mint on firm but well-integrated tannins, the wine shows good balance between wood and tannins and has a long appealing herbal finish. Drink now–2008. Score 89.

GUSTAVO & JO, CABERNET SAUVIGNON, 2000: Full-bodied, well rounded, with already soft tannins and good blackcurrant, plum and cherry aromas and flavors that linger very nicely on the palate, the wine also shows an appealing overlay of oak. Drink now. Score 89.

GUSTAVO & JO, CABERNET SAUVIGNON, 1999: Deep, almost impenetrable garnet in color, full-bodied, with now silky soft tannins and a ripe and complex core of currants, berries, leather and spices. On the long finish hints of dried herbs and espresso coffee. Drink now. Score 89.

GUSTAVO & JO, CABERNET SAUVIGNON, 1998: Medium to full-bodied, with fine balance between gently spicy, smoky wood and now silky smooth tannins. With still youthful blackcurrant and berry fruits, those matched by appealing olive and earthy streaks that run through to the long finish. Drink now. Score 90.

GUSTAVO & JO, CABERNET SAUVIGNON, 1997: Full bodied and complex but now moving gracefully from maturity to old-age. Tannins fully integrated, showing some appealing blackcurrant and berry flavors but those turning a bit acidic after a short while in the glass. Drink up. Score 88.

GUSTAVO & JO, FUMÉ BLANC, SHANI, 2005: Developed partly in stainless steel, partly in 300 liter Burgundy-style barrels, this medium to full-bodied, light-golden Sauvignon Blanc based wine combines grassiness and a hint of New Zealand style cat's pee together with Loire Valley crispness and fruitiness. Refreshing and easy to drink but still complex. Drink now–2008. Score 89.

Hakerem ✶✶

Founded in 2001 by Isaac Herskovitz and located in Beit-El near Hebron, this winery produces unoaked Cabernet Sauvignon and Merlot wines, drawing on grapes from various vineyards. Annual production is currently about 12,000 bottles.

HAKEREM, CABERNET SAUVIGNON, 2004: Deep ruby towards garnet in color, medium-bodied, with firm tannins and too generous hints of spicy oak and earthiness with aromas and flavors of currants and black cherries. Drink now. Score 84. **K**

HAKEREM, CABERNET SAUVIGNON, 2003: Medium-bodied, with soft, nicely integrated tannins and plum, cherry, berry and spice notes, this smooth wine ends with an appealing fruity finish. Drink now. Score 86. **K**

HAKEREM, CABERNET SAUVIGNON, 2002: Maturing now, its once dark garnet color now with generous hints of adobe brick, this medium to full-bodied oak-aged wine shows softened tannins and generous vanilla and smoky aromas and flavors, those well balanced by black fruits and hints of herbs and tobacco. Drink up. Score 86. **K**

HAKEREM, MERLOT, 2004: Medium-bodied, with plum, berry and currant fruits but marred by unclean earthy overtones, the wine is somewhat one dimensional. Drink up. Score 80. **K**

HAKEREM, MERLOT, 2003: Dark garnet toward purple in color, this medium-bodied, gently oaked wine shows good balance between soft tannins and ripe berry and currant fruits, along with a nice herbal-spicy finish. Drink now–2008. Score 86. **K**

Hamasrek ✶✶

Established by brothers Nachum and Hanoch Greengrass in 1999 on Moshav Beit Meir in the Jerusalem Mountains, this kosher boutique winery draws on grapes from their own area as well as from Zichron Ya'akov and the Upper Galilee. In 2000 the winery released 5,000 bottles of Merlot and Chardonnay and since then the winery has added Cabernet

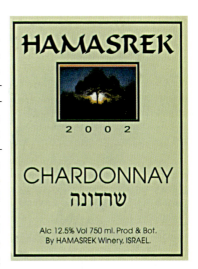

Sauvignon and Gewurztraminer to their line. Current production is about 20,000 bottles.

HAMASREK, CABERNET SAUVIGNON, 2003: Deep ruby towards garnet, medium to full-bodied, with firm tannins and generous wood but those yielding nicely to show blackcurrant and plum fruits on a lightly spicy background. Drink now. Score 86. **K**

HAMASREK, CABERNET SAUVIGNON, 2002: Dark garnet toward purple, medium to full-bodied with generous oak and firm tannins that tend to hide the currant and plum fruits. Somewhat one-dimensional. Drink up. Score 83. **K**

HAMASREK, CABERNET SAUVIGNON, 2001: Now mature and showing first signs of browning, this medium to full-bodied wine was developed in French oak for 19 months. Generous dusty, smoky oak, that balanced nicely by soft tannins and appealing currant and berry fruits. Drink up. Score 85. **K**

HAMASREK, MERLOT, 2003: Made entirely from Merlot grapes, reflecting its 18 months in *barriques* with dusty-smoky oak, and under that currant and blackberry flavors that never quite make it to the surface. Drink now. Score 83. **K**

HAMASREK, MERLOT, 2002: Dark royal purple, medium-bodied and with soft, well-integrating tannins opening to reveal generous blackberry, black cherry and cassis aromas and flavors. Drink now. Score 86. K

HAMASREK, MERLOT, 2001: Aged in French oak for 18 months, this deep purple, medium-bodied red has generous but well-integrated tannins and appealing berry, currant and herbal flavors and aromas. Drink up. Score 85. K

HAMASREK, MERLOT, 2000: Made entirely from Merlot grapes, this deep purple, medium-bodied, country-style wine had soft tannins, light earthy overtones and aromas and flavors of currants and mint in its youth, but now past its peak. Drink up. Score 80. K

HAMASREK, THE KING'S BLEND, LIMITED EDITION, JUDEAN HILLS, N.V.: A blend of Cabernet Sauvignon, Merlot and Zinfandel grapes from the 2003 and 2004 vintage. Medium to full-bodied, with chunky tannins, a strong influence of the wood and only bare hints of black fruits. Flat and one-dimensional. Drink now. Score 80. K

HAMASREK, CHARDONNAY, 2004: Light golden in color, medium-bodied, with spicy oak that comes together nicely with aromas and flavors of citrus and tropical fruits. Drink now. Score 85. K

HAMASREK, CHARDONNAY, 2003: Golden-straw in color, medium-bodied, with buttery overtones from the generous oak treatment, that matched nicely by natural acidity and aromas and flavors of melon, pears and tropical fruits. Drink up. Score 86. K

HAMASREK, CHARDONNAY, 2002: Developed *sur lie* in oak barrels for eight months, this medium-bodied, light golden wine shows appealing pineapple, citrus and pear aromas and flavors along with generous oak. Past its peak. Drink up. Score 84. K

HAMASREK, GEWURZTRAMINER, 2004: Although defined as semi-sweet, the wine shows deep sweetness set off nicely by natural acidity. Rich and soft but not flabby, with aromas and flavors of spices, honey, litchis and peaches, all coming together in a long finish. Drink now. Score 88. K

Hans Sternbach **

Founded by Gadi and Shula Sternbach in Moshav Givat Yeshayahu in the Judean Hills, the winery's first release was of 1,800 bottles from the 2000 harvest. With a new winery located on the Moshav and relying primarily on Cabernet Sauvignon grapes from their own nearby vineyards, production from the 2003 vintage was about 3,000 bottles and from the 2004 and 2005 vintages about 10,000 bottles. The winery produces wines in three series: Janaba Reserve, Nachal Hakhlil and Emek Haella.

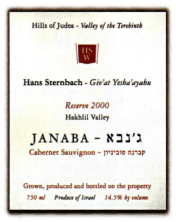

Janaba Reserve

JANABA RESERVE, CABERNET SAUVIGNON, HAKHLIL VALLEY, 2004: With firm, somewhat chunky tannins and generous spices from the oak casks in which it aged, those tending to overshadow elusive currant and blackberry fruits. Drink now–2008. Score 84.

JANABA RESERVE, CABERNET SAUVIGNON, HAKHLIL VALLEY, 2003: 100% Cabernet Sauvignon, this deep garnet towards royal purple, medium to full-bodied oak-aged red shows firm tannins that yield slowly to reveal blackcurrant and wild berry fruits. Marred somewhat by a bit of unwanted residual sugar. Drink now. Score 84.

JANABA RESERVE, CABERNET SAUVIGNON, HAKHLIL VALLEY, 2001: Aged in Bulgarian oak casks for 18 months, this dark cherry-red wine shows generous smoky and spicy oak, that well balanced by soft tannins, vanilla, and appealing currant, berry and black cherry fruits. Drink now. Score 85.

JANABA RESERVE, CABERNET SAUVIGNON, HAKHLIL VALLEY, 2000: Dark royal purple in color, medium to full-bodied, with firm tannins and a perhaps overly generous dose of wood, but with an array of currant, plum and berry fruits that open nicely in the glass. Drink now. Score 85.

Nachal Hakhlil

NACHAL HAKHLIL, CABERNET SAUVIGNON, 2003: Deep purple, medium to full-bodied, with firm, chunky tannins and aromas and flavors of currants and berries, this blend of 90% Cabernet Sauvignon and 10% Petite Sirah reflects its 12 months in oak with spicy and vanilla overtones. Drink now. Score 85.

Emek Haella

EMEK HAELLA, 2005: An unoaked blend of 80% Cabernet Sauvignon and 20% Merlot. Light in body, with soft tannins and berry-cherry fruits. A simple quaffer. Drink up. Score 81.

EMEK HAELLA, CABERNET SAUVIGNON, VALLELLA CLASSICO SUPERIORE, 2002: Like the Valpolicella Classico Superiore, this wine is also made by the *ripasso* method, but unfortunately, Cabernet Sauvignon grapes are not appropriate for the method. Light cherry colored, light to medium-bodied, the wine shows far too bitter overtones to the plum flavors that are here and therefore lacks balance. Drink up. Score 79.

Hatabor ★★

Located in the village of Kfar Tabor in the lower Galilee, this small winery was founded by Shimi Efrat in 1999 and released its first wines from the 2002 harvest. Grapes come primarily from nearby vineyards, and production is currently about 7,000 bottles annually with plans to expand to about 10,000.

HATABOR, CABERNET SAUVIGNON, 2003: Garnet towards purple in color, medium-bodied, with soft tannins and appealing currant, cassis and cherry fruits backed up nicely by a hint of spiciness. Drink now. Score 84.

HATABOR, CABERNET SAUVIGNON, 2002: Dark cherry-red toward garnet in color, medium-bodied, with moderately firm tannins and upfront berry, currant and cherry fruits. Drink now. Score 84.

HATABOR, MERLOT, 2002: Medium-bodied, with soft, well-integrated tannins and appealing berry and plum fruits set off by the hint of fresh herbs. A good quaffer. Drink now. Score 84.

HATABOR, CHARDONNAY, 2004: Golden straw in color, medium-bodied, with appealing citrus, tropical fruit and pear aromas and flavors. Drink now. Score 85.

HATABOR, CHARDONNAY, 2003: Light straw colored, medium-bodied, and with citrus, pineapple and melon flavors. Not traditional of Chardonnay but an acceptable quaffer. Drink up. Score 85.

HATABOR, SAUVIGNON BLANC, 2004: Light straw in color, light to medium-bodied, with crisp acidity backing up citrus and light grassy aromas and flavors. Drink now. Score 85.

HATABOR, SAUVIGNON BLANC, 2003: Light to medium-bodied, with refreshing litchi, melon and citrus aromas and flavors. Pleasant if not complex. Drink up. Score 80.

Hevron Heights ✴

Located in Kiryat Arba, not far from the heart of the city of Hebron, this winery was founded in 2001 by a group of French investors and initially produced about 150,000 bottles per year, the target audience being largely observant Jews abroad. The winery reports current production of about 600,000 bottles annually, and produces a line of varietal and blended wines of Cabernet Sauvignon, Merlot, French Colombard, Sauvignon Blanc, and Malbec grapes, drawing largely on grapes from the Judean Hills as well as vineyards near Hebron. The winery has a broad and somewhat confusing labeling system with a large number of series and brands including Hevron Heights, Noach, Hevron, Tevel, Efron's Cave, Shemesh, Pardess, Judea and Jerusalem Heights, some of which are also produced as private labels.

Hevron Heights

HEVRON HEIGHTS, CABERNET SAUVIGNON, SDEH CALEV, 2003: Deep garnet in color, medium to full-bodied, with soft tannins and currant and berry fruits matched nicely by hints of spices and mint. Drink now. Score 84. K

HEVRON HEIGHTS, CABERNET SAUVIGNON, JUDEAN HEIGHTS, 2002: Garnet towards royal-purple in color, medium to full-bodied, with firm, somewhat chunky country-style tannins opening in the glass to reveal currant, berry, and black cherry fruits. On the fruity finish look for hints of mint and cigar tobacco. Drink now. Score 83. K

HEVRON HEIGHTS, CABERNET SAUVIGNON, GIDEON, 2002: Dark inky purple in color and medium-bodied, the wine has chunky tannins, too much acidity and an overbearing influence of what appears to be oak. Over ripe and cloying. Drink up. Score 78. K

HEVRON HEIGHTS, CABERNET SAUVIGNON, ISAAC'S RAM, 2002: Medium-bodied, ruby towards garnet in color, with soft, near-sweet tannins and appealing berry, black cherry and currant fruits overlayed by hints of cigar tobacco and Oriental spices. Drink now. Score 84. K

HEVRON HEIGHTS, CABERNET SAUVIGNON, ISAAC'S RAM, 2001:
Deep but not clear garnet in color, this medium to full-bodied wine is packed with tannins and has such a high level of acidity that it makes the mouth pucker. Precious few fruits here; those present on a somewhat muddy background. Score 68. K

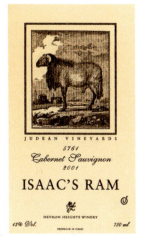

HEVRON HEIGHTS, MERLOT, JUDEAN HEIGHTS, 2002: Dark garnet in color, medium-bodied, with soft tannins, a judicious hand with wood and appealing black fruits backed up by light overlays of Mediterranean herbs and, on the finish, a hint of white chocolate. Drink now. Score 85. K

HEVRON HEIGHTS, MERLOT, PARDESS, 2002: Dark ruby towards garnet, medium bodied, with well integrated near-sweet tannins and appealing cassis, wild berry and citrus peel fruits, those supported by light hints of spices, tobacco and bittersweet chocolate. Drink now. Score 83. K

HEVRON HEIGHTS, MEGIDDO, 2002: The flagship wine of the winery, this unfiltered blend of Cabernet Sauvignon, Merlot and Syrah, aged in new French oak for 24 months and reflects that by a heavy dose of sweet and smoky wood. Gripping tannins that at least so far do not seem to integrate are hiding the currant, berry and very ripe plum flavors that are trying to make it to the surface. Drink up. Score 82. K

HEVRON HEIGHTS, SPECIAL RESERVE, 2001: A firmly tannic and far too oaked blend of Cabernet Sauvignon, Merlot and Shiraz. The vegetal and oak flavors dominate while the fruits never quite make it to the surface, and the wine lacks balance. Drink up. Score 72. K

HEVRON HEIGHTS, CABERNET-SAUVIGNON-MERLOT, JERUSALEM HEIGHTS, 2002: This unfiltered medium to full-bodied blend of 50% each Cabernet Sauvignon and Merlot, aged for 18 months in new American and French oak barrels, shows aromas and flavors of blackcurrants, wild berries and chocolate on a lightly spicy background. Drink now. Score 85. K

HEVRON HEIGHTS, TRIPLE RED, EFRON'S CAVE, 2003: Dark garnet in color, this medium-bodied, unoaked blend of one-third each Cabernet Sauvignon, Merlot and Syrah offers up soft tannins and forwards berry-cherry fruits. Drink up. Score 79. K

HEVRON HEIGHTS, TRIPLE PLUM, EFRON'S CAVE, 2003: A light to medium-bodied one dimensional blend of Cabernet Sauvignon, Merlot and Syrah (35%, 35% and 30% respectively) with forward plum and black cherry fruits. Drink up. Score 78. K

HEVRON HEIGHTS, VINYAMINA 160, N.V.: A half-dry red far too much like cough syrup in flavor and aromas. Score 60. K

HEVRON HEIGHTS, VILLAGE SUPERIOR, NOACH VILLAGES, N.V.: Dark cherry colored, light to medium-bodied, with far too ripe red fruits and unpleasant hints of bitterness and earthiness. Score 68. K

HEVRON HEIGHTS, CHARDONNAY, 2002: Too generously oaked and somewhat flat on the palate, this wine reveals only stingy pineapple and grapefruit flavors and none of the traits of Chardonnay. Drink up. Score 72. K

HEVRON HEIGHTS, SAUVIGNON BLANC FUMÉ, SHEMESH, 2004: Straw-colored, medium-bodied, with smoky oak and appealing citrus peel, tropical fruits, light herbal and grassy aromas and flavors. Not complex but pleasant. Drink now. Score 84. K

HEVRON HEIGHTS, MOSCATO, SHEMESH, 2004: Light lively golden straw in color, light in body, with moderate sweetness and distinctly floral on the nose and with an abundance of citrus and tropical fruits. Drink now. Score 83. K

HEVRON HEIGHTS, SAUVIGNON BLANC, SHEMESH, 2003: A wine that has gone wrong somewhere along the way, already going to brown and tasting more of vinegar than wine. Unscoreable. K

HEVRON HEIGHTS, WHITE, EFRON'S CAVE, 2003: Unoaked Sauvignon Blanc, light in color and body with refreshing citrus and herbal-mineral aromas and flavors. A simple entry-level wine. Drink up. Score 80. K

Noah

NOAH, CABERNET SAUVIGNON, TEVEL, 2004: Medium-bodied, with black cherry, blackberry, cedar and bell pepper notes along with a somewhat smoky oak finish. Drink now. Score 84. K

NOAH, CABERNET SAUVIGNON, TEVEL, 2002: Deep ruby towards garnet in color, with soft tannins and clean aromas and flavors of currants and raspberries. Not complex. Drink now. Score 82. K

NOAH, MERLOT, TEVEL, 2004: Medium-bodied, with super-soft tannins, bare hints of wood and generous berry, cherry and currant fruits. Drink now. Score 83. K

NOAH, MERLOT, TEVEL, 2002: Dark ruby towards garnet in color, medium-bodied, with chunky country-style tannins and generous wood. Appealing black fruits and a hint of tobacco here. Drink now. Score 84. K

NOAH, CABERNET SAUVIGNON-MERLOT, TEVEL, 2004: Medium-bodied, with soft tannins and gentle wood. On the nose and palate berry, black cherry and cassis fruits, those with hints of eucalyptus and espresso coffee. Drink now. Score 85. K

NOAH, CABERNET SAUVIGNON-MERLOT, TEVEL, 2002: Medium-bodied, with soft tannins and perhaps too generous acidity but with appealing aromas and flavors of currants and wild berries. Drink now. Score 83. K

NOAH, CABERNET-MERLOT, BLUSH WINE, MESSOPY, 2005: Dark-tinted pink, with raspberry, cassis, herbal and mineral aromas and flavors. Medium-bodied, somewhere between dry and off-dry. A good picnic wine. Drink up. Score 83. K

NOAH, PETITE SIRAH, GEDEON, 2005: Dark purple, medium-bodied, with chunky and somewhat coarse tannins, this distinct country-style wine shows skimpy berry and black cherry fruits, all with a not entirely wanted sweet aftertaste. Drink up. Score 78. K

NOAH, SAUVIGNON BLANC, TEVEL, 2005: Light to medium-bodied, with a few citrus and tropical fruits but with an unwanted hint of sweetness that will not be enjoyed by all. Drink now. Score 81. K

Kadesh Barnea *

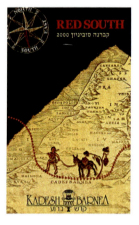

This Negev Desert winery was established in 1999 by Alon Tzadok on Moshav Kadesh Barnea and has its own vineyards near the ruins of the Byzantine city of Nitzana, near the Egyptian border. Releases to date have included only Cabernet Sauvignon and Merlot based wines and the winery is now developing further vineyards containing Petit Verdot and Shiraz grapes. Production for the 2004 and 2005 vintages was about 5,000 bottles and the wines have been kosher since the 2002 harvest.

KADESH BARNEA, CABERNET SAUVIGNON, RED SOUTH, 2004: Medium-bodied, with chunky tannins that seem not to want to integrate and only skimpy black fruits on a too herbal background. Drink from release. Tentative Score 80–82. K

KADESH BARNEA, CABERNET SAUVIGNON, RED SOUTH, 2003: Medium to full-bodied, firmly tannic, with hints of black cherry and plum fruits, those coming together with hints of green olives, herbs and chocolate. Drink now. Score 84. K

KADESH BARNEA, CABERNET SAUVIGNON, RED SOUTH, 2002: Medium-bodied, with tight tannins and green olive notes on the cherry and currant flavors along with hints of herbs. Drink up. Score 82. K

KADESH BARNEA, CABERNET SAUVIGNON, RED SOUTH, 2001: After 8 months in oak, this medium-bodied red is fairly stingy but has appealing currant, mineral and cedary oak aromas and flavors. Somewhat acidic and not a typical Cabernet. Drink up. Score 84.

KADESH BARNEA, CABERNET SAUVIGNON, RED SOUTH, 2000: Light to medium-bodied, with only modest hints of currant, cherry and berry fruits, along with hints of tea and rhubarb. Somewhat past its peak. Drink up. Score 79.

KADESH BARNEA, MERLOT, 2004: Medium-bodied, with chunky country-style tannins, and reflecting its 8 months in *barriques* with smoky and spicy oak. Look for aromas and flavors of black fruits and Mediterranean herbs. Drink now. Score 82. **K**

KADESH BARNEA, MERLOT, RED SOUTH, 2003: Generous black cherry, cedar and spice flavors but somewhat tannic and going sweet on the finish. Drink up. Score 80. **K**

KADESH BARNEA, CABERNET SAUVIGNON-MERLOT, GILAD, 2004: A medium-bodied blend of 50% each of Cabernet Sauvignon and Merlot. Sweet vanilla from the wood and near-sweet tannins here opening to reveal ripe plum and blackberry fruits. Drink now. Score 84. **K**

KADESH BARNEA, MERLOT-CABERNET SAUVIGNON, RED SOUTH, 2003: A pleasant if not distinctly country-style wine. Medium-bodied, with chunky tannins and showing an appealing berry-cherry personality, the fruits backed up nicely by hints of spiciness. Drink now. Score 84. **K**

Kadita ✶✶✶

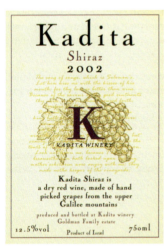

Jonathan Goldman made wines at his home in Bikta Bekadita in the Upper Galilee for several years before he released his first commercial output of 600 bottles in 2001, a blend of Cabernet Sauvignon and Merlot. Grapes are currently drawn from the winery's own nearby vineyards and from Kerem Ben Zimra. Production in 2004 and 2005 was 3,000 bottles.

KADITA, CABERNET SAUVIGNON, 2004: Youthful deep royal-purple in color, full-bodied, with generous soft tannins integrating nicely and concentrated black fruits, Mediterranean herbs, eucalyptus and hints of spicy cedar wood from the oak barrels. Long, concentrated and mouthfilling. Drink from release–2009. Tentative Score 88–90.

KADITA, CABERNET SAUVIGNON, 2003: A blend of grapes from two vineyards, one with volcanic soil, one with red soil, this still youthful deep royal-purple wine shows full body, firm tannins promising to integrate nicely and a tempting array of blackcurrant and wild berry fruits, those on a long, spicy tobacco and chocolate finish. Drink now–2009. Score 89.

KADITA, MERLOT, 2004: Full-bodied and aromatic, with firm but already well-integrating tannins and even at this early stage showing a tempting array of blueberry, raspberry and purple plum fruits, those on a background of chocolate and Mediterranean herbs. Drink from release–2008. Tentative Score 88–90.

KADITA, MERLOT, 2003: Full-bodied, concentrated, and intense, with generous soft tannins well balanced by near-sweet and smoky oak. Look for aromas and flavors of black cherries, blackberries and cassis as well as for hints of mocha and cigar tobacco on the long finish. Drink now–2008. Score 88.

KADITA, SHIRAZ, 2002: Made from grapes from a largely untended vineyard, this intense and concentrated wine is blended with 10% of Cabernet Sauvignon and aged in French oak for 20 months. Medium to full-bodied, with firm but well-integrating tannins and an appealing array of plum, berry and cassis fruits all on a background of generous black pepper, light earthiness and herbaceousness. Drink n\ow–2008. Score 89.

KADITA, CABERNET SAUVIGNON-MERLOT, 2003: Dark ruby toward garnet in color, medium to full-bodied, showing generous ripe berry and plum fruits and soft tannins, all balanced by vanilla, spices and herbal overtones. Drink now. Score 87.

KADITA, CABERNET SAUVIGNON-MERLOT, 2002: Medium to full-bodied, with generous tannins, those integrating nicely and set off well by blackcurrant, plum and wild berry fruits. Look as well for overlays of spices and toasty oak. Drink now. Score 86.

KADITA, CABERNET SAUVIGNON-MERLOT, 2001: Dark garnet toward purple in color, medium to full-bodied, with good balance between tannins, wood and acidity, this successful first release offers up appealing currant and berry fruits together with hints of vanilla and spices. Drink now. Score 86.

Karmei Yosef ★★★★

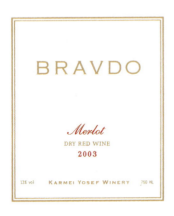

Founded in 2001 by Ben-Ami Bravdo and Oded Shosheyov, both professors of oenology at the Hebrew University of Jerusalem, the winery sits in the heart of a vineyard at Karmei Yosef on the western slopes of the Judean Mountains. This small winery released 2,800 bottles of its first wine in 2001 and current production is 18,000–20,000 bottles annually. Among the varieties under cultivation in the winery-owned vineyards are Cabernet Sauvignon, Merlot, Chardonnay, Carignan, French Colombard, Emerald Riesling and Muscat of Alexandria grapes.

KARMEI YOSEF, CABERNET SAUVIGNON, 2005: Dark garnet red, medium to full-bodied but remarkably light, round and soft on the palate with a well defined array of currant, blackberry, plum, sage and lead pencil aromas and flavors. Tannins and fruits rise nicely on the long and concentrated finish. Best 2008–2012. Tentative Score 91–93.

KARMEI YOSEF, CABERNET SAUVIGNON, BRAVDO, 2004: Medium to full-bodied, with soft near-sweet tannins integrating nicely with spicy wood, blackcurrant, wild berry and black cherry fruits. Soft, round and long. Best 2008–2012. Score 91.

KARMEI YOSEF, CABERNET SAUVIGNON, BRAVDO, 2003: A well-balanced, well structured blend of 80% Cabernet Sauvignon and 20% Merlot. Still young but already showing ripe, generous and mouthfilling aromas and flavors of plums, currants, black cherries and berries, with hints of minty spice and wood. On its way to becoming an elegant and graceful wine. Drink now–2010. Score 91.

KARMEI YOSEF, CABERNET SAUVIGNON, BRAVDO, 2002: This blend of 90% Cabernet Sauvignon and 10% Merlot, full-bodied, tight, but well focused and lively, has a leathery base with a complex array of ripe aromas and flavors of currants, black cherries and a tantalizing hint of anise, as well as an appealing hint of bitterness that makes itself felt on the long, fruity finish. Generous soft tannins and good balance. Drink now. Score 90.

KARMEI YOSEF, CABERNET SAUVIGNON, BRAVDO, 2001: Deep garnet toward purple, this oak-aged, unfiltered blend of 85% Cabernet Sauvignon and 15% Merlot is now showing excellent balance between soft, well-integrated tannins, natural acidity, wood and a tempting array of currant, blackberry and black cherry fruits, those on a background of toasted nuts, black licorice and Mediterranean herbs. Mouth-filling and delicious, the wine opens and then lingers long and gently. Drink now–2008. Score 91.

KARMEI YOSEF, MERLOT, BRAVDO, 2005: Dark ruby, medium-bodied and with fine balance between silky smooth tannins, gentle acidity and wood. An appealing array of blueberry, currant, coffee, mocha and black cherry aromas and flavors, all of which come together in a round and elegant package. Best 2008–2012. Tentative Score 90–92.

KARMEI YOSEF, MERLOT, BRAVDO, 2004: Oak-aged for 12 months, with 10% of Cabernet Sauvignon blended in, this medium-bodied red shows appealing smoky oak and moderately firm tannins well balanced with cassis, blueberry and black cherry fruits. On the long finish hints of anise, sweet cedar, sage and tobacco. Drink now–2010. Score 90

KARMEI YOSEF, MERLOT, BRAVDO, 2003: A rich, generous Merlot, with minty and licorice accents to ripe blackberry, currant, spice and anise flavors. Soft tannins well in balance with fruits and the first influence of the wood bode very nicely for the future development of this wine. Drink now–2010. Score 91.

KARMEI YOSEF, MERLOT, BRAVDO, 2002: Ripe, bold, well focused and delicious, with layer after layer of blueberry, plum and currant fruits, this medium-bodied wine boasts soft tannins along with hints of mocha and Mediterranean herbs that seem to dart in and out on the palate, all culminating in a long, near-sweet finish. Drink now. Score 90.

KARMEI YOSEF, CHARDONNAY, BRAVDO, 2005: Developed partly in stainless steel, partly *sur lie* in French and American *barriques*. Light golden in color, medium to full-bodied, crisply dry, with lively acidity well balanced by citrus, citrus peel, pineapple and melon fruits, and a gentle overlay of spicy oak. Promising long elegance. Drink now–2008. Score 90.

KARMEI YOSEF, CHARDONNAY, BRAVDO, 2004: Medium to full-bodied and rich, with light oak shadings and concentrated, complex and crisply dry aromas and flavors of citrus, citrus peel, melon and green apples. Drink now. Score 90.

Katlav ★★

Owner-winemaker Yossi Yittach founded this small winery on Moshav Nes Harim in the Jerusalem Mountains in 1996, and released his first wines from the 2000 vintage. The winery draws on Cabernet Sauvignon, Merlot and Syrah grapes from local vineyards and is currently releasing about 6,000 bottles annually.

KATLAV, CABERNET SAUVIGNON, 2004: Medium to full-bodied, dark royal purple in color, with tannins and spicy wood integrating nicely to show blackcurrant, blackberry and spicy plum aromas and flavors that linger nicely. Drink now–2008. Score 86. K

KATLAV, CABERNET SAUVIGNON, 2003: Dark garnet towards royal purple, medium to full-bodied with still firm tannins, the wine shows good balance between wood and fruits. On the nose and palate cassis, wild berries, spices and a welcome hint of smoke on a moderately-long finish. Drink now–2008. Score 86. K

KATLAV, CABERNET SAUVIGNON, 2002: Dark purple in color, this medium-bodied oak-aged wine, a blend of Cabernet Sauvignon with a small amount of Shiraz, offers up generous aromas and flavors of currants and wild berries, those complemented by a hint of spiciness. Somewhat one-dimensional. Drink up. Score 81. K

KATLAV, MERLOT, 2004: Medium-bodied, with soft but mouth-coating tannins and hints of spices. On the nose and palate cassis and berry fruits, those with an appealing hint of sage. Drink now. Score 86. K

KATLAV, CABERNET SAUVIGNON-MERLOT, WADI KATLAV, 2004: Appealing spices from first sip to the moderately-long finish highlighting soft tannins, gentle wood and black fruits. Drink now. Score 85. K

KATLAV, CABERNET SAUVIGNON-MERLOT, WADI KATLAV, 2003: A deep garnet blend of 60% Cabernet Sauvignon and 40%

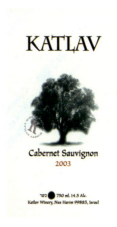

Merlot. Full-bodied, with firm tannins now softening and opening in the glass to reveal tempting currant, plum and berry fruits. Drink now. Score 86. K

Kfir ✶✶

Founded by Meir Kfir in the village Gan Yavne in the southern Coastal Plain, this small winery originally known as Gefen Adderet changed its name in 2006 to Kfir. The winery draws Cabernet Sauvignon, Merlot and Chardonnay grapes from the vineyards of Karmei Yosef, the Jerusalem Mountains and the Galilee, and is currently producing about 7,000 bottles annually.

KFIR, SHIRAZ, BAR, 2005: Ruby towards garnet in color, medium-bodied, with chunky, near-sweet tannins and showing basic plum and black cherry fruits, those with a hint of Oriental spices. Drink now. Score 84.

KFIR, AVICHAI, TEVA, 2003: A medium-bodied blend of 79% Merlot, 13% Cabernet Sauvignon and 8% Petite Sirah. Dark garnet, with soft tannins and appealing aroma and flavors of plums, black cherries and currants all on a lightly spicy background. Drink now–2008. Score 86.

KFIR, ZOHARA, TEVA 2003: Deep ruby towards garnet in color, this medium-bodied blend of Cabernet Sauvignon, Merlot and Argaman (68%, 22% and 10% respectively) shows light tannins and a fresh, lightly spicy berry-cherry personality. Drink now. Score 84.

KFIR, GALIA, BAR, 2005: Call this deep pink and unusual blend of white Riesling and red Petite Sirah grapes (70% and 30% respectively) blush or call it rosé as you like. Light to medium-bodied, floral and with a combination of strawberry and cassis liqueur aromas and flavors, a pleasant quaffer, best served very well chilled. Drink up. Score 85.

KFIR, CHARDONNAY, TEVA, 2004: With a distinct smoky-spicy overlay from the oak chips with which the wine was developed, that tending to overshadow the pear and melon aromas and flavors that remain somewhat muted throughout. Drink now. Score 83.

KFIR, VIOGNIER, BAR, 2005: Light golden straw in color, with generous fresh acidity keeping it lively. Aromas and flavors of peaches, melon, citrus and freshly cut hay. Not representative of the variety but appealing and refreshing. Drink up. Score 84.

KFIR, WHITE NIGHTS, TEVA, 2005: An off-dry blend of 85% Gewurztraminer and 15% Riesling, showing mango, pineapple and citrus peel aromas and flavors. With good acidity to keep it lively and refreshing. A pleasant aperitif. Drink now. Score 84.

La Terra Promessa ✷✷✷

Parma-born Sandro Pelligrini comes from a family of winemakers, and he and his wife Irit founded this small winery in 1998 at their home on Moshav Shachar on the fringes of the northern Negev Desert. The winery relies on Cabernet Sauvignon and Merlot grapes from the Upper Galilee and Ramat Arad, as well as from a vineyard near the winery with Shiraz, Zinfandel, Sangiovese and Petite Sirah. The winery is currently producing about 4,500 bottles annually, in three series; the premium Rubino Reserva, La Crime and La Terra Promessa.

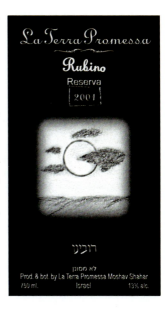

Rubino Reserva

RUBINO RESERVA, 2004: Dark garnet towards royal purple in color, full-bodied, with generous caressing tannins in fine balance with wood, natural acidity and fruits. On the nose and palate blackcurrants, blackberries and ripe plums, all with a hint of black truffles that makes itself felt on the finish. Drink now–2010. Score 89.

RUBINO RESERVA, 2003: Generous spicy oak on this full-bodied, softly tannic and well-balanced wine. Appealing aromas and flavors of blackcurrants, plums, and black cherries, those matched nicely by hints of cocoa and mint on the moderately-long finish. Drink now–2009. Score 88.

RUBINO RESERVA, 2002: A blend of 60% Cabernet Sauvignon and 40% Merlot, oak aged in used French *barriques* for 24 months. Full-bodied, with spicy wood balanced nicely by soft tannins and on the nose and palate black cherries, currants and berries. Long and generous. Drink now–2008. Score 87.

RUBINO RESERVA, 2001: A lightly oak-aged, dark garnet towards purple, medium to full-bodied blend of Cabernet Sauvignon and Merlot, with soft tannins now integrating nicely, hints of smoky oak from the wood and generous aromas and flavors of currant, wild berries and plums. A moderately-long, just spicy enough finish adds charm. Drink now. Score 88.

RUBINO RESERVA, 2000: Deep garnet-red, medium to full-bodied, with tannins now well integrated, showing an appealing herbal overlay over currant and plum fruits. Moderately long and mouth-filling. Drink up. Score 87.

RUBINO RESERVA, 1999: Medium to full-bodied, with still chunky country-style tannins and hints of berry, currant and plum fruits. A bit past its peak. Drink up. Score 85.

La Terra Promessa

LA TERRA PROMESSA, CABERNET SAUVIGNON, 2005: Deep garnet in color, medium-bodied, with soft tannins and an appealing hint of sweet herbs backing up generous plum and blackcurrant fruits. An excellent entry-level Cabernet. Drink from release. Tentative Score 85–87.

LA TERRA PROMESSA, CABERNET SAUVIGNON, 2004: Deep ruby towards garnet in color, aged in oak for 10 months and with soft tannins already integrating nicely. Aromas and flavors of currants, berries and cherries are matched by spicy wood and light minerals that linger comfortably in the background. Drink now–2008. Score 87.

LA TERRA PROMESSA, CABERNET SAUVIGNON, 2003: Medium to full-bodied, dense royal-purple towards black in color, with firm tannins now starting to integrate, this wine shows a gentle hand with the wood, and currant and black cherry fruits on a lightly spicy and herbal background. Drink now–2008. Score 87.

LA TERRA PROMESSA, CABERNET SAUVIGNON, 2002: Dark garnet toward purple, this medium-bodied red has firm and chunky country-style tannins, those matched nicely by plum, berry and black cherry fruits and light spiciness. Drink now. Score 85.

LA TERRA PROMESSA, CABERNET SAUVIGNON, 2001: An appealing deep purple in color, this medium-bodied wine has soft tannins and soft, smoky oak to match currant, wild berry and light herbal aromas and flavors that linger nicely on the palate. Drink now. Score 86.

LA TERRA PROMESSA, MERLOT, 2004: Aged 8 months in French oak *barriques*, deep royal purple towards garnet in color, medium-bodied and with soft tannins and a basic cherry-berry personality, that backed up by hints of spices and earthiness. Drink now. Score 86.

LA TERRA PROMESSA, MERLOT, 2003: Made entirely from Merlot grapes and with 8 months in oak, this calls to mind a Tuscan Merlot. Medium-bodied, unfiltered, with soft, sweet and already well-integrating tannins. Good plum, berry and black cherry fruits and a light hint of spices that linger nicely on the palate. Drink now. Score 87.

LA TERRA PROMESSA, SYRAH, 2005: Medium-dark garnet, medium to full-bodied, with appealing smoky oak and earthiness opening to reveal tempting black fruits and minerals. Generous and long. Drink from release–2009. Tentative Score 88–90.

LA TERRA PROMESSA, SYRAH, 2004: Deep inky purple in color and, medium to full-bodied, reflecting 16 months in oak with firm tannins and generous smoky wood, those in fine balance with plums, red berries, and spices, all leading to a long smoked-meat finish. Drink now–2009. Score 88.

LA TERRA PROMESSA, SYRAH, 2003: Dark and spicy, with firm tannins and generous oak in fine balance with wild berry, currant and cherry fruits, all of those with hints of anise and a light anise-leathery edge on the finish. Drink now–2008. Score 88.

LA TERRA PROMESSA, ZINFANDEL, 2004: Medium-bodied, with chunky country-style tannins, light wood influence, and on the nose and palate violets, hints of meatiness and an appealing hint of Brett to complement blackberry, cherry and cassis fruits. Drink now–2008. Score 86.

LA TERRA PROMESSA, ZINFANDEL, 2003: Inky purple in color, with generous acidity well balanced by wood and a fine array of wild berry, cherry and cassis aromas and flavors, all of which linger nicely on the palate. Drink now. Score 85.

LA TERRA PROMESSA, ZINFANDEL, 2002: Light cherry red in color, with only the barest hints of tannins and oak, this light to medium-bodied wine yields modest raspberry and cherry flavors, much like wines made from Gamay grapes rather than from Zinfandel. Drink up. Score 84.

LA TERRA PROMESSA, LA CRIME, 2005: Showing medium-bodied, with generous black fruit, tobacco and chocolate. Long, round and well-balanced. Drink now–2009. Score 86.

LA TERRA PROMESSA, LA CRIME, 2004: Syrah, Sangiovese and Cabernet Franc come together nicely in a medium to full-bodied red, showing gentle oak, soft tannins, and an appealing overlay of bitterness that highlights plum, berry, and lightly meaty-earthy aromas and flavors. Drink now–2008. Score 88.

LA TERRA PROMESSA, LA CRIME, 2003: A blend of 45% each Syrah and Sangiovese with the addition of 10% Cabernet Franc. Dark, deep and rich, full-bodied and with muscular tannins but those well balanced by smoky wood and generous berry-cherry and earthy aromas and flavors. Drink now–2008. Score 87.

LA TERRA PROMESSA, LA CRIME, 2002: An unfiltered, medium-bodied blend of half each of Sangiovese and Shiraz, reflecting its 14 months in oak with generous spicy oak and firm tannins, those nicely balanced by fresh berry, black cherry and earthy-mineral aromas and flavors. Drink up. Score 87.

LA TERRA PROMESSA, EMERALD RIESLING, 2005: Crisply dry and refreshing. On the nose and palate enough minerals and citrus peel that you might think you were drinking a Petit Chablis. A good choice for everyday quaffing. Drink now. Score 85.

LA TERRA PROMESSA, EMERALD RIESLING, 2004: Crisply dry, with aromas and flavors of summer fruits and green apples. Generously fruity but with good balancing acidity. A simple but lively and pleasant little wine. Drink up. Score 85.

Lachish ★★

Established on Moshav Lachish on the Central Plain by Oded Yakobson, Oscar Meisels and Gai Rosenfeld, this small winery relies entirely on Cabernet Sauvignon and Shiraz grapes from their own vineyards. Current production is about 3,000 bottles annually.

LACHISH, CABERNET SAUVIGNON, 2003: Dark ruby towards garnet in color, medium-bodied, with light oak influences and chunky country-style tannins. Appealing currant and berry fruits overlaid with light spices and a hint of herbaceousness. Drink now. Score 84.

LACHISH, SHIRAZ, 2003: Deep royal purple in color, showing soft tannins and a hint of spicy wood, along with aromas and flavors of ripe plums, wild berry and freshly picked mushrooms. Drink now. Score 84.

LACHISH, MERLOT, 2002: Garnet red with soft tannins integrated nicely, and appealing berry, black cherry and cassis fruits backed up by hints of spices and earthiness. Drink up. Score 84.

Latroun *

Located in an idyllic setting at the foothills of the Judean Mountains midway between Jerusalem and the coast, the Trappist monks at this monastery have been producing wine since their arrival from France in the 1890s. With over 400 dunams of land adjoining the monastery planted in grapes, the winery was the first to introduce Gewurztraminer, Riesling, Pinot Noir and Pinot Blanc grapes to the country and is currently producing about 300,000 bottles annually from twenty varieties of grapes.

LATROUN, CABERNET SAUVIGNON, 2005: Light to medium-bodied, soft, round and fruit-forward, a simple but pleasant quaffer. Drink now. Score 82.

LATROUN, CABERNET SAUVIGNON, 2004: Deep garnet red, medium-bodied, a distinctly country-style wine with simple currant and berry aromas and flavors. Drink now. Score 83.

LATROUN, MERLOT, 2005: Dark ruby in color, medium-bodied, with chunky tannins, this is a simple country-style wine with some berry, plum and near-sweet cassis aromas and flavors. Drink now. Score 81.

LATROUN, MERLOT, 2004: Royal purple, medium-bodied, with chunky tannins and simple berry-cherry aromas and flavors. Drink up. Score 79.

LATROUN, PINOT NOIR, 2005: Bright ruby towards garnet in color, medium-bodied, with soft tannins and gentle wood. Showing spicy berry-cherry aromas and flavors. Drink up. Score 82.

LATROUN, PINOT NOIR, 2004: Dark ruby in color, medium-bodied, with soft tannins. An odd sour aroma and flavor tends to hide the plum and berry fruits here. Drink up. Score 79.

LATROUN, PINOT NOIR, 2003: Deep ruby toward garnet in color, medium-bodied, with soft tannins but marred by somewhat stingy fruits and slightly exaggerated acidity. Drink now. Score 84.

LATROUN, ROSÉ, GRENACHE, 2005: Pale pink in color, light on the palate, with jammy strawberry and raspberry aromas and flavors. Drink up. Score 78.

LATROUN, ROSÉ, GRENACHE, 2004: Light in body, with skimpy strawberry and raspberry flavors. Generous hints of sweetness but not enough balancing acidity to keep it lively. Drink up. Score 78.

LATROUN, CHARDONNAY, 2005: Light to medium-bodied, with generous pineapple, apple and melon aromas and flavors. Drink up. Score 82.

LATROUN, CHARDONNAY, 2004: Medium-bodied, light golden in color, with pineapple and citrus fruits. A pleasant quaffer. Drink up. Score 84.

LATROUN, SAUVIGNON BLANC, 2005: Light straw in color, light to medium-bodied with citrus and herbal aromas and flavors. One dimensional and short. Drink up. Score 75.

LATROUN, SAUVIGNON BLANC, 2004: As light in color as in body, and dominated by grapefruit and bitter orange aromas and flavors. Drink up. Score 76.

LATROUN, DRY RIESLING, 2004: A simple little white, with floral and citrus aromas and flavors. Drink up. Score 79.

LATROUN, GEWURZTRAMINER, 2004: Light gold in color, medium-bodied and with generous aromas and flavors of citrus and summer fruit. Not traditional for Gewurztraminer. Drink now. Score 84.

LATROUN, PINOT BLANC, 2005: A simple, country-style white wine with grapefruit, pineapple and mineral aromas and flavors. Drink up. Score 78.

Lavie ⋆⋆

Located in the community of Ephrata not far from Jerusalem, the first wine of Asher Bentolila and Yo'av Guez was from the 2002 vintage. Drawing largely on grapes from the Jerusalem Mountains, the winery is currently producing about 1,500 bottles annually.

LAVIE, CABERNET SAUVIGNON, 2004: Medium-bodied, with soft tannins and a light hand with oak aging. Aromas and flavors of blackcurrants and blackberries matched nicely by light spicy and herbal notes. Drink now–2008. Score 85. K

LAVIE, CABERNET SAUVIGNON, 2003: Medium-bodied, with firm tannins that seem not to want to yield and holding back the plum and berry fruits that struggle to make themselves felt. Drink up. Score 84. K

LAVIE, CABERNET SAUVIGNON, 2002: Deep purple in color, this medium-bodied oak-aged wine shows clean and appealing aromas and flavors of blackberries, currants and spices on the first attack, those then complemented by light overtones of spices and green olives. Drink up. Score 85. K

Levron ✶

Established by Segal and Yehuda Levron, with their winery now located in their Haifa home, first releases are from the 2004 vintage. Drawing on Merlot and Cabernet Sauvignon grapes from Kerem Ben Zimra and the Gush Chalav area in the Galilee, the winery is currently producing 2,000 bottles annually and plans to expand to 6,000.

LEVRON, CABERNET SAUVIGNON, 2004: Medium-dark garnet in color, medium-bodied, with soft tannins and ripe plum, berry and smoky oak flavors. Drink now. Score 84.

LEVRON, MERLOT, 2004: Reflecting eight months aging in used oak barrels, this medium-bodied wine shows soft tannins, hints of vanilla and a pleasant berry-black cherry personality. Drink now. Score 85.

Maccabim★★

Founded in 2002 by Eytan Rosenthal, Gari Hochwald, Yo'av Heller and Ami Dotan in the community of Maccabim, at the foothills of the Jerusalem Mountains, and drawing grapes from that area as well as from the Galilee and the Ella Valley, this start-up winery's first release was of 1,200 bottles in 2002. Now producing Cabernet Sauvignon and Merlot wines, the winery releases 3,000 bottles annually.

MACCABIM, CABERNET SAUVIGNON, 2004: Deep garnet in color, medium to full-bodied, with spicy oak and soft tannins highlighting currant, black cherry and plum fruits. Drink now–2008. Score 85. **K**

MACCABIM, CABERNET SAUVIGNON, 2003: Dark ruby towards garnet, medium-bodied, with gentle oak influences and appealing currant and wild berry fruits. On the moderately-long finish look for hints of spices and vanilla. Drink now. Score 84. **K**

MACCABIM, CABERNET SAUVIGNON, BIN 9, 2002: Dark cherry red toward garnet in color, this medium-bodied, lightly oaked red shows soft tannins and appealing cherry-berry and currant fruits along with hints of spicy oak. Refreshing and pleasant. Drink up. Score 84. **K**

MACCABIM, MERLOT 2004: Medium-bodied, with soft tannins and hints of spicy wood, those showing blueberry, blackberry and black cherry fruits. Drink now. Score 84. **K**

MACCABIM, MERLOT, 2003: Garnet red, medium-bodied, with soft tannins integrating nicely to reveal cassis, plum and berry fruits on a lightly herbal background. Drink now. Score 84. **K**

Maor ✶

Established by Danny Maor on Moshav Ramot on the Golan Heights, the winery's first release was of 3,200 bottles from the 2003 vintage. Current production is about 10,000 bottles annually, drawing on grapes from the Golan Heights and the Upper Galilee, those including Cabernet Sauvignon, Merlot, Syrah, and Cabernet Franc.

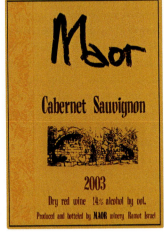

MAOR, CABERNET SAUVIGNON, 2004: Dark garnet in color, medium to full-bodied, with generous wood and firm tannins well balanced by fruits and acidity. On the nose and palate currants, wild berries and vanilla, all lingering nicely. Drink now–2008. Score 87.

MAOR, CABERNET SAUVIGNON, 2003: Deep, royal purple in color, full-bodied and concentrated, with rather firm tannins and a somewhat heavy hand with the oak, the wine shows aromas and flavors of very ripe plums and berries as well as hints of mocha and chocolate in the background. Drink now. Score 85.

Margalit *****

Among the first boutique wineries in the country, and the first to capture the imagination of sophisticated wine lovers. Founded in 1989, it was first located on Moshav Kfar Bilu near the town of Rehovot, and since 1994 has been set in a larger winery near the town of Hadera, at the foothills of Mount Carmel. Father and son team Ya'ir and Assaf Margalit are most renowned for their Bordeaux-style reds that are released in both a regular and a reserve series. In his role as a physical chemist, Ya'ir Margalit has published several well-known textbooks. Assaf, who studied in the agriculture faculty of Hebrew University at Rehovot, also trained in California.

Margalit's earliest release, in 1989, was of 900 bottles of Cabernet Sauvignon. More recent releases, including Cabernet, Merlot, Petite Sirah and Syrah are made primarily from grapes in their own vineyards in Kadita in the Upper Galilee, while the Cabernet Franc is grown in their Binyamina vineyard. Starting with the 2003 harvest, the winery released Enigma, its first Bordeaux-style blend, not a second wine but one that stands on its own within the Margalit répertoire. Production, including the occasional Chardonnay, currently varies at between 17,000–21,000 bottles annually.

Special Reserve

SPECIAL RESERVE, 2005: Full-bodied and concentrated, this muscular blend of 82% Cabernet Sauvignon and 18% Petite Sirah needs time for its elements to come together. Dark and almost searingly tannic now but already revealing the plum, berry, coffee and tobacco aromas and flavors that are going to make this an intense and complex wine. Best 2009–2015. Tentative Score 91–93.

SPECIAL RESERVE, CABERNET SAUVIGNON, 2004: A limited edition of 600 bottles, this full-bodied blend of 86% Cabernet Sauvignon and 14% Petite Sirah shows fine balance between tannins that are now integrating nicely, hints of sweet oak and generous but subdued blackcurrant, plum and chocolate aromas and flavors. Best 2008–2012. Score 91.

SPECIAL RESERVE, CABERNET SAUVIGNON, 2003: Rich, ripe and concentrated, with layer after layer of dark plum, currant, anise, mocha, black cherries and sage. An oak-aged blend of Cabernet Sauvignon and Petite Sirah (87% and 13% respectively), this distinctly Old World wine has excellent balance between wood, lively acidity and well-integrated tannins. Complex and long. Best 2008–2013. Score 93.

SPECIAL RESERVE, CABERNET SAUVIGNON, 2002: This blend of 80% Cabernet Sauvignon, 12% Petite Sirah and 8% Cabernet Franc is remarkably concentrated, intense, and heavy enough to chew, but through its muscles shows great elegance. Ripe currants, spices and cedar flavors on a complex leathery core and a long intense finish make this a wine difficult to match with food but excellent on its own or with fine aged cheeses. Drink now–2012. Score 93.

SPECIAL RESERVE, CABERNET SAUVIGNON, 2001: Dense and concentrated, this firmly tannic, full-bodied and rich blend of 85% Cabernet Sauvignon and 15% of Margalit's very special Petite Sirah needs time to develop, but as it does look for multiple layers of currants, wild berries, plums and black cherries along with toasty oak, minerals and just the right hints of earthiness and sage on the very long finish. Drink now–2012. Score 94.

SPECIAL RESERVE, CABERNET SAUVIGNON, 2000: Delicious, complex and so deep in color that it is almost black, this remarkably full-bodied, deep and concentrated blend of 80% Cabernet Sauvignon, 15% Petite Sirah and 5% Merlot boasts earthy currant, sage, black cherry and cedary oak flavors. As it develops look for coffee and tobacco notes. Drink now–2010. Score 93.

SPECIAL RESERVE, CABERNET SAUVIGNON, 1999: Harmonious, dense and tannic, this full-bodied and elegant blend of 87% Cabernet Sauvignon and 13% Carignan offers tempting spices and ripe fruit aromas and flavors of currants, plums, chocolate and coffee. Drink now–2012. Score 93.

SPECIAL RESERVE, CABERNET SAUVIGNON, 1998: This blend of 90% Cabernet Sauvignon and 10% remarkably concentrated Petite Sirah offers up a luxurious mouthful of ripe black cherry, currant, anise and plum flavors. Dark, hearty, rich and tannic, the wine is now beginning to turn silky and polished and has a long, mouth-filling finish. Drink now–2009. Score 92.

SPECIAL RESERVE, CABERNET SAUVIGNON, 1997: A blend of 85% Cabernet Sauvignon and 15% of the very special Petite Sirah that Margalit has managed to isolate and cultivate, this ripe, complex and full-bodied red has a lovely balance between currant, black cherry, spice, chocolate and cedary oak flavors, all of which seem to burst forth and blend together on the palate. Its once rough tannins are now integrating nicely and the wine shows a long, mouth-filling finish. Drink now–2008. Score 93.

SPECIAL RESERVE, CABERNET SAUVIGNON, 1995: Having lost its youthful rough edges, this full-bodied and harmonious wine now shows well-integrated tannins blending nicely with deep oak, tobacco, cherry and spicy flavors. Drink now. Score 91.

SPECIAL RESERVE, CABERNET SAUVIGNON, 1994: From a problematic vintage, and thus lacking the concentration and intensity felt in the 1993 wine, but still showing tempting currant, plum and berry aromas and flavors, those on a background of smoky oak and fresh forest. Somewhat past its peak. Drink up. Score 89.

SPECIAL RESERVE, CABERNET SAUVIGNON, 1993: Deep violet toward garnet and showing first hints of browning, this remains one of Margalit's finest efforts. A blend of Cabernet Sauvignon with 15% of deep and smooth Petite Sirah, this full-bodied wine boasts multiple layers of blackcurrants, dried fruits and vanilla as well as violets and plums. Even though somewhat past its peak, this seductive, tempting and well-structured wine continues to offer ample charms. Drink up. Score 92.

Margalit

MARGALIT, CABERNET SAUVIGNON, 2005: Medium to full-bodied, with fine balance between density and complexity, this rich, generous wine offers up currant, plum and berry fruits, those matched by appealing earthy-herbal overtones. Soft tannins and a hint of spicy oak here and, on the finish, a generous hint of blueberries. Best 2009–2015. Tentative Score 91–93.

MARGALIT, CABERNET SAUVIGNON, 2004: Dark garnet towards royal purple with orange reflections, this well-balanced, medium to full-bodied wine is showing generous currant and berry fruits, those matched nicely by spicy wood, dark chocolate and espresso coffee. Long and luxurious. Best 2008–2012. Score 92.

MARGALIT, CABERNET SAUVIGNON, 2003: Full-bodied and intense, but rich and well balanced, this blend of 88% Cabernet Sauvignon and 12% Cabernet Franc, both from the Kadita vineyard, is loaded with complex earthy currant, black cherry, anise and mocha aromas and flavors, those well set off by generous but smooth tannins. Look for an appealing leathery sensation on the long finish. Drink now–2012. Score 91.

MARGALIT, CABERNET SAUVIGNON, 2002: This full-bodied, well-balanced blend of 85% Cabernet Sauvignon, 8% Merlot and 7% Cabernet Franc is concentrated, its once firm tannins softening now and showing tempting aromas and flavors of blackcurrants, berries and game meat, together with a long finish. A complex and sophisticated wine. Drink now–2009. Score 92.

MARGALIT, CABERNET SAUVIGNON, 2001: A distinctly Old World wine, this dark, dense and richly flavored oak-aged blend of 90% Cabernet Sauvignon and 10% Merlot has generous currant, blackberry, sage and mineral aromas and flavors. Still firm tannins, those integrating nicely now, and a long finish with tempting coffee, dark chocolate and hints of licorice and mint. Drink now–2012. Score 93.

MARGALIT, CABERNET SAUVIGNON, LOT 37, 2001: Vastly different in style from every other Margalit wine released. The wine was aged in *barriques* for 2 years (all of Margalit's other wines have been aged for only 1 year), the blackcurrants that typify so many of the wines of this winery have been replaced here by plums, and the often-searing tannins that sometimes take years to integrate in the usual releases are already soft and well integrated and are now showing a sweet and dusty nature. Drink now–2012. Score 92.

MARGALIT, CABERNET SAUVIGNON, 2000: This full-bodied, still tannic blend of 88% Cabernet Sauvignon and 12% Merlot had some rough edges in its youth but has now come fully into its own. Look for an abundance of raspberry, black cherry, sage, and spicy aromas and flavors, all with delicious leathery, cedar wood overtones. Drink now–2008. Score 91.

MARGALIT, CABERNET SAUVIGNON, 1999: A blend of 84% Cabernet Sauvignon, 12% Merlot and 4% Petite Sirah, this oaked, full-bodied, ripe and complex wine shows good balance between wood and ripe cherry and berry flavors that come together in a long finish. Drink now–2008. Score 92.

MARGALIT, CABERNET SAUVIGNON, 1998: A blend of 90% Cabernet and 10% Merlot, this chewy, full-bodied red is packed with spicy currant and blueberry flavors alongside notes of pepper and cola for additional dimension. Still showing youthful and firm tannins, but those now softening and rounding off nicely. Drink now–2008. Score 91.

MARGALIT, CABERNET SAUVIGNON, 1997: Deep garnet-purple, this full-bodied blend of 85% Cabernet Sauvignon, 13% Merlot and 2% Petite Sirah has a complex core of currant, spices and cedar flavors along with hints of anise, tobacco and ripe cherries. Good balance, now well-integrated tannins and a long finish. Fully mature and not for further cellaring. Drink up. Score 88.

MARGALIT, CABERNET SAUVIGNON, 1996: Full-bodied but neither as tannic nor as heavy as some of Margalit's earlier efforts. Deep garnet red now, this distinctly Bordeaux-style red shows good balance between fruits, tannins and acidity, and is fleshy, elegant and long. Fully mature now. Drink up. Score 91.

MARGALIT, CABERNET SAUVIGNON, 1995: Medium to full-bodied, with soft and well-integrated tannins and generous aromas and flavors of black fruits, coffee and tobacco along with earthy-herbal notes, this well-balanced and well-structured wine offers up a generous mouthful. Not meant for further cellaring. Drink up. Score 91.

MARGALIT, CABERNET SAUVIGNON, 1994: Reflecting an overall poor vintage year, this wine is much lighter in style than Margalit's earlier efforts. Despite that, during its heyday the wine showed a deep purple color and intense blackcurrant aromas and flavors on a background of black pepper. Somewhat past its peak so drink up. Score 89.

MARGALIT, CABERNET SAUVIGNON, 1993: One of the best Cabernet wines ever made in Israel, this deep, concentrated and remarkably full-bodied wine was backward in its youth but when it did come into its own revealed delicious black and red fruits including cherries, plums and currants, as well as generous overtones of chocolate and cedar. Somewhat past its peak. Drink up. Score 90.

MARGALIT, MERLOT, 2004: Fresh, ripe and generous, with appealing blackberry, plum, cassis, mocha and vanilla aromas and flavors finishing with a hint of grilled herbs. Medium to full-bodied, with soft tannins, this gently spicy wine will be at its best now—2009. Score 90.

MARGALIT, MERLOT, 2002: Full-bodied, deep purple toward inky black in color and blended with 10% Cabernet Sauvignon to add backbone, this ripe, bold and delicious wine shows well-integrated tannins that give it a welcome softness, those matched nicely by aromas and flavors of plums, currants and black cherries, and a long spicy and cedar-flavored finish. Drink now–2012. Score 92.

MARGALIT, MERLOT, 2001: This complex, intense and well-balanced 85% Merlot and 15% Cabernet Sauvignon blend has abundant soft tannins and plenty of earthy and mineral notes overlaying spicy currant, wild berry and coffee aromas and flavors. Look for a long lingering finish with an array of hazelnuts, coffee and anise. Drink now–2010. Score 91.

MARGALIT, MERLOT, 2000: Remarkably tannic for a Merlot, this full-bodied wine which also contains 10% of Cabernet Sauvignon grapes is rich, ripe and concentrated, with layer after layer of currants, plums and black cherries, all with generous hints of tobacco, smoky oak and vanilla. Drink now–2008. Score 92.

MARGALIT, MERLOT, 1999: With smooth tannins and rich flavors that fill the mouth and then linger nicely, this well-balanced, full-bodied, bold, ripe and delicious wine shows layer after layer of plum, currant, and black cherry flavors as well as a long finish on which you will find nice herbal overtones. Drink now. Score 90.

MARGALIT, MERLOT, 1998: A full-bodied blend of 87% Merlot, 10% Cabernet Sauvignon and 3% Petite Sirah, with layers of ripe, spicy black cherry, currant, plum and mineral aromas and flavors. This rich, smooth, elegant and complex wine has remarkable depth and concentration. Drink now. Score 90.

MARGALIT, MERLOT, 1997: Bold, ripe and delicious, with multiple layers of plum, currant and black cherry aromas and flavors, smooth, nicely polished tannins, and a rich, deep finish. Fully mature. Drink up. Score 91.

MARGALIT, MERLOT, 1995: With a core of black cherry, currant, tea, herb and cedary oak flavors, this well-balanced, full-bodied and elegant red has ripe, well-rounded tannins and a long finish. Fully mature and not for further cellaring. Drink up. Score 90.

MARGALIT, CABERNET FRANC, 2004: Deeply fragrant, this full-bodied wine was blended with 10% of Merlot. Silky smooth tannins, black and red fruits, hints of tobacco and chocolate come together on a long, mouthfilling finish with an appealing hint of freshly turned earth. Drink now–2009. Score 91.

MARGALIT, CABERNET FRANC, 2003: Almost impenetrable deep purple in color, full-bodied, with excellent balance between soft, luxurious tannins and a tempting array of dark plum, wild berry and herbal aromas and flavors. Oak-aged, with the addition of 10% of Cabernet Sauvignon, the wine is mouthfilling and long, showing a tantalizing hint of mint on the finish. Drink now–2010. Score 90.

MARGALIT, CABERNET FRANC, 2002: This deep royal purple, full-bodied, concentrated Cabernet Franc with 12% Cabernet Sauvignon blended in, shows aromas and flavors of spicy plums and earthiness on first attack that yield to an array of currant, anise, chocolate and sweet cedar, all coming together in a long mouth-filling finish. The wine has soft tannins, generous oak, plenty of acidity and overall good balance. Drink now–2010. Score 92.

MARGALIT, CABERNET FRANC, 2001: This full-bodied, heavily oaked blend of 90% Cabernet Franc and 10% Cabernet Sauvignon is at the same time seductive, well balanced and supple. The wine has generous cherry, anise and currant fruits along with spicy and toasty aromas and flavors and a generous hint of mocha. The long finish boasts earthy and cedar wood flavors typical of the best wines made from this variety. Drink now–2009. Score 91.

MARGALIT, CARIGNAN, 1999: A delightful surprise because Carignan rarely produces a fine wine on its own. This full-bodied wine which also contains 5% of Cabernet Sauvignon grapes to round it out is still surprisingly closed when first poured, but given time to open in the glass bursts with raspberry and chocolate flavors and an almost floral bouquet. Drink now–2008. Score 90.

MARGALIT, ENIGMA, 2005: On the way to becoming Margalit's flagship wine, this oak-aged Bordeaux blend of Cabernet Sauvignon, Cabernet Franc and Merlot (60%, 22% and 18% respectively) shows ripe and intense medium to full-body, with cassis, violet and black cherry aromas and flavors matched by soft tannins. On the long finish, well integrated oak and hints of chocolate. Best 2008–2014. Tentative Score 92–94.

MARGALIT, ENIGMA, 2004: A blend of 60% Cabernet Sauvignon, 21% Cabernet Franc and 19% Merlot. A Bordeaux blend but with the clear Margalit signature, with generous but near-sweet soft tannins and a moderate hand with the wood, and even now showing dark purple plum and currant fruits, those matched nicely by spices and a hint of red licorice that creeps in on the long finish. Best 2008–2012. Score 93.

MARGALIT, ENIGMA, 2003: Living fully up to its earlier promise this Bordeaux blend of 70% Cabernet Sauvignon, 18% Merlot and 12% Cabernet Franc is showing remarkably rich, ripe and polished. Round and approachable, with a complex array of currant, plum and wild berry aromas and flavors, those well focused and long and matched by a gentle spiciness that runs through to the long finish. Drink now–2010. Score 92.

Meishar ★★★

Founded in 1991 by Ze'ev and Chaya Smilansky on Moshav Meishar in the southern coastal plains, this small winery relies entirely on its own vineyards of Cabernet Sauvignon, Merlot, Shiraz and Muscat grapes and currently produces about 7,000 bottles annually of red wines in a Reserve and a Meishar series.

Reserve

RESERVE 730, CABERNET SAUVIGNON, 2004: Destined for a total of about 18 months in oak, with its rough edges already smoothing out, and deep, firm tannins integrating nicely to show off black cherries, ripe currants, and light chocolate mousse flavors that sneak in quietly on the finish. Drink from 2008. Tentative Score 89–91.

RESERVE 730, CABERNET SAUVIGNON, 2002: Medium to full-bodied, dark garnet red, with still firm tannins but those starting to integrate nicely to reveal aromas and flavors of smoky oak, all well balanced with black fruits, Oriental spices and hints of chocolate and cigar tobacco on the moderately-long finish. Drink now. Score 88.

RESERVE 730, CABERNET SAUVIGNON, 2001: Dark cherry red toward garnet in color, this medium to full-bodied Cabernet was blended with 4% of Merlot to round it out. Its generous tannins balanced nicely with wood and fruits, the wine shows aromas and flavors of red currants and berries together with smoky oak and anise, as well as chocolate and mocha on the long finish. Drink now. Score 89.

RESERVE, CABERNET SAUVIGNON, 2000: Medium to full-bodied, with a rich array of berry, currant and plum fruits on a spicy oak background, the wine has good balance and tannins that are integrating nicely, as well as a long near-sweet finish. Drink now. Score 89.

RESERVE 730, CABERNET SAUVIGNON, 1999: Maturing nicely, this blend of Cabernet Sauvignon and Merlot, with the Cabernet dominating continues to show ripe blackcurrants and cherries along with tempting spicy and cedar aromas and flavors. Good balance between oak, fruits and smooth tannins, as well as a comfortably long finish. Drink up Score 90.

RESERVE, 730, MERLOT, 2005: Showing dark and spicy, with an enchanting earthy character that highlights cherry, blackberry and spice aromas and flavors. Long and mouthfilling. Drink from release–2010. Tentative Score 89–91.

RESERVE, 730, MERLOT, 2004: Made entirely from Merlot grapes, showing medium to full-body along with a gentle hand with the oak and generous earthy-herbal overtones, those in fine balance with ripe currant and blackberry fruits. On the long finish hints of Oriental spices and grilled meat. Drink now–2010. Score 89.

Meishar

MEISHAR, CABERNET SAUVIGNON, 2005: Dark garnet towards royal purple in color, medium to full-bodied, and with fine balance between still firm but already integrating tannins, spicy wood and well focused currant, dark plum and black cherry fruits. Hints of ground pepper and anise that linger nicely. Best from 2008. Tentative Score 90–92.

MEISHAR, CABERNET SAUVIGNON, 2004: Dark garnet in color, medium to full-bodied, with generous but soft tannins and smoky oak opening nicely to reveal aromas and flavors of blackcurrants, purple plums, white chocolate and spices. Long and mouthfilling. Drink now–2009. Score 89.

MEISHAR, CABERNET SAUVIGNON, 2003: Medium to full-bodied, with soft tannins and appealing currant and black cherry fruits set off nicely by hints of vanilla and spices. Drink now–2009. Score 89.

MEISHAR, CABERNET SAUVIGNON, 2002: Deep garnet in color with a hint of browning, full-bodied, with tannins almost fully absorbed and showing light chocolate and caramel hints over the currant and now hyper-ripe plum aromas and flavors. Not meant for further cellaring. Drink up. Score 86.

MEISHAR, CABERNET SAUVIGNON, 2001: Deep garnet, with generous but well-integrated tannins balanced nicely by smoky oak, this medium-bodied red offers up appealing plum, black cherry and blackcurrant aromas and flavors. Look as well for a hint of Oriental spices on the finish. Drink now. Score 88.

MEISHAR, CABERNET SAUVIGNON, 2000: This firm, intense and well-balanced red reveals currant and toasty oak flavors on a not overly imposing background of herbs and earthiness. Drink up. Score 88.

MEISHAR, CABERNET SAUVIGNON, 1999: Medium to full-bodied and with spicy, toasty oak flavors overlaying currant, berry and cherry flavors, the wine has a strong tannic finish. Fully mature. Drink up. Score 88.

MEISHAR, MERLOT, 2005: Medium-dark garnet in color, medium-bodied and with silky tannins allowing raspberry, blackberry and cassis fruits to show through nicely, those complemented by generous hints of cocoa and a light earthy-graphite sensation that lingers nicely. Potentially elegant. Drink from release–2010. Tentative Score 87–89.

MEISHAR, MERLOT, 2004: Dark royal purple in color, this gently oak-aged medium-bodied wine was blended with 13% of Cabernet Sauvignon. Long, soft and round with plum and blackberry fruits backed up by hints of nutmeg and freshly turned earth. Drink now–2009. Score 89.

MEISHAR, MERLOT, 2003: Dark brick-red, medium to full-bodied, with tannins integrating nicely and showing a generous array of blackberry, plum and black cherry fruits on a background of red licorice and chocolate. Drink now–2009. Score 89.

MEISHAR, MERLOT, 2002: Blended with 15% of Cabernet Sauvignon, this deep ruby toward garnet and full-bodied red shows good balance between firm but already well-integrating tannins, wood and fruits. Look for appealing plum, berry and blackcurrant fruits together with generous overlays of smoke and spices. Drink now. Score 87.

MEISHAR, SHIRAZ, 2005: Ripe and generous, with gamy and leathery notes that intertwine nicely with berry, black cherry, plum and smoky aromas and flavors. Round and long, with a hint of earthiness on the long finish. Best from 2008. Tentative Score 89–91

MEISHAR, SHIRAZ-MERLOT-CABERNET SAUVIGNON, #41, 2004: Dark garnet in color, medium-bodied, with sweet cedar and spicy oak overtones highlighting blackberries, black cherries and an array of herbs and spices. Look for hints of minerals and anise on the crisp finish. Drink now–2009. Score 89.

MEISHAR, SHIRAZ-MERLOT-CABERNET SAUVIGNON, #41, 2003: A blend of 40% each of Shiraz and Merlot and 20% Cabernet Sauvignon. Aged in oak for 8 months, medium-bodied, showing good balance between near-sweet tannins, spicy oak and fruits. On the nose and palate ripe plums, blackcurrants and blackberries matched by hints of earthiness and tobacco. Long and generous. Drink now–2010. Score 90.

MEISHAR, TACSUM, 2003: Perhaps the winemakers were in a playful mood when they named this wine by spelling "Muscat" backward. Made from Muscat Canelli grapes that were sun-dried and then frozen before pressing, this is a wine as much in the Italian *appasimento* style as it is an ice wine. Not so much full-bodied as it is "thick", the wine shows unabashed sweetness and a dark, burnished bronze color. Good balancing acidity and flavors of apricots, ripe peaches and honeydew melon keep it lively. Drink now–2009. Score 89.

Meister *

Founded by Ya'akov Meister in Rosh Pina and drawing on Cabernet Sauvignon grapes from his own vineyards as well as from other Galilee vineyards, this small winery released its first wines to the market with 2,000 bottles in 2003 and current production is about 5,000 bottles.

MEISTER, CABERNET SAUVIGNON, 2005: A somewhat cloudy garnet in color, with chunky country-style tannins and generous dusty oak. Some berry and currant fruits here but those with odd sweet and musky overlays. Drink up. Score 75.

MEISTER, CABERNET SAUVIGNON, 2004: Developed partly in used wood barrels and partly in stainless steel with the addition of oak chips, this medium-bodied, somewhat cloudy dark garnet wine shows chunky tannins and only skimpy berry and black-cherry fruits. Drink up. Score 70.

MEISTER, CABERNET SAUVIGNON, 2003: Already oxidizing, caramel and chocolate flavors dominating whatever black fruits struggle to make themselves felt. Coarse and biting. Score 65.

Miles ✶✶

Founded by vintner Eyal Miles in 2001 on Moshav Kerem Ben Zimra in the Upper Galilee, with its own vineyards containing Cabernet Sauvignon, Merlot, Sauvignon Blanc and Gewurztraminer, this winery is currently producing 6,000 bottles annually.

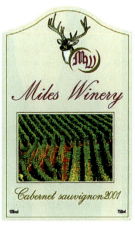

MILES, CABERNET SAUVIGNON, 2004: Dark garnet, medium to full-bodied, with generous soft tannins and spicy wood well balanced by appealing currant, berry and black cherry fruits as well as generous hints of Mediterranean herbs. Drink now–2008. Score 85. K

MILES, CABERNET SAUVIGNON, 2003: A medium-bodied, quaffing wine, garnet towards purple in color, with soft tannins, red fruits and a near-sweet finish. Drink now. Score 83. K

MILES, CABERNET SAUVIGNON, 2002: Aged in oak for 14 months, this medium to full-bodied deep garnet wine shows chunky tannins, generous wood, and currant, berry and pepper aromas and flavors, those somewhat hidden under earthy and herbal notes. A pleasant country-style wine. Drink now. Score 84. K

MILES, CABERNET SAUVIGNON, 2001: A country-style oak-aged wine, perhaps too rustic, with deep earthy and herbal notes almost hiding the plum, blackberry and vanilla flavors. Not meant for further cellaring. Drink up. Score 75. K

MILES, MERLOT, 2004: Medium-bodied, with firm tannins integrating nicely and well balanced with generous blueberry, black cherry and cassis fruits. A generous hint of spiciness adds charm to the moderately long finish. Drink now–2008. Score 85.

MILES, MERLOT, 2003: Garnet towards royal-purple, medium-bodied with soft well integrated tannins and not at all complex but rewarding aromas and flavors of blackberries, black cherries and plums. A good quaffer. Drink now. Score 85. K

MILES, MERLOT, 2002: Dark cherry red toward purple, this medium-bodied moderately tannic country-style wine offers up straightforward but appealing aromas and flavors of berries and plums on a light herbal background. Drink up. Score 85. K

MILES, MERLOT, 2001: After having spent 14 months in French oak casks, this young and intense medium-bodied wine is now showing cherry, anise, currant and cedar aromas and flavors. Plenty of tannins here but those nicely integrated in a well-balanced wine. Drink up. Score 86. K

MILES, SAUVIGNON BLANC, 2003: A light straw-colored medium-bodied white with appealing apple, grapefruit, and pineapple fruits, a light hint of spring flowers and good balancing acidity to add liveliness. Not complex but pleasant. Drink up. Score 85. K

MILES, SAUVIGNON BLANC, 2002: This light golden medium-bodied wine offers up generous summer fruit, citrus and floral notes all balanced nicely by fresh acidity. Somewhat past its peak. Drink up. Score 84. K

MILES, GEWURZTRAMINER, 2004: Light golden straw with a hint of bronze, medium-bodied and with good balancing acidity to show off the appealing spicy tropical fruits. Drink now. Score 86. K

MILES, GEWURZTRAMINER, DESSERT, 2004: Light golden in color, medium-bodied, with moderate sweetness set off nicely by refreshing acidity. On the nose and palate tropical fruits and honeyed apricots. Somewhat one dimensional but very pleasant. Drink now. Score 86. K

Mony ✳✳✳

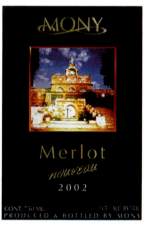

Located in the scenic foothills of the Jerusalem Mountains, on the grounds of the Dir Rafat Monastery, the winery was operated for many years by the resident monks. About three years ago control of the winery passed to the Ertul family, long-time vintners for the monastery. Grapes in the vineyards include Cabernet Sauvignon, Cabernet Franc, Merlot, Zinfandel, Shiraz, Carignan, Argaman, Petite Sirah, Chardonnay, Semillon, Emerald Riesling and other varieties. Annual production is about 22,000 bottles. The winery is currently producing wines in two series, Reserve and Mony, and from the 2005 vintage, the wines have been kosher.

Reserve

RESERVE, CABERNET SAUVIGNON, 2003: Medium-bodied, with gentle oak and soft tannins and showing generous ripe currant and wild berry flavors. On the background a nice spicy hint. Drink now. Score 85.

RESERVE, CABERNET SAUVIGNON, 2002: Medium to full-bodied with soft tannins, a marked but pleasant influence of smoky oak, well balanced by generous currant, berry and herbal aromas and flavors, all with a light spiciness to the moderately long finish. Drink now. Score 85.

RESERVE, MERLOT, 2003: Deep royal purple in color, medium-bodied, with appealingly spicy berry and cherry fruits and a hint of spicy oak on the moderately long finish. Drink now. Score 85.

RESERVE, MERLOT, 2002: Dark garnet red, medium to full-bodied, with still firm tannins but those set off nicely by spicy-smoky oak and generous currant and berry aromas and flavors. Drink now. Score 85.

RESERVE, SHIRAZ, 2003: Deep cherry towards garnet in color, with firm tannins needing time to settle down and generous spicy wood and vanilla. On the nose and palate a basically black cherry-plum personality, that with hints of leather, chocolate and licorice that come in on the medium-long finish. Drink now–2008. Score 86.

RESERVE, CHARDONNAY, 2004: With 8 months in oak, this medium-bodied, golden straw colored wine shows good balance between wood, acidity and fruits. Generous tropical fruits, citrus peel and melon aromas and flavors along with a hint of spices to add complexity. Drink now. Score 86.

RESERVE, CHARDONNAY, 2003: Made entirely from Chardonnay grapes, and with 60% of the wine aged in oak, this light golden-colored wine offers clean and fresh aromas and flavors of citrus, pineapple and melons, those just spicy enough and with just enough acidity to keep the wine lively. A hint of bitter almonds on the finish adds charm. Drink now. Score 86.

Mony

MONY, CABERNET SAUVIGNON, 2005: Lightly oaked, deep ruby in color, medium-bodied and with soft tannins and appealing red fruits. Not complex but generous and appealing. Drink now. Score 85. **K**

MONY, CABERNET SAUVIGNON, 2004: With only 3 months in oak, this medium-bodied red shows soft tannins and nice hints of spices and vanilla on a background of black fruits. Marred by a somewhat barnyardy aroma. Drink now. Score 84.

MONY, CABERNET SAUVIGNON, 2003: Deep garnet red, medium to full-bodied, with firm but well-integrating tannins and with traditional Cabernet aromas and flavors of currants, berries and a hint of spicy cedar wood. Well balanced and moderately long. Drink up. Score 85.

MONY, CABERNET SAUVIGNON 2002: Somewhat cloudy dark red in color, medium-bodied and with firm tannins that tend to hide the berry and currant fruits. A simple but pleasant country-style wine. Drink up. Score 83.

MONY, MERLOT, 2005: Ruby red, light to medium-bodied, with soft tannins and appealing currant and berry fruits. A good entry-level wine. Drink up. Score 83. K

MONY, MERLOT, 2004: Light in body, with almost unfelt tannins and berry, strawberry and cherry aromas. A simple quaffer. Drink now. Score 80.

MONY, MERLOT, 2003: Dark ruby towards garnet, medium to full-bodied, with firm tannins that need time to open to reveal the berry, black cherry and currant flavors that lie underneath as well as spicy oak and light herbal overlays. Drink now. Score 85.

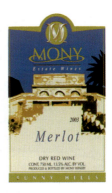

MONY, SHIRAZ, 2003: Dark cherry towards garnet red, with chunky, country-style tannins and reflecting its 12 months in oak with spices and hints of vanilla. Aromas and flavors of currants, black cherries and plums backed up by a hint of freshly tanned leather. An appealing entry-level wine. Drink now. Score 84.

MONY, CHARDONNAY, 2004: Light golden straw in color, this light to medium-bodied partially oak-aged white shows appealing apple, pear and mineral aromas and flavors. Not complex but a pleasant quaffer. Drink now. Score 84.

MONY, MUSCAT OF ALEXANDRIA, 2004: Light straw in color, light to medium-bodied, not complex but with appealing floral and citrus flower aromas and flavors on a lightly honeyed background. Drink now. Score 84.

Na'aman *

Founded by Rami and Betina Na'aman on Moshav Ramot Naftali in the Upper Galilee, this small winery released their first wines from the 2004 vintage. With their own vineyards containing Cabernet Sauvignon, Merlot, Petit Verdot and Shiraz grapes, releases from 2004 were just under 1,000 bottles and in 2005 about 4,000 bottles.

NA'AMAN, CABERNET SAUVIGNON, KEREM NA'AMAN, 2004: Medium to full-bodied, with chunky, country-style tannins and reflecting its 12 months in *barriques* with dusty and near-sweet cedar. On the nose and palate appealing blackberry and currant fruits, those with a light herbal overlay. Drink now. Score 84.

NA'AMAN, 50/50, 2004: Dark garnet in color, this medium-bodied blend of 50% each Cabernet Sauvignon and Merlot shows chunky tannins and generously spicy wood, those backed up by somewhat skimpy berry, currant and black cherry fruits. Pleasant but marred somewhat by a medicinal aroma that never quite fades. Drink now. Score 80.

Nahal Amud ✶

Established by Avi Abu in 1998 and located on Moshav Kfar Shamai near Sefad in the Upper Galilee, the winery draws on grapes from its own vineyards, those including Cabernet Sauvignon, Cabernet Franc, Merlot and Petite Sirah. Current production is about 5,000 bottles annually.

NAHAL AMUD, CABERNET SAUVIGNON, 2004: Medium-bodied, with coarse tannins and far-too generous and not entirely clean earthy overlays and only the skimpiest of black fruits. Drink up. Score 75. **K**

NAHAL AMUD, CABERNET SAUVIGNON, 2003: Developed partly in oak barrels and partly in glass demijohns, this unfiltered country style wine is more heavy than full-bodied and is lacking balance between its chunky tannins, high acidity and overripe fruits. Drink up. Score 72. **K**

NAHAL AMUD, CABERNET SAUVIGNON, 2002: With an unwelcome hint of sweetness that runs throughout and with intense herbal and earthy aromas and flavors and only stingy fruits, this wine lacks balance. Score 68. **K**

NAHAL AMUD, MERLOT, 2003: Dark but not fully clear royal purple, medium-bodied, with searing tannins and aromas and flavors that call to mind cherry liqueur. Score 68. **K**

NAHAL AMUD, CABERNET SAUVIGNON-MERLOT-SHIRAZ, 2003: Dark garnet in color, medium to full-bodied, firmly tannic, with plum and currant fruits pushed into the background by unwanted medicinal and earthy aromas and flavors. Drink up. Score 79. **K**

Nachshon ✱✱✱

Founded by Ariel Padawer in 1996 on Kibbutz Nachshon in the Ayalon Valley at the foot of the Jerusalem Hills, the winery, now under the supervision of winemaker Shlomi Zadok, raises its own Cabernet Sauvignon, Merlot, Shiraz, Cabernet Franc and Argaman grapes and produces about 20,000 bottles annually. Until 2003 the winery produced wines in four series, Ayalon, Sela, Pushkin and Nachshon but with the 2004 vintage, the Nachshon series was dropped.

Ayalon

AYALON, CABERNET SAUVIGNON, 2004: Tastings from two different barrels, one used French barrels and the other of new American oak, both perfectly dry but the first showing firm and almost sensually sweet tannins, a bare hint of vanilla and traditional blackcurrant fruits, the second softer and more round with comfortably yielding tannins and in addition to currant and berry fruits gentle overlays of sweet herbs and dark chocolate. Drink now–2008. Score 86.

AYALON, CABERNET SAUVIGNON, 2003: Made entirely from Cabernet Sauvignon grapes and aged for 25 months in new and one year old *barriques*, this medium to full-bodied, deep garnet red wine shows near-sweet tannins and hints of sweet cedar wood complemented nicely by spicy berry and currant fruits. Drink now. Score 87.

AYALON, CABERNET SAUVIGNON, 2002: Developed for two years in oak, this deep garnet blend of 66% Cabernet Sauvignon and 34% Merlot shows good balance between soft tannins, smoky wood and berry, currant and black cherry fruits. Drink now. Score 86.

AYALON, CABERNET SAUVIGNON, 2001: Deep royal purple and medium-bodied, the wine shows moderately firm tannins and generous, perhaps overly ripe flavors of currants and berries, but is a bit heavy on the oak. Drink up. Score 84.

AYALON, MERLOT, 2004: Deep cherry-ruby red in color, medium-bodied, with soft tannins, aromas and flavors of raspberries and cherries, the wine promises to be gently oaked, well rounded and nicely balanced. Drink now. Score 86.

AYALON, MERLOT, 2002: Dark royal purple in color, this blend of 66% Cabernet Sauvignon and 34% Merlot shows generous sweet cedar wood, currants, and plums, all with an appealing overlay of Mediterranean herbs. Drink up. Score 85.

AYALON, MERLOT, 2000: Medium to full-bodied, with herb and wild berry aromas and flavors backed up nicely by spices and mint. On the medium finish mineral and smoky accents. Somewhat past its peak. Drink up. Score 85.

AYALON, SYRAH, 2005: With the addition of 15% of Cabernet Sauvignon, this dark royal purple oak-aged wine opens with a light but tantalizing herbal nose and then goes on to show aromas and flavors of black cherries, cassis and blackberries, those backed up nicely by hints of tobacco and licorice. Drink from release–2009. Tentative Score 86–88.

AYALON, SYRAH, 2004: Youthful royal-purple in color, already showing a nice touch of sweet cedar wood, with firm but nicely yielding tannins. Aromas and flavors of currants, red berries, plums and hints of vanilla-scented oak. Good balance between tannins and wood ensures medium-term aging. Drink now–2008. Score 87.

AYALON, SYRAH, 2003: Medium-bodied, deep ruby in color, with soft tannins integrating well and ripe purple plum, blackberry and cherry fruits. Good balance between wood, tannins and acidity and an appealing spicy-earthy finish. Drink now. Score 87.

AYALON, CABERNET FRANC, 2005: Deep garnet towards royal purple, medium-bodied, with soft tannins integrating nicely, this blend of 86% Cabernet Franc and 7% each of Merlot and Petite Verdot was aged partly in French and partly in American oak. On the nose and palate generous earthy plum and currant fruits together with hints of citrus peel, cinnamon and tobacco. Drink from release–2009. Tentative Score 87–89.

AYALON, CABERNET-MERLOT, 2004: A blend of almost equal parts of Cabernet Sauvignon and Merlot with a small amount of Cabernet Franc, this dark, medium to full-bodied wine shows a generous hand on the oak, but that may well settle down with time. Beyond that, dusty tannins and good purple plum and blackcurrant aromas and flavors. Drink from release. Tentative Score 86–88.

AYALON, CABERNET SAUVIGNON-MERLOT, 2002: Medium-bodied, a blend of 66% Cabernet Sauvignon and 34% Merlot that spent two years in oak. Rich and round, with tannins nicely integrating and overall good balance. Drink up. Score 86.

Sela

SELA, FRENCH BLEND, 2005: Medium-dark garnet in color, with silky tannins, this blend of Syrah, Cabernet Sauvignon, Cabernet Franc and Petit Verdot (41%, 33%, 16% and 10% respectively) shows an appealing array of wild berries, currants and plums, those on a gently spicy background. Rich, round and moderately long. Drink from release–2009. Tentative Score 87–89.

SELA, FRENCH BLEND, 2003: A blend of Cabernet Sauvignon, Merlot, Cabernet Franc and Syrah (37%, 33%, 25% and 5% respectively), this smooth and round full-bodied red was aged in mostly new French oak for 16 months. Soft tannins well balanced by smoky oak and aromas and flavors of plums, cherries and raspberries. Drink now. Score 86.

SELA, FRENCH BLEND, 2002: Dark garnet toward purple, this blend of 50% Merlot, 33% Cabernet Sauvignon, 10% Syrah and 7% Cabernet Franc is medium-bodied and moderately tannic, showing an appealing touch of oak together with currant and berry fruits. Soft and generous but lacking depth. Drink up. Score 85.

SELA, AUSTRALIAN BLEND, 2002: A blend of 60% Shiraz and 40% Cabernet Sauvignon, this bright and supple wine offers up nice smoke-tinged berry and currant flavors. It has smooth tannins, moderate use of oak, and flavors that are tight and spicy through a medium-long finish. Drink up. Score 86.

SELA, MERLOT-CABERNET SAUVIGNON, 2001: An oak-aged blend of 50% each of Merlot and Cabernet Sauvignon. Low in both tannins and acidity, with the oak somehow dominating the too stingy berry and cherry aromas and flavors. Drink up. Score 80.

Nachshon

NACHSHON, CABERNET SAUVIGNON-MERLOT, 2002: A simple country-style wine with chunky tannins and a somewhat coarse influence of the wood and skimpy black fruits. Drink up. Score 84.

NACHSHON, CABERNET SAUVIGNON-MERLOT, 2000: Medium-bodied, smooth, with well-integrated tannins, those nicely balanced by currant, plum and tobacco aromas and flavors. Past its peak. Drink up. Score 84.

NACHSHON, MERLOT, 2002: Medium-dark garnet in color, medium-bodied with soft, well-integrated tannins and appealing blackberry, currant and cherry fruits. Look for hints of Oriental spices on the moderately-long finish. Drink up. Score 86.

Pushkin

PUSHKIN, 2005: This blend of Cabernet Sauvignon, Merlot, Cabernet Franc and Syrah (43%, 42%, 11% and 4% respectively) was aged partly in French *barriques* for 6–8 months and partly in stainless steel tanks. Medium-bodied, with soft tannins and aromas of spicy wood, raspberries and cassis. A good quaffer. Drink now. Score 85.

PUSHKIN, 2004: Dark garnet in color, this medium-bodied blend of 47% Cabernet Sauvignon, 35% Merlot, and 9% each of Cabernet Franc and Argaman shows a gentle wood influence, soft tannins and appealing berry-cherry and currant fruits. Not complex but round and easy to drink. Drink up. Score 85.

NACHSHON, PUSHKIN, 2003: A deep garnet red, medium-bodied blend of 60% Cabernet Sauvignon, 30% Merlot, 6% Argaman and 4%

Syrah, with light oak influence, soft tannins and appealing berry-cherry and currant fruits. Drink now. Score 86.

NACHSHON, PUSHKIN, 2002: Medium-bodied, this oak-aged blend of Cabernet Sauvignon and Merlot offers up clean, round flavors of currants and berries on a lightly tannic and spicy background. Drink up. Score 84.

Nashashibi ✹✹

Owned by brothers Munir and Nashashibi Nashashibi and located in the village of Eehbelin in the heart of the Carmel Mountains, on a site where wine has been made since Roman times, this winery is now producing 5,000 bottles annually of Chardonnay and Cabernet Sauvignon. Grapes come from the Upper Galilee as well as from their own vineyards at the foothills of the Carmel Mountains.

NASHASHIBI, CABERNET SAUVIGNON, 2004: Medium-dark garnet in color, medium-bodied, with firm, almost chunky tannins that give the wine a distinct country-style. Appealing aromas and flavors of spicy oak, cassis and blackberries. Drink now. Score 85.

NASHASHIBI, CABERNET SAUVIGNON, 2003, SPECIAL RESERVE: Dark ruby towards garnet, medium to full-bodied, with soft tannins and forward berry and black cherry fruits and a hint of spices that runs throughout. Drink now. Score 85.

NASHASHIBI, CABERNET SAUVIGNON, 2002, SPECIAL RESERVE: Medium to full-bodied with rich aromas and flavors of blackcurrants, chocolate and tobacco, the wine is mouth-filling and moderately long. Drink now. Score 85.

NASHASHIBI, CABERNET SAUVIGNON, 2001, SPECIAL RESERVE: Dark garnet with some browning, medium to full-bodied with plum, currant and herbal aromas but somewhat flat on the palate. Drink up. Score 84.

Natuf ✦✦

Founded by Meir Akel and Ze'ev Cinamon on Moshav Kfar Truman in the Central Plains not far from Ben Gurion Airport, this winery draws on grapes from the Ayalon Valley, and its first releases have been of Cabernet Sauvignon and a sweet, Port-style Merlot from the 2000 vintage. Current production is about 4,500 bottles annually.

NATUF, CABERNET SAUVIGNON, 2004: Dark ruby in color, medium to full-bodied, with firm tannins integrating nicely with smoky wood and forward cassis, black cherry and berry fruits, those matched by hints of sweet herbs. Drink now. Score 86.

NATUF, CABERNET SAUVIGNON, 2003: Ruby towards garnet red, medium-bodied, with chunky tannins and aromas and flavors of ripe berries, plums and cassis as well as a bare hint of sweet chocolate on the finish. An appealing country-style wine. Drink now. Score 85.

NATUF, CABERNET SAUVIGNON, 2002: A pleasant country-style wine, medium to full-bodied with chunky tannins, firm texture, and appealing cassis, berry and plum fruits. Drink up. Score 85.

NATUF, CABERNET SAUVIGNON, 2001: With somewhat chunky tannins, this medium to full-bodied wine offers up a pleasing berry-cherry and plum personality and good length. Drink up. Score 85.

NATUF, CABERNET SAUVIGNON, 2000: A blend of 85% Cabernet Sauvignon and 15% Merlot, this deep purple wine spent 14 months in small oak barrels and shows medium to full-body and good balance between moderate, well-integrated tannins, currants and plum fruits, as well as an appealing hint of spiciness at the end. Fully mature. Drink up. Score 84.

Neot Smadar ✶✶

This small winery, the southernmost in the country, is located on an oasis on Kibbutz Neot Smadar in the Jordan Valley, 60 kilometers north of Eilat. The winery released its first wines from the 2001 vintage and since its inception has relied entirely on organically raised grapes of Cabernet Sauvignon, Merlot, Chardonnay, Sauvignon Blanc and Muscat Canelli, all grown in vineyards on the *kibbutz*. Due to the unique climate conditions, theirs is invariably the earliest harvest in the country. Winemakers Orit Idan and Ruth Haluf are currently producing about 4,000 bottles annually.

NEOT SMADAR, CABERNET SAUVIGNON, 2004: Medium-bodied, with soft tannins and lightly spicy oak. Nicely balanced and showing berry and cherry aromas and flavors. Not typical of the variety but a pleasant quaffer. Drink now. Score 84.

NEOT SMADAR, CABERNET SAUVIGNON, 2003: Moderately tannic, medium-bodied and with fresh berry-cherry flavors, but somewhat flabby and lacking in liveliness, this wine raises the question of whether Cabernet Sauvignon is a good choice for lowland-desert cultivation. Drink now. Score 83.

NEOT SMADAR, CABERNET SAUVIGNON, 2002: Medium-bodied, with soft tannins and currant, cassis and light herbal-spicy aromas and flavors. Drink up. Score 84.

NEOT SMADAR, MERLOT, 2004: Deep royal purple in color, medium-bodied, with soft tannins and appealing aromas and flavors of blackberries, minerals and spices. Drink now–2008. Score 86.

NEOT SMADAR, MERLOT, 2003: Medium to full-bodied, deep royal purple in color and with generous mineral, herbal and green olive overlays. Somewhat atypical for Merlot, this wine has good balance and depth, and a surprisingly long and tannic finish. Drink now. Score 86.

NEOT SMADAR, MERLOT, 2002: Medium-bodied and rather light in color, with soft tannins and appealing black fruits, those perhaps somewhat too dominated by the wood in which the wine developed. Drink up. Score 84.

NEOT SMADAR, CABERNET SAUVIGNON-MERLOT, 2003: A blend of 85% Cabernet and 15% Merlot, still somewhat tannic and rough because of its youth, but showing good balance and a promise to reveal nice currant, berry and herbal aromas and flavors. Drink now. Score 87.

NEOT SMADAR, CHARDONNAY, 2005: Dark straw in color, medium-bodied, with generous acidity and minerality backing up tropical fruits and melon aromas and flavors. Not complex but refreshing and appealing. Drink now. Score 85.

NEOT SMADAR, CHARDONNAY, 2004: Lightly oaked, medium-bodied, with generous minerality and aromas and flavors of grapefruit, green apple and melon. Crisp, clean and refreshing. Drink now. Score 85.

NEOT SMADAR, CHARDONNAY, 2003: Light golden straw in color, this medium-bodied, gently oaked Chardonnay shows refined citrus, green apple and pineapple fruits, those complemented nicely by crisp acidity and appealing mineral undertones. Past its peak. Drink up. Score 86.

NEOT SMADAR, SAUVIGNON BLANC, FUMÉ, 2004: Light to medium-bodied, mineral rich, with moderate smoky and spicy oak highlighting summer fruits, citrus and grassy aromas and flavors. Drink now. Score 85

NEOT SMADAR, SAUVIGNON BLANC, FUMÉ, 2003: Golden straw in color, medium-bodied and reflecting just the right hint of smoky-toasted oak on a background of grassy and citrus aromas and flavors. Drink up. Score 85.

NEOT SMADAR, SAUVIGNON BLANC, 2003: Light golden straw in color, this light to medium-bodied wine offers up appealing peach and melon fruits along with mineral-crisp acidity. Drink up. Score 83.

Noga ✶

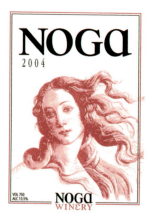

Owned by the Harari family and located between Gedera and Moshav Kidron on the Southern Plains, the winery released its first wines, 2,000 bottles, from the 2004 vintage. The winery currently produces two wines, Noga and Tom, blends of Cabernet Sauvignon and Merlot.

NOGA, 2004: A dark royal purple blend of 80% Merlot and 20% Cabernet Sauvignon, oak-aged for 12 months. Medium to full-bodied, with generous smoky wood, medicinal aromas and a potent alcoholic aroma that dominates and hides the black fruit. Drink now. Score 78.

TOM, 2004: Dark garnet towards purple, this blend of 80% Cabernet Sauvignon and 20% Merlot was aged in oak for 12 months. Medium to full-bodied, with currant and berry fruits buried under firm tannins and a far too strong sense of alcohol. Drink now. Score 78.

Odem Mountain ✯✯✯

Founded by Michael Elfasi and his sons Adam and Yishay in 2003 and situated in a newly constructed and thoroughly modern facility on Moshav Odem in the northern Golan Heights, the winery relies on grapes grown in its own vineyards, including one organic vineyard, as well as from other vineyards on the Golan and in the Upper Galilee. Currently producing wines based on Cabernet Sauvignon and Merlot, the winery is considering future releases of Sauvignon Blanc and Pinot Noir. Production for 2003 was 6,500 bottles and for 2004 and 2005 about 30,000 in the Reserve series, in the mid-range Nimrod and Odem Mountain series and under the label 'Volcanic' for wines made from organic grapes.

Reserve

RESERVE, CABERNET SAUVIGNON, 2005: Deep garnet towards royal purple in color, medium to full-bodied, with generous soft tannins and spicy wood in good balance with blackberry, currant and cassis fruits and, on the moderately long finish hints of cedar and freshly cut herbs. Drink from release–2010. Tentative Score 88–90.

RESERVE, CABERNET SAUVIGNON, 2004: Dark garnet towards black in color, full-bodied and already reflecting soft tannins and moderate wood influence. Traditional Cabernet Sauvignon aromas and flavors of blackcurrants and blackberries come together with hints of lead-pencil and sweet cedar. Drink now–2009. Score 89.

RESERVE, CABERNET SAUVIGNON, 2003: Dark ruby towards garnet in color, medium to full-bodied, with generous tannins and wood influence now starting to integrate. Needs time in the glass to open but when it does look for appealing black fruits, spices and chocolate leading to a long finish. Drink now. Score 87.

RESERVE, MERLOT, 2005: Dark ruby towards garnet in color, medium-bodied, with soft tannins and smoky, vanilla laded wood, those integrating nicely to show an appealing range of black fruits. Deep and long. Drink from release–2009. Tentative Score 87–89.

RESERVE, MERLOT, 2004: Deep purple, with gentle spices and hints of vanilla from the oak and an appealing array of aromas and flavors that includes wild berries, black cherries, and chocolate. Long and mouthfilling. Drink now–2008. Score 88.

RESERVE, MERLOT, 2003: Dark almost impenetrable garnet towards purple, medium to full-bodied, reflecting firm tannins and smoky oak from its 15 months in new and used oak *barriques*. Look for aromas and flavors of currants, plums and blueberries, those with hints of tobacco and vanilla on the finish. Drink now. Score 87.

Volcanic

VOLCANIC, 2004: Fermented partly in stainless steel and then allowed to undergo malolactic fermentation in French oak *barriques*, this medium to full-bodied, deep garnet colored wine shows primarily herbal aromas and flavors when first poured but then opens nicely in the glass to reveal currant and purple plum fruits. Drink now. Score 86.

Odem Mountain

ODEM MOUNTAIN, CABERNET SAUVIGNON, 2005: Dark ruby towards garnet in color, medium-bodied, with soft tannins integrating nicely and well balanced by spicy oak. On the spicy nose and palate, traditional Cabernet blackcurrant and wild berry fruits. Drink from release–2009. Tentative Score 86–88.

ODEM MOUNTAIN, CABERNET SAUVIGNON, 2004: Medium to full-bodied, deep garnet in color, with firm tannins just starting to reside, those balanced nicely by smoky oak and aromas and flavors of blackcurrants, plums and chocolate. Drink now. Score 87.

ODEM MOUNTAIN, CABERNET SAUVIGNON, 2003: Deep royal purple in color, medium-bodied and reflecting its 6 months in oak with an overlay of spices and vanilla. Look for aromas and flavors of blackcurrants and blackberries on a background of citrus peel and chocolate. Drink now. Score 86.

ODEM MOUNTAIN, MERLOT, 2004: Dark garnet towards purple, medium to full-bodied, with firm tannins already integrating nicely and generous ripe plum, black cherry and berry fruits backed up nicely by hints of spices and vanilla. Drink now–2008. Score 87.

ODEM MOUNTAIN, MERLOT, 2003: Medium-dark purple in color, medium to full-bodied, with well-integrating tannins and aromas and flavors of black cherries, berries and vanilla. Lacking backbone and somehow one dimensional. Drink up. Score 84.

Nimrod

NIMROD, CABERNET SAUVIGNON, 2005: Medium-bodied, with soft tannins, smoky oak and appealing aromas and flavors of currants, blackberries and spices, all lingering nicely. Drink from release–2009. Tentative Score 86–88.

NIMROD, CABERNET SAUVIGNON, 2004: Medium to full-bodied, with soft tannins integrating nicely, a nice hint of oak from having spent eight months in *barriques*, with flavors and aromas of black fruits along with hints of anise and chocolate. Round and generous. Drink now. Score 86.

NIMROD, CABERNET SAUVIGNON 2003: Garnet towards purple in color, medium-bodied, with soft tannins and sweet cedar wood. Black cherry, currant and hints of spices on the moderate finish. Drink now. Score 85.

NIMROD, MERLOT, 2004: Deep ruby towards purple, medium-bodied, with soft, well integrated tannins, and a gentle hand with the wood. Blackcurrants, berries and a nice hint of spiciness on the nose and palate. Drink now. Score 85.

NIMROD, CABERNET SAUVIGNON-MERLOT, 2004: Ruby towards garnet in color, medium-bodied, with soft tannins and generous but not overpowering oak. Cassis, blackberry and plum fruits with a nice hint of dark chocolate on the finish. Drink now. Score 86.

NIMROD, CABERNET SAUVIGNON-MERLOT, 2003: Dark ruby towards garnet in color, medium-bodied with light tannins and a bit of excess acidity, this blend of 60% Cabernet Sauvignon and 40% Merlot spent 15 months in oak. Opens nicely on the palate to reveal berry, plum and red currant fruits. Drink up. Score 85.

Pelter ★★★★

Established in 2002 on Kibbutz Ein Zivan on the Golan Heights by Tal Pelter, who studied oenology and worked at several wineries in Australia, the winery plans to move soon to nearby Kibbutz Merom Golan. Drawing on Cabernet Sauvignon, Merlot, Cabernet Franc, Shiraz, Grenache, Merlot and Chardonnay grapes from the Golan, the Upper Galilee and the Jerusalem Mountains, the winery, one of only four in the country to produce a sparkling wine, releases wines in two series: T-Selected and Pelter. Production from the 2002 vintage was about 4,000 bottles and current production is 30,000–35,000 bottles annually.

T-Selection

T-SELECTION, CABERNET SAUVIGNON, 2004: Dark, dense and concentrated, spicy and complex, with muscular and earthy currants and blackberries backed up by herbal and spicy oak, all with a generous dose of firm tannins but those all turning smooth and polished as they open to reveal tempting mineral, sage and cedar flavors. Long and generous and with the promise for true elegance. Drink from release–2012. Tentative Score 92–94.

T-SELECTION, SHIRAZ, 2004: Destined to develop for 18–20 months in French oak and already showing the kind of balance and structure that bodes well for the future. Full-bodied, deeply tannic and concentrated enough to be thought of as chewy, but under that, red currants, plums and red berries along with black pepper, rosemary, thyme and a very appealing hint of peppermint. Drink now–2012. Score 91.

T-SELECTION, CABERNET FRANC, 2004: Dark purple towards black in color, lush and elegant with a rich array of ripe raspberry, plum and berry fruits, those matched nicely by herbal and chocolate aromas and flavors. Firm tannins, especially on the finish but with just the right levels of French oak influence and both balance and structure that bode well for the future. Best 2008–2012. Tentative Score 90–92.

T-SELECTION, CABERNET FRANC, T-SELECTION, 2003: Oak aged for 14 months in new French *barriques*. Smooth, rich and supple, with ripe plum, currant and berry fruits together with an array of mocha, tobacco and espresso coffee, all complemented nicely by a hint of vanilla-scented oak. Finishes tannic so give this one some time to show its elegance. Best 2008–2012. Score 90.

T-SELECTION, SHIRAZ-GRENACHE, 2004: Medium-dark garnet towards royal purple in color, full-bodied, with generous tannins well balanced by the influence of aging in French oak casks for 14 months. Distinctive, ripe and luxurious, with near-sweet plum, blueberry and citrus peel intertwined beautifully with spicy, herbal and pomegranate aromas and flavors. Drink now–2014. Score 92.

T-SELECTION, SHIRAZ-GRENACHE, 2003: Almost impenetrably purple towards black in color, this rich, big and juicy wine is absolutely loaded with blackberry and plum fruits, those set off nicely by hints of cloves, coffee, citrus peel and black pepper, all on super-soft tannins. Generous, long and mouthcoating, a harmonious wine that will develop nicely in the bottle. Best 2008–2012. Score 91.

Pelter

PELTER, CABERNET SAUVIGNON-SHIRAZ, 2003: Deep ruby towards garnet, medium-bodied, with good balance between soft, well-integrating tannins, vanilla and herbal overtones and appealing currant, blackberry and red plum fruits. Long, but with a hint of bitterness that creeps in on the finish. Drink now. Score 86.

PELTER, CABERNET SAUVIGNON-MERLOT-CABERNET FRANC, 2004: A blend of 90% Cabernet Sauvignon with 5% each of Merlot and Cabernet Franc. Deep ruby towards garnet in color, medium to full-bodied, showing a rich core of berry and currant flavors, those with herbal and cedar overlays, all on a background of supple tannins. Long and generous. Best 2008–2012. Score 91.

PELTER, CABERNET SAUVIGNON-MERLOT-CABERNET FRANC, 2003: Medium to full-bodied, round and generous with silky soft tannins allowing us to focus on blueberry, plum, cola and light herbal-spicy notes, all leading to a long and satisfying finish. Drink now–2010. Score 90.

PELTER, CABERNET-MERLOT-CABERNET FRANC, 2002: Dark garnet in color, medium to full-bodied, and with an appealing berry-black cherry personality. Soft tannins, overall good balance, and a mouth-filling finish. Drink now. Score 86.

PELTER, CABERNET SAUVIGNON-SHIRAZ, 2004: Aged in American oak for 18 months, this blend of 50% each of Cabernet Sauvignon and Shiraz shows a medium-dark garnet color, a strong acidic backbone and appealing spices and vanilla from the wood, none of which hold back layers of blackberry, cherry, herbal and earthy aromas and flavors. Good concentration, ripeness and smoothness lead to a long and generous finish. Drink now–2012. Score 91.

PELTER, CABERNET SAUVIGNON-SHIRAZ, 2003: Dark ruby in color, medium to full-bodied, with soft tannins integrating nicely. On the nose and palate berry, currant, plum and tobacco aromas, those opening in the glass to reveal hints of espresso and chocolate. Drink now–2009. Score 88.

PELTER, CABERNET SAUVIGNON-SHIRAZ, 2002: Medium-bodied, dark garnet in color, this oak-aged blend of 65% Cabernet Sauvignon and 35% Shiraz shows appealing herbal and leathery overlays, those nicely highlighting blackcurrant, plum and spicy oak aromas and flavors. Drink now. Score 87.

PELTER, CHARDONNAY, UNOAKED, 2005: Lovely! Fresh and lively, with generous but not at all overbearing acidity showing appealing peach, apricot and tropical fruits on a background that tantalizes with hints of freshly cut grass. Drink now. Score 90.

PELTER, SAUVIGNON BLANC, 2005: Blended with 10% of Semillon, unoaked, as are all of Pelter's white wines, this crisp and refreshing wine offers up bright and generous aromas and flavors of guava, grapefruit and green apples and, lurking in the background, a nearly unconscious hint of celery. Not for long-term cellaring but delicious and enchanting. Drink now. Score 91.

PELTER, SAUVIGNON BLANC, 2004: Crisp, clean and straightforward, light golden straw in color, medium-bodied, with good balancing acidity allowing appealing citrus, melon and light grassiness to show through. Drink now. Score 87.

PELTER, SAUVIGNON BLANC, 2003: Golden straw in color, this medium-bodied, crisply acidic and almost flinty-dry white offers up generous aromas and flavors of citrus and melon fruits, those on a background of a light hint of freshly mown grass. Drink up. Score 86.

PELTER, SAUVIGNON BLANC, 2002: An Australian-style blend of 90% Sauvignon Blanc and 10% Semillon, this white wine is far too light in body and color, showing stingy grassy, grapefruit and pineapple aromas and flavors, followed by a hint of grassy bitterness on the finish. Somewhat past its peak. Drink up. Score 82.

PELTER, SEMILLON, 2003: Partly fermented in stainless steel, and part in *barriques* for two months. Perhaps the very first truly successful local dry Semillon, with a character of herbal and pepper aromas and flavors highlighting citrus, pears and green apples, all leading to a long and spicy finish. Approachable and thoroughly enjoyable, young but with the definite potential to develop and flesh out with appropriate cellaring. Drink now–2008. Score 91.

PELTER, BLANC DE BLANC BRUT, 2ND EDITION, N.V.: Pelter's second release of a sparkling wine, this too to be released as a non-vintage wine but with Chardonnay grapes entirely from the 2003 vintage. Gentle yeast and hints of nicely toasted white bread with sharp bubbles that go on and on. Fresh, aromatic, well focused and intense, with grapefruit and lime fruits backed up by hints of cloves, ginger and roasted nuts. Drink now–2010. Score 90.

PELTER, BLANC DE BLANC, BRUT, 1ST EDITION, N.V.: Although categorized as a non-vintage sparkling wine, the grapes for this bottling all come from the 2002 vintage. With a long, high mousse, sharp bubbles and a marked overlay of yeast, this Chardonnay-based wine also shows tropical fruits and citrus peel aromas and flavors, those together with a tempting hint of bitter oranges that arise on the long finish. Not for long-term cellaring but delicious now. Score 89.

Psagot**

Located in the northern Jerusalem Mountains, overlooking Wadi Kelt (Nachal Prat), the winery was founded by Na'ama and Ya'akov Berg, who planted their first vineyards in 1998. The oak *barriques* used by the winery are stored in a cave containing ancient pressing facilities, which maintains 90% humidity and temperatures up to 18 degrees Celsius. The winery is currently producing a Cabernet Sauvignon, a Merlot, a Viognier and a Chardonnay as well as a Port-style wine. Production for 2004 was 15,000 bottles and for 2005 about 17,000 bottles.

PSAGOT, CABERNET SAUVIGNON, 2004: Generous oak and firm, country-style tannins, those opening to reveal blackberry, black cherry and currant fruits along with hints of tobacco and herbs. Well balanced and moderately-long. Drink now. Score 85. **K**

PSAGOT, CABERNET SAUVIGNON, RESERVE, 2003: Intense oak and vanilla overshadowing soft tannins and moderate levels of currant and plum fruits. Drink up. Score 80. **K**

PSAGOT, MERLOT, 2004: Aged in French and American oak barrels, this generously oaky, dark garnet and distinctly plummy wine shows medium-body, soft tannins and a hint of spiciness. Drink now–2008. Score 85. **K**

PSAGOT, EDOM, 2004: A blend of 75% Cabernet Sauvignon and 25% Merlot, reflecting its 14 months in *barriques* with firm but nicely integrating tannins, spicy and vanilla-rich oak and, on the nose and palate, blackberries, currants and an appealing hint of freshly turned earth. A solid effort, with a long berry-rich finish. Drink now–2008. Score 87. **K**

PSAGOT, CHARDONNAY RESERVE, 2004: Aged for 10 months in 300 liter French oak barrels, this crisp and lively wine shows appealing aromas and flavors of citrus and tropical fruits on first attack, those yielding nicely to pear and vanilla on the finish. Drink now. Score 87. K

PSAGOT, VIOGNIER, 2005: Medium-bodied, crisply dry, with floral and mineral overlays showing peach, melon and pear fruits. Long and generous. Drink now. Score 87. K

Ra'anan ✶✶

Established by Ra'anan Margalit in 1994 on Moshav Ganei Yochanan in the Southern Plains and utilizing Cabernet Sauvignon, Merlot and Chardonnay grapes from his own vineyards, those located near the winery as well as at Karmei Yosef, current production of the winery is about 8,000 bottles annually. In order to avoid confusion with the Margalit winery, the owner changed the name from Ra'anan Margalit to Ra'anan with the releases of the 2003 vintage.

RA'ANAN, CABERNET SAUVIGNON, RESERVE, 2004: With its chunky and somewhat coarse tannins, this is a country-style wine but one with charm, showing currant, plum and wild berry aromas and flavors. Drink now. Score 85.

RA'ANAN, CABERNET SAUVIGNON, RESERVE, 2003: A country-style wine, the best to date from this winery. Medium-bodied, with chunky and firm tannins but those yielding in the glass to reveal smoky wood, black plums and cassis flavors. Drink now. Score 85.

RA'ANAN MARGALIT, CABERNET SAUVIGNON, 2002: Dark garnet and medium-bodied, this red has generous tannins, wood and cherry, plum and spices. A pleasant country-style wine. Drink up. Score 83.

RA'ANAN MARGALIT, CABERNET SAUVIGNON, 2001: Medium-bodied, with firm tannins that promise to integrate nicely and appealing black cherry and currant fruits as well as hints of spicy oak. Past its peak. Drink up. Score 84.

RA'ANAN MARGALIT, CABERNET SAUVIGNON, 2000: A country-style, medium-bodied wine with chunky tannins that go nicely with black fruits, spices and a light earthy-herbal overlay. Well past its peak. Drink up. Score 79.

RA'ANAN, MERLOT, 2003: Medium-bodied, with soft tannins and hints of spicy oak. Aromas and flavors of black cherries and wild berries. Drink now. Score 84.

RA'ANAN, MERLOT, 2002: Garnet towards purple, medium-bodied, with soft tannins and a pleasant berry-cherry personality. Drink up. Score 82.

RA'ANAN MARGALIT, MERLOT, 2001: Dark cherry red toward purple, medium-bodied, with moderate tannins and appealing flavors of black cherries and wild berries. Lacking depth or complexity and somewhat past its peak. Drink up. Score 82.

RA'ANAN MARGALIT, MERLOT, 2000: Garnet colored and medium-bodied, with soft tannins and forward berry, cherry and currant fruits, those hindered by a not entirely clean and somewhat overly alcoholic finish. Well past its peak. Drink up. Score 74.

RA'ANAN, MERLOT-CABERNET SAUVIGNON, 2003: Garnet towards purple in color, with soft tannins integrating nicely and on the nose and palate spicy cedar, berry and cassis fruits. Drink now. Score 84.

RA'ANAN, MERLOT-CABERNET SAUVIGNON, 2002: A medium-bodied blend of 80% Merlot and 20% Cabernet Sauvignon. Sweet tannins, light wood influence and ripe berry-cherry fruits. Drink up. Score 84.

RA'ANAN, CHARDONNAY, 2003: Dark golden straw in color, medium-bodied, with aromas and flavors of citrus, pineapple and green apples. Drink up. Score 84.

Ramim **

Founded in 1999 on Moshav Shachar in the Southern Plains by Nechemia Ya'akobi and Nitzan Eliyahu, the latter of whom is also the winemaker, and producing their first wines from the 2000 harvest, the winery draws grapes from three self-owned vineyards, in Kfar Yuval and Safsufa, both on the Lebanese border, and on Moshav Shachar. Red varieties include Cabernet Sauvignon, Merlot, Sangiovese, Cabernet Franc, Syrah from France and Shiraz from Australia, as well as early plantings of Barbera, and Nebbiolo. White varieties include Zinfandel, Chardonnay, Gewurztraminer, Riesling, Semillon and Muscat.

The winery, which relies on Hungarian, French and American oak barrels, releases wines in four series: Special Reserve, Reserve, Ramim and Yuval. Production in 2002 was 22,000 bottles, in 2003, 55,000 bottles, in 2004 about 75,000 bottles, and in 2005 about 80,000 bottles. The wines have been kosher since the 2003 vintage.

Special Reserve

SPECIAL RESERVE, CABERNET SAUVIGNON, 2002: This blend of 85% Cabernet Sauvignon, 10% Merlot and 5% Cabernet Franc is best described as wood-driven, the smoky oak and tannins so dominant that they all but suppress whatever black fruits struggle to make themselves felt. Drink now–2008. Score 83.

SPECIAL RESERVE, MERLOT, 2002: Dark, almost impenetrable garnet towards black in color, aged in barrels for a lengthy 29 months, now so dominated by wood that it is difficult to find either the tannins or the fruits here. Drink up. Score 82.

Reserve

RESERVE, CABERNET SAUVIGNON, 2002: Aged for 15 months in 400 liter Hungarian oak barrels, this deep cherry-red toward garnet wine shows solid tannins, those well balanced by vanilla and spiciness from the wood and a generous array of blackcurrant and blackberry fruits. Drink now. Score 86.

RESERVE, MERLOT, 2002: Aged for 14 months in new Hungarian oak barrels, the wine shows a few off aromas when first poured, but those fade quickly in the glass making place for aromas and flavors of plums and black cherries, vanilla and sweet cedar. Somewhat acidic. Drink now. Score 84.

Ramim

RAMIM, CABERNET SAUVIGNON, SHACHAR, 2003: Oak-aged in 165-liter Hungarian oak barrels, this medium-bodied red shows firm but well integrated tannins and an array of currant and plum fruits on a spicy background with appealing herbal hints coming in on the finish. Drink now. Score 86. K.

RAMIM, CABERNET SAUVIGNON, 2002: Oak aged for 15 months and with the addition of 6% Merlot, this dark ruby towards garnet wine shows medium-body, soft near-sweet tannins and aromas and flavors of raspberries and cassis on a background of spices and smoky oak. Drink now. Score 85.

RAMIM, CABERNET SAUVIGNON, PSAGOT, 2002: A minor variation on a theme of the wine reviewed above, this one with only 3% of Merlot. Deep garnet in color, medium-bodied, and when first poured showing somewhat coarse tannins that tend to dominate, reflecting its 15 months in oak. Given considerable time in the glass these recede and allow the currant, berry and black cherry flavors to show through. Drink now. Score 85.

RAMIM, CABERNET SAUVIGNON, 2001: Blended with 14% of Merlot and aged in oak for 18 months, this medium to full-bodied country-style wine shows generous chunky tannins, those melding nicely with plum, blackberry and cassis flavors. Some spices coming in from mid-palate and leading to a medium-long finish. Drink up. Score 82.

RAMIM, MERLOT, SHACHAR, 2003: Aged in small oak casks, with just firm enough tannins balanced nicely by vanilla and spices from the wood, the wine shows good spicy plum and black cherry fruits as well as hints of tobacco and cocoa on the long finish. Drink now. Score 85. **K**

RAMIM, MERLOT, PSAGOT, 2002: Aged in oak for 28 months. Medium to full-bodied, with super-generous spicy wood and an overabundance of acidity, both of which work hard to hide the red berry, cassis and black cherry fruits that fight to make themselves felt. Drink up. Score 83.

RAMIM, MERLOT, 2001: With the addition of 14% Cabernet Sauvignon to add backbone, this medium-bodied, moderately tannic wine shows a modest band of currant and plum fruits, those on a background of spices and Mediterranean herbs. An unwelcome note of earthiness comes in on the finish. Drink up. Score 82.

RAMIM, SANGIOVESE, 2003: Aged in 165-liter Hungarian oak barrels, this deep garnet toward royal purple, medium-bodied red has generous but soft and well-integrated tannins, but hardly any aromas, and flavors of plum, berry and cassis that fade too quickly. Drink now. Score 84. **K**

RAMIM, CABERNET FRANC, 2004: Deep ruby towards garnet, with gripping tannins that need time to settle down, but intrinsic good balance that promises that the plum, wild berry and wood-inspired spices and vanilla will show through nicely. Drink now. Score 85. **K**

RAMIM, CABERNET FRANC, 2003: This dark ruby toward garnet, medium to full-bodied oak-aged red shows appealing black fruit, cassis and spicy flavors but hardly any aromas. Drink up. Score 84. **K**

RAMIM, BARBERA, PSAGOT, 2003: Aged in small barrels for 1 year, medium-bodied, with soft tannins nicely integrated with smoky oak and appealing currant, cherry, berry and earthy notes. Drink now. Score 86. **K**

RAMIM, CABERNET SAUVIGNON-MERLOT, 2004: A deep garnet, medium-bodied blend of 55% Cabernet Sauvignon and 45% Merlot, aged in oak for about 6 months. Soft tannins and good balance with aromas and flavors of ripe berries and plums as well as hints of sweet cedar and vanilla. Drink now–2008. Score 86. **K**

RAMIM, CABERNET SAUVIGNON-MERLOT, 2003: Aged in small oak barrels for 6 months, this blend of Cabernet Sauvignon, Merlot, Pinot

Noir and Syrah (54%, 31%, 8% and 7% respectively) has dark purple color, medium body, soft tannins and berry, currant and plum fruits on a lightly earthy-vanilla background. Somewhat short on the finish. Drink now. Score 85. K

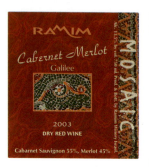

RAMIM, CABERNET SAUVIGNON-MERLOT, PSAGOT, 2002: A blend of 60% Cabernet Sauvignon and 40% Merlot, aged in oak for 28 months. Too generous wood, tannins that seem firm at one moment and soft at another, and a generous spicy and vegetal overlay not fully in balance with blackberry, currant and plum fruits. Drink now. Score 84.

RAMIM, CHARDONNAY, SHACHAR, 2004: Oak aged, golden straw in color, medium-bodied, showing smoky oak, green apple and citrus peel aromas, all on a somewhat acidic background. Drink up. Score 82. K

RAMIM, CHARDONNAY DESSERT WINE, 2003: Appealing in its youth but now falling apart and showing oily, earthy and herbal aromas. Drink up. Score 75. K

RAMIM, WHITE RIESLING, SHACHAR, 2004: Semi-dry, light and fruity, with generous acidity to keep it lively. Flavors of citrus and tropical fruits. Drink up. Score 83. K

RAMIM, RIESLING, SCHACHAR, 2003: Light to medium-bodied, semi-dry, and with skimpy citrus and summer fruits. A bit flat. Drink up. Score 80. K

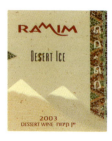

RAMIM, CHARDONNAY, DESSERT ICE, 2003: Showing dramatically better than at an earlier tasting, almost as if my palate was discerning two different wines. Medium-bodied, dark golden in color, with generously sweet kiwi, pineapple and citrus fruits backed up by gentle acidity. At its best served icy-cold. Drink now. Score 84. K

RAMIM, CABERNET FRANC, DESSERT ICE, 2003: Strawberry colored, light to medium-bodied, tutti-fruity in flavor, unabashedly sweet and without enough balancing acidity. Score 70. K

Yuval

YUVAL, CABERNET SAUVIGNON, 2003: Medium-bodied, with gripping tannins and generous wood but those yielding nicely to reveal currant, berry and herbal aromas and flavors. A rather standard but pleasant wine. Drink now. Score 85. K

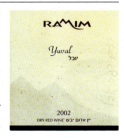

YUVAL, MERLOT, 2003: Deep cherry towards garnet red, medium-bodied, with soft tannins, this is a smooth, well-balanced wine showing lightly spicy berry, cherry and plum flavors and aromas. Somewhat internationalized in style. Drink now. Score 85. K

YUVAL, CABERNET SAUVIGNON-MERLOT, 2003: Deep ruby towards garnet, medium-bodied, and with soft tannins and moderate oak. On the nose and palate currants, plums and berries leading to a medium-long finish. Not complex but appealing. Drink now. Score 85. K

YUVAL, CABERNET SAUVIGNON-MERLOT, 2002: This medium-dark garnet-red, medium-bodied blend of 58% Cabernet Sauvignon and 42% Merlot was aged in small oak barrels for 15 months. With tannins integrating nicely and good balance between tannins, wood and black fruits, this is a soft and smooth if not overly complex wine. Drink up. Score 86.

Ramot Naftali ✶✶

Founded on Moshav Ramot Naftali in the Upper Galilee in 2003 by vintner Yitzhak Cohen working with winemaker Tal Pelter, this small winery owns vineyards planted with Cabernet Sauvignon, Merlot, Shiraz, Petit Verdot and Malbec. Production from the 2003 vintage was 1,300 bottles and 6,000 bottles will be released from the 2004 vintage.

RAMOT NAFTALI, CABERNET SAUVIGNON, RESERVE, 2003: Dark ruby towards garnet, medium to full-bodied, reflecting its 18 months in French oak with generous wood but that in good balance with tannins and fruit. On the first attack, tobacco and espresso, those yielding nicely to aromas of ripe berries and currants. Drink now–2009. Score 87.

Recanati ★★★★

Established in 2000, this modern winery located in the Hefer Valley in the north part of the Sharon region relies on grapes from their own as well as contract vineyards, primarily in the Upper Galilee. Under the supervision of California trained winemaker Lewis Pasco, the winery currently produces wines in several series: the top-of-the-line Special Reserve wines, which are often blends of Cabernet Sauvignon and Merlot; and two varietal series, Reserve and Recanati, which now include Cabernet Sauvignon, Merlot, Syrah, Petite Sirah, Chardonnay and most recently Sauvignon Blanc. The winery also has a popularly priced series named Yasmine. Production in 2002 was 230,000 bottles and in 2003, 500,000. Output for 2004 and 2005 was about 700,000 bottles and future target production is over one million bottles, 30% of which are destined for export. Winery owner Lenny Recanati is currently negotiating the purchase of land in the Judean Hills on which to build a new and larger winery to replace the existing facility.

Special Reserve

SPECIAL RESERVE, 2004: An oak-aged blend of 92% Cabernet Sauvignon and 8% Merlot. Youthful royal purple, full-bodied, with silky smooth tannins and smoky, toasty oak that yield to reveal rich spicy currant, wild berry, black cherry and mineral-minty sensations that come in on the long finish. Best 2008–2012. Tentative Score 91–93. **K**

SPECIAL RESERVE, 2003: A blend of grapes from vineyards at Manara and Kerem Ben Zimra, this deep, broad, gently tannic blend of 72% Cabernet Sauvignon and 28% Merlot combines Cabernet currants, cassis and spicy-herbal overtones with typical Merlot softness. Good balance between wood, tannins and fruit and a long finish. Best 2008–2012. Score 92. K

SPECIAL RESERVE, 2001: An oak-aged blend of 96% Cabernet Sauvignon and 4% Merlot, this full-bodied, deep garnet toward purple wine offers tempting currant, blackberry and raspberry fruits, those backed up nicely by generous but soft and well-integrated tannins and a nice touch of oak. Drink now–2008. Score 90. K

SPECIAL RESERVE, 2000: Aged 18 months in new French oak, this full-bodied now well-matured blend of 50% each of Cabernet Sauvignon and Merlot, with its once tight tannins now softened, shows good balance between tannins, fruit and smoky oak. With tempting currant, black cherry and vanilla aromas and flavors, and herbal, earthy and leathery notes on the long finish. Not for further cellaring and with a good deal of variation between bottles. Drink up. Score 90. K

Reserve

RESERVE, CABERNET SAUVIGNON, 2004: Deep garnet in color, this medium to full-bodied wine with tannins softening nicely shows aromas and flavors of currants and black cherries as well as hints of spicy wood and Mediterranean herbs. Drink now–2010. Score 89. K

RESERVE, CABERNET SAUVIGNON, 2003: Ripe and rich, well balanced, with medium to full-body and soft tannins, traditional Cabernet currant and berry fruits as well as hints of anise and light toasty oak flavors. Drink now–2010. Score 90. K

RESERVE, CABERNET SAUVIGNON, 2002: Firm tannins here, but given time to open in the glass the wine shows sweet cedar, smoky oak, currant, plum and anise flavors. Somewhat short and perhaps lacking the structure for further cellaring. Drink now. Score 87. K

RESERVE, CABERNET SAUVIGNON, 2001: Dark in color, and firmly tannic but with concentrated currant, berry and spicy aromas and flavors, the wine has a welcoming hint of raspberries on the long finish. Elegant and complex. Drink now. Score 90. K

RECANATI

RESERVE, CABERNET SAUVIGNON, 2000: Having lost the freshness and first flush of youth, now with hints of browning. Generous oak here and still some black fruits, truffles and leather. Drink up. Score 87. **K**

RESERVE, MERLOT, 2004: A single-vineyard wine, with grapes harvested at Manara. Medium to full-bodied, with firm tannins yielding nicely and well balanced by sweet oak, currant, black cherry, earthy and herbal aromas and flavors. Chocolate and appealing anise flavors on the long finish. Drink now–2011. Score 90. **K**

RESERVE, MERLOT, 2003: With firm tannins giving a solid backbone, sweet oak that makes itself felt from first attack to the long finish, and layers of currant, black cherry, mocha and chocolate, a concentrated and graceful wine. Drink now–2009. Score 90. **K**

RESERVE, MERLOT, 2002: Showing cherry and wild berry fruits backed up by hints of tea, herbs and cedar wood. Not overly complex and with a still tannic edge that lingers into the finish. Drink now. Score 87. **K**

RESERVE, MERLOT, 2001: Dark, deep and mysterious, this tempting medium to full-bodied wine has plenty of smooth tannins and abundant dark fruit, chocolate, vanilla and smoky-herbal aromas and flavors. Drink now. Score 90. **K**

RESERVE, MERLOT, 2000: Deep royal purple, this medium to full-bodied red offers aromas and flavors of blackcurrants, purple plums, eucalyptus and sage. Still somewhat heavy on the oak, but well structured and balanced enough to carry that. Drink up. Score 89. **K**

RESERVE, SHIRAZ, 2004: Ripe and supple, with black cherry, herbal and beefy aromas and flavors, those coming together with firm tannins and sweet cedar wood. On the long appealingly tannic finish, toasted bread and mocha. Drink now–2009. Score 89. **K**

RESERVE, PETITE SIRAH-ZINFANDEL, 2004: Aged in American oak, this dark garnet blend of 70% Petite Syrah and 30% Zinfandel is packed with ripe blueberry, blackberry, plum, pepper, licorice and mineral aromas and flavors. Generous but not exaggerated oak and tannins, those in fine balance with the fruits. Drink now–2010. Score 90. **K**

RESERVE, PETITE SIRAH-ZINFANDEL, 2003: A dark garnet blend of 80% Petite Syrah and 20% Zinfandel, aged in American oak. Tannic, concentrated, full-bodied and with expressive spicy plum and black cherry fruits, those matched nicely by spicy, earthy overlays and a light hint of asphalt on the finish. Drink now. Score 89. **K**

RESERVE, CHARDONNAY, 2003: Deep golden, smooth and supple, with a pleasant earthy accent to pineapple, hazelnut and mineral notes, this stylish wine offers up appealing oak seasoning, a light buttery note and a round and mouth-filling finish. Drink now. Score 89. K

RESERVE, CHARDONNAY, 2002: Oak aged for about 9 months, still zesty and with a golden color, the wine shows pear and hazelnut, as well as generous buttery-smoky oak aromas and flavors on the finish. Drink up. Score 88. K

Recanati

RECANATI, CABERNET SAUVIGNON, 2004: Deep ruby towards garnet, medium to full-bodied, with near-sweet tannins and generous currant and berry fruits, those backed up by smoky wood and earthiness. Drink now–2008. Score 87. K

RECANATI, CABERNET SAUVIGNON, 2003: Medium-bodied, with soft tannins and appealing berry, currant and plum fruits, all with a hint of spice on the background. Drink now. Score 85. K

RECANATI, CABERNET SAUVIGNON, 2002: Soft tannins, inviting currant and plum flavors, and hints of spices and herbs make this medium to full-bodied wine is just a bit past its peak. Drink up. Score 85. K

RECANATI, CABERNET SAUVIGNON, 2001: Medium-deep garnet toward purple in color, the wine shows appealing plum, currant and blackberry fruits overlaid by pleasant spicy hints. Perhaps somewhat heavy on the oak but that settling in nicely with the tannins and fruits. Drink up. Score 85. K

RECANATI, MERLOT, 2004: Medium-bodied, soft but concentrated, with a core of currant, blackberry and cherry fruits matched nicely by cedar and anise. Well balanced and with a moderately long finish on which hints of exotic spices make themselves felt. Drink now–2008. Score 88. K

RECANATI, MERLOT, 2003: Smooth, ripe and fruity, with cherry, berry, earthy and herbal aromas and flavors. Young and vibrant, with good balance between tannins and fruits. Drink now. Score 86. K

RECANATI, MERLOT, 2002: Medium-bodied, somewhat on the earthy side, with wild berry and juniper accents along with sweet cedar and spices. Round but a bit tight. Drink up. Score 85. **K**

RECANATI, MERLOT, 2001: After 8 months in oak, this medium-bodied red may not have too many complexities but it is still an appealing wine, with cherry, currant and blueberry flavors along with a bit of toasty oak, and modest tannins that are felt mostly on the finish. Somewhat past its peak. Drink up. Score 86. **K**

RECANATI, SHIRAZ, 2004: Aged in French and American oak, medium to full-bodied, with near-sweet tannins, a gentle hand with spicy oak and a primarily plum-based personality. Generous and appealing but lacking the balance for more than short-term cellaring. Drink now. Score 87. **K**

RECANATI, SHIRAZ, 2003: Aged for 12 months in new French and American oak, this dark ruby towards purple, medium-bodied wine shows moderate near-sweet tannins and good balance along with enchanting aromas and flavors of jammy fruits, those with spicy, peppery and licorice overtones, all reflecting the judicious use of oak. Drink now–2008. Score 89. **K**

RECANATI, BARBERA, 2004: Made entirely from grapes from the Manara vineyard, this youthful royal purple towards dark garnet colored, medium to full-bodied red shows excellent balance between gentle oak, acidity and a tempting array of plum, black cherry and currant fruits, those matched nicely by overtones of freshly turned earth and chocolate. As the wine develops in the bottle look for hints of tobacco and white truffles. Drink now–2010. Score 90. **K**

RECANATI, BARBERA, 2003: Aged for 9 months in used French *barriques*, this pleasant little cherry towards garnet colored, medium-bodied wine has light tannins allowing the cherry and berry flavors to come through nicely. Lacking complexity but pleasant. Drink now. Score 88. **K**

RECANATI, CHARDONNAY, 2005: Light golden straw in color, medium-bodied, with crisp minerality and tempting aromas and flavors of citrus, melon and green apples. Lively and refreshing. Drink now. Score 87. **K**

RECANATI, CHARDONNAY, 2004: Golden straw in color, medium-bodied, with aromas and flavors of tropical fruits, melon and citrus. Lively, complex, round and long with a light mineral-yeasty finish. Drink now. Score 87. **K**

RECANATI, CHARDONNAY, 2003: Developed *sur lie* for 8 months, this medium to full-bodied Chardonnay reflects just a hint of wood over appealing citrus and tropical fruits. Good balancing acidity here and a nice hint of spiciness Drink now. Score 88. K

RECANATI, CHARDONNAY, 2002: Light golden straw in color, with generous litchis and pineapple fruits and good acidity. Somewhat past its peak and now showing a butternut-caramel hint on the finish. Drink up. Score 85. K

RECANATI, SAUVIGNON BLANC, 2005: A lively straw in color, this unoaked white shows medium body and, on the nose and palate, crisp citrus and summer fruits. Not complex but clean, crisp and refreshing. Drink now. Score 88. K

RECANATI, SAUVIGNON BLANC, 2004: Light straw colored, medium-bodied, not specially aromatic but with very appealing summer fruits on a grassy, earthy background. Drink now. Score 87. K

RECANATI, SAUVIGNON BLANC, 2003: This unoaked, fresh and lively medium-bodied white starts off with earthy-mineral aromas, those yielding nicely to guava, citrus, grass and nectarine flavors. Drink up. Score 86. K

Yasmine

YASMINE, RED, 2005: A somewhat hodge-podge blend of Cabernet Sauvignon, Merlot, Shiraz and Pinot Noir treated to oak chips while developing. Ruby towards purple in color, light to medium-bodied, with silky soft tannins and a basically berry-cherry and chocolate personality. Lacking complexity but a soft, smooth quaffer. Drink up. Score 85. K

YASMIN, RED, 2004: Dark cherry red in color, medium-bodied, with soft tannins, gentle wood and blackberry and currant fruits. Drink up. Score 84. K

YASMIN, WHITE, 2005: Light golden straw in color, light to medium-bodied, with grapefruit and nectarine aromas and flavors. A good summertime quaffer. Drink up. Score 85. K

YASMIN, WHITE, 2004: A pleasant little white with aromas and flavors of citrus and summer fruit. Crisp, clean and refreshing. Drink up. Score 84. **K**

Red Poetry ✶✶

Established in 2001 by Dubi Tal on Havat Tal on the western slopes of the Judean Mountains, the winery has its own vineyards with Cabernet Sauvignon, Merlot, Cabernet Franc, Petit Verdot, Shiraz, Petite Sirah, Sangiovese, Riesling and Gewurztraminer grapes. Current production is 3,000 bottles annually.

RED POETRY, CABERNET SAUVIGNON, 2003: Ruby towards royal purple in color, medium-bodied, with soft, near-sweet tannins and generous oak, but those opening to show currant, berry and cherry fruits on a lightly spicy background. Drink now–2008. Score 85.

RED POETRY, CABERNET SAUVIGNON, RESERVE, 2003: Generous spicy wood and firm tannins not all that well balanced, with medium body. Despite that, appealing blackcurrant and plum fruits, generous spices and a light herbal finish. Drink now. Score 85.

RED POETRY, CABERNET SAUVIGNON, RESERVE, 2002: Dark garnet towards royal purple, medium-bodied, with mouth-coating tannins and generous smoky oak that yield slowly to reveal straightforward but appealing currant, berry and spicy aromas and flavors. Drink now. Score 84.

RED POETRY, CABERNET SAUVIGNON, 2002: Dark garnet in color, medium-bodied, with near sweet ripe fruits and with an aroma of decaying mushrooms. Drink up. Score 75.

RED POETRY, CABERNET SAUVIGNON, 2001: Medium to full-bodied, deep garnet in color, and with simple plum and wood-imparted flavors that are hidden under biting tannins and a too herbal overlay that runs throughout. Drink up. Score 78.

RED POETRY, MERLOT, 2004: Dusty garnet red in color, medium-bodied with rather gripping tannins, this oak-aged red shows minimal red fruits. Lacking balance and meant for early drinking. Drink from release. Tentative Score 78–80.

RED POETRY, MERLOT, 2003: Brownish-red, with soft tannins, and a good deal of acidity throwing the wine out of balance and giving the black fruits a distinctly sour flavor. Score 70.

RED POETRY, MERLOT, 2002: Blended with 10% of Cabernet Franc, this once dark garnet wine is now going to brown and caramelizing. Past its peak. Drink up. Score 73.

RED POETRY, MERLOT-SHIRAZ-CABERNET SAUVIGNON, EHRLICH, 2002: Oak aged for 12 months, dark cherry red towards garnet, medium-bodied, with firm tannins that tend to hold back whatever black fruits are here. Drink up. Score 76.

RED POETRY, SHIRAZ-CABERNET SAUVIGNON, 2002: Medium-bodied, with soft, nicely integrating tannins set off well by hints of spicy oak. On the nose and palate blackberry, currant and plum fruits. Round and easy to drink. Drink up. Score 83.

RED POETRY, CABERNET FRANC-MERLOT, 2003: Medium-bodied, with chunky, country-style tannins and an overly generous dose of smoky wood. A few spicy berry and currant fruits here but short and one-dimensional. Drink up. Score 79.

RED POETRY, RHINE RIESLING, 2004: Categorized as dry but on the palate half-dry, with perhaps too generous acidity. Lacking varietal traits but with some clean summer fruits and citrus. An acceptable quaffer. Drink up. Score 83.

Rosh Pina *

Set in the village of Rosh Pina in the Galilee, this small winery was founded by Ya'akov Blum in 2001 and released its first wines in 2002. The winery draws on grapes from the Galilee, those including Cabernet Sauvignon, Shiraz and Carignan. The winery is currently releasing about 4,000 bottles annually.

ROSH PINA, CABERNET SAUVIGNON, PNINA, 2004: Medium-bodied, dark brick red, with chunky tannins, this simple country-style wine offers up only skimpy berry and plum flavors. Drink up. Score 76.

ROSH PINA, CABERNET SAUVIGNON, 2003: Medium-bodied, with somewhat coarse tannins, but beyond that appealing currant and berry flavors and aromas. Drink up. Score 79.

ROSH PINA, MERLOT, 2003: Coarse enough to be thought of as vulgar, with chunky tannins, far too much acidity and earthy and only bare hints of wild berry fruits. Drink up. Score 70.

ROSH PINA, MERLOT, 2002: Chunky, a bit coarse on the palate and with basic black fruits, this distinctly country-style wine lacks breadth, depth, length or charm. Drink up. Score 74.

ROSH PINA, SHIRAZ, 2003: Dark but not fully clear garnet in color, with chunky country-style tannins and a bit of coarseness. On the nose and palate black cherry and cassis fruits, those with a somewhat exaggerated earthy character. Drink up. Score 76.

ROSH PINA, SHIRAZ, 2002: With modest tannins and an earthy, leathery character, but with enough cherry and wild berry flavors to give the wine some interest. Drink up. Score 76.

ROSH PINA, CABERNET-MERLOT-SHIRAZ, 2003: Ruby towards garnet in color, medium-bodied, far too acidic, with chunky tannins and skimpy berry and black fruit aromas and flavors. Drink up. Score 76.

ROSH PINA, CARIGNAN, PNINA DESSERT WINE, 2003: Burnished copper in color, as sweet as treacle, with far too little acidity to make it lively and fruits that are best described as muddy. Score 60.

Rota *

Established by Erez Rota on Moshav Tsafririm at the foothills of the Jerusalem Mountains in 2001 and re-located in 2005 to the Rota Ranch in the Negev Heights. The winery released its first wines in 2002 and current production is about 5,000 bottles annually.

ROTA, CABERNET SAUVIGNON, SHUA, 2003: Deep garnet towards purple, medium-bodied, with near-sweet tannins and clean aromas and flavors of plums, black cherries and cassis. Simple but appealing. Drink now. Score 84.

ROTA, MERLOT, SHUA, 2003: Dark cherry-red, medium-bodied but somewhat flabby and only skimpy berry fruits that make themselves felt. Drink up. Score 82.

ROTA, CABERNET-MERLOT, 2003: Unoaked, medium-bodied and somewhat on the simple side, but with just enough plum, black cherry and herbal aromas and flavors to hold interest. Drink up. Score 82.

ROTA, CABERNET-MERLOT, 2002: With clean aromas and flavors of berries and cherries, this soft, fresh and only moderately tannic wine is pleasant, although lacking complexity. Drink up. Score 83.

Rozenbaum ✶

Founded by Avi Rozenbaum in 1998, this small winery is located on Kibbutz Malkiya in the Upper Galilee near the Lebanese border. Grapes, including Cabernet Sauvignon, Merlot, Sangiovese, Chardonnay and Muscat of Alexandria, come from the Kadesh Valley. Production in 2003 was of 7,000 bottles, no wines were produced in 2004 and, with a new partner, production started again with the 2005 harvest.

ROZENBAUM, CABERNET SAUVIGNON, 2003: Medium-dark garnet, medium-bodied, with chunky, country-style tannins and overly generous acidity that give the red fruits here distinctly sour note. Drink up. Score 78.

ROZENBAUM, CABERNET SAUVIGNON, 2002: Dark garnet in color, medium-bodied, with firm and almost searing tannins holding back whatever fruits struggle, not fully successfully, to make themselves felt. Drink up. Score 78.

ROZENBAUM, MERLOT, 2002: Chunky tannins, medium-body and aromas and flavors of black fruits, but reflecting a rather heavy hand with the oak. A country-style wine meant for early drinking. Drink up. Score 84.

ROZENBAUM, MERLOT, 2001: Light to medium-bodied, on the alcoholic side, and with plums and black cherries that bring to mind fruit-juice concentrates. Past its peak. Drink up. Score 70.

ROZENBAUM, BLEND, 2002: An oak-aged blend of 66% Cabernet Sauvignon and 34% Merlot. Chunky, on the coarse side but with some appealing spicy cherry and berry fruits. Drink up. Score 75.

Ruth **

Founded by Tal Ma'or and located in Kfar Ruth, adjoining the city of Modi'in, this family-owned winery produced several hundred bottles of wine from the 2002 vintage and current production is 4,000 bottles annually. Grapes, including Cabernet Sauvignon, Merlot and Shiraz are harvested from vineyards on the central plain and in the hills of Jerusalem.

Reserve

RESERVE, CABERNET SAUVIGNON, 2003: Medium-bodied, with chunky, country style tannins opening slowly to show skimpy blackcurrant and berry fruits. Drink now. Score 82. **K**

RESERVE, CABERNET SAUVIGNON, 2002: Medium to full-bodied, with generous oak and firm tannins that tend to hide the black fruits and spices that are here. Drink now. Score 82. **K**

RESERVE, MERLOT, 2003: Medium-bodied, with acidity so puckering that you cannot tell where the sour sensations stop and the citrus peel and sour cherry flavors start. Lacking balance or charm. Drink up. Score 75. **K**

Ruth

RUTH, CABERNET SAUVIGNON, 2003: Dark ruby towards garnet in color, medium-bodied, with soft tannins, hints of smoky oak, and berry, cherry and currant fruits that open nicely on the palate. Not complex but generous and satisfying. Drink now. Score 86. **K**

RUTH, CABERNET SAUVIGNON, 2002: Deep garnet in color, medium to full-bodied, with soft well integrated tannins and generous currant, berry and cherry fruits. Good balance between smoky wood, fruits and a hint of tobacco on the finish. Drink now. Score 87. **K**

RUTH, MERLOT, 2004: Medium-bodied with chunky tannins, but those well balanced by smoky wood and appealing aromas and flavors of black fruits. Lacking complexity but appealing. Drink now. Score 84. **K**

RUTH, MERLOT, 2003: A somewhat dusty garnet red in color, with chunky country style tannins, this medium-bodied red shows muted aromas and flavors of berries and black cherries. Drink up. Score 84. **K**

RUTH, CABERNET SAUVIGNON-MERLOT, 2004: Medium dark garnet in color, with soft tannins and medium-body. On the nose and palate clean blackcurrant and berry aromas as well as a hint of spices. Drink now. Score 85. **K**

RUTH, MERLOT-SHIRAZ, 2003: Dark royal-purple, with generous acidity but scarcely any tannins, this medium-bodied blend of equal parts of Merlot and Shiraz was developed in oak for 10 months. Appealing aromas and flavors of plums and black berries and, starting on mid-palate, an earthy-herbal overlay. Serve lightly chilled. Drink now. Score 85. **K**

Salomon *

Located on Moshav Amikam in the Ramot Menashe forest not far from Zichron Ya'akov, this winery was founded in 1997 by Itamar Salomon. For several years the winery prepared only small quantities of wine for home consumption, and the first commercial release was from the 2002 vintage. Grapes are currently drawn from the Golan Heights but the winery is planting its own vineyards with Cabernet Sauvignon, Merlot, Cabernet Franc and Shiraz grapes. Production was about 2,500 bottles in 2004 and 5,000 in 2005.

SALOMON, CABERNET SAUVIGNON, 2004: Medium-bodied, with coarse tannins that seem not to want to settle down and dominating whatever black fruits are lying underneath. Drink from release. Tentative Score 82–84.

SALOMON, CABERNET SAUVIGNON, 2003: Dark garnet but not fully clear, and medium-bodied with chunky, somewhat coarse tannins, but under those generous plum and black cherry fruits. Lacking complexity, but pleasant. Drink now. Score 84.

SALOMON, MERLOT, 2004: Deep garnet in color, medium-bodied, with soft tannins and generous berry, cherry and cassis fruits. Not complex but appealing. Drink now. Score 84.

SALOMON, MERLOT, 2003: Somewhat over-extracted and showing hyper-ripe, almost sweet fruits, and fairly deep tannins for a Merlot. Simple but pleasant. Drink now. Score 84.

SALOMON, MERLOT-CABERNET SAUVIGNON 2003: Dark ruby towards garnet, medium-bodied, with soft tannins and appealing berry and plum aromas, those with a tempting spicy overlay. Drink now. Score 85.

Saslove ★★★★

Established by Barry Saslove in 1998 on Kibbutz Eyal in the Sharon region, this boutique winery has vineyards in the Upper Galilee currently planted with Cabernet Sauvignon, Merlot, Syrah, and Sauvignon Blanc grapes, and plans to grow Cabernet Franc, Petit Verdot, and Gewurztraminer grapes in the future. Current production of red wines is in three series: Reserved, Adom and Aviv, and the winery occasionally produces white wines as well. Production has grown steadily, from 35,000 bottles in 2002 to 55,000 in 2005. Projected production for 2006 is about 80,000 bottles. Beginning with the 2003 harvest Saslove has also produced two kosher Cabernet Sauvignon wines under the label "K by Saslove", using the facilities of Carmel in Zichron Ya'akov and currently producing about 10,000 bottles under this label. In the near future operations will shift to a new winery now under construction, not far from the Saslove-owned vineyards.

Reserved

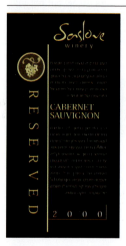

RESERVED, CABERNET SAUVIGNON, 2003: Medium to full-bodied, deep garnet with purple and orange reflections and fine balance between oak, spices, and firm but nicely integrating tannins. An oak-aged blend of 88% Cabernet Sauvignon and 12% Merlot, showing aromas and flavors of currants, black cherries and raspberries. Supple and elegant with a long blackberry and herbal finish. Drink from release–2010. Score 91.

RESERVED, CABERNET SAUVIGNON, 2002: Taking on a nose of sweet herbs, this dark garnet, full-bodied wine is maturing nicely, continuing to show currant, vanilla and herbal aromas and flavors that come together nicely and lead to a long, rich finish. Drink now–2008. Score 89.

RESERVED, CABERNET SAUVIGNON, 2000: Full-bodied, deep garnet toward purple, showing good balance between wood, well-integrated tannins and fruits. The wine shows cassis and berry fruits together with appealing spices, and on the finish a generous overlay of Mediterranean herbs comes in. Drink now. Score 91.

RESERVED, CABERNET SAUVIGNON, PRIVATE EDITION, SAGOL, 2000: Dark royal purple in color, this medium to full-bodied, well-balanced and moderately long wine spent 14 months in French oak barrels and now shows soft, well-integrated tannins, a gentle influence of smoky oak, and generous blackcurrant and plum fruits backed up nicely by Oriental spices, vanilla and chocolate. Drink now. Score 89.

RESERVED, CABERNET SAUVIGNON, 1999: Dark, deep and elegant, this delicious full-bodied wine has sweet plum, black cherry and red currant aromas and flavors, all opening slowly on the palate together with herbs, vanilla and a light hint of mint. Well balanced and with well-integrated tannins, the wine has a pleasingly long finish. Drink now. Score 92.

RESERVED, CABERNET SAUVIGNON, 1998: With a generous core of ripe cherries, wild berries, red currants, plums, vanilla and spices, this well made and complex wine borders on elegance. After 21 months in new oak casks the wine has a fairly tannic finish. Showing first signs of aging. Drink up. Score 90.

RESERVED, MERLOT, 2003: Medium-dark garnet with orange reflections, medium to full-bodied, with generous but well integrating tannins set off nicely by spicy and vanilla hints from the wood and appealing black cherry, plum and berry fruits. Long and mouthfilling. Drink now–2009. Score 89.

RESERVED, CHARDONNAY, 2002: This wine has generous oak on a tight firm frame, but given time to open in the glass reveals appealing flavors of citrus, pear and pineapple that fill the mouth nicely, and culminates in a lightly spicy finish. Somewhat past its peak. Drink up. Score 86.

RESERVED, GEWURZTRAMINER, DESSERT, JASMINE, 2004–2005: Made from Gewurztraminer grapes harvested in 2004 and 2005 in the Upper Galilee, this unabashedly sweet wine seems to have gone seriously wrong. Even though the wine offers honeyed summer and tropical fruits, it is too alcoholic and has an unwanted medicinal overlay. Score 65.

RESERVED, GEWURZTRAMINER DESSERT, JASMINE, 2002–2003: A blend of Gewurztraminer grapes from two harvest years that was aged in oak and reinforced to obtain a 14% alcohol content. This frankly sweet wine has good balancing acidity and generous aromas and flavors of litchis, pineapple, ripe peaches and lilacs, as well as a hint of bitterness on the finish that will appeal to some. Drink now. Score 87.

Adom

ADOM, CABERNET SAUVIGNON, 2004: Still in embryonic form, the wood just beginning to make itself felt but already showing fine balance between tannins, natural acidity and generous fruits, all on a full-bodied frame. Look for currant, black plum and toasted citrus peel on first attack, those followed by appealing herbal and tobacco notes. Drink from release–2010. Tentative Score 88–90.

ADOM, CABERNET SAUVIGNON, 2003: Still young but already ripe and smooth, the wine shows an attractive array of flavors that include currants, cherries, herbs, and vanilla. The tannins and structure of this well-balanced and complex red bode well for its aging potential. Drink now–2009. Score 90.

ADOM, CABERNET SAUVIGNON, 2002: Showing beautifully now with full body and with generous currant and berry fruits, those matched nicely by exotic spices and hints of sweet cedar. Tannins need a bit of time to recede. Drink now–2008. Score 90.

ADOM CABERNET SAUVIGNON, 2001: Deep garnet red, full-bodied, and showing good balance between sweet and smoky wood, now softening tannins and generous currant, blackberry and ripe plum fruits. Appealing hints of mint, chocolate and now even a tantalizing hint of cigar tobacco on the moderately long finish. Drink now. Score 90.

ADOM, CABERNET SAUVIGNON, 2000: Made entirely from Cabernet Sauvignon grapes and aged for 14 months in new and old French and American *barriques*, this attractive red shows currant, berry and smoky oak aromas and flavors. It has good balance, integrated tannins and a medium-long finish. Drink now. Score 88.

ADOM, MERLOT, 2003: Shows exuberant blackberry and cassis fruits and a toasty oak accent as well as licorice and spice aromas and flavors. Look for hints of chocolate and coffee that will increase as the wine continues to develop. Drink now–2010. Score 90.

…………………………………………………………………………SASLOVE

Aviv

AVIV, CABERNET SAUVIGNON, 2005: Dark garnet in color, medium to full-bodied with still firm tannins needing a bit of time to integrate but already with a generous array of blackcurrant and blackberry fruits, those with an appealing spicy overlay. Drink from release–2009. Tentative Score 88–90.

AVIV, CABERNET SAUVIGNON, 2004: Dark garnet red, medium to full-bodied, with soft, mouth-coating tannins. Good balance here and a tempting array of currant, plum and spices, those backed up by hints of vanilla and green olives. Drink now–2008. Score 88.

AVIV, CABERNET SAUVIGNON, 2003: Deep garnet red, medium-bodied, with firm tannins that coat the mouth nicely, those balanced by spicy oak and appealing currant and black cherry fruits. Drink now. Score 87.

AVIV, CABERNET SAUVIGNON, 2002: Dark and firmly tannic, with concentrated sweet cedar and smoke now blended comfortably with berry and currant fruits. Drink now. Score 88.

AVIV, CABERNET SAUVIGNON, 2001: A deep purple medium-bodied wine with red currants, black cherry, Oriental spices and a light welcome touch of earthiness. Drink up. Score 89.

AVIV, CABERNET SAUVIGNON, 2000: Made entirely from Cabernet Sauvignon grapes, this exuberant medium-bodied wine is packed with soft tannins, currant, cherry and plum flavors, and just the right hint of vanilla and spices. Drink up. Score 88.

AVIV, MERLOT, 2005: Medium-bodied, with caressing, near-sweet tannins and a generous array of black fruits backed up nicely by earthy, herbal and chocolate aromas and flavors that linger nicely on the palate. Drink from release–2009. Tentative Score 88–90.

AVIV, MERLOT, 2004: Medium to full-bodied, with well-integrating tannins, spicy oak and appealing berry, black cherry and cassis aromas and flavors, those with hints of red licorice, chocolate and Mediterranean herbs. Drink now–2008. Score 88.

AVIV, MERLOT, 2003: Medium-bodied, deep royal purple towards garnet in color, with soft tannins and light spicy oak set off well by currant, berry and cherry fruits. On the finish hints of white chocolate and mocha. Drink now. Score 87.

AVIV, MERLOT, 2002: Fresh and exuberant, medium to full-bodied, and garnet toward purple in color, the wine was aged for 6 months in French and American oak and now shows tannins that start off firmly but open in the glass to reveal a pleasing berry and black cherry personality, the fruits complemented nicely by spicy chocolate and coffee flavors. Look as well for hints of smoky oak and toasted white bread on the medium-long finish. Drink up. Score 89.

AVIV, MERLOT, 2001: Comfortably reflecting the 5 months that it spent in small oak casks, this deep purple medium-bodied wine has plenty of black fruits, currant and spices. What gives the wine an appealing "twist" is its almost sweet finish, yielding vanilla beans and Mediterranean herbs. Drink up. Score 90.

AVIV, MARRIAGE, 2005: A medium to full-bodied blend of Merlot, Cabernet Sauvignon and Syrah (60%, 32% and 8% respectively), showing good balance between soft tannins, wood and fruits. On the nose and palate dark plums, cassis and berries that come together nicely. Soft and caressing. Drink from release–2009. Tentative Score 87–89.

AVIV, MARRIAGE, 2004: A blend of 60% Merlot, 36% Cabernet Sauvignon and 4% Syrah, all from the Upper Galilee, developed on oak chips for 6 months. Dark garnet in color, with soft tannins integrating nicely with vanilla and white pepper, those on a background of blackberries, currants and Mediterranean herbs. Drink now–2008. Score 87.

AVIV, MARRIAGE, 2003: This deep royal purple, full-bodied blend of 60% Merlot, 39% Cabernet Sauvignon and 1% Syrah shows generous but almost sweet tannins coming together nicely with vanilla-rich American oak, spices and appealing berry, currant and black cherry fruits. On the pleasingly long finish look as well for hints of cigar tobacco. Drink now–2008. Score 88.

Saslove

SASLOVE, SAGOL, PRIVATE EDITION, 2000: Dark royal purple in color, this medium to full-bodied wine spent 14 months in French oak barrels. With soft, well-integrated tannins, a gentle influence of smoky oak and generous blackcurrant and plum fruits backed up nicely by Oriental spices, vanilla and chocolate, this is a well balanced and moderately long wine. Somewhat past its peak. Drink up. Score 88.

SASLOVE, SAUVIGNON BLANC, 2001: Light golden straw in color, this medium-bodied wine has appealing aromas and flavors of citrus and tropical fruits and just the right level of grassy herbaceousness. Well past its peak. Drink up. Score 86.

SASLOVE, BLANC DE NOIRS, 2004: Pale pink towards peach in color, made entirely from Cabernet Sauvignon grapes that were allowed minimum skin contact, with medium body and a surprisingly high 14.7% alcohol. With aromas and flavors of strawberries, blackberries and citrus. Fresh and fun to drink, especially when well chilled. Drink now. Score 87.

K By Saslove

K BY SASLOVE, CABERNET SAUVIGNON, 2004: Medium-bodied, generously but softly tannic, with currant and plum aromas and flavors, those on a generously spicy background. Drink now–2008. Score 86. **K**

K BY SASLOVE, CABERNET SAUVIGNON, 2003: Light to medium-bodied, perhaps a bit thin on the palate, with some berry, currant, and herbal flavors but those somehow never coming together. Drink now. Score 84. **K**

K BY SASLOVE, CABERNET SAUVIGNON, MEDITERRANEAN, 2003: Made entirely from Cabernet Sauvignon grapes from the Kayumi Vineyard in the Galilee and aged in new French oak barrels for 6 months, this deep royal purple, medium-bodied wine seems fairly aggressive, with a green, herbal character that hides the cherry and plum flavors. Rough on the finish. Drink now. Score 83. **K**

Sassy *

Sasson Bar-Gig set up this small winery in 2000 in the town of Bat Yam on the outskirts of Tel Aviv. The winery draws on grapes from Gush Etzion and the Golan Heights, and is currently producing about 4,000 bottles annually, the reds aged in oak for about 12 months.

SASSY, CABERNET SAUVIGNON, 2003: Medium-bodied, with somewhat coarse tannins and too-generous smoky, dusty oak and on the nose and palate skimpy berry and cherry fruits. Drink up. Score 79.

SASSY, CABERNET SAUVIGNON, 2002: Showing better now than in its youth, this garnet red, medium-bodied wine continues to offer very earthy aromas and flavors but now also reveals some plum and berry fruits. Drink up. Score 80.

SASSY, CABERNET SAUVIGNON, 2001: A medium-bodied country style wine with chunky tannins, a high level of acidity and a bitterness that overpowers the black fruits. Drink up. Score 74.

SASSY, MERLOT, 2003: Medium-bodied, with firm tannins and generous wood influence and opening to reveal jam-like aromas and flavors of plums and currants. Drink now. Score 82.

SASSY, MERLOT, 2002: Deep garnet in color, this medium to full-bodied wine is a step-up for Sassy. Generous tannins here, but those integrating nicely and coming together with aromas and flavors of sweet cedar, berries and black cherries, all backed up by hints of spices that lead to a moderately long finish. Drink up. Score 83.

SASSY, CABERNET SAUVIGNON-MERLOT, 2002: Medium-bodied, with chunky tannins and aromas and flavors of berries and black cherries. A simple but appealing country-style wine. Drink up. Score 84.

Savion ★★★

Founded in 2000 by Ashi Salmon and Eli Pardess on Moshav Nataf in the Jerusalem Mountains and with new vineyards in which they are raising their own Cabernet Sauvignon and Merlot, this winery is currently releasing about 2,000 bottles annually.

SAVION, CABERNET SAUVIGNON, 2004: Medium to full-bodied, with generous tannins and spicy cedar wood balanced nicely by currant and berry fruits, those supported nicely by aromas and flavors of Mediterranean herbs and, on the moderately long finish, a hint of white chocolate. Drink now–2009. Score 88.

SAVION, CABERNET SAUVIGNON, 2003: Dark royal purple towards black, medium to full-bodied, with firm tannins well balanced by smoky wood and an array of red currants and wild berries. On the moderately-long finish hints of herbaceousness and chocolate. Drink now–2009. Score 89.

SAVION, CABERNET SAUVIGNON, 2002: Deep youthful garnet towards royal purple in color, with still firm tannins that need time to integrate but with good balance between currant, berry and plum fruits and spicy wood, this tempting wine needs some time to show its elegance. Drink now–2008. Score 86.

SAVION, CABERNET SAUVIGNON, 2001: Full-bodied, with good balance between generous but soft tannins and fruits, this blend of 90% Cabernet Sauvignon and 10% Merlot spent 12 months in *barriques*, that reflected by hints of smoke, vanilla and cedar wood on a background of currant, plum and berry fruits. A long, just spicy enough finish. Drink now. Score 89.

SAVION, CABERNET SAUVIGNON, 2000: A blend of primarily Cabernet Sauvignon with small percentages of Merlot and Syrah, this deep purple toward black, rather Australian-style wine spent 12 months in small oak barrels and shows soft tannins and plenty of fruit on its medium to full-bodied frame. Drink now. Score 89.

Sde Boker ★★★

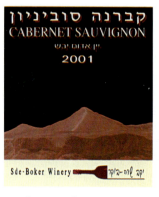

Located on Kibbutz Sde Boker in the heart of the Negev Desert, this small winery was founded in 1998 by former Californian Zvi Remick who studied winemaking at California's Napa Valley College. Relying on Cabernet Sauvignon, Merlot, Carignan, Zinfandel, Sauvignon Blanc and Chardonnay grapes grown in the desert, production currently varies between 2,000–3,000 bottles annually.

SDE BOKER, CABERNET SAUVIGNON, 2003: Medium to full-bodied, opening nicely to reveal its intrinsic good balance between gentle wood, soft tannins and tempting blackcurrant, cherry and spicy aromas and flavors. Long, complex and generous. Drink now–2009. Score 88.

SDE BOKER, CABERNET SAUVIGNON, 2002: A good effort considering the limitations of the 2002 vintage, with plenty of ripe plum, currant and berry flavors but not enough tannins or body. Drink now. Score 85.

SDE BOKER, CABERNET SAUVIGNON, 2001: Dark royal purple in color, this well-balanced, medium to full-bodied red reflects its 23 months in oak casks with abundant vanilla, toasty oak and cedar flavors, those with currant and berry fruits. Drink now–2008. Score 88.

SDE BOKER, CABERNET SAUVIGNON, 2000: Made entirely from Cabernet Sauvignon grapes, this medium-bodied red has ample soft tannins and an array of plum, currant and spicy flavors, as well as attractive overlays of vanilla and black olives that make themselves felt on the finish. Drink up. Score 86.

SDE BOKER, CABERNET SAUVIGNON, 1999: Somewhat on the rustic side, this medium-bodied, unfiltered wine has moderate tannins and green olive and herbal flavors, those matched with just enough cherry and plum flavors. Slightly past its peak. Drink up. Score 86.

SDE BOKER, MERLOT, 2003: Dark ruby to garnet in color, medium-bodied, with firm but nicely yielding tannins and a generous hint of oak. On the nose and palate red currant, cherry and berry fruits, all on an appealingly spicy background. Drink now–2009. Score 88.

SDE BOKER, MERLOT, 2002: An appealing medium-bodied wine with wild berry, herbal and mineral aromas and flavors and soft tannins, but turning somewhat thin on the finish. Drink now. Score 86.

SDE BOKER, MERLOT, 2000: Medium-bodied, gentle and well-balanced, with abundant black cherries and plums along with gentle hints of mint and spices. Drink now. Score 85.

SDE BOKER, MERLOT, 1999: Medium-bodied and with soft tannins, this wine had in its youth a good interplay between ripe currant, plum, spice and mint flavors, but is now showing age. Drink up. Score 84.

SDE BOKER, ZINFANDEL, 2004: A generous, hearty rustic wine with lots of personality. Medium-bodied, and on the nose and palate aromas and flavors of black cherries, pomegranate, cola and toasted rye bread. A charmer. Drink now. Score 88.

SDE BOKER, ZINFANDEL, 2003: Medium-bodied but with good solidity. Appealing wild berry, cherry and anise flavors that open nicely to a lightly tannic and mineral finish. Not a great Zinfandel but a very nice one indeed. Drink now. Score 87.

SDE BOKER, CARIGNAN, 2003: Light to medium-bodied, with a nice chewy sensation and bright and lively on the palate, showing purple plum and spice flavors that linger nicely. An appealing little wine. Drink now. Score 86.

Sea Horse ★★★★

Ze'ev Dunie founded this boutique winery in 2000 on Moshav Bar Giora in the Jerusalem Mountains, after retiring from partnership in the Agur winery where he had made his first Elul wine. Now he has his own vineyards planted in Syrah and Zinfandel, and draws on Cabernet Sauvignon and Merlot from the Upper Galilee. The winery has grown from initial production of 1,800 bottles from the 2001 vintage to about 15,000 bottles annually. Releases include two Cabernet Sauvignon based wines, Elul and Fellini; two Zinfandel based wines, Lennon and Take Two; two Syrah based wines, Camus and Antoine; and in selected years, Munch, which is made entirely from Petite Sirah grapes.

Elul

ELUL, 2004: A blend of Cabernet Sauvignon, Syrah and Petite Sirah (75%, 20% and 5% respectively) aged for about 18 months in French and American oak. Dense and concentrated, ultra-dark garnet in color, full-bodied and loaded with muscular tannins that will turn plush and rich with time. On the nose and palate currant, plum, wild berry and mineral flavors, those yielding on a remarkably long finish to bittersweet chocolate, espresso and Mediterranean herbs. Drink from release–2012. Tentative Score 92–94.

ELUL, 2003: This well-balanced blend of Cabernet Sauvignon, Syrah and Petite Sirah (85%, 10% and 5% respectively) shows rich and quiet elegance. Ripe black cherry, currant and berry fruits overlayed nicely by hints of anise, spicy oak and light earthiness, all of which come to a long and generous finish. Drink now–2012. Score 92.

ELUL, 2002: Deep garnet towards royal purple in color, this full-bodied blend of 85% Cabernet Sauvignon, 9% Merlot and 6% Syrah, shows generous but soft and well-integrating tannins and jammy currant and berry aromas and flavors, set off by spices and toast, all showing appealing overtones of Mediterranean herbs. Plush and elegant, with a long finish that yields bittersweet chocolate Drink now–2009. Score 92.

ELUL, 2001: Maturing nicely, this full-bodied blend of 70% Cabernet Sauvignon, 28% Merlot and 2% Syrah has settled down, its once chunky tannins now softened and integrating nicely. On the nose and palate currant, black cherry, mineral and herbal aromas and flavors all with a gentle hint of minty-vanilla on the finish. Drink now–2008. Score 91.

ELUL, 2000: Aging gracefully now, this oak-aged blend of Cabernet Sauvignon and Syrah (70% and 30% respectively) continues to show fine balance and length. Spicy currant and purple plum fruits here on a lightly herbal finish. Drink now. Score 91.

ELUL, 1999: A blend of 70% Cabernet Sauvignon and 30% Merlot, this full-bodied wine was aged for 14 months in small oak barrels. Tight, with firm but well-integrated tannins and with an appealing earthiness to its plum, currant and spicy flavors, the wine is now somewhat past its peak but is still showing good balance and finesse. Drink up. Score 87.

Sea Horse

SEA HORSE, ANTOINE, TETE DE CUVEE, 2004: Made from low yield, organically raised Syrah vines, aged in Burgundy barrels for 16 months, this dark purple towards black wine is plump, rich and well balanced. Full-bodied, with spicy and peppery overlays highlighting plum, currant and wild berry flavors, those along with just the barest hint of Brett to add a pleasing earthy charm to the wine. Destined for elegance. Best 2008–2012. Score 91.

SEA HORSE, ANTOINE, 2004: Dark garnet towards royal purple in color, full-bodied, with firm tannins but with fine balance and structure. On the nose and palate an appealing array of plum, blackberry, and licorice, those matched nicely by near-sweet oak, all leading to a long, generously spicy finish. Drink now–2011. Score 91.

SEA HORSE, ANTOINE, 2003: Made from 100% Syrah grapes, this is a rich and complex wine, with smoky, meaty overlays on a delicious array of berry, black cherry, spices and currants. Firm but supple tannins and tempting anise, leathery and earthy notes on the long finish. Only a single barrel was made. Drink now–2010. Score 91

SEA HORSE, MUNCH, 2003: Named as a tribute to artist Edward Munch, this 100% Petite Sirah spent 16 months in French and American oak. The best Petite Sirah ever from Israel, this exotic, spicy and complex wine shows layers of wild berry, plum, currant and black cherry fruits together with a generous peppery overlay and supple tannins. Drink now–2009. Score 91.

SEA HORSE, PETITE SIRAH, 2002: Dark, dense and rich, with aromas and flavors of wild berries, minerals and leather, those backed up nicely by crushed black pepper. Lots of tannins here, but those well in balance with the wood and fruits. Drink now. Score 88.

SEA HORSE, FELLINI, 2004: An impenetrable purple towards inky-black, this blend of 50% each of Syrah and Cabernet Sauvignon reflects its 16 months in oak with a supple and gentle but lively style. Look for tempting earthy and spicy aromas and flavors to complement wild berry, rhubarb, and currant fruits, all lingering nicely on the mouthfilling finish. Drink now–2010. Score 90.

SEA HORSE, FELLINI, 2003: This blend of 60% Syrah and 40% Cabernet spent 18 months in French and American oak. Complex, with tempting spiciness overlaying wild berry, blackcurrant and meaty plums, and with a tantalizingly sweet edge. Well balanced and moderately long. Drink now–2009. Score 90.

SEA HORSE, FELLINI, 2002: This medium to full-bodied blend of 90% Cabernet Sauvignon and 10% Petite Sirah is warm and elegant, and has distinctly Mediterranean aromas and flavors of fresh herbs and spicy vanilla notes that give an added dimension to the currant and black cherry fruits. Supple tannins, good balance and concentration come together nicely in this oak-aged blend. Drink now. Score 89.

SEA HORSE, CAMUS, 2004: Syrah with 6% Petite Sirah. Medium to full-bodied, aged for about 12 months in oak, showing generous acidity, soft tannins and spicy wood. Opens to show blackcurrant, blackberry, tobacco and licorice. Needs time to come together. Drink now–2010. Score 90.

SEA HORSE, CAMUS, 2003: Dark garnet red, full-bodied, with still firm tannins well balanced by spicy wild berry and cherry fruits, the wine boasts an appealing leathery edge on the finish. Rich and complex. Drink now–2009. Score 90.

SEA HORSE, CAMUS, 2002: Dark garnet toward royal purple, this medium to full-bodied red made primarily from oak-aged Shiraz shows deep raspberry flavors with floral accents, but with enough tannins to keep it firm. Clean and long, with hints of black pepper and licorice aromas and flavors, it has a moderately long, near-sweet finish. Drink now. Score 90.

SEA HORSE, LENNON, TETE DE CUVEE, 2004: Made from low yield organically raised Zinfandel vines, blended with 5% of Petite Sirah, full-bodied, fruit forward and with a whopping 15.6% alcohol, but with the balance and structure to carry it. Tightly focused currants, plums and wild berries matched nicely by pepper and mocha from the oak. Drink now–2010. Score 91.

SEA HORSE, LENNON, 2004: Made from low yield vines, high in alcohol, and with the addition of 5% Petite Sirah, this version leaning to red berries, red plums and cassis. Reflecting 14 months in American and French oak with peppery, vanilla and eucalyptus flavors, this well-structured wine shows firm and concentrated. Drink now–2009. Score 89.

SEA HORSE, LENNON, 2003: A medium to full-bodied blend of 95% Zinfandel and 5% Petite Sirah. With 14 months in American oak this moderately tannic wine shows good concentration of ripe juicy cherry and wild berry flavors as well as an appealing pepper and anise edge. Drink now–2008. Score 90.

SEA HORSE, TAKE TWO, 2004: Dark ruby towards garnet, this blend of 88% Zinfandel, 10% Petite Sirah and 2% Cabernet Sauvignon shows light meaty and leathery notes. Smooth and round, with wild berry and cassis fruits that make themselves felt nicely. Drink now–2008. Score 89.

SEA HORSE, TAKE TWO, 2003: A blend of 90% Zinfandel, 9% Petite Sirah and 1% Cabernet Sauvignon, this medium to full-bodied wine reflects its eight months in American oak with good balance between tannins, wood and fruits. A true Zinfandel personality, round and juicy with spicy berry and cherry flavors on which you will find a firm tannic edge and a moderately-long tar and anise finish. Drink now–2008. Score 89.

SEA HORSE, TAKE TWO, 2002: This second wine of the winery is a blend of 67% Merlot, 25% Cabernet Sauvignon and 8% Petite Sirah that spent 8 months in American and French oak. Dark cherry red in color and medium-bodied but somewhat light on the palate, the wine has low tannins, lively acidity, and raspberry and black cherry flavors. Drink now. Score 86.

Segal ★★★★

Established in the 1950s as Ashkelon Wines and later taking on the name of the family that owned it, Segal was until the mid-1980s one of the more up-market wineries of the country. In 2001 the company was bought out by Barkan Wineries, but kept its name. Under winemaker Avi Feldstein, with quality vineyards in several regions of the Upper Galilee, and operating now in Barkan's state-of-the-art facilities at Kibbutz Hulda, the winery is now producing several good wines, including Single Vineyard and Unfiltered wines, both from Cabernet Sauvignon grapes. Other series are Ben Ami, Marom Galil (including those wines labeled *Single* and *Fusion*), Rehasim, the single vineyard Dovev varietal wines, Batzir and the popularly-priced Shel Segal series. The winery relies on Cabernet Sauvignon, Merlot, Argaman, Chardonnay, Sauvignon Blanc, Emerald Riesling, and French Colombard grapes, and current production is about 1.5 million bottles annually, of which nearly one million are in the Shel Segal series.

Single Vineyard

SINGLE VINEYARD, CABERNET SAUVIGNON, KEREM DISHON, 2002: Layers of jammy berry and strawberry fruits on spicy currants, anise, tar and sweet cedar, all along with a touch of green olive that works its way into the finish. Full-bodied and complex with firm but polished tannins. Drink now–2008. Score 89. **K**

SINGLE VINEYARD, KEREM DISHON, 2001: Deep royal purple in color, with blackberry, blackcurrant and plum fruits, this full-bodied wine was aged in oak for 18 months. Showing good balance between fruits, wood and moderately firm but well integrating tannins, this complex wine has a long, near-sweet finish. Drink now–2008. Score 91. **K**

SINGLE VINEYARD, CABERNET SAUVIGNON, KEREM DISHON, 2000: Made entirely from Cabernet Sauvignon grapes, this well-balanced, deep garnet toward royal purple wine reflects its 18 months in small oak casks by showing generous vanilla and smoke, those on a background of currant, berry, plum and spices. Drink now. Score 91. K

SINGLE VINEYARD, MERLOT, DOVEV, 2002: Garnet towards black, medium to full-bodied, soft on the palate despite firm tannins and with tempting aromas and flavors of blackberries, plums and sweet herbs. Drink now–2008. Score 89. K

SINGLE VINEYARD, CHARDONNAY, DOVEV, 2004: Light gold in color, medium-bodied, with crisp minerals in the background yielding nicely to a rich array of spring flowers, summer fruits and melons. Tempting and long. Drink now–2008. Score 90. K

Unfiltered

UNFILTERED, CABERNET SAUVIGNON, 2002: Aged in oak for 18 months, full-bodied, rich and ripe, with fine balance between generous soft tannins and smoky oak. On the nose and palate currants, berries, plums, vanilla and on the long finish light herbs, black pepper and chocolate. Long, mouthfilling and destined for elegance. Drink now–2010. Score 91. K

UNFILTERED, CABERNET SAUVIGNON, 2001: Dark garnet in color, full-bodied and reflecting its 22 months in oak with generous vanilla and toasty oak. Concentrated, complex and tannic but now opening very nicely indeed, and showing appealing currant, plum and black cherry fruits, those on a background of oriental spices, all coming to a long, complex finish. Drink now–2009. Score 90. K

UNFILTERED, CABERNET SAUVIGNON, 2000: Deep garnet in color, this wine spent 20 months in new French and American oak. Now showing full-bodied, and matured nicely, with its currant, berry and earthy-herbal aromas and flavors now showing overlays of chocolate and mint. Drink now. Score 90. K

SEGAL, CABERNET SAUVIGNON, UNFILTERED, 1999: Full-bodied, still showing good balance and well-focused black cherry, wild berry and currant fruits along with hints of herbs and spices, but now throwing a generous amount of sediment. Still drinking nicely but not for much longer cellaring. Drink up. Score 89. **K**

Rehasim

REHASIM, CABERNET SAUVIGNON, DISHON, 2004: Dark, youthful royal-purple in color, intense and concentrated, with a rich array of currant, tobacco, sage and cedar wood aromas and flavors. Fine balance between wood, tannins and acidity yield a ripe and supple Cabernet. Drink now–2010. Score 90. **K**

REHASIM, CABERNET SAUVIGNON, DOVEV, 2003: Medium to full-bodied, with soft tannins. Rich, round, supple and generous, with layers of blueberries, currants, plums and sweet cedar, those on a generous but not at all offensive background of dusty oak. Drink now–2009. Score 88. **K**

REHASIM, CABERNET SAUVIGNON, DOVEV, 2002: Made entirely from Cabernet Sauvignon grapes, aged for 20 months in primarily French oak *barriques*, this medium-bodied, soft and round wine offers up enticing aromas of currants, mocha and minerals, those backed up by chewy but nicely yielding tannins. Worth decanting. Drink now–2008. Score 90. **K**

REHASIM, MERLOT, DOVEV, 2004: Dark garnet in color, this medium to full-bodied, herbal and spicy and generously tannic wine shows the kind of balance and structure that even at this early stage bode well for its future. Aromas and flavors of black cherries, blackberries and currants matched nicely by spicy oak accents and on the long finish hints of espresso and dark chocolate. Best 2008–2012. Score 90. **K**

REHASIM, MERLOT, DOVEV, 2003: Deep and dark, ripe and luxurious, with generous black cherry, blackberry, plum, mocha and vanilla aromas and flavors on a soft, round and almost caressing background. Drink now–2010. Score 91. **K**

REHASIM, MERLOT, DOVEV, 2002: Reflecting its 19 months in *barriques*, shows generous oak but that in fine balance with mouthcoating tannins, the rough edges coming together in surprisingly soft and round ways. On the nose and palate appealing berry, black cherry and cassis fruits, all on a just spicy enough background. Drink now–2008. Score 88. **K**

Ben Ami

BEN AMI, CABERNET SAUVIGNON, 2004: Medium-bodied, with soft tannins and generous hints of smoky wood opening to reveal wild berry, currant and cassis fruits. Drink now. Score 85. K

BEN AMI, CABERNET SAUVIGNON, 2003: Deep garnet towards royal purple, medium-bodied and with chunky, country style tannins. Appealing plum and berry fruits are matched nicely by a light herbaceousness. Drink now. Score 85. K

BEN AMI, CABERNET SAUVIGNON, 2002: Dark garnet in color, medium-bodied, with generous soft tannins integrating nicely and aromas and flavors of currants, plums and berries as well as hints of wood and herbs. Drink up. Score 86. K

BEN AMI, MERLOT, 2002: Dark garnet in color, medium-bodied, with chunky, country-style tannins and with aromas and flavors of plums and berries. Marred perhaps by a heavy herbal overtone. Drink up. Score 84. K

BEN AMI, MERLOT, 2001: Firm and tight when first poured, but after a few minutes in the glass it opens to show a compact personality with currant, herbal and cedar notes, all on a moderately tannic and cedarwood background. Past its peak. Drink up. Score 85. K

Marom Galil

MAROM GALIL, CABERNET SAUVIGNON, SINGLE, 2004: Oak-aged, made from grapes from several different Galilee vineyards. Traditional Cabernet aromas and flavors of currants and blackberries, those backed up by hints of bittersweet chocolate and minerals. Drink now–2010. Score 88. K

MAROM GALIL, CABERNET SAUVIGNON, SINGLE, 2002: Cabernet Sauvignon from four Galilee vineyards, aged for 18 months in French and American oak. Medium to full-bodied, with soft tannins and generous wood integrating nicely to reveal currant and blackberry fruits, those complemented by hints of cigar tobacco, earthy-minerals and light herbaceousness. Drink now. Score 88. **K**

MAROM GALIL, CABERNET SAUVIGNON, 2002: Deep garnet towards inky purple, medium to full-bodied, with firm tannins comfortably balanced by sweet cedar wood, blackcurrants and ripe plum fruits. A long cola-berry finish. Drink now–2008. Score 87. **K**

MAROM GALIL, CABERNET SAUVIGNON, 2001: Inky purple to black in color, medium to full-bodied, and reflecting its 18 months in oak with generous sweet and smoky oak, those well balanced by firm but well integrating tannins and a rich array of blackcurrant, cassis and wild berry fruits. Long and complex. Drink now. Score 89. **K**

MAROM GALIL, MERLOT, SINGLE, 2004: Generous oak and firm tannins in this still youthful wine, but with good balance and structure to assure that these will settle down nicely to reveal a medium to full-bodied red with red and black berry fruits, cassis, and hints of spices and eucalyptus on the nose and palate. As the wine develops look for a candied citrus peel finish. Drink now–2010. Score 87. **K**

MAROM GALIL, MERLOT, SINGLE, 2003: Despite its name, not a single vineyard wine and not even a single variety wine, this blend of 85% Merlot and 15% Cabernet Franc comes from various vineyards in the upper Galilee. Reflecting 14 months in oak with good balance between spicy wood and now softening tannins and revealing ripe red plums, cassis and citrus peel, all with a light hint of sweetness. Drink now. Score 86. **K**

MAROM GALIL, MERLOT, 2003: Deep ruby towards garnet, medium-bodied, with soft tannins integrating nicely and currant and wild berry fruits. A bit heavy on the oak. Drink now–2008. Score 87. **K**

MAROM GALIL, MERLOT, 2002: Medium to full-bodied, this blend of 85% Merlot and 15% Cabernet Sauvignon has firm tannins and generous wood, those balanced nicely by plum, berry and currant fruits. Round and mouthfilling. Drink now. Score 87. **K**

MAROM GALIL, RED, FUSION, 2004: Ruby towards purple in color, an unoaked, medium-bodied and softly tannic blend of 60% Merlot and 20% each of Cabernet Sauvignon and Cabernet Franc. Nothing complex but fresh aromas of blackcurrants and berries as well as a hint of herbaceousness. Drink now. Score 85. **K**

MAROM GALIL, CABERNET SAUVIGNON-MERLOT, 2003: Dark garnet red, medium-bodied with somewhat chunky tannins but with generous berry and black cherry fruits. A pleasant quaffer. Drink now. Score 84. K

MAROM GALIL, RED, 2003: Light to medium-bodied, with soft tannins this blend of Cabernet Sauvignon and Shiraz has a distinctly berry-cherry personality. Drink up. Score 83. K

MAROM GALIL, CHARDONNAY, SINGLE, 2004: A lively golden colored Chardonnay from four different Galilee vineyards, aged partly in oak for seven months. Medium-bodied, with generous oak and lively acidity and aromas and flavors of ripe melons, pineapple and pears matched by a gentle nutty overlay. Drink now. Score 87. K

MAROM GALIL, CHARDONNAY, 2003: Not subjected to the usual process of malolactic fermentation, this rich, round and spicy white offers up toasty vanilla and caramel nuances to complement pineapple, melon and citrus fruits on a generous oaky background, culminating in a long finish. Drink up. Score 89. K

MAROM GALIL, WHITE, FUSION , 2005: An unoaked blend of Chardonnay, French Colombard and Sauvignon Blanc. Light golden straw in color, super-fruity on the nose, medium-bodied, with lively acidity and generous citrus, peach and tropical fruit flavors. Lacking complexity but delightful. Drink now. Score 87. K

MAROM GALIL, FUSION, LEVAN, 2004: A partly oaked blend of Chardonnay and French Colombard, with generous acidity highlighting pineapple, peach and melon aromas and flavors. A good quaffer. Drink now. Score 85. K

MAROM GALIL, WHITE, 2003: Light golden straw in color, this simple blend of Sauvignon Blanc and Chardonnay shows some citrus and green apple aromas and flavors along with generous acidity to keep the wine lively. Drink up. Score 82. K

Shel Segal

SHEL SEGAL, CABERNET SAUVIGNON, 2004: Lightly oak aged, dark ruby towards garnet in color, medium-bodied, with soft tannins and forward berry, cherry and currant fruits. Drink now. Score 84. K

SHEL SEGAL, CABERNET SAUVIGNON, 2003: Oak aged for about 8 months, dark garnet in color, medium-bodied, with chunky, country-style tannins and a few berry and black cherry fruits. Drink up. Score 84. **K**

SHEL SEGAL, CABERNET SAUVIGNON, 2002: Made entirely from Cabernet Sauvignon grapes and aged in oak barrels for 8 months, this medium-bodied wine with black fruits and moderate tannins shows very few of the varietal traits of Cabernet Sauvignon. Drink up. Score 81. **K**

SHEL SEGAL, MERLOT, 2002: A medium-bodied blend of 90% Merlot and 10% Cabernet Sauvignon, this deep garnet-colored wine was aged for 8 months in American oak casks and now shows plenty of vanilla and oak along with some black fruits but lacks backbone and depth. Drink up. Score 80. **K**

SHEL SEGAL, DRY RED, 2004: A simple country-style wine, a bit coarse but with berry and black cherry fruits to make it quaffable. An acceptable entry-level wine. Drink now. Score 80. **K**

SHEL SEGAL, DRY RED, 2003: This blend of 65% Argaman filled out with Merlot and Petite Sirah has dark color but light body with no noticeable tannins and only a few black fruits. Drink up. Score 75. **K**

SHEL SEGAL, EMERALD RIESLING, 2005: Semi-dry, floral on the nose and palate and with basic citrus fruits. Drink up. Score 79. **K**

SHEL SEGAL, DRY WHITE, 2005: A basic white for those just starting to drink wines. Soft and easy to drink but with not much to recommend it. Drink up. Score 78. **K**

SHEL SEGAL, DRY WHITE, 2004: A dry white, a blend of French Colombard, Sauvignon Blanc and Emerald Riesling. With grapefruit and tropical fruits aromas and flavors. Simple but quaffable. Drink up. Score 80. **K**

Smadar *

Established by Motti Sela in 1998 and located in Zichron-Ya'akov, this winery produces wines from nearby vineyards owned by the family, those containing Cabernet Sauvignon, Merlot and Carignan grapes. Production is currently about 6,000 bottles annually.

SMADAR, CABERNET SAUVIGNON, 2004: Dark royal purple in color, medium-bodied, with generous tannins and wood, those receding in the glass to reveal blackberry and currant fruits. Not complex but appealing. Drink now. Score 84.

SMADAR, CABERNET SAUVIGNON, 2003: Dark ruby towards garnet, with firm tannins and perhaps too generous an impact from the wood, but with berry, currant and black cherry fruits and a light herbaceousness that make themselves felt. Somewhat short and one dimensional. Drink now. Score 83.

SMADAR, CABERNET SAUVIGNON, 2002: Dark royal purple in color, medium to full-bodied, with chunky tannins and moderate wood influence, and aromas and flavors of blackberry and currant fruits as well as a hint of earthiness. Perhaps a bit coarse but a pleasant country-style wine. Drink now. Score 84.

SMADAR, MERLOT, 2004: Medium-bodied, with generous, somewhat chunky tannins but opening to show black fruits. An appealing country-style wine. Drink now. Score 84.

SMADAR, MERLOT, 2002: Dark ruby with a hint of browning. Medium-bodied, with firm tannins and generous wood that tend to hide the black cherry and berry fruits. Drink now. Score 84.

SMADAR, CARIGNAN, 2004: Dark ruby in color, medium-bodied, with soft tannins. Aromas and flavors of jammy berries and black cherries. Drink now. Score 80.

SMADAR, CARIGNAN, 2003: Bright light garnet red, medium-bodied, with almost unfelt tannins and aromas and flavors of wild berries and cherries. Drink up. Score 82.

Sode Hayain ✶✶

Founded by Reuven Cohen and located on Moshav Tirat Yehuda in the central plains, the winery produces about 3,500 bottles annually, drawing on Cabernet Sauvignon and Merlot grapes from vineyards in different parts of the country.

SODE HAYAIN, CABERNET SAUVIGNON, REUBEN'S WINE, 2002: Dark garnet towards purple in color, medium to full-bodied, with chunky, country-style tannins and perhaps too ample influence of the oak barrels, showing vanilla, spices and herbs overlaying the currant and berry fruits. Drink now. Score 85. **K**

SODE HAYAIN, MERLOT, REUBEN'S WINE, 2003: Reflecting 18 months in oak with firm tannins and generous smoky cedar. Opens to reveal generous plum, cassis and berry fruits, those turning a bit jammy on the finish. Drink now. Score 84. **K**

SODE HAYAIN, MERLOT, REUBEN'S WINE, 2002: Medium-bodied, with soft tannins but with generous spicy and toasted bread from the oak in which it aged that tend to hide the plum and berry fruits. Drink now. Score 85. **K**

Soreq ★★★

Originally a partnership of Yossi Shacham, his son Nir and Barry Saslove, this small winery was founded in 1994 on Moshav Tal Shachar, which is situated at the foot of the Jerusalem Mountains between the Ayalon and Soreq Valleys. After Saslove resigned to open his own winery in 1998, Nir Shacham took over as winemaker and has recently taken on full ownership. The winery relies entirely on Cabernet Sauvignon and Merlot grapes grown in its own vineyards, and releases wines in Special Reserve and regular editions. Current production is about 6,000–7000 bottles annually.

Special Reserve

SPECIAL RESERVE, CABERNET SAUVIGNON, 2001: Medium to full-bodied, the wine shows generous tannins well balanced by spicy wood and tempting currant, plum and berry fruits along with hints of smoke and chocolate, on a medium-long finish. Drink now. Score 89.

SPECIAL RESERVE, CABERNET SAUVIGNON, 2000: Full-bodied, the wine shows generous tannins that are now integrating nicely, along with rich aromas and flavors of blackcurrant and berry fruits, those complemented nicely by toasted oak and spices. On the long finish look for hints of chocolate and mint. Drink up. Score 88.

SPECIAL RESERVE, CABERNET SAUVIGNON, 1999: Rich, muscular and full-bodied, but elegant and sophisticated, with currants, black cherries, violets and dried herbs. Rich in tannins that promise to integrate nicely. Drink up. Score 89.

SPECIAL RESERVE, CABERNET SAUVIGNON, 1998: This deep purple toward garnet, medium to full-bodied wine opens with an attack of stewed, almost sweet black fruits. Given time in the glass, these yield to appealing aromas and flavors of cassis, plums and herbs, all on a moderately long finish. Past its peak. Drink up. Score 85.

SPECIAL RESERVE, CABERNET SAUVIGNON, 1997: Medium-bodied, dark, deep and long, with spicy currants running throughout, and a long finish yielding appealing hints of anise, peppermint and vanilla. Past its peak. Drink up. Score 85.

SPECIAL RESERVE, CABERNET SAUVIGNON, 1996: Dark ruby toward purple in its youth, this medium to full-bodied wine may be beginning to lighten slightly in color, but still shows deep fruit flavors, smooth tannins and appealing oak overtones. Long and gentle, with hints of spices on the finish. Past its peak. Drink up. Score 86.

SPECIAL RESERVE, MERLOT, 2001: Deep garnet red, medium to full-bodied, with generous soft tannins integrating nicely with generous oaky-vanilla aromas and flavors, those opening to reveal plum and blackberry fruits and a long, moderately sweet finish. Drink now. Score 89.

SPECIAL RESERVE, MERLOT, 2000: Dark garnet towards royal purple, medium to full-bodied, with good balance between wood, soft tannins and ripe black fruits. Now fully mature. Drink up. Score 87.

SPECIAL RESERVE, MERLOT, 1999: An almost inky dark medium to full-bodied Merlot, with excellent balance between soft tannins, ample but not exaggerated oak, well-delineated black fruits and enchanting herbal overtones. Drink up. Score 89.

Soreq

SOREQ, CABERNET SAUVIGNON, 2004: Full-bodied enough to be thought of as "thick", remarkably concentrated and with moderate, near-sweet tannins and generous vanilla imparted from the oak barrels in which it is aging. On the nose and palate sweet plums and berries along with a hint of red licorice. Drink now–2009. Score 88.

SOREQ, CABERNET SAUVIGNON, TAL SHACHAR, 2002: Reflecting its 18 months in *barriques* with generous sweet cedar and vanilla and firm tannins, those balanced well with currant, plum and wild berry fruits and an appealingly long finish rich in espresso and tobacco notes. Drink now. Score 88.

SOREQ, CABERNET SAUVIGNON, TAL SHACHAR, 2001: 100% Cabernet Sauvignon aged for 18 months in French and American oak *barriques*, this medium-bodied red shows basic good balance between wood, soft tannins and somewhat dominating oak. The wine shows plum, blackcurrant and black cherry fruits on a generous smoky oak background. Drink now. Score 86.

SOREQ, MERLOT, TAL SHACHAR, 2002: Dark royal purple in color, medium-bodied, with soft tannins and gentle wood. Aromas and flavors of spicy plum, berry and cassis. Drink now. Score 87.

SOREQ, MERLOT, TAL SHACHAR, 2001: This medium-bodied, moderately tannic wine is dominated by wood that overshadows the plum and currant fruits. Past its peak. Drink up. Score 85.

Srigim ✶

Founded by Uriel Harari and Moti Mordechai on Moshav Srigim in the Ella Valley in 2000, this small winery released its first wines from the 2002 harvest. Drawing on grapes from the Judean Mountains, the Ella Valley and Gush Etzion, the winery has chosen to concentrate entirely on Cabernet Sauvignon. Production for the 2004 and 2005 vintages was 2,500 bottles.

SRIGIM, CABERNET SAUVIGNON, 2004: Garnet towards royal purple in color, this oak-aged wine shows firm tannins and ample oak. On the nose and palate near-jammy blackberry, blueberry and cassis fruits. Drink now. Score 83.

SRIGIM, CABERNET SAUVIGNON, 2003: Aged in oak for 12 months, this deep royal purple in color, full-bodied red offers firm tannins and generous oak, those complemented by super-ripe, almost jammy black plum and berry fruits. Drink now. Score 85.

SRIGIM, CABERNET SAUVIGNON, BICURIM, 2002: Dark garnet but not as clear as one might hope for, with chunky tannins and raspberry, cherry and currant aromas and flavors. A simple country-style wine. Drink up. Score 82.

Tabor ★★★★

Founded in 1999 by several grape-growing families in the village of Kfar Tabor in the Lower Galilee, this modern winery draws on white grapes largely from their own vineyards near Mount Tabor and on red grapes from the Upper Galilee. Initial production was of 20,000 bottles and current production is about 270,000 bottles annually. Several years ago, partial control of the winery was bought by the Central Bottling Corporation, the local producer of Coca Cola, and in October of 2005 the company increased their holdings in the winery to 51%.

European-trained winemaker Arieh Nesher is currently releasing wines in three series. The top-of-the-line label is Mes'cha, a series of varietal wines that now includes Cabernet Sauvignon, Merlot and Chardonnay, those to be joined shortly by Gewurztraminer. A second label, Tabor-Adama, reflects the type of soils in the vineyards. In reading the labels it may be useful to know that *adama* translates into soil; *gir* is chalky soil; *terra rosa* is red earth; *charsit* is clay and *bazelet* refers to volcanic soil. There is also a more basic series released under the label Tabor.

Mes'cha

MES'CHA, 2003: A blend of Cabernet Sauvignon, Merlot and Shiraz (80%, 15% and 5% respectively), this deep garnet, medium to full-bodied wine reflects its 18 months in oak with still firm tannins, those integrating nicely and opening to reveal blackcurrant, berry and plum fruits on a background of spicy wood and Mediterranean herbs. Generous, well-balanced and long. Drink now–2009. Score 90. **K**

MES'CHA, 2002: A blend of Cabernet Sauvignon and Merlot, this medium to full-bodied red shows firm tannins integrating nicely now with spicy oak and generous currant and wild berry fruits, those matched by hints of spices, earthiness and tobacco on the finish. Drink now–2008. Score 88. **K**

MES'CHA, CABERNET SAUVIGNON, 2001: Dark garnet red, medium to full-bodied, with good balance between firm but nicely integrating tannins, spicy oak and an appealing array of blackcurrant, plums, smoke and fresh earthy aromas and flavors. Long and mouthfilling. Drink now–2008. Score 90. **K**

MES'CHA, CABERNET SAUVIGNON, 2000: Full-bodied, concentrated and intense, this deeply tannic wine opens slowly in the glass to show black fruits, cigar tobacco, tar, and earthy aromas and flavors. Still firm and muscular, but finally showing signs of opening. Drink now. Score 89. **K**

MES'CHA, CABERNET SAUVIGNON-MERLOT, 2001: A full-bodied blend of 80% Cabernet Sauvignon and 20% Merlot, the wine was aged partly in new oak and partly in one-year-old barrels for 14 months and shows excellent focus and tempting flavors of currants, spices and cedar along with a leathery note that runs throughout. Drink now. Score 91. **K**

MESCHA, CHARDONNAY, 2004: Deep gold in color, medium to full-bodied, with appealing pear, citrus flavors and a hint of mango on a background of spicy oak along with a round buttery texture. Good balance between wood, acidity and fruits. Drink now. Score 89. **K**

MES'CHA, CHARDONNAY, 2003: Golden straw in color, this medium to full-bodied white reflects its 4 months in oak with hints of smoky and spicy wood together with rich, lightly creamy layers of pear, honey and apricots. Complex and long. Drink now. Score 90. **K**

Adama

ADAMA, CABERNET SAUVIGNON, BAZELET, 2005: Dark, deep and round, showing good balance between wood, soft tannins and a tempting array of cassis, berry, citrus peel and earthy-herbal aromas and flavors. Drink from 2008. Tentative Score 88–90. **K**

ADAMA, CABERNET SAUVIGNON, BAZELET, 2004: Deep garnet in color, with deep purple and orange reflections, medium to full-bodied, and with good balance between smoky wood, acidity and fruits. On the nose and palate concentrated currant and blackberry fruits matched by espresso and vanilla. Seductive and elegant. Drink now–2010. Score 90. **K**

ADAMA, CABERNET SAUVIGNON, TERRA ROSA, 2005: Deep garnet in color, with soft, near-sweet tannins and hints of spices and vanilla from the wood in which it is developing. On the nose and palate red plums, blackberries and blackcurrants, those complemented by hints of earthy minerals. Drink from 2008. Tentative Score 88–90. K

ADAMA, CABERNET SAUVIGNON, TERRA ROSA, 2004: Dark garnet, medium to full-bodied, with spicy wood, soft tannins integrating nicely and red currant, blackberry and plum on the nose and palate, those backed up by an appealing hint of earthiness that lingers nicely. Drink now–2008. Score 88. K

ADAMA, CABERNET SAUVIGNON, TERRA ROSSA, 2003: Dark royal purple, almost inky, this medium to full-bodied red is already showing appealing currant, cherry and spice flavors and aromas. Inherent good balance between soft tannins, acidity and fruits and an appealing spicy finish. Drink now. Score 87. K

ADAMA CABERNET SAUVIGNON, TERRA ROSA, 2002: Dark, tight and firm but well focused and opening nicely in the glass to reveal an array of ripe cherry, currant, spice, anise and lightly toasty oak flavors. Supple and well focused with just the right hints of tannins that come to the fore on the long finish. Drink now. Score 88. K

ADAMA, MERLOT, BAZELET, 2005: Showing medium to full-body, promising hints of vanilla from American oak and spicy wood from French. Soft tannins here well balanced by good acidity, raspberry and cassis aromas and flavors, and a light earthy overtone. Promising soft, round elegance. Drink from release–2010. Tentative Score 88–90. K

ADAMA, MERLOT, BAZELET, 2004: Medium to full-bodied, dark garnet towards royal purple in color, with generous wood influence and deep tannins in fine balance with blackcurrant, plum and wild berry fruits. On the moderately-long finish, hints of eucalyptus and chocolate. Drink now–2008. Score 88. K

ADAMA, MERLOT, BAZELET, 2003: Opening beautifully now, reflecting its 12 months in oak with appealing smoky and vanilla overlays and showing tempting blackcurrant, purple plum and berry fruits. A distinctly French-style wine, well balanced and generous. Drink now. Score 89. K

ADAMA, MERLOT, BAZELET, 2001: Deep garnet in color and reflecting its aging in French and American oak with hints of vanilla and smoke, this medium to full-bodied red is aromatic, round and mouth-filling. Features currant, spice and black cherry flavors, smooth and polished tannins, and a rich finish, with fruits that fan out beautifully on the palate. Drink now. Score 89. K

ADAMA, MERLOT, GIR, 2005: Developing in French oak, medium-dark ruby towards garnet in color, with near-sweet tannins set off nicely by a hint of bitter herbs and those showing hints of spicy cedar, blackcurrants, and berries. Best 2008–2010. Tentative Score 87–89. **K**

ADAMA, MERLOT, GIR, 2004: Medium-bodied, with gentle spicy oak influences and soft tannins integrating nicely, with raspberry, blackberry, cassis and light earthy overtones. A round, smooth and near-elegant wine. Drink now–2008. Score 89. **K**

ADAMA, MERLOT, GIR, 2003: Dark garnet in color, medium-bodied, and somewhat internationalized in style, with soft tannins, hints of sweet cedar wood and forward plum and currant fruits. Turns a bit more complex on the lightly herbal finish. Drink now. Score 88. **K**

ADAMA, MERLOT, GIR, 2002: Dark cherry red toward garnet, this medium-bodied, lightly oaked wine has a somewhat muted nose but shows very well on the palate, opening to reveal dark plums, currants, smooth tannins and a rich lingering finish. Drink up. Score 87. **K**

ADAMA, SHIRAZ, CHARSIT, 2004: Full-bodied, with soft tannins, good hints of smoky oak and sweet cedar, and generous black plums, berries and currants. Still in its infancy but showing promise to be a simultaneously complex and easy-to-drink wine. Drink from release–2008. Tentative Score 89–91. **K**

ADAMA, SHIRAZ, CHARSIT, 2003: Deep garnet, medium to full-bodied, with firm tannins but those well integrated with spicy oak, vanilla and generous red plum and currant fruits. On the long finish, appealing light meaty and herbal overtones. Drink now–2009. Score 89. **K**

ADAMA, CABERNET FRANC, ROSÉ, CHARSIT, 2005: With a deep pink color that typifies peaches in their first bloom, this wine shows appealing currant, red berry and rose petal aromas and flavors, those hinting of earth on the finish. A 14% alcohol content, medium-bodied, delicious, crisply dry rosé for fun quaffing or as a comfortable match with fish, seafood or poultry dishes. Drink now. Score 88. **K**

ADAMA, CABERNET FRANC, ROSÉ, CHARSIT, 2004: Bright cherry red in color, this medium-bodied crisply dry wine shows good balancing acidity and appealing berry, cherry and plum aromas and flavors. A well made round rosé. Drink up. Score 87. **K**

ADAMA, CHARDONNAY, BAZELET, 2005: Fermented in *barriques* with no malolactic fermentation encouraged. Clean, crisp and fresh, medium-bodied, with citrus and peach fruitiness matched nicely by gentle wood and lively acidity leading to a long finish. Drink now. Score 88. **K**

ADAMA, CHARDONNAY, BAZELET, 2004: Light gold, medium-bodied, with citrus and tropical fruits on a lightly earthy background. Good balancing acidity keeps the wine lively and hints of earthiness and herbaceousness add complexity. Drink now. Score 88. K

ADAMA, CHARDONNAY, BAZELET, 2003: Golden straw in color, with green reflections, this supple wine has a pleasing earthy accent to its citrus, hazelnut and pineapple notes. Appealing ripe pear flavors on the finish make this a deep, complex and satisfying wine. Drink now. Score 89. K

ADAMA, CHARDONNAY, GIR, 2004: Crisp, clean and with abundant minerals on the nose and palate, those matched well by citrus and melon fruits. Calls to mind a Petit Chablis. Drink now. Score 87. K

ADAMA, CHARDONNAY, GIR, 2003: Reflecting three months in new French and American oak, this light to medium-bodied straw colored wine shows an appealing touch of spicy-vanilla laden wood together with green apple and citrus fruits. Not long or complex, with a hint of bitterness now creeping in but still quite pleasing. Drink now. Score 86. K

ADAMA, SAUVIGNON BLANC, GIR, 2005: Light straw in color, this unoaked white starts off with subdued aromas and flavors but given time in the glass opens to reveal crisply dry, mineral-rich citrus and nut aromas and flavors. Round and full of flavor. Drink now. Score 88. K

ADAMA, SAUVIGNON BLANC, GIR, 2004: Unoaked, crisply dry with light herbal and earthy hints on a background of grapefruit, orange peel and minerals. Fresh, refreshing and generous. Drink now. Score 88. K

ADAMA, SAUVIGNON BLANC, CHARSIT, 2004: Lightly oaked (2 months in *barriques*), light gold in color, medium-bodied and with lively grassy, citrus and citrus peel aromas and flavors, calling to mind the wines of France's Loire Valley. Refreshing, complex and with a long finish. Drink now. Score 88. K

Tabor

TABOR, CABERNET SAUVIGNON, 2004: Dark ruby towards garnet in color, medium-bodied, with silky-smooth tannins and appealing currant and wild berry fruits. Nothing complex here but remarkably pleasant. A very good choice as an everyday wine. Drink now. Score 86. K

TABOR, CABERNET SAUVIGNON, 2003: Deep royal purple, showing herbal and black olive flavors backed up nicely by currants and wild berries. Soft tannins and good balance make the wine drinkable now. Score 86. **K**

TABOR, MERLOT, 2003: Medium-bodied, with soft tannins and generous berry and black cherry fruits. Not complex but pleasant. Drink now. Score 85. **K**

TABOR, SHIRAZ, 2003: Dark purple in color, with true Shiraz characteristics, and at this stage still brooding and very firm, the wine opens in the glass to reveal hints of licorice and game together with firm tannins and deep raspberry, floral accents. Clean and long, a fine Mediterranean version of Shiraz. Drink now. Score 88. **K**

TABOR, CHARDONNAY, 2005: Clean, crisp and refreshing. Medium-bodied, with forward aromas and flavors of citrus and peaches and crisp minerality. Drink now. Score 87. **K**

Tanya ★★

Located in the town of Ofra at the foot of the Hebron Mountains, this winery established by Yoram Cohen released its first wines in 2002. Drawing on Cabernet Sauvignon and Merlot grapes from Gush Etzion and the Golan Heights, the winery produced 6,500 bottles in 2004 and about 13,000 bottles in 2005.

Reserve

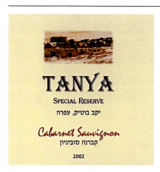

RESERVE, CABERNET SAUVIGNON, 2004: Medium-bodied, softly tannic, with generous but not overpowering smoky oak and appealing aromas and flavors of blackcurrants, berries and dark chocolate, all with a bitter hint that will appeal to some. Drink from release. Tentative Score 83–85. **K**

RESERVE, CABERNET SAUVIGNON, 2003: Dark cherry red, medium to full-bodied, with firm but already well-integrating tannins and a light influence of oak. Aromas and flavors of currants, plums, Mediterranean herbs and a hint of tobacco. Drink now–2008. Score 84. **K**

RESERVE, CABERNET SAUVIGNON, 2002: Medium-bodied and deep garnet in color, with firm but well-integrated tannins and a nice hint of wood after 4 months in small barrels. Barnyard aromas are present when first poured, but those fade away to reveal aromas and flavors of black fruits and herbs. Drink now. Score 84. **K**

RESERVE, MERLOT, 2004: Garnet red in color, medium to full-bodied, with soft tannins and spicy oak. Aromas and flavors of blackberries, currants and chocolate. Not complex but appealing. Drink now. Score 85. **K**

RESERVE, MERLOT, 2003: Medium-bodied, with chunky tannins and a too generous smoky-spicy influence of the oak, this holding back whatever black fruits are here. Drink up. Score 82. **K**

RESERVE, MERLOT, 2002: Dark cherry-red in color, this wine reflects its 7 months in oak with surprisingly firm tannins and very generous toasted oak aromas and flavors, both of which come together to hide the plum and berry flavors that struggle to make themselves felt. Drink now. Score 83. **K**

RESERVE, BLEND, 2004: A dark garnet, medium-bodied and softly tannic blend of 70% Cabernet Sauvignon and 30% Merlot. On the nose and palate currants, raspberries and a generous hint of herbaceousness. Drink now. Score 84. **K**

Tanya

TANYA, CABERNET SAUVIGNON, 2004: Medium-dark garnet in color, medium-bodied, with chunky, country-style tannins. Flavors of blackcurrants and blackberries but one dimensional and short. Drink now. Score 80. **K**

TANYA, MERLOT, 2004: Full-bodied, firmly tannic, with very generous smoky wood hiding the berry and black cherry aromas and flavors that try to make themselves felt. Drink now. Score 78. **K**

TANYA, MERLOT-CABERNET SAUVIGNON, 2003: An oak-aged blend of 70% Merlot and 30% Cabernet Sauvignon. Medium to full-bodied, with firm tannins, too-deep earthy aromas and flavors and lacking fruit. Perhaps better with time. Drink up. Score 78. **K**

Tishbi ✶✶✶

Following the initiatives of Baron Edmond de Rothschild, the Tishbi family started to plant vineyards in 1882 on the slopes of Mount Carmel near the town of Zichron Ya'akov and continued to cultivate vines throughout the next hundred years. In 1985, Jonathan Tishbi, a fourth generation member of the family, launched this family-owned winery in the nearby town of Binyamina, initially named Habaron as homage to Baron Rothschild, and later renamed Tishbi.

With Golan Tishbi serving as senior winemaker the winery has made the leap from 650,000–870,000 bottles to an output of nearly 1,000,000 annually. Drawing on grapes from their own vineyards as well as from vineyards in the Jerusalem region and the Upper Galilee, the winery produces several series, the top-of-the-line being the age-worthy Cabernet Sauvignon, Merlot and Chardonnay wines in the Jonathan Tishbi Special Reserve series. These are followed by varietal wines in the Estate and Vineyards series, and by the more popularly priced wines in the Tishbi series and the recently discontinued Baron series. The winery also produces a sparkling wine and a Port-style wine.

Special Reserve

SPECIAL RESERVE, CABERNET SAUVIGNON-MERLOT, 2004: Dark garnet in color, medium to full-bodied, this oak-aged blend of 55%

Cabernet Sauvignon and 45% Merlot was made entirely from grapes harvested at Sde Boker in the Negev. Good balance between still firm tannins, spicy wood and black fruits, those matched by tobacco and chocolate leading to a long finish. Drink from release–2010. Tentative Score 88–90. **K**

SPECIAL RESERVE, CABERNET SAUVIGNON, BEN ZIMRA, 2002: Deep purple in color, ripe, bold and concentrated, the wine has solid and chewy tannins, those well balanced by oak. On the nose and palate spicy currant and berry fruits. Drink now–2008. Score 90. **K**

SPECIAL RESERVE, CABERNET SAUVIGNON, GUSH ETZION, 2002: Medium to full-bodied, well balanced, with surprisingly soft tannins and aromas and flavors of currant, cherry, plum and wild berry fruits, just the right hint of wood, and a hint of anise on the medium finish. Drink now. Score 88. **K**

SPECIAL RESERVE, CABERNET SAUVIGNON, BEN ZIMRA, 1999: Ripe and harmonious, this well balanced wine offers up fresh cherry, spice and plum flavors along with supple tannins, all overlaid by appealing hints of earthiness and herbs. Drink now. Score 90. **K**

SPECIAL RESERVE, CABERNET SAUVIGNON, SDE BOKER, 1999: Perhaps reflecting the origin of the grapes in the Negev Desert, the wine is not so much earthy or herbal but instead is marked by distinct flavors of green olives and spices. Full-bodied, with tannins that integrate nicely now, it also shows ripe and well focused black cherry and currant flavors along with an appealing long finish. Drink now. Score 89. **K**

SPECIAL RESERVE, CABERNET SAUVIGNON, KFAR YUVAL, 1999: With earthy currant and cherry flavors emerging through firm tannins, this rich and concentrated wine is now showing the smooth and supple texture promised in its youth. Drink now. Score 88. **K**

SPECIAL RESERVE, CABERNET SAUVIGNON, 1998: Fully mature now but as it was during its extreme youth, a well-balanced, well-proportioned wine with generous cassis, plum, berry and spicy overtones. Full-bodied, with now soft and integrated tannins and a generous toasty oak overlay, and hints of anise and chocolate on the finish. Drink up. Score 90. **K**

SPECIAL RESERVE, MERLOT, KEREM KFAR YUVAL-GUSH ETZION, 2002: Mature now but still graceful. With a deep, almost inky garnet color and generous but smooth tannins, this supple and well-balanced medium to full-bodied wine shows plums, ripe cherry, chocolate and gentle cedar-oak aromas and flavors along with a sweet and spicy herbal finish. Drink now. Score 90. **K**

SPECIAL RESERVE, MERLOT, 1999: This deep garnet, full-bodied wine, with far more tannins than one usually anticipates in a Merlot, is nevertheless rich and flavorful, and has good balance between tannins, the oak in which it was aged, and fruits, those including spicy black cherry, plum, currant and mineral flavors. Drink up. Score 89. **K**

SPECIAL RESERVE, CHARDONNAY, GUSH ETZION, 2004: Aged in 300 liter French barrels, this deep golden, full-bodied and buttery-creamy white shows appealing pear and vanilla aromas and flavors. At this stage somewhat dominated by the wood. Drink now. Score 86. **K**

SPECIAL RESERVE, CHARDONNAY, 2003: Aging 4 months in new French oak barrels, this light golden colored, medium-bodied wine shows gentle touches of vanilla, spicy oak, pineapple and citrus aromas and flavors. Drink up. Score 87. **K**

Estate

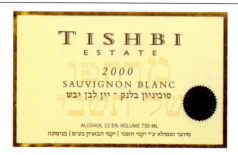

ESTATE, CABERNET SAUVIGNON, 2004: Medium to full-bodied, with silky smooth tannins and layers of currant, berry and plum fruits, those matched nicely by hints of spicy wood and a light herbal overlay. Drink now–2008. Score 87. **K**

ESTATE, CABERNET SAUVIGNON, 2003: Deep garnet, medium to full-bodied, with an appealing earthy overtone to currant and berry fruits. Fading quickly. Drink up. Score 84. **K**

ESTATE, CABERNET SAUVIGNON, 2002: Oak-aged for 12 months in small casks, this dark garnet medium to full-bodied wine offers up generous but soft and already nicely integrating tannins, appealing currant, plum and wild berry fruits, and hints of vanilla and smoky oak. Drink up. Score 87. **K**

ESTATE, CABERNET SAUVIGNON, 2001: Surprisingly light in color, this medium-bodied, moderately tannic wine shows fresh currant, berry and plum notes, and nicely reflects its 18 months in oak with a finish of spicy oak. Drink up. Score 86. **K**

ESTATE, CABERNET SAUVIGNON, 2000: Medium-bodied, with soft tannins that are already well integrated and traditional blackcurrant and spicy aromas and flavors. Somewhat past its peak. Drink up. Score 85. **K**

ESTATE, MERLOT, 2004: Made from grapes from Sde Boker in the Negev, this soft, medium-bodied wine offers a few berry and spice flavors but seems badly out of balance and even at this early stage is showing signs of browning. Drink from release. Tentative Score 80–82. **K**

ESTATE, MERLOT, 2003: Deep garnet red, medium-bodied, with firm tannins that yield in the glass. Good balance between lightly smoky wood and plum and currant fruits all leading to a moderately long finish. Drink now. Score 86. **K**

ESTATE, MERLOT, 2002: A blend of 92% Merlot and 8% Cabernet Sauvignon, this dark, medium to full-bodied wine is somewhat closed on the nose but shows tempting berry, black cherry and currant flavors, those coming together with good hints of the oak and a medium-long finish. Drink up. Score 87. **K**

ESTATE, MERLOT, 2001: After 18 months in oak this medium to dark royal purple, medium-bodied blend of 85% Merlot and 15% Cabernet Sauvignon shows soft tannins and generous hints of vanilla from the oak as well as good plum and berry fruits, all on a lightly spicy background. Somewhat past its peak. Drink up. Score 84. **K**

ESTATE, MERLOT, 2000: An oak-aged blend of 85% Merlot and 15% Cabernet Sauvignon, this medium-bodied wine shows appealing berry and black cherry fruits along with smooth tannins and overlays of vanilla and spices. Drink up. Score 85. **K**

ESTATE, PINOT NOIR, 2004: Light wood influences, soft tannins, medium-bodied, with berry, plum and light earthy-mineral hints leading to a medium-long finish. A good quaffer. Drink now. Score 85. **K**

ESTATE, PINOT NOIR, 2003: Aged in new and old oak, this attractive medium to full-bodied wine offers up light earthy, mineral and herbal overtones on a background of wild berries and red plums. Drink now. Score 87. **K**

ESTATE, CHARDONNAY, 2005: Unoaked, with a crisp and mineral-rich nature and showing generous citrus, green apple and melon aromas and flavors. Refreshing and complex. Drink now. Score 86. **K**

ESTATE, CHARDONNAY, 2004: Made from organically raised grapes from the Gush Etzion region, this unoaked wine shows some melon and pear fruits but is lacking in acidity and somewhat flat on the palate. Drink now. Score 82. **K**

ESTATE, SAUVIGNON BLANC, 2005: Light, almost watery in color, but given time to open in the glass rich aromas and flavors of lightly grassy and herbal apple and melons. Not a lively wine but one that sits comfortably on the palate. Drink now. Score 85. **K**

ESTATE, SAUVIGNON BLANC, 2004: Light straw in color, medium-bodied and aromatic, with summer fruit and green apples on the palate. Good balance between natural acidity and fruits. Drink now. Score 87. **K**

ESTATE, SAUVIGNON BLANC, 2003: Light gold in color, with orange and green tinges, this medium-bodied white offers up appealing aromas and flavors of citrus, green apples and melon fruits on a crisply fresh background. Drink now. Score 86. **K**

ESTATE, LATE HARVEST RIESLING, 2004: Made from Emerald Riesling grapes. Floral on the nose, with ripe peach and apricot fruits. Moderate sweetness set off nicely by acidity makes for a pleasant quaffer. Drink now. Score 85. **K**

ESTATE, LATE HARVEST RIESLING, 2003: Made from Emerald Riesling grapes, this light to medium-bodied wine offers up simple but lively aromas and flavors of summer fruits and vanilla. Drink now. Score 83. **K**

ESTATE, WHITE RIESLING, 2004: Light straw colored, medium-bodied, with tropical and citrus fruits along with a hint of litchis. Not complex but dry, lively and pleasant. Drink now. Score 85. **K**

ESTATE, WHITE RIESLING, 2003: Golden straw colored, medium-bodied, with citrus-litchi and traditional and rather marked petrol aromas that often typify Riesling. Dry, well balanced and with a lingering finish. Drink now. Score 87. **K**

ESTATE, FRENCH COLOMBARD, LATE HARVEST, 2004: Aged in brandy barrels, flowery and cloying, with far too much residual sugar and not enough balancing acidity. Drink up. Score 78. K

Vineyards

VINEYARDS, CABERNET SAUVIGNON, 2004: Dark cherry red in color, medium-bodied with soft, almost unfelt tannins, and cassis, blueberry and plum flavors all on a somewhat sweet finish. Drink now. Score 84. K

VINEYARDS, CABERNET SAUVIGNON, 2003: Medium-bodied, with moderate tannins integrating nicely and appealing currant and berry fruits. Not complex but pleasant. Drink up. Score 85. K

VINEYARDS, CABERNET SAUVIGNON, 2002: Reflecting the problematic 2002 vintage, this medium-bodied blend of 85% Cabernet Sauvignon and 15% Merlot shows soft tannins and hints of wood but only modest fruits and a fairly short finish. Drink up. Score 85. K

VINEYARDS, MERLOT, 2004: Dark cherry red to purple in color, medium-bodied, with soft tannins and forward plum and black cherry fruits. Look as well for hints of smoky oak and Mediterranean herbs. Drink now. Score 85. K

VINEYARDS, MERLOT, 2003: Garnet red in color, this medium-bodied blend of 85% Merlot and 15% Cabernet Sauvignon offers up spicy plum and currant fruits and light hints of smoky, spicy oak. Perhaps a bit astringent. Drink now. Score 86. K

VINEYARDS, MERLOT, 2002: Ruby toward purple, medium-bodied, with soft, almost unfelt tannins and berry and currant fruits. A pleasant little wine. Drink up. Score 85. K

VINEYARDS, CARIGNAN, 2004: A wine made especially for Ikea, labeled as 85% Carignan and 15% Cabernet Sauvignon but with a remarkable resemblance to the Tishbi Cabernet-Petite Sirah blend of the same year. A pleasant quaffer. Drink now. Score 84. **K**

VINEYARDS, CARIGNAN, 2002: Blended with about 10% of Cabernet Sauvignon to add depth and "bite", this medium-bodied wine offers up tempting currant, berry and black cherry fruits along with a generous overlay of chocolate. Somewhat acidic. Drink up. Score 86. **K**

VINEYARDS, SAUVIGNON BLANC, 2004: Pale golden straw in color, unoaked and crisply dry with some grapefruit and pineapple fruits. Drink now. Score 84. **K**

VINEYARDS, SAUVIGNON BLANC, 2003: Light straw colored, this light to medium-bodied wine offers up appealing light herbal flavors to go with summer fruits and a bare hint of grassiness. Drink now. Score 85. **K**

VINEYARDS, EMERALD RIESLING, 2004: Semi-dry, with grapefruit and green apple and a reasonable level of sweetness. An acceptable entry-level wine. Drink up. Score 84. **K**

VINEYARDS, DRY MUSCAT, 2004: Medium-bodied, crisply dry, with apple, pineapple and summer fruits. An appealing and refreshing white. Drink up. Score 84. **K**

VINEYARDS, DRY MUSCAT, 2003: Made from Muscat of Alexandria grapes but lacking the usual flowery and sweet aroma, this crisply dry wine offers up simple fruity and minty pleasures. Not complex but pleasant. Drink up. Score 84. **K**

Tishbi

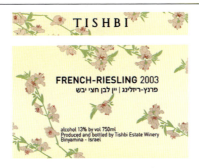

TISHBI, CABERNET SAUVIGNON-PETITE SIRAH, 2005: Dark ruby red, with soft tannins and an appealing array of raspberry, cassis and black cherry fruits. A good quaffer. Drink now. Score 85. **K**

TISHBI, CABERNET SAUVIGNON-PETITE SIRAH 2004: Cherry red, fresh, lively and with soft tannins and berry-cherry fruits. Drink now. Score 84. **K**

TISHBI, CABERNET-PETITE SIRAH, 2003: Light to medium-bodied, this dark cherry-colored blend of 70% Cabernet Sauvignon and 30% Petite Sirah has fresh and fruity aromas and flavors of black cherries and berries. Light and pleasant on the palate. Drink now. Score 84. **K**

TISHBI, CABERNET-PETITE SIRAH, 2002: Medium-bodied and low in tannins, this deep ruby-colored wine shows berry and currant flavors. Drink up. Score 83. **K**

TISHBI, JUNIOR, 2005: Ruby red, light to medium-bodied, with soft but chunky country-style tannins and appealing berry, cherry fruits. An appealing entry-level wine. Drink up. Score 80. **K**

TISHBI, SAUVIGNON BLANC, 2004: Light golden straw in color, a simple but pleasant little wine with grapefruit, passion fruit and spicy pear aromas and flavors. Drink up. Score 83. **K**

TISHBI, SAUVIGNON BLANC, 2003: Light straw in color, with generous citrus, tropical fruit aromas and flavors. Not much similarity to Sauvignon Blanc, but an appealing quaffing wine. Drink up. Score 84. **K**

TISHBI, EMERALD RIESLING, 2004: Perhaps a bit too sweet for a semi-dry wine, but with clean, appealing citrus and floral aromas and flavors. Drink now. Score 81. **K**

TISHBI, FRENCH COLOMBARD-EMERALD RIESLING, 2004: Off-dry, with simple citrus, apple and floral aromas and flavors. Drink now. Score 82. **K**

TISHBI, FRENCH COLOMBARD-EMERALD RIESLING, 2003: Off dry, with appealing grapefruit and green apple aromas and flavors. A simple but pleasant quaffing wine. Drink up. Score 83. **K**

TISHBI, MUSCAT OF ALEXANDRIA, 2004: As always, floral and packed with tropical fruits and apple aromas. A pleasant little semi-dry white. Drink up. Score 82. **K**

TISHBI, SPARKLING WINE, 2003: Made entirely from French Colombard grapes the wine shows flavors that are somewhere between off-dry and sour, with no mousse to speak of and bubbles that fade far too quickly. This is a wine with little to recommend it. Score 70. **K**

TISHBI, BRUT, 2000: Made from French Colombard grapes, traditionally used to make Cognac and Armagnac brandies, this vintage Brut is fruity but lacks depth or body, and is overly acidic. The bubbles are far too large for a wine made in the traditional Champagne method. Drink up. Score 78. **K**

TISHBI BRUT, N.V.: In its youth, like the vintage version, the wine had strong but attractive overtones of yeast as well as pleasant apple, pear and citrus flavors, but lately some bottles have been corked and others disclosed as lifeless. At its best, the wine earned a Score of 87. **K**

Tulip ★★★

Located near the town of Kiryat Tivon, not far from Haifa, this winery is an effort of the Itzhaki family, with Doron Itzhaki serving as the winemaker. Drawing largely on Cabernet Sauvignon, Merlot, Syrah, Sauvignon Blanc and Chardonnay grapes from Kerem Ben Zimra, other locations in the Upper Galilee and Karmei Yosef, the winery released 27,000 bottles from the 2004 vintage and 45,000 from the 2005 vintage.

The winery is currently releasing wines in four series: varietal Grand Reserve and Reserve; Mostly (blended wines); and Just (single vineyard wines). The winery also releases a Port-style reinforced red wine.

Grand Reserve

GRAND RESERVE, CABERNET SAUVIGNON, 2003: Made entirely from Cabernet Sauvignon grapes and destined for about 18 months of oak aging, this full bodied, deep garnet colored and still firmly tannic wine already shows the promise of elegance. Aromas and flavors of black fruits, citrus peel, chocolate and Mediterranean herbs here. Drink now–2009. Score 88.

GRAND RESERVE, 1999: Medium to full-bodied and with surprisingly moderate tannins and wood influence considering that it was aged in a combination of new and old oak *barriques* for an extraordinarily long 32 months. Showing somewhat better than at an earlier tasting, now revealing currant, raspberry and black cherry fruits. Lacking complexity and showing signs of aging. Drink up. Score 80.

Reserve

RESERVE, CABERNET SAUVIGNON, 2004: Dense royal-purple towards black, full-bodied, deeply tannic and with generous wood influence but with balance and structure that bodes well for the future. As the wine develops look for spicy blackcurrant, cassis, chocolate and a light overlay of cigar tobacco. Drink from release–2009. Score 89.

RESERVE, CABERNET SAUVIGNON, 2003: Deep garnet towards black, medium to full-bodied and reflecting 14 months in small oak barrels with vanilla, spicy wood and appealing black fruits. Firm tannins here but good balance bodes well for the future. Drink now–2008. Score 89.

RESERVE, SYRAH, 2004: Full-bodied, with generous dusty, smoky oak and firm tannins but those well balanced with black fruits, chocolate and earthy-animal aromas and flavors. Needs time to settle down but bodes well for the future. Drink now–2010. Score 88.

Mostly

MOSTLY, MERLOT, 2004: Garnet towards royal purple in color, this medium-bodied blend of 77% Merlot and 23% Cabernet Sauvignon shows soft tannins integrating nicely, a judicious hand with oak, and appealing red currant and wild berry fruits. Soft, round, generous and moderately long. Drink now–2008. Score 87.

MOSTLY, SHIRAZ, 2004: Dark ruby towards garnet in color, this blend of Shiraz and Cabernet Sauvignon (75% and 25% respectively) was aged primarily in new barrels. Medium to full-bodied, with plum, currant and berry fruits backed up by appealing hints of earthiness and freshly tanned leather. Drink now–2008. Score 87.

MOSTLY, SAUVIGNON BLANC, 2004: Dark straw in color, portions of this medium-bodied blend of Sauvignon Blanc and Chardonnay (75% and 25% respectively) were oak fermented and aged *sur lie* before the final blend was made. Generous melon, pear and citrus fruits backed up nicely by light herbaceousness. Drink now. Score 87.

Just

JUST, CABERNET SAUVIGNON, 2004: Dark royal purple, developed in French and American oak for eight months. Showing good balance between spicy wood, soft, well integrating tannins and wild berry and currant fruits. Look for hints of vanilla and Mediterranean herbs on the finish. Drink now. Score 86.

JUST, MERLOT, 2004: Deep ruby in color, medium-bodied, with black fruits complemented by hints of chocolate and espresso coffee. Well balanced and moderately long. Drink now–2008. Score 86.

JUST, SHIRAZ, 2005: Oak aged for about 12 months, medium-bodied, with still firm tannins but those in good balance with spicy wood and earthy, plum and spicy aromas and flavors. Drink from release–2008. Tentative Score 84–86.

JUST, SAUVIGNON BLANC, 2004: Light straw colored, light to medium bodied, clean, crisp and refreshing, with pineapple, green melon and citrus fruits on a generously acidic and spicy background. Drink up. Score 86.

Tzora ★★★★

Set on Kibbutz Tzora at the foothills of the Jerusalem Mountains and overlooking the Soreq Valley, this *kibbutz*-owned winery released its first wines, 1,500 bottles, from the 1993 vintage. Current production is about 60,000 bottles annually.

Ronnie James, who has been the winemaker since the winery's inception, releases varietal wines as well as blends based on Cabernet Sauvignon, Merlot, Sauvignon Blanc, Chardonnay, Johannisberg Riesling and Muscat of Alexandria, many of those as single-vineyard wines. James has succeeded as very few winemakers do to consistently represent a specific Mediterranean *terroir*. As to the winery's labels, it is difficult to divide the wines into specific series or to know from year to year precisely which wines will be released in which series. Starting with the releases of the 2002 vintage the wines of Tzora have been kosher.

TZORA, CABERNET SAUVIGNON, NEVE ILAN, SPECIAL SELECTION, 2003: Aged in oak casks for 20 months, this medium to full-bodied blend of 66% Cabernet Sauvignon and 34% Merlot shows almost impenetrable garnet in color. Firm tannins and spicy wood are well balanced by blackcurrant, wild berry and plum fruits on an earthy, mineral-rich background. Drink now–2010. Score 88. **K**

TZORA, CABERNET SAUVIGNON, NEVE ILAN, MISTY HILLS, 2003: A blend of 85% Cabernet Sauvignon and 15% Merlot, aged in oak for 20 months. Deep purple towards black in color, with generous tannins and wood but those in good balance with blackcurrant, purple plum and blackberry fruits. Drink now–2009. Score 89. **K**

TZORA, CABERNET SAUVIGNON, NEVE ILAN, 2003: Dark garnet towards purple, medium to full-bodied, with still firm tannins but those starting to integrate and already revealing smoky oak and a pleasing earthiness on a background of currants and plums. Drink now–2010. Score 87. **K**

TZORA, CABERNET SAUVIGNON, GIVAT HACHALUKIM, 2003: Dark garnet in color, medium to full-bodied, with appealing aromas and flavors of plums and currants and a light earthiness that come together nicely. Well balanced and long. Drink now–2010. Score 89. **K**

TZORA, CABERNET SAUVIGNON, ILAN, BIN 72, 2001: Medium to full-bodied, now dark garnet in color and with still firm tannins. On the nose and palate fresh currant, berry and plum fruits, those with overlays of herbs, espresso coffee and a hint of leather. Long and mouthfilling. Drink now. Score 90.

TZORA, CABERNET SAUVIGNON, ILAN, 2001: Mature now, its tannins and wood fully integrated, the fruits still generous, with blackcurrant and plum fruits but showing distinct signs of aging in the form of a molasses-like sweetness that is starting to creep in. A mere shadow of its once excellence. Drink up. Score 82.

TZORA, CABERNET SAUVIGNON, GIVAT HACHALUKIM, RESERVE, 2001: Dark garnet in color, the once searing tannins of this oak-aged blend of 90% Cabernet Sauvignon and 10% Merlot have finally receded and now show excellent balance with wood, black fruits and herbaceousness, all on a light peppery background. Drink now. Score 89.

TZORA, CABERNET SAUVIGNON, GIVAT HACHALUKIM, 2001: This dark ruby toward purple, medium-bodied single vineyard wine has moderate, well-integrated tannins, generous fruits that include red currants and black cherries, and light touches of herbaceousness and white pepper. Not overly complex but a wine that makes for easy drinking. Drink up. Score 87.

TZORA, CABERNET SAUVIGNON, 2000: Aged for 20 months in *barriques*, this intense wine is living up to its promise and shows a dark ruby toward purple color and a complex interplay on the palate between blackcurrants, blackberries, pepper, sage and spicy cedar aromas and flavors. Look as well for hints of dark chocolate, eucalyptus and leather on the long finish. Drink now–2008. Score 92.

TZORA, CABERNET SAUVIGNON, TZORA VINEYARDS, 2000: This medium to full-bodied wine has firm tannins and needs time to open in the glass to reveal its wild berry, plum, violet, vanilla and chocolate aromas and flavors. Drink up. Score 89.

TZORA, CABERNET SAUVIGNON, BIN 64, SPECIAL SELECTION, 1999: A blend of 85% Cabernet Sauvignon and 15% Merlot, this complex, concentrated and full-bodied wine spent 20 months in oak before bottling. It has a garnet toward purple color, abundant but now well-integrated tannins, and aromas and flavors of currant and blackberry fruits, those nicely matched by vanilla and a tantalizing hint of spicy cedar wood on the finish. Drink now. Score 89.

TZORA, CABERNET SAUVIGNON, BIN 72, SPECIAL SELECTION, 1999: Even though this wine was made from the same grapes and received the same treatment as the wine reviewed above, the grapes came from different rows in the same vineyard. The two wines are far from identical, this one being darker in color and having more of an earthy-herbal than a fruit personality and with tannins firm enough to hide whatever spices, vanilla and cedar wood present here. Drink now. Score 88.

TZORA, CABERNET SAUVIGNON, MISTY HILLS, 1999: Firm and chewy, with firm tannins and delicious black cherry, currant and wild berry flavors, all overlaid by spices, vanilla and cedar wood flavor. Drink up. Score 88.

TZORA, CABERNET SAUVIGNON, SPECIAL SELECTION, NEVE ILAN, 1999: Dark purple toward black, with brownish overtones and now coming into its own, this medium to full-bodied wine offers up generous blackcurrant, wild berry, spice and vanilla flavors along with just the right touch of the oak in which it developed. Drink up. Score 87.

TZORA, MERLOT, NEVE ILAN, 2003: Full-bodied, deep garnet in color, with soft tannins. Round and soft with rich plum and black cherry fruits and just the right hint of spicy oak. Drink now–2008. Score 88. **K**

TZORA, MERLOT, SHORESH, 2003: A simple Merlot, medium-bodied with soft tannins, plenty of acidity, perhaps too much, and appealing plum and berry fruits. Drink now–2007. Score 86. **K**

TZORA, MERLOT, ESTATE WINE, 2003: Rustic in style, rough and chewy with a range of flavors that include herbs, tea, spices and leather but lacking the rich Merlot flavors that should have been there. Past its peak. Drink up. Score 79. **K**

TZORA, MERLOT, ILAN, 2001: This medium to full-bodied blend of 90% Merlot and 10% Cabernet Sauvignon reflects the two years it spent in new and old oak with generous but soft tannins and tempting red currant and berry flavors, those on a background of Mediterranean herbs and vanilla. Just enough spiciness here to add interest along with a medium-long finish. Drink up. Score 89.

TZORA, MERLOT, 1997: Smooth and harmonious, with black cherry, currant and wild berry flavors, a hint of anise and sweet toasted oak flavors that linger on the palate, this is a wine that is simultaneously elegant and easy to drink. Past its peak. Drink up. Score 84.

TZORA, CABERNET SAUVIGNON-MERLOT, SAGIV, 2004: Oak-aged for 14 months, this medium-bodied blend of 80% Cabernet Sauvignon and 20% Merlot shows dark garnet, softly tannic and with generous spicy wood. On the nose and palate wild berries, plums and vanilla, all with a light peppery overlay. Drink now–2008. Score 85. K

TZORA, CABERNET SAUVIGNON-MERLOT, NEVE ILAN, SPECIAL SELECTION, 2003: Dark royal purple in color, with soft, already well-integrating tannins, this blend of 50% each Cabernet Sauvignon and Merlot offers generous currant and berry fruits on a long smoky finish. Drink now–2009. Score 87. K

TZORA, CABERNET SAUVIGNON-MERLOT, MISTY HILLS, 2000: Full-bodied, with cedary oak overlaying rich levels of currants, black cherries, berries and plums, the wine has a long mouth-filling finish. Drink now. Score 87. K

TZORA, MERLOT-CABERNET SAUVIGNON, ILAN, MISTY HILLS 2003: This blend of 60% Merlot and 40% Cabernet Sauvignon has deep ruby towards purple color, medium to full-body chunky, country style tannins, and generous oak on a rich spicy black fruit background. Mouthfilling and long. Drink now–2009. Score 87. K

TZORA, CABERNET SAUVIGNON-ZINFANDEL, 2003: Aged in oak casks for 8 months, this medium-bodied blend of 67% Cabernet Sauvignon and 33% Zinfandel is a bit stingy on the nose but offers generous flavors of berries, black cherries and spices. Drink up. Score 85. K

TZORA, SHORESH, JERUSALEM HILLS, 2003: A medium-bodied blend of Cabernet Sauvignon and Merlot grapes from a variety of vineyards. Appealing, fairly sharp berry and plum flavors, somewhat coarse tannins and a good deal of heat give the wine a distinct rustic style. Drink now. Score 85. K

TZORA, STONE RIDGE, 2002: A medium-bodied blend of 60% Cabernet Sauvignon and 40% Merlot, this garnet red wine spent 8 months in new oak barrels. With currant, plum and berry fruits that make themselves apparent on the first attack, on a lightly spicy background and matched by soft tannins, this is not a wine for long-term cellaring. Drink up. Score 85. K

TZORA, JOHANNISBERG RIESLING, 2005: Light gold in color, bright and lively, with peach, apple and spicy floral aromas and flavors that linger nicely on the palate. Drink now. Score 87. K

Vanhotzker ✯✯

Founded by Eli Vanhotzker in 2004, the winery has its own vineyards with Cabernet Sauvignon and Merlot grapes on the slopes of Mount Meron in the Upper Galilee. Releases, entirely of Cabernet Sauvignon from the 2004 and 2005 vintages, were of 1,500 bottles, and projected production from the 2006 vintage is 3,000 bottles, that to include the winery's first Merlot.

VANHOTZKER, CABERNET SAUVIGNON, 2004: Medium to full-bodied, with generous soft tannins and spicy oak already integrating nicely and showing good balance with blackcurrant, plum and blackberry fruits. Generous and moderately long. Drink now–2008. Score 87. **K**

Villa Wilhelma *

Founded in 2003 by Motti Goldman and Amram Surasky and located on Moshav Bnei Atarot not far from Ben Gurion Airport on the central plain, the winery draws its red grapes from the vineyards of Karmei Yosef at the foothills of the Jerusalem Mountains. Wines are released in a Grand Reserve and regular series, and the winery released 3,500 bottles from the 2003 vintage, 14,000 from the 2004 vintage and 17,000 from the 2005 vintage.

Grand Reserve

GRAND RESERVE, CABERNET SAUVIGNON, 2003: Dark garnet, full-bodied and reflecting 18 months in oak with firm, somewhat dominating tannins, yielding slowly to reveal currant, blackberry and tar aromas and flavors along with hints of smoky wood and oriental spices. Drink now. Score 86.

GRAND RESERVE, MERLOT, 2003: Medium to full-bodied, garnet towards dark royal purple in color, with dusty cedar wood and generous acidity and near-sweet tannins. On the nose and palate, wild berries, purple plums and hints of spices. Drink now. Score 85.

GRAND RESERVE, MEDOCABERNET, 2004: Named after Bordeaux's Medoc wines, this medium to full-bodied red shows generous spicy and smoky wood after having spent 20 months in oak, along with aromas and flavors of wild berries, cassis and Mediterranean herbs. Drink now. Score 85.

GRAND RESERVE, GRAND CHARDONNAY, 2004: Developed for only 10 months in French oak but somehow extremely oaky, the wine picked up not so much the spices or vanilla of the wood but the sap, and took on a deep, almost maple syrup-like color. Medicinal on the nose, and on the palate only skimpy fruits and an odd bitterness that comes in on the finish. Drink up. Score 70.

Villa Wilhelma

VILLA WILHELMA, CHARDONNAY, 2004: Dark golden, almost as if going to brown, dominated by bitter almonds and wood sap that hide the fruit. Score 68.

VILLA WILHELMA, SAUVIGNON BLANC, 2005: Light straw in color, opening with strong sulphur and earthy aromas that linger on and interfere with whatever fruits may be here. Score 72.

VILLA WILHELMA, EMERALD RIESLING, 2005: Categorized as half-dry but lacking acidity and sweetness. Floral and medicinal on the nose, and with a distinct hint of sour pineapple juice on the palate. Score 60.

VILLA WILHELMA, MUSCAT OF ALEXANDRIA, DESSERT WINE, 2003: Made from late-harvested grapes and developed *sur lie*, its fermentation stopped by the addition of grape brandy, the wine is golden-maple syrup in color, aggressively floral on the nose and lacks acidity. Its cloying sweetness doesn't yield fruits on the palate but rather a distinct caramel flavor. Score 60.

Vitkin ★★★

Established by Doron and Sharona Belogolovsky on Moshav Kfar Vitkin on the central Coastal Plain, this winery released its first wines from the 2002 vintage. Winemaker Assaf Paz relies on Cabernet Sauvignon, Merlot, Zinfandel, Carignan, Cabernet Franc, Syrah, Tempranillo, Petit Verdot, Petite Sirah, Viognier, French Colombard, Johannisberg Riesling, Gewürztraminer and Muscat grapes from vintners in the Jerusalem hills as well as several other parts of the country. The winery is currently producing 25,000–30,000 bottles annually.

VITKIN, CABERNET SAUVIGNON, 2002: Medium-bodied, with soft, well-integrating tannins, this moderately oaked wine offers up a generous berry-black cherry personality, the fruits complemented nicely by overlays of spices and vanilla. Drink now. Score 85.

VITKIN, CARIGNAN, 2004: Dark garnet towards royal purple in color, now showing full-bodied and with good balance between wood, soft tannins and fruits. Earthy and spicy, with appealing plum, black cherry and cassis aromas and flavors, those opening on the finish to hints of chocolate, Mediterranean herbs and mint. Drink now–2010. Score 89.

VITKIN, CARIGNAN, 2003: Oak-aged with 10% of Petit Verdot added. Dark garnet red, the wine reflects its year in French oak barrels with generous smoke and vanilla, those matched nicely by soft tannins and generous plum and wild berry fruits. Drink now. Score 87.

VITKIN, CARIGNAN, 2002: Deep royal purple in color, medium-bodied and with generous black fruits and spices but closed because the massive tannins have never receded. Drink now. Score 85.

VITKIN, CABERNET FRANC, 2005: Full-bodied, firmly tannic, muscular and already showing generous spicy oak and, from first attack to the long finish, a tempting overlay of Madagascar green peppercorns. Opens with ripe cherries and herbs, those yielding to layers of currant, black cherry, plum and wild berry fruit, and finishing with a long herbal note. Best from 2008. Tentative Score 90–92.

VITKIN, CABERNET FRANC, 2004: Deep, almost impenetrable royal purple in color, this blend of 90% Cabernet Franc and 10% Petit Verdot shows fine balance between wood, moderately-firm tannins and vegetal-fruity characteristics. On first attack pepper and spicy wood, that followed by blackcurrants, plum and blackberry fruits, all supported by hints of cloves, oriental spices and on the long and mouthfilling finish, freshly picked Mediterranean herbs. Best 2008–2011. Score 90.

VITKIN, CABERNET FRANC, 2003: Dark garnet towards royal purple in color, this oak-aged, medium to full-bodied blend of 90% Cabernet Franc, 6% Petit Verdot and 4% Cabernet Sauvignon offers generous dark plum, black cherry and spice flavors, all complemented nicely by chocolate notes. On the clean, long finish look for hints of kirsch liqueur. Drink now. Score 87.

VITKIN, CABERNET FRANC, 2002: Spicy and fruity, with plum and currant flavors, this soft, medium-bodied wine yields an appealing hint of cloves on the finish. Drink now. Score 84.

VITKIN, PINOT NOIR, 2005: Medium-bodied and remarkably fresh, with soft tannins that show a harmonious blending with raspberry, blackberry and cherry fruits, those on a background of persimmons, hazelnuts and even a hint of cola. Going for elegance and not power. Drink from release–2009. Tentative Score 87–89.

VITKIN, PINOT NOIR, 2004: Reflects its 14 months in small oak casks with spicy wood and soft tannins. Dark cherry red and medium-bodied, with black cherry, currant and purple plum fruits and showing hints of chocolate and light earthiness. Drink now–2008. Score 87.

VITKIN, PINOT NOIR, 2003: A blend of Pinot Noir, Petit Verdot and Cabernet Sauvignon (90%, 6% and 4% respectively) that was aged in used oak for about 12 months. This deep cherry towards garnet, medium-bodied, very softly tannic wine offers up appealing berry, cherry and currant fruits on a background of vanilla and mocha. Drink now–2008. Score 87.

VITKIN, PETITE SIRAH, 2005: At this stage a monster, impenetrably dark in its purple-black color, already taking on deep spices from the wood and with tannins firm enough that you feel you could almost drive stakes into the wine. Given time in the glass the wine shows hints of what waits in the future, opening to reveal generous layers of black and red fruits, spices and an overlay of deep herbaceousness. Best 2008–2010. Tentative Score 90–92.

VITKIN, PETITE SIRAH, 2004: Deep, dark and intense, reflecting its 16 months in partly new French oak, with fine balance between firm tannins, sweet cedar and spicy oak. This concentrated wine opens slowly in the glass but when it does open it explodes with blackberry, plum, mineral, meaty and herbal aromas and flavors. Long, tannic and with a gentle hint of bittersweet chocolate on the finish. An elegant wine. Drink now–2010. Score 91.

VITKIN, PETITE SIRAH, 2003: Dark ruby towards garnet, this medium to full-bodied and moderately tannic blend of 90% Petite Sirah and 10% Cabernet Franc developed for 14 months in oak. Aromas and flavors of blackberries and purple plums and a long spicy finish. Drink now. Score 86.

VITKIN, CLASSIC, 2004: Aged in *barriques* for 10 months, this medium-bodied, well-balanced, softly tannic blend of Shiraz, Cabernet Sauvignon and Carignan shows appealing red berries and cherries on first attack, those turning to currants, spring flowers and spices that linger nicely. Drink now. Score 86.

VITKIN, CLASSIC, 2003: An unlikely blend of 40% Cabernet Sauvignon, 35% Syrah and 25% Carignan each vinified separately and aged in oak for 6 months before blending and another 6 months afterwards. Medium-bodied, with soft, somewhat flabby tannins, and with berry-cherry and currant flavors that fail to come together. Drink now. Score 85.

VITKIN, PINK, 2005: A crisply dry blend of Syrah, Carignan, Tempranillo and Cabernet Franc somewhere in color between strawberry-red and shocking pink. Light to medium-bodied, with fresh acidity and aromas and flavors of strawberries and raspberries, those with light peppery overtones, all of which linger nicely on the palate. Drink now. Score 87.

VITKIN, ROSÉ, 2004: A blend of Tempranillo, Syrah and Carignan (50%, 30% and 20% respectively), not so much pink as bright cherry red, light, dry and lively, the wine shows aromas and flavors of strawberry, cassis and orange peel. Drink up. Score 85.

VITKIN, RED DESSERT WINE, N.V.: A medium to full-bodied blend of Petite Sirah, Carignan, Cabernet Sauvignon and Petit Verdot, reinforced with white alcohol to 17% strength, and on the nose candied fruits, strawberries, exotic spices, and chocolate, its generous sweetness balanced nicely by good natural acidity. Drink now. Score 89.

VITKIN, JOHANNISBERG RIESLING, 2004: Perhaps the first Israeli white to show the oily, floral, kerosene-like aromas of fine Alsace or Rhine Rieslings. Gold in color, medium-bodied, with good balancing acidity, refreshingly dry and showing appealing citrus, melon and summer fruits. Drink now–2008. Score 88.

VITKIN, JOHANNISBERG RIESLING, 2003: Deep golden straw colored, medium-bodied and showing aromas and lightly spicy flavors of citrus, green gage plums and spring flowers. Drink now. Score 86.

VITKIN, GEWÜRZTRAMINER, 2003: Made entirely from Gewurztraminer grapes and developed *sur lie* in stainless steel, this medium-bodied dry white is generous with its traditional Gewurztraminer flavors and aromas of litchis, and spicy summer fruits. Drink now. Score 86.

VITKIN, BLANC, 2005: A medium-bodied, partly oak-aged blend of Viognier, French Colombard and Gewurztraminer (45%, 40% and 15% respectively. On the nose generous flowers and on the palate orange, orange blossoms and tropical fruits, those matched by hints of litchis, rose petals and tapioca. Drink now. Score 87.

VITKIN, BLANC, 2004: A blend of 45% each Viognier and French Colombard and 10% Gewurztraminer, each fermented separately before blending. Light golden straw in color, with good balance between fruits, acidity and a hint of freshly cut grass. Flowery on first attack but that receding to reveal generous citrus and peach aromas and flavors complemented by a hint of freshly cut grass and hay. Drink now. Score 85.

VITKIN, BLANC, 2003: Light to medium-bodied, this lively unoaked blend of 60% Viognier and 40% French Colombard offers pleasant notes of lime and orange peel. Clean and refreshing, a good quaffer. Drink up. Score 85.

VITKIN, RIESLING, LATE HARVEST, 2004: With about 20% of the grapes in this wine affected by botrytis, this lightly funky, bronzed-gold colored wine shows unabashed near-honeyed sweetness, and on the nose and palate dried apricots, tropical fruits and wild spring flowers. Drink now–2009. Score 86.

VITKIN, LATE HARVEST RIESLING, 2003: Medium-bodied, thick in texture and unabashedly sweet, this dessert wine offers aromas and flavors of dried peaches, orange peel and wild flowers. Good balancing acidity adds liveliness. Drink now. Score 85.

Yaffo ★★★

Founded in Jaffa in 1998 by Moshe and Anne Celniker and today located in the basement of their home in the Tel Aviv suburb of Ramat Hachayal, this small winery is currently producing about 10,000 bottles annually. Grapes, primarily Cabernet Sauvignon and Merlot, come from kibbutz Netiv Halamed Hey in the Jerusalem Hills and from the Golan Heights. The winery also produces a Port-style wine.

YAFFO, CABERNET SAUVIGNON, 2004: Dark ruby towards garnet, medium-bodied, with chewy tannins integrating nicely with black fruits, spices and an appealing herbal overlay. Drink now–2008. Score 86.

YAFFO, CABERNET SAUVIGNON, 2003: Deep garnet towards royal purple, this still firmly tannic, medium to full-bodied and generously oaked wine shows structure and balance that bode well for its future. Already showing aromas and flavors of spicy black fruits, freshly picked herbs and an appealing earthy undercurrent that lingers nicely on the palate. Drink now–2008. Score 86.

YAFFO, CABERNET SAUVIGNON, 2002: Dark in color, this medium to full-bodied oak-aged wine shows soft tannins along with blackcurrant, cherry and berry aromas and flavors. Light spices and herbs come together on a round, moderately long finish. Drink now. Score 87.

YAFFO, CABERNET SAUVIGNON, 2001: Deep garnet red, this medium-bodied wine was aged in French and American oak barrels and now shows generous currant and black cherry aromas and flavors, those coming together nicely with a light spiciness and Mediterranean herbs. Look for an appealing gentle earthiness and a green olive finish. Drink up. Score 87.

YAFFO, MERLOT, 2004: Reflecting twelve months in *barriques* with hints of spices and vanilla and with soft tannins integrating nicely. On the nose and palate blueberry, blackberry and plum fruits. Moderately long and with a hint of milk chocolate on the finish. Drink now–2008. Score 87.

YAFFO, MERLOT, 2003: Medium to full-bodied, with soft tannins integrating nicely and generous plum, cassis and spicy oak aromas and flavors. Drink now–2008. Score 86.

YAFFO, MERLOT, 2002: Medium-bodied, with generous soft tannins and berry, black cherry, and appealing vanilla-spicy hints that come in from mid-palate. Good touches of sweet wood and a light herbaceousness. Drink now. Score 86.

YAFFO, MERLOT, 2001: Medium-bodied, with moderate tannins, plenty of black fruits and hints of vanilla and toasty oak all coming together on a moderately long finish. Drink up. Score 86.

YAFFO, ROUGE, 2004: A blend of 45% each of Merlot and Cabernet Sauvignon and 10% of Shiraz, with light oak influences, silky tannins and generous black fruits and spices leading to a mouthfilling finish. Drink now–2008. Score 86.

YAFFO, ROUGE, 2003: Deep garnet in color, medium-bodied and with soft tannins, this blend of Cabernet Sauvignon and Merlot shows generous ripe plum, currant and berry aromas and flavors. Moderately long. Drink up. Score 86.

YAFFO, ROUGE, 2002: A blend of 45% each of Cabernet Sauvignon and Merlot and 10% of Shiraz, this soft and round red offers up appealing berry, cherry and currant fruits together with well-integrated tannins and good acidity. Not complex but a pleasant quaffer. Drink up. Score 86.

YAFFO, BLANC, CHARDONNAY, 2004: The color of damp straw, medium-bodied and showing appealing aromas and flavors of citrus and melon. Light mineral and flowery overlays. Drink now. Score 86.

Yatir ★★★★

Set in a state-of-the-art winery at the foot of the Judean Hills, and under the supervision of Australian-trained winemaker Eran Goldwasser, this boutique winery, a joint venture between Carmel and the vintners of the Yatir region, released its first wines from the 2001 vintage. Releases now include the age-worthy Ya'ar Yatir (Yatir Forest) and Yatir wines as well as the new, earlier-approachable Forester-Lodge. Drawing its name from the Yatir Forest, located in the Judean Hills, the winery is cultivating its own vineyards with Cabernet Sauvignon, Merlot, Shiraz, Sauvignon Blanc, Chardonnay and Shiraz grapes. Current production is about 100,000 bottles annually.

Ya'ar Yatir (Yatir Forest)

YATIR, YA'AR YATIR, 2004: Showing the potential for true elegance. Full-bodied and solid, with soft tannins, smoky wood and vanilla, all in fine balance with ripe blueberry, blackcurrant, and plum flavors. Look as well for an appealing earthy undercurrent leading to a long and generous finish. Best 2008–2014. Tentative Score 90–92. **K**

YATIR, YA'AR YATIR, 2003: A blend of 85% Cabernet Sauvignon and 15% Merlot reflecting its 12 month development in *barriques* with gently spicy and lightly dusty wood and showing fine balance between tannins, wood and acidity. Well focused and on the palate light herbal and white pepper traits underlying rich blueberry and blackcurrant fruits. Long, and destined for elegance. Best 2008–2012. Score 92. **K**

YA'AR YATIR, 2002: Made from 100% Cabernet Sauvignon grapes, this dark garnet toward purple, full-bodied wine is now showing still firm tannins and gentle and well-integrated smoky oak and sweet cedar aromas, those coming together very nicely with aromas and flavors of ripe currant and purple plum fruits as well as generous hints of chocolate and mint. Drink now–2010. Score 90. **K**

YA'AR YATIR, 2001: As youthful on the nose and palate as it is in its dark ruby toward purple color, this medium to full-bodied blend of 85% Cabernet Sauvignon and 15% Merlot is already showing good integration between soft tannins and oak, and rich, still quite forward aromas and flavors of currants, wild berries and cherries. The spicy oak and generous minerals are integrating nicely and yielding a luxurious and elegant wine. Drink now–2009. Score 91. **K**

Yatir

YATIR, CABERNET SAUVIGNON, 2005: Tasted from several different barrels, one in which the wine underwent extended skin contact and the other a shorter period of contact, the first with sweet, soft tannins, the second with gripping tannins, but both with fine balance and showing the potential for traditional Cabernet currant, berry and spicy aromas and flavors and, with a bit of luck as the wine continues to develop, cigar box aromas. Best 2008–2012. Tentative Score 90–92.

YATIR, CABERNET SAUVIGNON, 2002: Young and tight but well focused, with deep, firm tannins and ripe flavors of cherries, currants, anise and nice touches of earth and minerals. Distinctly Mediterranean, the wine is drinking nicely now but will cellar well. Drink now–2009. Score 91. **K**

YATIR, MERLOT, 2005: Medium to full-bodied, with generous near-sweet tannins, this seductive wine is already showing delicious blueberry, blackberry, mocha and vanilla flavors. Plush and round, on the way to becoming a delicious, complex and concentrated wine. Drink from release–2012. Tentative Score 90–92. **K**

YATIR, MERLOT, RAMAT ARAD, 2002: Full-bodied, tannic and muscular for a Merlot, but with balance between wood, fruits and acidity that gives the wine grace and elegance. Black plums, wild berries and currants here, together with freshly picked Mediterranean herbs and a hint of granite that comes in on the long finish. Drink now–2009. Score 91. **K**

YATIR, MERLOT, 2001: Deep garnet toward royal purple in color, full-bodied, and with generous tannins well balanced by plum, currant and blackberry fruits as well as generous hints of minerals and herbs. Drink now. Score 91. **K**

YATIR, SHIRAZ, 2005: A dark, almost impenetrable garnet towards royal purple in color and packed with firm tannins at this early stage, but with the balance and structure to indicate a fine future. Red currants, cherries and berries here, those matched nicely by pepper and oriental spices. Long and generous. Best 2008–2011. Tentative Score 89–91. **K**

YATIR, CABERNET SAUVIGNON-MERLOT, 2001: A blend of 60% Cabernet Sauvignon and 40% Merlot, this medium to full-bodied wine shows a dark royal purple color, soft, already well-integrated tannins and generous blackcurrant, plum, berry, and earthy-mineral aromas and flavors. Look as well for hints of spicy oak that develop from mid-palate. Drink now. Score 89. K

YATIR, CABERNET SAUVIGNON-MERLOT-SHIRAZ, 2004: Full-bodied, with depth and concentration but never losing sight of elegance. Deep royal purple in color, with near-sweet tannins and appealing smoky and light vegetable overlays highlighting aromas and flavors of ripe plums, blackberries, cherry, and licorice. On the long finish a tantalizing hint of spicy oak. Drink now–2012. Score 91. K

YATIR, CABERNET SAUVIGNON-MERLOT-SHIRAZ, 2003: A blend this year of 56% Cabernet Sauvignon, 33% Merlot and 11% Shiraz. Aged in oak for one year, this medium to full-bodied wine shows ripe berry, cherry and currant fruits, those with just a hint of toasted oak, all backed up with vanilla and spicy aromas and flavors. Long and caressing. Drink now–2011. Score 90. K

YATIR, CABERNET SAUVIGNON-MERLOT-SHIRAZ, 2002: A blend of 75% Cabernet Sauvignon and 15% Merlot with 10% of Shiraz, this inky purple towards black, medium to full-bodied wine spent one year in new and used oak casks. Showing good balance between smoky wood, generous but soft tannins, plum and currant fruits, black pepper and a very appealing overlay of near-sweet herbaceousness, all leading to a long, satisfying finish. Drink now–2008. Score 88. K

YATIR, ROSÉ, 2005: Made entirely from Syrah grapes that were allowed only one hour of skin contact and then treated to cold fermentation, this stylish wine has surprising depth and complexity for a rosé. With dried cherry, rose petal, spice and mineral flavors, this salmon-colored wine has just a hint of oak and a lightly spicy finish to tantalize. Drink now. Score 88. K

YATIR, SAUVIGNON BLANC, 2005: Aged in half new, half one-year-old *barriques* for three months, this light golden, medium-bodied white shows fresh, concentrated and vibrant aromas and flavors of passion fruit, green apples, hay, honeysuckle and citrus peel. Crisp, elegant and harmonious. Drink now–2008. Score 92. **K**

YATIR, SAUVIGNON BLANC, 2004: This bright straw-colored wine shows remarkable freshness together with well enunciated aromas of citrus, tropical fruits and light grassy-herbaceousness. Medium-bodied, with crisp acidity, a tantalizing hint of the oak in which it developed for several months, and a long and complex finish. Drink now. Score 90. **K**

YATIR, SAUVIGNON BLANC, 2003: Light gold in color, with orange and green tints, this well balanced white was aged *sur lie*. Full bodied, with traditional Sauvignon Blanc aromas and flavors of fresh-mown grass and herbs matched nicely by quince and pear fruits as well as hints of pepper, walnut and vanilla, all leading up to a long mouth-filling finish. Somewhat oaky but graceful and harmonious. Drink up. Score 89. **K**

Forester-Lodge

YATIR, FORESTER-LODGE, 2004: A medium-bodied blend of 75% Merlot and 25% Cabernet Sauvignon, aged for 8 months in *barriques*. A lovely, silky-smooth red with red berry, cherry and cassis aromas and flavors, just the right hint of toasty oak, soft tannins and a long-caressing finish. Drink now–2008. Score 89. **K**

Ye'arim ★★★

Located in the village of Givat Ye'arim near Jerusalem, this small winery is owned by Sasson Ben-Aharon who is also the winemaker for Binyamina Wineries. With vineyards in the Judean Mountains, the winery produced 1,000 bottles from the 2000 vintage, 2,000 from the 2003 vintage and 3000 from 2004 and 2005.

YE'ARIM, CABERNET SAUVIGNON, SASSON'S WINE, 2002: Garnet-red in color, medium to full-bodied, showing soft, well-integrated tannins and spicy cedar from its 18 months in oak. With generous aromas and flavors of currants, ripe berries, sweet herbs and vanilla. Drink now–2008. Score 87.

YE'ARIM, CABERNET SAUVIGNON, SASSON'S WINE, 2000: Dark-garnet colored, this medium-bodied unfiltered blend of 95% Cabernet Sauvignon and 5% Merlot was aged in French oak *barriques* for 14 months and shows soft tannins and some spicy oak. Fully mature now and taking on a light herbal overlay but still showing appealing berry, currant and black cherry flavors. Drink up. Score 85.

YE'ARIM, MERLOT, SASSON'S WINE, 2003: Made entirely from Merlot grapes, garnet towards purple in color, well-balanced and medium-bodied. With soft tannins, and reflecting 15 months in French oak with a gentle touch of spicy wood. Aromas and flavors of cherries, wild berries and tobacco as well as an appealing hint of minty-chocolate on the finish. Drink now–2008. Score 86.

YE'ARIM, MERLOT, SASSON'S WINE, 2001: Showing better than at earlier tastings, this medium-bodied blend of 92% Merlot and 8% Cabernet Sauvignon offers up subdued but appealing aromas and flavors of cassis, plums and blackberries. Drink now. Score 84.

YE'ARIM, MERLOT, SASSON'S WINE, 2000: Medium to full-bodied and deep ruby toward garnet in color, with soft tannins and generous but not overwhelming wood, this unfiltered blend of 92% Merlot and 8% Cabernet Sauvignon was aged for 14 months in oak. Smooth, rich and mouth-filling but not for further cellaring. Drink up. Score 86.

Yehuda ✶

Located on Moshav Shoresh in the Jerusalem Mountains, this winery was founded by Avi Yehuda in 1998. Cabernet Sauvignon, Merlot and Sauvignon Blanc grapes come from the winery's own nearby vineyards as well as from Moshav Shoresh. Current production is 2,000–3,000 bottles annually.

YEHUDA, CABERNET SAUVIGNON, 2003: A country-style, somewhat coarse, medium-bodied wine with chunky tannins and showing only skimpy black fruits. Drink now. Score 79.

YEHUDA, CABERNET SAUVIGNON, 2002: Dark ruby towards garnet in color, medium-bodied, with firm tannins that fail to integrate with the wood, both of those holding back whatever fruits may be here. A country-style wine showing too earthy barnyard sensations. Drink now. Score 77.

YEHUDA, CABERNET SAUVIGNON, 2001: Deep cherry red in color and medium-bodied, with chunky tannins and generous blackberry and cassis aromas and flavors overlaid by sweet herbs, this is a simple and distinctly country-style wine. Drink up. Score 79.

YEHUDA, MERLOT, 2003: Garnet red, softly tannic and with its berry and plum fruits marred by a lightly muddy sensation. Drink up. Score 72.

YEHUDA, MERLOT, 2002: Light garnet with a bit of browning showing early aging. Soft tannins and stingy with its plum and wild berry fruits. Drink up. Score 77.

YEHUDA, MERLOT, 2001: With soft tannins and offering up a modest range of plum and cherry flavors, this soft, simple, vaguely oaky wine finishes with rather coarse tannins. Drink up. Score 78.

YEHUDA, MERLOT-CABERNET SAUVIGNON, 2001: A successful medium-bodied and moderately tannic blend of 40% Merlot and 60% Cabernet Sauvignon. The wine was aged in oak for several months and shows hints of vanilla and anise, with a pleasing core of cherries and wild berries. Drink up. Score 86.

Yiftah'el ✶

Founded in 1999 in the community of Alon Hagalil in the Upper Galilee, owner-vintners Tzvika Ofir and Avner Sofer rely on Cabernet Sauvignon, Merlot, Petite Sirah and Sangiovese grapes from their own vineyards. Current production is about 10,000 bottles.

YIFTAH'EL, CABERNET SAUVIGNON, 2004: Oak-aged for about 12 months, showing firm tannins and generous spicy wood along with currant and berry fruits. Somewhat coarse on the palate. Drink now. Score 78.

YIFTAH'EL, MERLOT, 2003: Reflecting its 12 months in oak with generous tannins and vanilla, the wine shows as well some berry-black cherry fruits. One dimensional and short. Drink up. Score 82.

YIFTAH'EL, SANGIOVESE, 2004: A rustic wine, deep garnet in color, medium to full-bodied, with almost coarse tannins, too generous acidity and a slightly dusty fruit character, with too marked hints of earthy, tar and herbal aromas and flavors that tend to dominate. Drink up. Score 75.

YIFTAH'EL, SANGIOVESE, 2003: Light cherry red in color, with only scarce tannins and berry, strawberry and banana aromas and flavors. Drink up. Score 80.

YIFTAH'EL, PETITE SIRAH, 2004: Dark cherry red towards garnet, with chunky, country-style tannins and with primary aromas and flavors of very ripe plums. Starts off near-sweet and turns somewhat bitter on the finish. Drink up. Score 80.

YIFTAH'EL, CABERNET-MERLOT, 2002: A medium-bodied, lightly tannic oak-aged blend of 60% Cabernet Sauvignon and 40% Merlot. Not complex but pleasant. Drink up. Score 83.

Yuval Ben-Shoshan ✶

Established by agronomist Yuval Ben-Shoshan on Kibbutz Bror Hail in the Negev Desert, this winery released its first wine from the vintage of 1998. Grapes, including Cabernet Sauvignon and Merlot, are currently drawn from the area of Kerem Ben Zimra in the Galilee. The winery's production is currently about 4,000 bottles annually.

YUVAL BEN-SHOSHAN, CABERNET SAUVIGNON, AVDAT, 2003: Not living up to its earlier promise and now fading and showing medium-body, soft tannins and only a few currant and plum fruits, those being hidden by barnyard aromas that are hard to get by. Drink up. Score 76.

YUVAL BEN-SHOSHAN, CABERNET SAUVIGNON, AVDAT, 2002: Deep garnet red, medium to full-bodied, with generous tannins well balanced by hints of spicy oak, and blackcurrant and anise aromas and flavors. Drink now. Score 87.

YUVAL BEN-SHOSHAN, MERLOT, AVDAT, 2004: Light, diluted ruby in color, lacking body, with only the vaguest hint of tannins and stingy, almost watery berry and black cherry fruits. Drink now. Score 78.

YUVAL BEN-SHOSHAN, MERLOT, AVDAT, 2003: Medium-bodied, with firm but well-integrating tannins and appealing plum, black cherry and smoky wood aromas and flavors. Well balanced and appealing. Drink now. Score 86.

YUVAL BEN-SHOSHAN, CABERNET SAUVIGNON-MERLOT, 2001: Harmonious and smooth, with soft ripe tannins and an attractive core of currant, cherry and wild berry flavors and aromas. Well focused and with flavors that linger nicely. Drink now. Score 88.

YUVAL BEN-SHOSHAN, CABERNET SAUVIGNON-MERLOT, 2000: Medium to full-bodied, this garnet red, unfiltered blend of 70% Cabernet Sauvignon and 30% Merlot shows good black fruits, hints of spices and a light vanilla overlay. Somewhat one-dimensional. Drink up. Score 85.

Zauberman ★★★★

Founded in 1999 by Itzik Zauberman and located in the town of Gedera in the Southern Plains, this small winery draws on organically raised grapes from its own vineyards nearby as well as using grapes from Karmei Yosef. Current production is about 3,000 bottles annually.

ZAUBERMAN, CABERNET SAUVIGNON, LIMITED EDITION, 2002: Deep garnet red, full-bodied, with intense tannins and powerful wood, those needing time to settle down and integrate with plum, currant and spicy and earthy aromas and flavors. Drink now–2009. Score 90.

ZAUBERMAN, CABERNET SAUVIGNON, LIMITED EDITION, 2001: Dark royal purple toward black in color, full-bodied, concentrated and tannic, with aromas and flavors that include dried plums and cherries, red berries, chocolate, honey and spices, This powerful, near-massive and complex wine, made by drying the grapes before pressing them much in the way that Italian Amarone is made, is approachable now if given at least 30 minutes in the glass to open. Drink now–2012. Score 93.

ZAUBERMAN, CABERNET SAUVIGNON, 2000: Well balanced, dark and rich, this concentrated wine shows good currant, plum, vanilla and herbal aromas and flavors well balanced by tannins and wood. Rich bittersweet overtones call to mind wines made in Italy by the *ripasso* method. Long and mouth-filling. Drink now–2009. Score 90.

ZAUBERMAN, MERLOT, 2004: Dark, almost impenetrable garnet, full-bodied, with soft tannins, spicy oak, and plum, currant and berry fruits. Long and generous. Drink from release–2009. Tentative Score 89–91.

ZAUBERMAN, MERLOT, 2003: Dark ruby towards garnet, medium to full-bodied and with good balance between smoky oak, caressing tannins and black fruits. Drink now–2009. Score 89.

ZAUBERMAN, MERLOT, 2002: Deep garnet toward royal purple in color, this medium to full-bodied unfiltered wine shows good balance between smoky oak, soft tannins and fruits. The wine has aromas and flavors of berries, currants and anise along with a generous earthiness on a moderately long finish. Drink now. Score 91.

ZAUBERMAN, MERLOT, 2001: The best Merlot ever from this winery, and one of the best ever made in Israel. Remarkably rich and full-bodied, this deep garnet toward purple wine shows delicious plum, cherry and currant fruits along with anise, vanilla and spicy oak and a complex and long finish. Still young and tight, but already well focused and harmonious. Drink now–2008. Score 93.

ZAUBERMAN, MERLOT, 2000: Medium to full-bodied, and firmer in texture than most local Merlot wines, the wine shows good balance between wood, acidity and fruits and abundant blackberry, cherry, anise and vanilla flavors. Supple, spicy and generous, with a long finish. Drink now. Score 89.

ZAUBERMAN, MERLOT, 1999: This blend of 94% Merlot and 6% Cabernet Sauvignon was aged in new French oak barrels for 8 months and has smooth tannins and attractive cherry, herbal and wood flavors, as well as intrinsically good balance. Drink up. Score 86.

Zemora ★★★

Set in a facility in Moshav Beit Zayit in the Jerusalem Mountains, winemaker Baruch Yosef released his first wines from the 2000 vintage. Grapes are drawn largely from the Jerusalem Mountain area and include Cabernet Sauvignon, Merlot, Cabernet Franc, Shiraz, Petit Verdot, Sangiovese, Viognier and Chardonnay, some of which are being raised organically. Production for 2003 was 7,000 bottles and 35,000–40,000 bottles are being released from the 2005 vintage. Starting with the 2004 vintage, the wines have been kosher.

ZEMORA, CABERNET SAUVIGNON, 2005: Still in embryonic form but already showing medium to full-body, soft tannins, hints of vanilla and spices from the wood in which it is aging, and appealing blueberry and currant fruits. Soft, round and finely balanced. Drink from release–2010. Tentative Score 87–89. **K**

ZEMORA, CABERNET SAUVIGNON, 2004: Blended with just 3% of Merlot, this generously oak-aged, medium-bodied and softly tannic wine shows distinct red fruits (raspberries, red currants and red plums), those with just enough spiciness to add complexity. Drink from release. Tentative Score 85–87. **K**

NOTE: The winery's 2003 Cabernet Sauvignon was released in two versions, the one referred to below as Version 1 having been made from grapes from the center of the country, and the other, Version 2, from grapes from the Northern Galilee. As will be seen in the tasting notes, the wines are considerably different. Unfortunately, there is a single label for the two versions.

ZEMORA, CABERNET SAUVIGNON, VERSION 1, 2003: Blended with 15% of Merlot, this oak-aged wine shows overall good balance, medium-body and soft tannins. Look for plum, blackcurrant, orange peel and light herbal aromas and flavors. Drink now–2008. Score 85.

ZEMORA, CABERNET SAUVIGNON, VERSION 2, 2003: Dark garnet towards royal purple in color, medium to full-bodied, with firm tannins that yield slowly but comfortably to reveal blackcurrant and black cherry fruits, those supported nicely by spicy oak and an appealing herbal-earthy finish. Drink now–2009. Score 87.

ZEMORA, CABERNET SAUVIGNON, 2002: Garnet toward deep purple in color, this medium to full-bodied, softly tannic wine shows appealing currants, wild berries and spices, along with a generous hint of sweet cedar on the finish. Has a somewhat heavy hand with the oak. Drink now. Score 86.

ZEMORA, CABERNET SAUVIGNON, 2001: Royal purple in color, this ripe and smooth wine has a supple texture, a generous core of currant, cherry and berry flavors, and soft tannins that make themselves felt primarily on the finish. Drink up. Score 86.

ZEMORA, MERLOT, 2004: Dark garnet red, medium to full-bodied, with generous soft tannins and smoky wood opening nicely to reveal blackberry, black cherry and cassis fruits, those on a nicely spicy background. Drink now–2008. **K**

ZEMORA, MERLOT, 2003: Dark ruby towards garnet, medium-bodied, with soft tannins, generous wood and forward berry and cherry fruits. Somewhat one dimensional. Drink now. Score 84.

ZEMORA, MERLOT, 2002: Medium-bodied, with gentle tannins and appealing berry, black cherry, anise and black pepper aromas and flavors, together with very generous wood that will not be to everyone's taste. Drink now. Score 86.

ZEMORA, MERLOT, 2001: Dark cherry red toward garnet, with firm but well-integrated tannins and tempting blueberry, blackberry and currant aromas and flavors, this medium to full-bodied wine shows good balance between fruits, tannins and a gentle wood. Drink up. Score 85.

ZEMORA, SHIRAZ, 2005: An organic wine, oak-aged and relying on wild yeasts. Dark royal purple, medium to full-bodied, with intense currant, stewed plum and black cherry aromas and flavors, and an appealing light beefy overlay. Somewhat on the acidic side. Drink from release. Tentative Score 85–87. **K**

ZEMORA, CABERNET FRANC, 2005: Dark in color, full-bodied, with chewy tannins and smoky oak opening to reveal plum and black cherry notes, those supported by leather and cedar and leading to vanilla and spices on a moderately long finish. Best 2008–2011. Tentative Score 86–88. **K**

ZEMORA, CABERNET FRANC, 2003: Made from grapes from the Meron vineyards, this medium-bodied red shows chunky, country-style tannins, a generous hand with the oak reflecting a good deal of smoke and vanilla, those overshadowing somewhat the plum and berry flavors. Drink now. Score 85.

ZEMORA, CABERNET FRANC, 2002: Medium to full-bodied and dark garnet in color, with a distinct country-style coarseness that is set off by berry, cherry and plum fruits. Ripe and mouthfilling. Drink now. Score 85.

ZEMORA, PETIT VERDOT, 2005: Dark purple in color, opening with a floral nose and showing spicy oak and soft tannins in fine balance with a core of plum, blueberry and currant fruits. Makes up for its lack of complexity with a long and harmonious finish. Drink from release–2009. Tentative Score 87–89. K

ZEMORA, SANGIOVESE, 2004: Ruby red, medium-bodied, with perhaps too generous acidity. A few cherry-berry fruits are not enough to save the wine. Drink now. Score 79. K

ZEMORA, SANGIOVESE, 2003: Blended with 15% of Cabernet Sauvignon but still lacking backbone and showing rather flabby tannins. Light to medium-bodied, perhaps even a bit diluted on the palate, with skimpy berry-black cherry fruits. One dimensional and short. Drink now. Score 83.

ZEMORA, CASTRA, 2003: An almost impenetrably dark garnet in color, medium to full-bodied, with still firm tannins integrating nicely. A well-balanced blend of 75% Cabernet Sauvignon, 20% Cabernet Franc and 5% Merlot, showing up-front cherry and blackberry aromas and flavors, those complemented by spicy, smoky cedar. Drink now–2010. Score 90.

ZEMORA, CABERNET SAUVIGNON-CABERNET FRANC, 2003: A generously oak-aged blend of 60% Cabernet Sauvignon and 40% Cabernet Franc, showing chunky tannins and heavy spices but those balanced nicely by appealing currant, berry and black cherry fruits. Not complex or long but a good quaffer. Drink now. Score 85.

ZEMORA, RED, 2004: A blend of Cabernet Sauvignon, Merlot and Shiraz (70%, 24% and 6% respectively), the grapes blended before oak aging. Medium to full-bodied, with firm tannins, generous spicy-smoky oak and appealing plum, berry and cassis fruits. Round and mouthfilling but somewhat short. Drink now. Score 84. K

ZEMORA, RED, 2001: A blend of 70% Cabernet Sauvignon and 30% Merlot that reflects its 24 months in *barriques* with a rather heavy hand of smoky oak. Low in tannins, round and with uncomplicated black fruits. Drink up. Score 84.

ZEMORA, CHARDONNAY, 2005: Lightly oak-aged and with a deep golden color, this medium-bodied white offers up peach, melon and citrus aromas and flavors. Not complex but appealing. Drink now–2008. Score 87. K

ZEMORA, CHARDONNAY, 2004: Dark golden-straw in color, medium to full-bodied, with pineapple, guava and citrus fruits on a generously oaked but creamy background. Drink up. Score 86. K

ZEMORA, VIOGNIER, 2005: Golden-straw in color, medium-bodied, with fresh citrus, guava and pear fruits matched nicely by a silky texture. On the finish hints of honey and figs. Drink from release. Score 87. K

Afterword

Dessert Wines

Since the time of the ancient Romans, sweet white wines have been among the most coveted wines in the world. That desirability has never abated, and today wine lovers can enjoy superior sweet wines made in Sauterne, Barsac, and the Loire Valley in France, the magnificent ice wines of German and Austria, and the superb Tokaji wines in Hungary. Even though Israeli sweet wine cannot compete with those, several local wineries are producing sweet whites of notably high quality.

The secret of sweet wines, which are often known as dessert wines, lies in their balance, for in addition to flavors reminiscent of apricots, citrus and citrus peel, grapes and honey, these wines, perhaps more than any others, must have fine balancing acidity to keep them from appearing cloying. At their very best such wines are big and luscious, have an intensely rich texture, a flowery bouquet and unmatched elegance, and their delicate sweetness is the result of great expense.

To many, the greatest sweet wines are those made from grapes affected by *botrytis cinerea*. Known as noble rot, botrytis is a fungus that attacks grapes, shrivels them, drains them of water and concentrates their sugar. Because the Israeli climate is not often conducive of botrytis, only one fully botrytized wine was ever made in the country—the 1998 Late Harvest Sauvignon Blanc of the Golan Heights Winery. Since that harvest, not enough grapes have been affected by botrytis to replicate that superb wine, but that has not prevented vintners from isolating small sections of their wineries and there exposing late-harvested grapes to *botrytis* spores to encourage the development of sweetness. The result in the Golan Heights Winery's Noble Semillon, has been commendable. At Carmel, winemakers found a small area within one vineyard with grapes impacted by botrytis and then blended those grapes with others to produce a special Single Vineyard wine, the Late Harvest Gewurztraminer of Kerem Shual.

The sweet wines known as *Eiswein* in German and Ice Wine in English were originally made in Germany in the 18th century, but now are produced in Canada and New Zealand as well. The process of making those wines involves allowing the grapes to freeze on the vine in temperatures of 7 degrees Celsius (20 degrees Fahrenheit) or below, and then pressing them while they are still frozen. This process leaves the must concentrated and very sweet. In warmer areas, this can be carried on by cryo-extraction, a technique in which the grapes are frozen in the winery. In Israel, the Golan Heights Winery was the first to produce such a wine, Heightswine. That wine was made from Gewurztraminer grapes in their Yarden series in 1998, and has appeared successfully every year since. Several other local wineries have also been using cryo-extraction, but those have met only with moderate success.

In addition to relying on Semillon, Sauvignon Blanc and Gewurztraminer grapes, other local dessert wines have relied on late-harvested Muscat and Johannisberg Riesling grapes, and many of those from Carmel, the Golan Heights Winery, Vitkin, Dalton and Tishbi have met with high levels of success, the wines often honeyed, floral and fruity. Another commendable example of a wine that might well be thought of as a dessert wine is the lightly *frizzante* Moscato of the Golan Heights Winery.

Even though most people drink sweet wines primarily with or as desserts, these wines can serve as excellent aperitifs, as accompaniments to first courses such as goose liver, and to Thai and other spicy dishes, especially those that contain coconut milk. Such wines are also excellent accompaniments to Parmesan, sweet Gorgonzola, well-aged Cheddar and hard or soft goats' milk cheeses. Since the wine should always be sweeter than the dessert with which it is served, it is difficult to match sweet wines with chocolate, but they will be ideal matches to cheesecakes, ripe fruits and fruit-based desserts. Whenever served, these wines are at their best when served chilled to 4–6 degrees Celsius (40–43 degrees Fahrenheit).

Because such wines can be intensely sweet, one rarely drinks them in large quantities and service is often in smaller than usual glasses. Recognizing this, many of the finest dessert wines are bottled in 375 ml. bottles, this allowing a small bottle to comfortably serve six to eight people.

A Guide to Tasting Wines

Wine tasting is not a complex or difficult task. All that is required is the use of one's senses of sight, smell and taste. Before setting out to taste wines, try to eliminate as many distractions as possible. During the actual tasting, for example, extraneous aromas (e.g. food, perfume and aftershave lotion) should be avoided as they interfere with the ability to appreciate the aromas and bouquet of the wine. Also, during a tasting, try as hard as possible to ignore the comments by others in order not to be influenced by their opinions. Be sure to use high quality glasses (ideally of thin crystal) as this enhances the flavors and aromas of wines. A separate glass should be provided for each wine, this allowing the taster to return to earlier tasted wines in order to make comparisons. The glasses should be, of course, perfectly clean, without any aroma of soap or detergent. Glasses should be filled to no more than 20% of their capacity as this will give ample room for swirling the wine, that process serving to aerate and release the more subtle aromas and flavors of the wine being tasted.

Basic Rules for tasting wines

- Professionals can sample fifty or more wines at a single sitting, but it is widely agreed that in a private tasting, alone at home or at a friendly gathering, the number of wines for tasting should not exceed eight.
- White wines should be tasted before reds, and within

each group wines that are light in body should be tasted before fuller-bodied wines. When tasting wines of the same variety, such as Cabernet Sauvignon or Merlot, always start with the youngest wines and end with the most mature.

- Wines should be served at their proper temperatures. Young reds should be opened about fifteen or twenty minutes before the tasting, and more mature reds about half an hour before they are poured.
- You can either place the bottles on the table with the labels exposed or place each bottle in a paper bag, each bag identified only by a number, for a blind tasting. I prefer blind tastings, for the power of suggestion is strong and it is difficult to be entirely objective vis à vis a label of a prestigious Chateau.
- Wines should be arranged on the table in the order they are to be tasted. I suggest using a felt-tipped pen to put a number on each bottle and then to mark the corresponding number on the base of each glass in order to avoid any confusion.
- Professional wine tasters spit the wine in order to avoid intoxication, but there is no need to spit at a home tasting where much of the pleasure comes from drinking the wine. For those that choose to spit, prepare adequate receptacles (clay jugs, low vases and Champagne buckets are ideal).
- Allow half a bottle per person. That is to say, for eight people you will need four bottles. When pouring during the tasting, remember that the average sampling should be small enough to allow room for swirling the wine in the glass. Whatever wines are left over after the actual tasting can be served with the meal or snacks afterward.
- Use a tasting form such as that illustrated in the following section or record your impressions on a piece of paper. Making notes helps people make up their minds before they commit themselves.
- Food should be served after a wine tasting and never

before or during because food changes the taste of wine. If you must have something on the table, use unsalted and sugar-free white bread.

Wine Appreciation

1. VISUAL APPEARANCE

In order to best see the color and clarity of a wine, hold your glass against a white background (a white tablecloth or even a blank sheet of white paper will do) and tilt the glass away from yourself slightly so that the exposed surface is larger. Red wines can be anywhere from bright cherry red in color to dark and opaque, in fact almost black. Although most white wines will have a light golden-straw color, they can range from almost colorless to deep golden, and rosé or blush wines are only rarely true pink and can vary from purple-pink to orange or even bright ruby red. Whatever the color, the wine should be perfectly clear. Wines that have thrown a sediment will become clear as the sediment settles.

Consider whether the color is deep or pale and whether it is vivid and youthful or browning and perhaps showing age. While the glass is tilted look as well at the rim (that point where the wine meets the glass), for it is not generally a positive sign if the color at the rim fades to an almost watery consistency. After noting the qualities of the color, swirl the wine in the glass gently and then hold it up to see the legs or tears—these are the threads of wine that appear and linger on the inside of the glass. These are an accurate indicator of the alcohol level in the wine; the broader and more viscous the legs, the greater the alcohol content and, according to many, a good indicator of the wine's ability to age. At the same time, note whether the wine is *frizzante*, that is to say, whether it has tiny little bubbles in it. Although this is acceptable in some white wines (e.g. Muscadet de Sevres et Maine *sur lie*, Vinho Verde, Moscato d'Asti), and occurs in many white wines when they have been overly chilled, such bubbles indicate a fault in nearly all red wines. When evaluating Champagnes or other sparkling wines, the bubbles should be sharp, small and long lasting, rising from a central point in the glass.

A hint: Never taste wines under fluorescent light as this makes all red wines appear brown.

2. SMELL

It surprises many to realize that people with a normal sense of smell can identify more than 1,000 different aromas. That should not be daunting, however, as the process of identifying aromas is a largely automatic one and although we may sometimes "struggle" to distinguish between the aroma of a blackberry or raspberry, our associations with aromas are quite strong. In order to best evaluate and appreciate the aromas of a wine, swirl the glass rapidly for a few seconds, place your nose well into the glass and inhale deeply through your nostrils.

One of the first sensations to be evaluated is the alcohol content of the wine. If the wine appears to be highly alcoholic, ask yourself whether it is a fortified wine (e.g. Sherry, Port, Madeira) or whether the strong alcoholic aromas reflect a fault. After that, consider whether the wine smells as youthful or as mature as it appears to the eye, whether the aromas are smooth and harmonious, whether they are distinctive, bland or reticent and whether they are simple or complex. Consider as well whether there is a creamy, spicy or vanilla note to the aromas as this may give a hint about whether the wine was aged in oak. Also consider whether the wine has any "off" aromas that may indicate a fault. With a bit of practice it becomes possible for many to identify from aroma alone the variety of the grape used and even the region in which the wine was made.

A hint: a slight musky aroma can add great charm but when exaggerated almost always reveals a fault in the wine.

3. TASTE

When actually setting out to taste the wine, take a good mouthful, close the lips firmly and swirl the wine vigorously in order to coat the entire mouth. This is important because

AFTERWORD

ROGOV'S GUIDE TO ISRAELI WINES RATING CHART

Name of Wine: Date of Tasting:
Vintage Year: Date Obtained:
Country of Origin: Price:
Wine Region:

	COMMENTS

VISUAL APPEARANCE: (0–5 POINTS)
 	
 Clarity: (*cloudy, dull, clear, brilliant*)
 Depth and Intensity of Color (*watery, pale, medium, deep, dark*)
 Color: White Wines—green tinge, pale yellow, yellow, gold, brown
     Red Wines—purple, garnet, red, brown
 Viscosity: Light sparkle, watery, normal, heavy, oily
 	
 Champagnes Only:
     Length of mousse
     Finesse and Sharpness of bubbles
     Duration of bubbles
	Points: ____

AROMAS AND BOUQUET: (0–15 POINTS) Attractiveness (*neutral, clean, attractive, outstanding, off*) Aroma and Bouquet (*fruits and others*) (*none, light, positive, identifiable*) Intensity (*pleasant, complex, powerful, overpowering*)	Points: ____
FLAVORS AND PALATE IMPRESSIONS (0–15 POINTS) Sweetness (*bone dry, dry, medium-dry, medium-sweet, very sweet*) Acidity (*flat, refreshing, marked, tart*) Body (*very light and thin, light, medium, full-bodied, heavy*) Tannin—(*Red wines only*) (*astringent, hard, dry, soft*) Tactile impression (*slight sparkle, watery, normal, heavy, oily*) Flavor (*stingy, medium, generous, exaggerated*) Taste Sensations (*fruits, oak, vanilla, spices, herbs, etc*) Alcohol (*low, medium, ideal, high*) Finish (*Length*) (*short, medium, long, very long*) Balance (*unbalanced, well balanced, very well balanced*)	Points: ____
OVERALL IMPRESSION (0–15 POINTS) Coarse, poor, acceptable, fine, outstanding	Points: ____
To arrive at a final score, add up the points in each of the boxes and add 50.	Score: ____

different taste sensations are perceived by different parts of the mouth (sweetness on the tip of the tongue, sourness on the sides, bitterness on the back and the roof of the mouth, saltiness on the fronts and side of the tongue). Some tasters also draw a bit of air into the mouth believing this will accentuate the flavors.

The first thing to be noted is whether the flavors are in accord with the aromas of the wines. Then, with the wine lingering in the mouth, identify the various taste sensations imparted. Ask yourself: are the flavors pronounced and easily identifiable or somewhat confused; is the wine clean or muddy; are the tannins, acidity, wood and fruits in balance; are the tannins and wood in good proportion to the fruits; is the level of sweetness appropriate for the wine?

Keep in mind that the major goal of tasting is not only to evaluate a wine but to determine whether it is to your taste. Wine tasting is not a guessing game but with increased practice and repeated tastings, many come to the point where they can identify and discuss the grape variety, area of origin and age and quality of the wines they are tasting.

A hint: A wine dominated by a single flavor is one-dimensional and thus lacking excitement.

Among the fruit aromas and flavors to be sought in white wines: citrus (especially lemon, grapefruit, lime and citrus peel), apple, melon, pear, peach, apricot, grapes, figs and, especially in sweet dessert wines, dried fruits. Also in white wines look for hints of grassiness, herbaceousness, honey, and a creamy sensation. Fruits to be found in red wines include, among others, black and red currants (sometimes referred to as cassis), plums and a variety of berries. Other taste sensations that may be imparted by red wines are chocolate, coffee and tobacco. In both reds and whites look for aromas and flavors imparted by oak aging, those including spicy or smoky oak, sweet cedar, asphalt and vanilla. Be aware that some of the aromas and flavors traditionally found in a red may appear in a white and vice versa.

TASTING FORMS

Because few of us have perfect memories, one of the very best aids in tasting wines is to use an organized sheet for keeping notes. Such sheets, used by professional wine tasters as well as amateurs, help to organize our thoughts and to leave a permanent record for future reference with which to compare the same wine or similar wines. The act of writing our reactions down also serves to implant our thoughts in long-term memory.

The tasting form that is illustrated on the opposite page (and is in larger format on the inside of the dust jacket of this book) is meant for those purposes. Readers may feel free to reproduce this form for their own use or for the use of friends, and should the original be lost, a downloadable and printable copy can be found at:

www.tobypress.com/rogov/tasting.pdf

Several Words about Scores

A great many people walk into wine stores and order this or that wine entirely on the basis of its high score. This is a mistake. A score is nothing more than a critic's attempt to sum up in digits the overall quality of a wine. Scores can provide a valid tool, especially when awarded by experienced critics, but they should not be separated from the tasting notes that precede them; for although a score may be a convenient summary, it says nothing about the style, personality or other important traits of the wine in question and therefore cannot give the consumer a valid basis for choice.

There are, however, three major advantages to scores. First of all, scores can serve as initial guides for the overall impression of the wine in question. Second, scores also give an immediate basis for comparison of that wine to others in its category and to the same wine of the same winery from earlier years. Finally, such scores give valuable hints as to whether the wine in question is available at a reasonable value for one's money.

The scores awarded in this book should be taken as merely one part of the overall evaluation of the wine, the most important parts of which are the tasting notes that give details about the body, color, aromas, flavors, length and overall style of the wine. It is also important to keep in mind that scores are not absolute. The score earned by a light and hyper-fruity wine made from Gamay grapes, a wine meant to be consumed in its youth, cannot be compared to that given to a deep, full-bodied wine made from a blend of Cabernet Sauvignon, Merlot and Cabernet Franc, the peak of drinking for which may come only five, ten or even thirty years later on. Numerical comparisons between the wines of the great Chateaux of Bordeaux and those meant to be consumed within weeks or months of the harvest is akin to comparing, by means of a single number, the qualities of a 1998 Rolls Royce and a 1965 Volkswagen Beetle.

Even if there was a perfect system for rating wines (and I do not believe such a system exists), no two critics, no matter how professional or well intentioned they may be, can be expected to use precisely the same criteria for every facet of every wine they evaluate. Even when similar scoring systems are used by different critics, readers should expect to find a certain variation between them. The trick is not in finding the critics with whom you always agree, but those whose tasting notes and scores give you direction in finding the wines that you most enjoy.

My own scoring system is based on a maximum of 100 points interpreted as follows:

95–100	Truly great wines
90–94	Exceptional in every way
86–89	Very good to excellent and highly recommended
81–85	Recommended but without enthusiasm
70–79	Average but at least somewhat faulted
Under 70	Not recommended

Glossary of Wine Terminology

ACIDIC: A wine whose level of acidity is so high that it imparts a sharp feel or sour taste in the mouth.

ACIDITY: An important component of wine. A modicum of acidity adds liveliness to wine, too little makes it flat and dull, and too much imparts a sour taste. The acids most often present in wines are tartaric, malic and lactic acids.

AFTERTASTE: The flavors and aromas left in the mouth after the wine has been swallowed.

AGGRESSIVE: Refers to the strong, assertive character of a young and powerful wine. Aggressive wines often lack charm and grace.

ALCOHOL CONTENT: Percent by volume of alcohol in a wine. Table wines have usually between 11.5–13.5% in alcohol content but there is an increasing demand for wines as high as 15–16%.

ALCOHOLIC: A negative term, referring to wines that have too much alcohol and are thus hot and out of balance.

AROMA: Technically this term applies to the smells that come directly from the grapes, whereas bouquet applies to the smells that come from the winemaking process. In practice the two terms are used interchangeably.

ASTRINGENT: A puckering sensation imparted to the wine by its tannins. At a moderate level, astringency is a positive trait. When a wine is too astringent it is unpleasant.

ATTACK: The first sensations imparted by a wine.

ATYPICAL: A wine that does not conform to its traditional character or style.

AUSTERE: A wine that lacks fruits or is overly tannic or acidic.

BALANCED: The term used to describe a wine in which the

acids, alcohol, fruits, tannins and influence of the wood in which the wine was aged are in harmony.

BARNYARD: Aromas and flavors that call to mind the barnyard, and when present in excess impart dirty sensations, but when in moderation can be pleasant.

BARREL: The wood containers used to ferment and hold wine. The wood used in such barrels is most often French or American oak but other woods can be used as well.

BARREL AGING: The process in which wines mature in barrels after fermentation.

BARRIQUE: French for "barrel" but specifically referring to oak barrels of 225 liter capacity in which many wines are fermented and/or aged.

BIG: A term used to describe a wine that is powerful in flavor, body or alcohol.

BLANC DE BLANCS: White wines made entirely from white grapes.

BLANC DE NOIRS: White wines made from grapes usually associated with red wines.

BLEND: A wine made from more than one grape variety or from grapes from different vintages. Some of the best wines in the world, including most of the Bordeaux wines, are blends of different grapes selected to complement each other.

BLUSH WINE: A wine that has a pale pink color imparted by very short contact with the skins of red grapes.

BODY: The impression of weight or fullness on the palate. Results from a combination of fruits and alcohol. Wines range from light to full-bodied.

BOTTLE AGING: The process of allowing wine to mature in its bottle.

BOTRYTIS CINEREA: Sometimes known as "noble rot", this is one of the few fungi that is welcomed by winemakers, for as it attacks the grapes it shrivels them, drains the water and concentrates the sugar, thus allowing for the making of many of the world's greatest sweet wines.

BOUQUET: Technically, the aromas that result from the winemaking process, but the term is used interchangeably with aroma.

GLOSSARY OF WINE TERMINOLOGY

BRUT: Bone dry. A term used almost exclusively to describe sparkling wines.

BUTTERY: A positive term for rich white wines, especially those that have undergone malolactic fermentation.

CARBONIC MACERATION: Method of fermenting red wine without crushing the grapes first. Whole clusters of grapes are put in a closed vat together with carbon dioxide, and the fermentation takes place within the grape berries, which then burst.

CARAMELIZED: A wine that has taken on a brown color, and sweet and sour aromas and flavors, often due to exposure to oxygen as the wine ages.

CHARACTER: Balance, assertiveness, finesse and other positive qualities combine to create character. The term is used only in the positive sense.

CHEWY: Descriptive of the texture, body and intensity of a good red wine. A chewy wine will be mouth-filling and complex.

CLONE: A vine derived by vegetative propagation from cuttings, or buds from a single vine called the mother vine.

CLOYING: A wine that has sticky, heavy or unclean aromas or flavors.

COARSE: A wine that is rough or overly alcoholic. Appropriate in some country-style wines but not in fine wines.

CORKED: A wine that has been tainted by TCA (2,4,6-Tricholoraniole), increasingly caused by faulty corks. TCA imparts aromas of damp, moldy and decomposing cardboard to a wine. Sometimes only barely detectable, at other times making a wine unapproachable.

COUNTRY-STYLE: A simple wine that is somewhat coarse but not necessarily unpleasant.

CREAMY: A soft, silky texture.

CRISP: A clean wine with good acidity.

DENSE: Full in flavor and body.

DEPTH: Refers to complexity and intensity of flavor.

DESSERT WINE: A sweet wine. Often served as an accompaniment to goose-liver dishes at the start of a meal.

DIRTY: A wine typified by off aromas or flavors resulting from either poor vinification practices or a faulty bottling process.

DRINKING WINDOW: The predicted period during which a wine will be at its best.

DRY: The absence of sugar or sweetness.

EARTHY: Sensations of freshly turned soil, minerals, damp leaves and mushrooms.

ELEGANT: A wine showing finesse or style.

EVERYDAY WINES: Inexpensive, readily available and easy to drink wines, lacking sophistication but at their best pleasant accompaniments to food.

FAT: A full bodied wine that is high in alcohol or glycerin but in which the flavor overshadows the acidity, giving it a heavy, sweetish sensation. A negative term.

FERMENTATION: A process by which yeast reacts with sugar in the must, resulting in the creation of alcohol.

FILTRATION: Usually done just prior to bottling, the process of filtering of the wine in order to remove large particles of sediment and other impurities. Over-filtration tends to rob wines of their aromas and flavors.

FINESSE: Showing great harmony. Among the best qualities of a good wine.

FINISH: The aromas and flavors that linger on the palate after the wine has been swallowed.

FIRMNESS: The grip of a wine, determined by its tannins and acidity.

FLABBY: The opposite of crisp, often a trait of wines that lack acidity and are thus dull and weak.

FLAT: Synonymous to flabby.

FLINTY: A slightly metallic taste, sometimes found in white wines such as Chardonnays. A positive quality.

FORTIFIED WINE: A wine whose alcoholic strength has been intensified by the addition of spirits.

FRIZZANTE: Lightly sparkling.

GRASSY: A term often used to describe white wines made from Sauvignon Blanc and Gewurztraminer grapes.

GREEN: In the positive sense, wines that are tart and youthful but have the potential to develop. In the negative sense, a wine that is unripe and sour.

GLOSSARY OF WINE TERMINOLOGY

HARD: A sense of austerity usually found in young, tannic red wines before they mellow and develop with age.

HARSH: Always a negative term, even more derogatory than "coarse".

HERBACEOUS: Implies aromas and flavors of grass, hay, herbs, leather and tobacco.

HOT: The unpleasant, sometimes burning sensation left on the palate by an overly alcoholic wine.

ICE WINE: A dessert wine made by a special method in which the grapes are left on the vine until frozen and then pressed while still frozen. Only the water in the grape freezes and this can be removed, leaving the must concentrated and very sweet. In warm weather areas the freezing process may be done in the winery.

INTERNATIONALIZED WINES: Reds or whites that are blended to please any palate. At their best such wines are pleasant, at their worst simply boring.

INTENSE: A strong, concentrated flavor and aroma.

LATE HARVEST: In such a harvest grapes are left on the vines until very late in the harvest season, the purpose being to obtain sweeter grapes that will be used to make dessert wines.

LEES: Sediments that accumulate in the bottom of the barrel or vat as a wine ferments.

LEGS: The "tears" or stream of wine that clings to a glass after the wine has been swirled.

LENGTH: The period of time in which the flavors and aromas of a wine linger after it has been swallowed.

LIGHT: Low in alcohol or body. Also used to describe a wine low in flavor.

LIVELY: Clean and refreshing.

LONG: A wine that offers aromas and flavors that linger for a long time after it has been swallowed.

LONGEVITY: The aging potential of a wine, dependent on balance and structure.

MALOLACTIC FERMENTATION: A second fermentation that can occur naturally or be induced, the purpose of which is to convert harsh malic acid to softer lactic acid.

MATURE: A wine that has reached its peak after developing in the bottle.

MELLOW: A wine that is at or very close to its peak.

METHODE CHAMPENOISE: The classic method for making Champagne by inducing a second fermentation in the bottle.

MID-PALATE: Those aroma and taste sensations felt after the first attack.

MOUSSE: The foam and bubbles of sparkling wines. A good mousse will show long-lasting foam and sharp, small, concentrated bubbles.

MOUTH FILLING: A wine that fills the mouth with satisfying flavors.

MUST: The pre-fermentation mixture of grape juice, stem fragments, skins, seeds and pulp, that results from the grape crushing process.

NOUVEAU: Term that originated in Beaujolais to describe very young, fruity and light red wines, often made from Gamay grapes and by the method of carbonic maceration. Such wines are always meant to be consumed very young.

NOSE: Synonymous with bouquet.

OAK: The wood most often used to make the barrels in which wines are fermented or aged. The impact of such barrels is reflected in the level of tannins and in its contribution to flavors of smoke, spices and vanilla to the wines.

OAKED: A wine that has been fermented and/or aged in oak barrels.

OXIDIZED: A wine that has gone off because it has been exposed to oxygen or to high temperatures.

PEAK: The optimal point of maturity of a given wine.

PERSONALITY: The overall impression made by an individual wine.

RESIDUAL SUGAR: The sugar that remains in a wine after fermentation has been completed.

RICH: A wine with full flavors and aromas.

RIPASSO: A second fermentation that is induced on the lees of a wine made earlier.

ROBUST: Assertive, full-bodied and characteristic of good

GLOSSARY OF WINE TERMINOLOGY

red wines at a young age, or country style wines that are pleasingly coarse.

ROTTEN EGGS: Describes the smell of hydrogen sulfide (H2S). Always an undesirable trait.

ROUND: A wine that has become smooth as its tannins, acids and wood have integrated.

RUSTIC: Synonymous with country-style.

SHARP: Overly acidic.

SHORT: A wine whose aromas and flavors fail to linger or to make an impression after the wine has been swallowed.

SIMPLE: A wine that has no nuances or complexity.

SMOKY: A flavor imparted to a wine from oak casks, most often found in unfiltered wines.

SMOOTH: A wine that sits comfortably on the palate.

STALE: A wine that has lost its freshness, liveliness or fruitiness.

STEWED: The sensation of cooked, overripe or soggy fruit.

STINGY: A wine that holds back on its aromas or flavors.

SULFITES: Usually sulfur dioxide that is added to wine to prevent oxidation.

SUR LIE: French for "on the lees". A term used to describe the process in which a wine is left in contact with its lees during fermentation and barrel aging.

SUR-RIPE: Grapes that have been allowed to develop on the vine to their maximum point of ripeness and sweetness.

TANNINS: Phenolic substances that exist naturally in wines and extracted from the skins, pips and stalks of the grapes, as well as from development in new oak barrels. Tannins are vital for the longevity of red wines. In young wines, tannins can sometimes be harsh, but if the wine is well balanced they will blend with other substances in the wine over time, making the wine smoother and more approachable as it ages.

TANNIC: A wine still marked by firm tannins. In their youth, many red wines tend to be tannic and need time for the tannins to integrate.

TCA: 2,4,6-Tricholoraniole. See "corked".

TERROIR: The reflection of a vineyard's soil, altitude, microclimate, prevailing winds, and other natural factors that impact on the quality of the grapes, and consequently on the wines produced from them.

THIN: Lacking in body or fruit.

TOASTING: Searing the inside of barrels with an open flame when making the barrels. Heavy toasting can impart caramel-like flavors to a wine; medium toasting and light toasting can add vanilla, spices or smokiness to the wine, all positive attributes when present in moderation.

VANILLA: Aroma and flavor imparted to wines from the oak barrels in which they age.

VARIETAL WINE: A wine that contains at least 85% of the grape named on the label.

VARIETAL TRAITS: The specific colors, aromas and flavors traditionally imparted by a specific grape variety.

VEGETAL: An often positive term used for a bouquet of rounded wines, in particular those made from Pinot Noir and Chardonnay grapes whose aromas and flavors often call to mind vegetables rather than fruits.

VINTAGE: (a) Synonymous with harvest; (b) A wine made from grapes of a single harvest. In accordance with EU standards, a vintage wine must contain at least 85% grapes from the noted year.

WATERY: A wine so thin that it feels diluted.

WOOD: Refers either to the wood barrels in which the wine ages or to a specific aroma and flavor imparted by the barrels.

YEAST: A kind of fungus, vital to the process of fermentation.

Contacting the Wineries

Agur Winery
Meshek 17,
Moshav Agur 99840
Tel: 02 9910483 Fax: 02 9910483
yashuv@netvision.net.il

Alexander Winery
Meshek 112,
Moshav Beit Yitzhak 42970
Tel: 09 8822956 Fax: 09 8872076
a_wine@netvision.net.il

Aligote Winery
Moshav Gan Yoshiya 38850
Tel: 054 4748893 Fax: 04 6258492
aligote@aviv-flowers.co.il

Alon Wineries
Moshav Alonei Aba 36005
Tel 054 4237745 Fax: 04 9800727
alonwine@netvision.net.il

Amphorae Vineyard
POB 12672 Herzliya 46733
Tel 04 9840702 Fax: 04 9704318
gil@amphorae-v.com
www.amphorae-v.com

Amram's Winery
Moshav Ramot Naftali 13830
Tel/Fax: 04 6940039
amramswin@hotmail.com

Anatot Winery
POB 3390
11 Anatot St
Givat Ze'ev 90917
Tel: 02 5860187 Fax: 02 5362565
Aharon@anatotwinery.co.il
www.anatotwinery.co.il

Assaf Winery
POB 69, Katzrin
Kidmat Tzvi 12421
Tel: 04 4779722 Fax 04 6963014
kedemas@walla.com

Avidan Winery
253 Weizmann Street,
Ra'anana 43721
Tel: 09 7719382 Fax: 09 7712679
avidanwine@walla.com

Bar Winery
22 Ha'avoda Street,
Binyamina 30500
Tel: 04 6388545
alanbar@zahav.net.il

Baram Winery
Kibbutz Baram 13860
Tel: 052 8313208
dror@baram.org.il

Barkai Vineyards
Meshek 14,
Moshav Roglit 99865
Tel/Fax: 02 9993281
barkaimi@bezeqint.net

Barkan Wine Cellars
POB 146, Kibbutz Hulda 76842
Tel: 08 9355858 Fax: 08 9355859
winery@barkan-winery.co.il
www.barkan-winery.co.il

Bashan Winery
Moshav Avnai Eitan 12925,
Golan Heights
Tel 057 7691124 Fax: 04 6762618
bashanwinery@013.net

Bazelet Hagolan Winery
POB 77, Moshav Kidmat Tsvi,
Katzrin 12421,
Tel: 04 6827223 Fax: 04 6820084
bazelet@netvision.net.il
www.bazelet-hagolan.co.il

Beit-El Winery
Beit-El 90628
Tel/Fax: 02 9971158
hmanne@netvision.net.il

Benhaim Winery
34 Sderot Ben-Zvi,
Ramat-Gan 52247
Tel: 03 6762656
benhaim@benhaim.co.il
www.benhaim.co.il

Ben Hanna Winery
POB 115, Shilat 73188
Tel: 052 5434253
wine@ben-hanna.com
www.ben-hanna.com

Binyamina Wine Cellars
POB 34, Binyamina 30550
Tel: 04 6388643 Fax: 04 6389021
info@binyaminawines.co.il
www.binyaminawines.com

Birya Winery
Birya 13805
Tel: 052 5405223 Fax: 04 6923815
drporat@zahav.net.il

Bnai Baruch Winery
POB 1552, Ramat Gan 52115
Tel 054 6696704 Fax: 03 9226741
Boris_beloter@yahoo.com

Bustan Winery
POB 55, Moshav Sharei Tikva 44860
Tel: 054 4892757
bustanwinery@yahoo.com

Bustan Hameshusheem Winery
Moshav Had Ness 12950
Tel: 052 4358407

Carmel Winery
Rishon Letzion, Zichron Ya'akov
Tel: Rishon Letzion 03 9488888
Tel: Zichron Ya'akov 04 6390105
www.carmelwines.co.il

Domaine du Castel
Moshav Ramat Raziel 90974
Tel: 02 5342249 Fax: 02 5700995
castel@castel.co.il
www.castel.co.il

The Cave
c/o Binyamina Winery,
POB 34, Binyamina 30550
Tel: 04 6388643 Fax: 04 6389021
thecave@zahav.net.il

Chateau Golan Winery
Moshav Eliad 12927
Tel: 04 6600026 Fax: 04 6600274
shatoltd@netvision.net.il
www.chateaugolan.com

Chillag Wine
39 Leonardo da Vinci Street,
Tel Aviv 64955
Tel: 054 4562057 Fax: 03 69121903
chillag@netvision.net.il

Clos de Gat
Kibbutz Har'el 99740
Tel: 02 9993505 Fax; 02 9993350
harelca@netvision.net.il
www.closdegat.com/intro.html

Dalton Winery
Dalton Industrial Park,
Merom Hagalil 13815
Tel: 04 6987683 Fax: 04 6987684
info@dalton-winery.com
www.dalton-winery.com

Dicos Winery
Meshek 37,
Moshav Ginaton 73110
Tel: 08–9243135

Efrat Wine Cellars
1 Steinberg Street,
Motza, Jerusalem 90822
Tel: 02 5346022 Fax: 02 5340760
office@efratwine.co.il
www.efrat-winery.co.il

Ella Valley Vineyards
Kibbutz Netiv Halamed Hey 99855
Tel: 02 9994885 Fax: 02 9994876
ella@ellavalley.com

Essence Winery
Ma'aleh Tsvi'a 20129
Tel: 04 6619058 Fax: 04 6619054
essencewines@zvia.org.il

Flam Winery
9 Avshalom Street,
Rishon Le Zion 75285
Tel: 02 9929924 Fax: 02 9929926
golanfla@netvision.net.il

Galai Winery
Moshav Nir Akiva 85365
Tel: 08 9933713 Fax: 08 9931287
galai-winery@bezeqint.net
www.galai-winery.com

Galil Mountain Winery
Kibbutz Yiron 13855
Tel: 04 6868740 Fax: 04 6868506
winery@galilmountain.co.il
ww.galilmountain.co.il

Gat Shomron Winery
Karnei Shomron 44855
Tel: 050 7264855
na_lior@walla.co.il

Gesher Damia Winery
2 Hatavor Street,
Pardes Hannah-Karkur 37011
Tel/Fax: 04 6377451
damiya@walla.co.il

Ginaton Winery
Meshek 19,
Moshav Ginaton 73110
Tel: 050 3932403 Fax: 08 9254841
ginaton1999@walla.co.il

Givon Winery
POB 140, Givon Hachadasha 90901
Tel: 02 5362966
info@givonwine.com
www.givonwine.com

Golan Heights Winery
POB 183, Industrial Zone, Katzrin 12900
Tel: 04 6968420 Fax: 04 6962220
ghwinery@golanwines.co.il
www.golanwines.co.il

Greenberg Winery
51 Hameginim Street,
Herzliya 46686
Tel: 052 3237689
elegant@netvision.net.il

Gush Etzion Winery
POB 1415, Efrat 90435
Tel: 02 9309220 Fax: 02 9309156
winery@actcom.co.il
www.gushetzion-winery.com

Gustavo & Jo Winery
19 Marvah Street,
Kfar Vradim 25147
Tel: 04 9972190
boia@netvision.net.il

Hakerem Winery
POB 645, Qiryat Arba 90100
Tel: 02 9961120

Hamasrek Winery
Moshav Beit Meir 90865
Tel: 02 5701759 Fax: 02 5336592
hamasrek@netvision.net.il
www.hamasrek.com

Hans Sternbach Winery
Meshek 83,
Moshav Giv'at Yeshayahu 99825
Tel: 02 9990162 Fax: 02 9911703
sk-Gadi@zahav.net.il

Hatabor Winery
POB 22, Kfar Tavor 15241
Tel: 04 6767889
ssiecodo@zahav.net.il

Hevron Heights Winery
Moshav Geulim 42820
Tel: 09 8943711 Fax: 09 8943006
mm@churchill.fr

Kadesh Barnea Winery
Meshek 43,
Moshav Kadesh Barnea 85513
Tel: 08 6555849 Fax: 08 6571323
winerykb@012.net.il

Kadita Winery
POB 1052, Safed
Bikta Bekadita
Tel: 050 6933219
winery@kadita.co.il
www.kadita.co.il/winery/intro.html

Karmei Yosef Winery
Karmei Yosef 99797
Tel: 08 9286098
bravdo@bravdo.co.il
www.bravdo.com

Katlav Winery
Meshek 8,
Moshav Nes Harim 99885
Tel/Fax: 02 5701404
yosss@bezeqint.net

Kfir Winery
POB 4125, Gan Yavne 70800
Tel: 08 8570354 Fax: 08 8673708
meirkfir@gmail.com
www.kfir-winery.co.il

CONTACTING THE WINERIES

La Terra Promessa Winery
Meshek 44,
Moshav Shachar 79335
Tel: 08 6849093 Fax: 151 50684775
laterrapromessa@bezeqint.net

Lachish Winery
Moshav Lachish 79360
Tel: 054 7920151
galiam@bezeqint.net

Domaine de Latroun
Latroun Monastery 99762
Tel: 08 9255180

Lavie Winery
Rehov Shemen Zeit 15/2,
Ephrata 90435
Tel: 02 9938520

Levron Winery
Rehov Orbach 10,
Haifa 34985
Tel: 04 8344837 Fax: 04 824 6724

Maccabim Winery
Maccabim-Re'ut 71908
Tel: 050 8503362
info@maccabimwinery.com

Maor Winery
Moshav Ramot,
Golan Heights 12948
Tel: 052 8515079
danny@maorwinery.com
www.maorwinery.com

Margalit Winery
POB 4055, Caesarea 38900
Tel: 050 5334433 Fax: 04 6262058
a_m_n_l@netvision.net.il
www.margalit-winery.com

Meishar Winery
Meshek 41,
Moshav Meishar 76850
Tel: 08 8594759
zosh_s@netvision.net.il
www.meishar.co.il

Meister Winery
33 Schoonat Hashalom,
Rosh Pina 12000
Tel: 054 4976940
meister@bezeqint.net
www.ruth-meister.co.il

Miles Winery
Moshav Kerem Ben Zimra 13815
Tel: 04 6980623
milso13.013.net.il

Mony Winery
POB 275, Beit Shemesh 99000
Dir Rafat Monastery,
Tel: 02 9916629 Fax: 02 9910366
monywines@walla.co.il
www.ymp.co.il/moni/

Na'aman Winery
Meshek 90,
Moshav Ramot Naftali, 13830
Tel: 04 6944463 Fax: 04 6950062
naaman@017.net.il
www.naamanwine.co.il

Nahal Amud
Meshek 17,
Moshav Kfar Shamai 20125
Tel: 04 6989825

CONTACTING THE WINERIES

Nachshon Winery
Kibbutz Nachson 99760
Tel: 08 9278641 Fax: 08 9278607
winery@nachshon.co.il
http://winery.nachshon.org.il

Nashashibi Winery
Kfar Eehbelin 30012
Tel: 054 6387191
nash_win@hotmail.com

Natuf Winery
Meshek 45,
Kfar Truman 73150
Tel: 052 2608199
natuf@012.net.il

Neot Smadar Winery
Kibbutz Neot Smadar 88860
Tel: 08 6358111

Noga Winery
POB 111, Gedera 70700
Tel 08 8690253
nogawinery@bezeqint.net

Odem Mountain Winery
Moshav Odem 12473
Tel/Fax: 04 6871120
megolan@012.net.il

Pelter Winery
POB 136, Kibbutz Merom Golan 12436,
Tel: 052 8666384 Fax: 04 6850343
tal@pelterwinery.co.il
www. pelterwinery.co.il

Psagot Winery
Psagot 90624
Tel: 02 545942802 Fax: 02 9978222
info@ psagotwines.com
www. psagotwines.com

Ra'anan Winery
Moshav Ganei Yochanan 31, 76922
Tel: 08 9350668
orsss@zahav.net.il

Ramim Winery
Meshek 64,
Moshav Shachar 79335
Tel: 054 4608080 Fax: 08 6849122
enrade@multinet.net.il

Ramot Naftali Winery
Moshav Ramot Naftali 13830
Tel: 04 6940371 Fax: 04 6902661
Yitzhak3@012.net.il

Recanati Winery
POB 12050, Industrial Zone, Emek Hefer
Tel: 04 6222288 Fax: 04 6222882
info@recanati-winery.com
www.recanati-winery.com

Red Poetry Winery
Havat Tal,
Karmei Yosef 99797
Tel: 08 9210352
talfarm@bezeqint.net

Rosh Pina Winery
Rosh Pina 12000
Tel: 050 5271073

Rota Winery
Havat Rota,
DN Halutza 85515
Tel: 054 4968703 Fax: 03 9732278
rotawinery@walla.com

Rozenbaum Winery
Kibbutz Malkiya 13845
Tel: 050 5423046 Fax: 09 8996316
aviroze@bezeqint.net

CONTACTING THE WINERIES

Ruth Winery
Kfar Ruth 73196
Tel: 050 6980098
maortal@012.net.il

Salomon Winery
Moshav Amikam 37830
Tel: 04 6380475

Saslove Winery
POB 10581, Tel Aviv 69085
Tel: 09 7492697 Fax: 03 6492712
winery@saslove.com
www.saslove.com

Sassy Winery
24 Sderot Ha'atzmaut,
Bat Yam 59378
Tel: 052 2552012

Savion Winery
Bareket Street 41,
Mevaseret Zion 90805
Tel: 02 5336162

Sde Boker Winery
Kibbutz Sde Boker 84993
Tel: 050 7579212 Fax: 08 6560118
winery@ sde-boker.org.il
www. sde-boker.org.il/winery

Sea Horse Winery
Moshav Bar Giora 99880
Tel: 050 7283216 Fax: 02 5709834
info@seahorsewines.com
www.seahorsewines.com

Segal Wines
Kibbutz Hulda 76842
Tel: 08 9358860 Fax: 08 9241222
segal@segalwines.co.il

Smadar Winery
31 Hameyasdim Street,
Zichron-Ya'akov 30900
Tel: 04 6390777

Sode Hayain Winery
Moshav Tirat Yehuda 73175
Tel: 03 9712048
wine4u@bezeqint.net
www.wine4u.co.il

Soreq Winery
Moshav Tal Shachar 78805
Tel: 08 9450844 Fax: 08 9370385
soreq@barak.net.il

Srigim Winery
POB, 174 Moshav Srigim 99835
Tel: 050 6991398 Fax: 02 9991512
ursl10@netvision.net.il

Tabor Winery
POB 422, Kfar Tavor 15241
Tel 04 6760444, Fax: 04 6772061
twc@twc.co.il
www.taborwinery.co.il

Tanya Winery
DN Mizrach Binyamin
Ofra 90627
Tel: 054 4354034
Yoram5733@walla.co.il

Tishbi Estate Winery
33 Hameyasdim Street,
Zichron Ya'akov 30900
Tel: 04 6389434 Fax: 04: 6280223
tishbi_w@netvision.net.il
http://www.tishbi.com/

Tulip Winery
24 Hacarmel Street,
Kiryat Tivon 36081
Tel/Fax: 04 9830573
tulip@tulip-winery.co.il

Tzora Vineyards
Kibbutz Tzora
DN Shimshon 99803
Tel: 02 9908261 Fax: 02 9915479
info@tzorawines.com
www.tzorawines.com

Vanhozker Winery
Moshev Meron, Marom haGalil 13910
Tel/Fax: 04 6989063
Elivan1@bezeqint.net

Villa Wilhelma Winery
Meshek Goldman,
Moshav Bnai Atarot 60991
Tel: 054 4564526
Motti_goldman@yahoo.com

Vitkin Winery
POB 267, Kfar Vitkin 40200
Tel: 09 8663505 Fax: 03 7256258
vtknwine@netvision.net.il

Yaffo Winery
15 Rozov Street,
Tel Aviv 69716
Tel: 03 6474834
yaffowine@zahav.net.il
www.yaffowinery.com

Yatir Winery
POB 5210, Arad
Tel: 08 9959090 Fax: 08 9959050
y_yatir@zahav.net.il
www.yatir.net

Ye'arim Winery
Moshav Givat Ye'arim 90970
Tel: 052 5791080
sassons_wine@hotmail.co.il

Yehuda Winery
Moshav Shoresh 90860
Tel: 054 4638544 Fax: 02 5348100
yekev_yehuda@neve-ilan.co.il

Yiftah'el Winery
Alon Hagalil 17920
Tel: 04 9865811
hadassr@bezeqint.net

Yuval Ben-Shoshan Winery
Kibbutz Bror-Hail 79152
Tel: 08 6803321 Fax: 08 6803667
niva_yuval@walla.com

Zauberman Winery
50 Piness Street,
Gedera 70700
Tel: 08 8594680
www.zaubermanwines.com

Zemora Winery
POB 451
Mevaseret Tzion 90805
Tel: 052 2636850 Fax: 02 5346166

Index of Wineries

Agur 31
Alexander 33
Aligote 38
Alon 40
Amphorae 42
Amram's 47
Anatot 48
Assaf 50
Avidan 51

Bar 53
Baram 55
Barkai 56
Barkan 57
Bashan 67
Bazelet Hagolan 68
Beit-El 71
Benhaim 72
Ben-Hanna 76
Ben-Shoshan *see*
    Yuval Ben-Shoshan
Binyamina 78
Birya 88
Bnai Baruch 89
Bravdo *see* Karmei Yosef
Bustan 90
Bustan Hameshusheem 93

Carmel 95
Castel 109
Cave, The 115
Chateau Golan 117
Chillag 123
Clos de Gat 126

Dalton 129

Dico's 137
Domaine de Latroun *see*
    Latroun
Domain de Castel *see* Castel

Efrat 138
Ella Valley 144
Essence 149

Flam 151

Galai 156
Galil Mountain 158
Gamla *see* Golan Heights
    Winery
Gat Shomron 164
Gefen Adderet *see* Kfir
Gesher Damia 165
Ginaton 166
Givon 168
Golan *see*
    Golan Heights Winery
Golan Heights Winery 169
Greenberg 191
Gush Etzion 193
Gustavo & Jo 195

Hakerem 198
Hamasrek 199
Hans Sternbach 201
Har'el *see* Clos de Gat
Har Odem *see*
    Odem Mountain
Hatabor 203
Hevron Heights/Noah 204

Kadesh Barnea 208

Kadita 210
Karmei Yosef 212
Katlav 215
Katzrin *see*
    Golan Heights Winery
Kfir 217

La Terra Pomessa 219
Lachish 223
Latroun 224
Lavie 226
Levron 227

Maccabim 228
Maor 229
Margalit 230
Meishar 238
Meister 242
Miles 243
Mony 245

Na'aman 248
Nahal Amud 249
Nachshon 250
Nashashibi 255
Natuf 256
Neot Smadar 257
Noah *see* Hevron Heights
Noga 260

Odem Mountain 261
Orna Chillag *see* Chillag

Pelter 265
Psagot 269

Ra'anan 271
Ramim 273
Ramot Naftali 278
Recanati 279
Red Poetry 286
Rosh Pina 288

Rota 289
Rozenbaum 290
Ruth 291

Salomon 293
Saslove 294
Sasson's *see* Ye'arim
Sassy 300
Savion 301
Sde Boker 302
Sea Horse 304
Segal 309
Smadar 316
Sode Hayain 317
Soreq 318
Srigim 321

Tabor 322
Tanya 328
Terra Promessa *see*
    La Terra Promessa
The Cave *see* Cave, The
Tishbi 330
Tulip 339
Tzora 342

Vanhotzker 347
Villa Wilhelma 348
Vitkin 350

Yaffo 355
Yarden *see*
    Golan Heights Winery
Yatir 357
Ye'arim 361
Yehuda 363
Yiftah'el 364
Yuval Ben-Shoshan 365

Zauberman 366
Zemora 368

About the Author

Daniel Rogov is Israel's most influential and preeminent wine critic. He writes weekly wine and restaurant columns in the respected newspaper *Haaretz*, and contributes regularly to two prestigious international wine books—Hugh Johnson's *Pocket Wine Book* and Tom Stevenson's *Wine Report*.

The fonts used in the book are from the Chaparral family

The Toby Press publishes fine writing,
available at bookstores everywhere. For more information,
please contact *The* Toby Press at www.tobypress.com